Sasanian Persia

EDINBURGH STUDIES IN ANCIENT PERSIA

Dealing with key aspects of the ancient Persian world from the Achaemenids to the Sasanians: its history, reception, art, archaeology, religion, literary tradition (including oral transmissions) and philology, this series provides an important synergy of the latest scholarly ideas about this formative ancient world civilisation.

SERIES EDITOR
Lloyd Llewellyn-Jones, Cardiff University

EDITORIAL ADVISORY BOARD
Touraj Daryaee
Andrew Erskine
Thomas Harrison
Irene Huber
Keith Rutter
Jan Stronk

TITLES AVAILABLE IN THE SERIES

Courts and Elites in the Hellenistic Empires: The Near East After the Achaemenids, c. 330 to 30 BCE
By Rolf Strootman

Greek Perspectives on the Achaemenid Empire: Persia through the Looking Glass
By Janett Morgan

Semiramis' Legacy: The History of Persia According to Diodorus of Sicily
By Jan P. Stronk

ReOrienting the Sasanians: East Iran in Late Antiquity
By Khodadad Rezakhani

Sasanian Persia: Between Rome and the Steppes of Eurasia
Edited by Eberhard W. Sauer

FORTHCOMING TITLES

The Bactrian Mirage: Iranian and Greek Interaction in Western Central Asia
By Michael Iliakis

Plutarch and the Persica
By Eran Almagor

Visit the Edinburgh Studies in Ancient Persia website at
edinburghuniversitypress.com/series/esap

Sasanian Persia

Between Rome and the Steppes
of Eurasia

Edited by Eberhard W. Sauer

EDINBURGH
University Press

Edinburgh University Press is one of the leading university presses in the UK. We publish academic books and journals in our selected subject areas across the humanities and social sciences, combining cutting-edge scholarship with high editorial and production values to produce academic works of lasting importance. For more information visit our website: edinburghuniversitypress.com

© editorial matter and organisation
Eberhard W. Sauer, 2017
© the chapters their several authors, 2017

Edinburgh University Press Ltd
The Tun – Holyrood Road, 12(2f) Jackson's Entry, Edinburgh EH8 8PJ

Typeset in 11/13pt Sabon by
Servis Filmsetting Ltd, Stockport, Cheshire

A CIP record for this book is available
from the British Library

ISBN 978 1 4744 0101 2 (hardback)
ISBN 978 1 4744 0102 9 (webready PDF)
ISBN 978 1 4744 2068 6 (epub)
ISBN 978 1 4744 5230 4 (paperback)

The right of Eberhard W. Sauer to be identified as the editor of this work has been asserted in accordance with the Copyright, Designs and Patents Act 1988, and the Copyright and Related Rights Regulations 2003 (SI No. 2498).

Contents

List of Illustrations vii
Acknowledgements xv
Notes on Contributors xvii
Series Editor's Preface xx

1 Introduction 1
 Eberhard W. Sauer

 PART I SURPLUS PRODUCTION, URBAN GROWTH
 AND THE ENVIRONMENT

2 Sasanian Cities: Archaeological Perspectives on the Urban
 Economy and Built Environment of an Empire 21
 St John Simpson

3 Palaeoecological Insights into Agri-Horti-Cultural and
 Pastoral Practices Before, During and After the Sasanian
 Empire 51
 *Lyudmila Shumilovskikh, Morteza Djamali, Valérie
 Andrieu-Ponel, Philippe Ponel, Jacques-Louis de Beaulieu,
 Abdolmajid Naderi-Beni and Eberhard W. Sauer*

4 Animal Exploitation and Subsistence on the Borders of
 the Sasanian Empire: From the Gorgan Wall (Iran) to the
 Gates of the Alans (Georgia) 74
 *Marjan Mashkour, Roya Khazaeli, Homa Fathi,
 Sarieh Amiri, Delphine Decruyenaere, Azadeh Mohaseb,
 Hossein Davoudi, Shiva Sheikhi and Eberhard W. Sauer*

PART II FRONTIERS AND FRONTIER LANDSCAPES

5 The Northern and Western Borderlands of the Sasanian Empire: Contextualising the Roman/Byzantine and Sasanian Frontier 99
Dan Lawrence and Tony J. Wilkinson

6 Connectivity on a Sasanian Frontier: Route Systems in the Gorgan Plain of North-East Iran 126
Kristen Hopper

7 The Sasanian Empire and the East: A Summary of the Evidence and its Implications for Rome 151
Warwick Ball

PART III CONTESTED TERRITORIES AND CULTURAL CONTACTS BETWEEN PERSIA AND ROME

8 Minority Religions in the Sasanian Empire: Suppression, Integration and Relations with Rome 181
Lee E. Patterson

9 A Contested Jurisdiction: Armenia in Late Antiquity 199
Tim Greenwood

10 Cultural Contacts Between Rome and Persia at the Time of Ardashir I (c. AD 224–40) 221
Pierfrancesco Callieri

PART IV IMPERIAL POWER BALANCE AND INTERNATIONAL RELATIONS

11 Innovation and Stagnation: Military Infrastructure and the Shifting Balance of Power Between Rome and Persia 241
Eberhard W. Sauer, Jebrael Nokandeh, Konstantin Pitskhelauri and Hamid Omrani Rekavandi

12 The Arabian Frontier: A Keystone of the Sasanian Empire 268
Craig Morley

13 The India Trade in Late Antiquity 284
James Howard-Johnston

Index 305

List of Illustrations

COVER IMAGES

The Sasanian Empire's relations with its neighbours as portrayed on Sasanian rock reliefs (from top to bottom):

- Relief at Naqsh-e Rostam (VI): victorious King Shapur I (c. AD 240–72) and his vanquished Roman enemies, emperors Philip I (AD 244–9) and Valerian (AD 253–60), taken prisoner of war in AD 260, the former kneeling, the latter standing.
- Relief at Bishapur (VI) of disputed date, but often attributed to Shapur II (AD 309–79): Iranians with booty from an eastern campaign, including an elephant with a mahout.
- Relief at Darabgird: King Shapur I (c. AD 240–72), triumphing over defeated Roman enemies. It features probably the same emperors as Naqsh-e Rostam above, as well as the corpse of Gordian III (AD 238–44) under the hoofs of the king's horse.
- Relief at Bishapur (IV): Bahram II (AD 276–93) receives a delegation of nomads with dromedaries, perhaps from Arabia or possibly from Sagestan (southern Afghanistan).

The precise chronology of the reliefs and the identification of the figures shown, notably the kneeling and standing Roman emperors, has been the subject of much academic debate, which there is no space to summarise and discuss here. See recently Callieri 2014: 129–61 with sources, notably Herrmann 1980, 1981, 1983 and 1989 and Trümpelmann 1975. See also Weber 2009: 605–9 and the stimulating work by Overlaet 2009, even if the editor does not follow the proposed identification of the standing emperor in the Darabgird, Bishapur (II) and (III) reliefs as Uranius Antoninus, in the light of the broad similarity of the scene with that on the Naqsh-e Rostam relief and the lack of evidence that the enigmatic usurper suffered defeat at the hands of Shapur I or ceded Emesa's holy black stone to the king. This is not to deny the importance of Overlaet's work. Indeed, the proposed interpretation of a heavy oval object featuring twice on the Bishapur (III) relief as a *baitylos* (sacred stone) taken as war booty is attractive, even if it need not have been the one from Emesa. Evidently, however, each relief depicts a sequence of events: the death of Gordian III/submission of Philip I in AD 244 and the encounter with/capture of a third emperor, probably Valerian in AD 260. As these two events are clearly not contemporary, there is no reason why the postulated capture of a *baitylos*, whether taken in AD 253 or on another campaign, could not feature on reliefs carved (or re-carved) in the AD 260s.

References

Callieri, P. (2014), *Architecture et représentations dans l'Iran Sassanide*, Studia Iranica, Cahier 50, Paris: Association pour l'Avancement des Études Iraniennes.
Herrmann, G. (1980), *Iranische Felsreliefs E: The Sasanian Rock Reliefs at Bishapur*, 1, Iranische Denkmäler, 9, Berlin: Reimer.
Herrmann, G. (1981), *Iranische Felsreliefs F: The Sasanian Rock Reliefs at Bishapur*, 2, Iranische Denkmäler, 10, Berlin: Reimer.
Herrmann, G. (1983), *Iranische Felsreliefs G: The Sasanian Rock Reliefs at Bishapur*, 3, Iranische Denkmäler, 11, Berlin: Reimer.
Herrmann, G. (1989), 'The Sasanian Rock Reliefs at Naqsh-i Rustam', in G. Herrmann and D. N. MacKenzie, *Iranische Felsreliefs I*, Iranische Denkmäler, 13, Berlin: Reimer, pp. 9–33.
Overlaet, B. (2009), 'A Roman Emperor at Bishapur and Darabgird: Uranius Antoninus and the Black Stone of Emesa', *Iranica Antiqua*, 44, pp. 461–530.
Trümpelmann, L. (1975), *Iranische Felsreliefs B: Das Sasanidische Felsrelief von Dārāb*, Iranische Denkmäler, 6, Berlin: Reimer.
Weber, U. (2009), 'Wahrām II., König der Könige von Ērān und Anērān', *Iranica Antiqua*, 44, pp. 559–643.

TEXT IMAGES

Fig. 2.1 Map showing the approximate extent of the Sasanian Empire and some of the principal sites (drawing: P. Goodhead).   23
Fig. 2.2 Aerial view of Ardashir Khurrah (from Google Earth, 2013).   24
Fig. 2.3 Schematic map showing major Sasanian sites in the Ctesiphon conurbation, including the location and reconstructed extent of Ctesiphon, Veh Ardashir, Aspanabr

(i.e. 'Asfanabr') and Veh-az-Antiok-Khusro, the earlier city sites of Seleucia and Valasapat, the present course of the River Tigris and the position of its palaeo-channels, and the alignment of First World War trenches following ancient canal beds (after Simpson 2015: 8, fig. 1.2). 25
Fig. 2.4 Aerial view of Darabgird (from Google Earth, 2012). 27
Fig. 2.5 Aerial view of Bishapur/Bay-Shapur (from Google Earth, 2012). 28
Fig. 2.6 Plan of the remains at Gondeshapur (after Adams and Hansen 1968: fig. 1). 29
Fig. 2.7 Aerial view of Eyvan-e Karkha (from Google Earth, 2012). 30
Fig. 2.8 Plan of the inverted siphon and bridge at Gondeshapur (after Adams and Hansen 1968: fig. 2). 31
Fig. 2.9 Aerial view of unexcavated Sasanian new foundation south-west of Samawah (from Google Earth, 2012). 32
Fig. 2.10 Aerial view of unexcavated Sasanian new foundation at Qasr Muqatil (?) (from Google Earth, 2013). 33
Fig. 2.11 View of unexcavated Sasanian new foundation at Dezeridan (?) (from Google Earth, 2013). 34
Fig. 2.12 Map of Sasanian sites and canals in central and southern Iraq, based on surface surveys and satellite imagery (after Simpson 2015: 19, fig. 1.5). 36
Fig. 2.13 Plan of Ruqbat al-Mada'in, showing details of the architecture visible on the surface (after Finster and Schmidt 1976: 153–57, figs 80–4). 37
Fig. 2.14 Plan of the excavated area at Veh Ardashir (after Simpson 2015: 10). 39
Fig. 2.15 Multi-phase plan of the excavated architecture on the citadel of Qasr-e Abu Nasr (after Whitcomb 1985: fig. 30). 42
Fig. 2.16 Oblique aerial view of Merv looking north: the Sasanian city site is on the right with its citadel at the top; the site on the left is its medieval successor (from Google Earth, 2009). 43
Fig. 3.1 Map of Sasanian Empire with location of palaeoecological sites discussed in the text. 52
Fig. 3.2 Palaeoecological diagram of Lake Neor (selected curves). 55
Fig. 3.3 Palaeoecological diagram of Gomishan Lagoon (selected curves). 55

Fig. 3.4 Palaeoecological diagram of Lake Kongor (selected curves). 56
Fig. 3.5 Palaeoecological diagram of Tuska Tchal peat bog (selected curves). 57
Fig. 3.6 Palaeoecological diagram of Lake Almalou (selected curves). 57
Fig. 3.7 Palaeoecological diagram of Lake Van (selected curves). 58
Fig. 3.8 Palaeoecological diagram of Lake Bouara (selected curves). 59
Fig. 3.9 Palaeoecological diagram of Lake Zeribar (selected curves). 59
Fig. 3.10 Palaeoecological diagram of Lake Parishan (selected curves). 60
Fig. 3.11 Palaeoecological diagram of Lake Maharlou (selected curves). 61
Fig. 3.12 Example of pastoralism on the Neor plateau: (a) landscapes around the lake (photo P. Ponel); (b) *Gymnopleurus* sp., a dung beetle species swarming on human faeces in the Zagros Mountains (photo P. Ponel). 66
Fig. 4.1 Location map with key sites. 76
Fig. 4.2a Evolution of the faunal spectra in Trench F using the NISP (number of identified specimens). 86
Fig. 4.2b Evolution of the faunal spectra in Trench F, based on the weight of bones. 87
Fig. 4.3 Size variation in the sheep (*Ovis*) population of Dariali Fort, compared to other assemblages belonging to the Iron Age, antiquity and modern times. 89
Fig. 4.4 Size variation in the goat (*Capra*) populations at Dariali Fort, compared to other assemblages belonging to the Iron Age, antiquity and modern times. 90
Fig. 4.5 Size variation in the cattle (*Bos*) population at Dariali Fort, compared to other assemblages belonging to the Iron Age, antiquity and modern times. 91
Fig. 5.1 Map showing the location of the case study areas discussed. Background SRTM DEM courtesy of the U.S. Geological Survey. 101
Fig. 5.2 Map of the Khandaq Shapur region. Black squares are modern towns, white circles are ancient sites and white lines represent sections of the Khandaq Shapur. Background SRTM DEM courtesy of the U.S. Geological Survey. 105

Fig. 5.3 Map of the Khabur Basin region. White circles are ancient sites, black on white lines represent survey limits. Background SRTM DEM courtesy of the U.S. Geological Survey. 107

Fig. 5.4 Graph of settlement density (number of sites/survey area in km^2) by survey across the Khabur Basin (arranged west to east). 108

Fig. 5.5 Map of the coastal strip between the Caspian Sea and the Upper Caucasus. White circles are ancient sites and white lines represent linear barriers. Background SRTM DEM courtesy of the U.S. Geological Survey. 110

Fig. 5.6 CORONA image of Torpakh Qala. Mission 1110–1057DA111 acquired 24 May 1970, reproduced courtesy of the U.S. Geological Survey. 111

Fig. 5.7 CORONA image of Qal'eh Pol Gonbad. Mission 1103–2218DA035 acquired 7 May 1968, reproduced courtesy of the U.S. Geological Survey. 112

Fig. 5.8 Map of the Ghilghilchay Wall sections and fortifications. Background CORONA Mission 1110–1057DA111 acquired 24 May 1970, reproduced courtesy of the U.S. Geological Survey. 113

Fig. 5.9 Map of the southern Caucasus region (excluding the Dariali Pass). Background SRTM DEM courtesy of the U.S. Geological Survey. 116

Fig. 6.1 Locations mentioned in the text. Elevation data: SRTM 90m resolution (data available from the U.S. Geological Survey). 128

Fig. 6.2 Map of the Gorgan Plain showing the Gorgan Wall and archaeological sites of all periods mapped on CORONA imagery. Sites and features mentioned in the text are marked. Elevation data: SRTM 90m resolution (data available from the U.S. Geological Survey). 129

Fig. 6.3 Possible crossing points of the Gorgan Wall. The Sarli Makhtum canal flowing through a gap in the wall into the ditch on its northern side (left); Qizlar Qal'eh, an earlier site incorporated into the Gorgan Wall (centre); and Forts 12 and 13 on the Gorgan Wall (right) on the CORONA imagery. CORONA images from 6 October 1969 (data available from the U.S. Geological Survey). 135

Fig. 6.4 Hollow ways visible on the CORONA imagery near Forts 12 and 13. CORONA image from 6 October 1969 (data available from the U.S. Geological Survey). 137

Fig. 6.5 A possible mid- to late Sasanian route system based on the alignment of forts, campaign bases, urban sites (Sauer et al. 2013; Wilkinson et al. 2013: 102–45) and a mountain pass. Note the location of a possible Sasanian site in the pass (Abbasi 2011: 217–18). Elevation data: SRTM 90m resolution (data available from the U.S. Geological Survey). 139

Fig. 6.6 Earlier hollow ways cut by the Gorgan Wall. Elevation data: SRTM 90m resolution. CORONA image from 6 October 1969 (data available from the U.S. Geological Survey). 142

Fig. 7.1 Map of the Sasanian Empire (from Wiesehöfer 1996, reproduced by kind permission of Josef Wiesehöfer). 152

Fig. 7.2 Map of early Sasanian sites in Afghanistan, third to fourth century (from Ball 1982). 154

Fig. 7.3 A case of mistaken location: the Sar-e Pol relief in Iran confused with Sar-e Pol in Afghanistan? (after Herzfeld 1941). 157

Fig. 7.4 Interpretive drawing by Anne Searight of the Ghulbiyan painting (after Grenet and Lee 1998, reproduced by kind permission of the authors). 158

Fig. 7.5 The Ghulbiyan painting (copyright© J. L. Lee 2006; by kind permission, all rights reserved). 159

Fig. 7.6 The Rag-e Bibi relief (copyright© J. L. Lee 2004; by kind permission, all rights reserved). 160

Fig. 7.7 The Sasanian fort of Kohna Masjid at Surkh Kotal. 161

Fig. 7.8 The Sasanian-period Buddhist stupa-monastery complex of Guldara. 163

Fig. 7.9 Sogdian wall painting from Panjikent, now in the Hermitage, St Petersburg. 165

Fig. 7.10 Donors from Cave 8 at the Buddhist cave paintings at Qizil in Xinjiang. 165

Fig. 7.11 Detail of the Kucha reliquary (after Bussagli 1978). 166

Fig. 7.12 Sasanian-derived dress in modern Kandahar. 167

Fig. 7.13 Sasanian silver ewer from Ningxia, now in the Yinchuan Museum. Compare with Fig. 7.14. 168

Fig. 7.14 Sasanian silver ewer from Perm in northern Russia, now in the Hermitage. 168

Fig. 7.15 Sasanian-derived gold and silver plate of the ninth–tenth century in the Museum of the Institute of Archaeology in Akademgorodok. 169

Fig. 7.16 Delegates to the Tang court at the vast Tang necropolis at Qianling. 172

Fig. 10.1 Ardashir Khurrah (southern central Fars, Iran): Takht-e Neshin, general view before the excavations (photo P. Callieri). 223

Fig. 10.2 Ardashir Khurrah (southern central Fars, Iran): Takht-e Neshin, the south-east face of the *chahar taq* (photo D. M. Meucci). 223

Fig. 10.3 Tang-e Ab (southern central Fars, Iran): Firuzabad I rock relief (photo P. Callieri). 225

Fig. 10.4 Tang-e Ab (southern central Fars, Iran): Firuzabad II rock relief (photo P. Callieri). 226

Fig. 10.5 Naqsh-e Rajab (central Fars, Iran): Naqsh-e Rajab III rock relief (after Hinz 1969: pl. 57). 226

Fig. 10.6 Naqsh-e Rostam (central Fars, Iran): Naqsh-e Rostam I rock relief (photo P. Callieri). 227

Fig. 10.7 Salmas (eastern Azerbaijan, Iran): Salmas rock relief (after Hinz 1969: pl. 69). 227

Fig. 10.8 Tang-e Sarvak (Khuzestan, Iran): Rock III, relief (after Vanden Berghe and Schippmann 1985: pl. 47). 231

Fig. 11.1 The Sasanian Empire at its greatest extent in c. AD 619–28. 245

Fig. 11.2 The Arch of Septimius Severus at Rome, commemorating the Parthian Wars of the AD 190s. 249

Fig. 11.3 Rock relief at Bishapur (II): Shapur I triumphant over the dead Gordian III (AD 238–44), a kneeling emperor, probably Philip I (AD 244–9), and a standing emperor, probably Valerian, taken prisoner of war in AD 260. (See above, 'Cover Images', on the proposed identification of the figures.) 249

Fig. 11.4 Dura-Europos on the River Euphrates, taken by Shapur I with overwhelming force in AD 256. 251

Fig. 11.5 Recent excavations by the University of Edinburgh and Tbilisi State University have shown that the well-built mortared outer walls (right) and casemates of Dariali Fort, blocking the key route across the Caucasus, most probably date to the AD 390s or early fifth century when the site was under Sasanian control. 253

Fig. 11.6 Plan of Fort 4, based on fieldwork by the ICHHTO, the University of Edinburgh and Abingdon Archaeological Geophysics. The neat organisation of space, with barracks providing accommodation for a permanent

Fig. 11.7 At c. 170ha, perhaps the largest fortress in the late antique world: Qalʻeh Gabri near Varamin, a probable Sasanian campaign base. 258

Fig. 11.8 Hypothetical schematic deployment scheme of the Sasanian field army and its possible use of large (c. 125–70ha: large squares) and medium-size (c. 30–70ha: small squares and rectangles) campaign bases. 258

Fig. 11.9 The Sasanian Empire was the first mega-empire to control temporarily the main passes across Europe's highest mountain range, the Caucasus. View from Dariali Fort over the narrow gorge north. 260

Fig. 11.10 The coastal section of the Ghilghilchay Wall in modern Azerbaijan, with its tower mounds, survives in places to a height of up to 7m and must have been much higher prior to the decay of its mudbricks: a possible indicator how high the robbed-out Gorgan and Tammisheh Walls, made of sought-after fired bricks, may have been. 261

Fig. 11.11 A tower on Chirakh Qala, a fortification on the Ghilghilchay Wall, may perhaps have originated as a Sasanian fire temple, with the spaces between the pillars blocked up later. 262

TABLES

Table 3.1 List of sites. 53
Table 4.1a Trench F on Dariali Fort. Taxonomic distribution of bone fragments. 80
Table 4.1b Trench F on Dariali Fort. Taxonomic distribution by bone weight (in grams). 82
Table 11.1 The archaeology of Roman and Partho-Sasanian military infrastructure (disregarding long walls and military equipment). 256
Table 12.1 Sasanian coins found in eastern Arabia. 270

Acknowledgements

We are indebted to the European Research Council and the British Institute of Persian Studies for enabling us to hold a conference session on 'The Sasanian Empire and Rome' on 14 November 2013. This was part of the conference on 'Persia & Rum' in the eternal city, Rome, whose very name embodied the west even long after it had ceased to be the capital of the Mediterranean world's most powerful empire. So many institutions and individuals have offered support to this venture in particular, and the 'Persia and its Neighbours' project in general, that it is impossible to list them all, and we can name only a few. Without the kind support of the presidents of the British Institute of Persian Studies, Dr Vesta Sarkhosh Curtis and Professor Ali Ansari, this conference would never have taken place. Dr Lloyd Ridgeon played an important role too, as did other members of the council. The British School at Rome and its president, Professor Christopher Smith, were perfect hosts. The reunion of these two overseas academic institutions, one at Rome and one in Persia, epitomised the theme of our conference, the encounters between the Persianate world, the west and its neighbours elsewhere. Much work on organisational matters rested on the shoulders of Paul Churchill, who deserves credit for everything running like clockwork. We are very grateful to the contributors and the audience for stimulating debate. We are indebted to Edinburgh University Press for publishing this volume and all their editorial efforts, especially to Ellie Bush, James Dale, Carol Macdonald, Rebecca Mackenzie, the series editor, Professor Lloyd Llewellyn-Jones, and our admirably diligent copy-editor, Fiona Sewell, who has saved us from many imperfections.

The research of several contributors has been made possible through the generous support of the European Research Council via the 'Persia and its Neighbours' project. We are very grateful to our outstanding multinational teams excavating and surveying in Georgia, Iran, Azerbaijan and Oman – and most of all to the late Professor Tony Wilkinson (1948–2014), co-investigator on our current and previous Sasanian projects, without whose fundamental contribution these projects might never have received permission and funding and certainly would have been less successful.

Notes on Contributors

Sarieh Amiri is a graduate student at the University of Tehran.

Valérie Andrieu-Ponel is Associate Professor, Aix-Marseille Université, and affiliated to the Institut Méditerranéen de Biodiversité et d'Ecologie marine et continentale (IMBE), Aix-Marseille Université et Université d'Avignon.

Warwick Ball was formerly Acting Director of the British Institute of Afghan Studies.

Jacques-Louis de Beaulieu is Emeritus Research Director (DR), Centre National de la Recherche Scientifique (CNRS), and affiliated to the Institut Méditerranéen de Biodiversité et d'Ecologie marine et continentale (IMBE), Aix-Marseille Université et Université d'Avignon.

Pierfrancesco Callieri is Professor of Archaeology of Pre-Islamic Iran at the Department of Cultural Heritage, University of Bologna, campus of Ravenna, and co-director of the Iranian–Italian Joint Archaeological Mission in Fars.

Hossein Davoudi is a doctoral student at Tarbiyat Modares University.

Delphine Decruyenaere is a Master's student at the Muséum National d'Histoire Naturelle in Paris.

Morteza Djamali is Research Scientist (CR), Centre National de la Recherche Scientifique (CNRS), and affiliated to the Institut Méditerranéen de Biodiversité et d'Ecologie marine et continentale (IMBE), Aix-Marseille Université et Université d'Avignon.

Homa Fathi is a BA student at Payam Noor University.

Tim Greenwood is Senior Lecturer in the Department of Mediaeval History, University of St Andrews.

Kristen Hopper is a PhD student and Research Assistant on the 'Persia and its Neighbours' project, Department of Archaeology, Durham University.

James Howard-Johnston is Emeritus Fellow of Corpus Christi College, Oxford, and was formerly University Lecturer in Byzantine Studies, Faculty of History, University of Oxford.

Roya Khazaeli is a graduate student at the University of Tehran.

Dan Lawrence is Lecturer in the Archaeology of the Ancient Near East and Director of the Archaeology Informatics Lab, Department of Archaeology, Durham University.

Marjan Mashkour is Research Director (DR), Archéozoologie, Archéobotanique (UMR 7209), Centre National de la Recherche Scientifique (CNRS), Muséum National d'Histoire Naturelle in Paris, Université Pierre et Marie Curie, Sorbonne Universités.

Azadeh Mohaseb is a Post-Doctoral Fellow, Archéozoologie, Archéobotanique (UMR 7209), Centre National de la Recherche Scientifique (CNRS), Muséum National d'Histoire Naturelle in Paris, Université Pierre et Marie Curie, Sorbonne Universités.

Craig Morley is a recent PhD graduate, Department of Archaeology, Classics and Egyptology, University of Liverpool.

Abdolmajid Naderi-Beni is Research Scientist, Iranian National Institute for Oceanography and Atmospheric Sciences, Tehran.

Jebrael Nokandeh is Director of the National Museum of Iran, Tehran, and Research Fellow at the Research Institute of Cultural Heritage and Tourism (RICHT).

Hamid Omrani Rekavandi is Director of the Great Gorgan Wall Cultural Heritage Base, Iranian Cultural Heritage, Handcraft and Tourism Organization, Gorgan.

Lee E. Patterson is Associate Professor, Department of History, Eastern Illinois University.

Konstantin Pitskhelauri is Assistant Professor at Ivane Javakhishvili Tbilisi State University and Head of the Archaeological Unit at the National Agency for Cultural Heritage Preservation of Georgia.

Philippe Ponel is Research Director (DR), Centre National de la Recherche Scientifique (CNRS), and affiliated to the Institut

Méditerranéen de Biodiversité et d'Ecologie marine et continentale (IMBE), Aix-Marseille Université et Université d'Avignon.

Eberhard W. Sauer is Professor of Roman Archaeology, School of History, Classics and Archaeology, University of Edinburgh.

Shiva Sheikhi is a doctoral student, Paris-Sorbonne University (Paris IV), and affiliated to Archéozoologie, Archéobotanique (UMR 7209), Centre National de la Recherche Scientifique (CNRS), Muséum National d'Histoire Naturelle in Paris, Université Pierre et Marie Curie, Sorbonne Universités.

Lyudmila Shumilovskikh is a member of scientific staff of the Department of Palynology and Climate Dynamics, Georg-August-Universität Göttingen.

St John Simpson is a senior curator in the Department of the Middle East in the British Museum.

Tony J. Wilkinson was Professor of Archaeology, Department of Archaeology, Durham University. He sadly passed away before the completion of this volume.

Series Editor's Preface

Edinburgh Studies in Ancient Persia focuses on the world of ancient Persia (pre-Islamic Iran) and its reception. Academic interest in and fascination with ancient Persia have burgeoned in recent decades and research on Persian history and culture is now routinely filtered into studies of the Greek and Roman worlds; biblical scholarship too is now more keenly aware of Persian-period history than ever before; while, most importantly, the study of the history, cultures, languages and societies of ancient Iran is now a well-established discipline in its own right.

Persia was, after all, at the centre of ancient world civilisations. This series explores that centrality throughout several successive 'Persian empires': the Achaemenid dynasty (founded c. 550 BCE) saw Persia rise to its highest level of political and cultural influence, as the Great Kings of Iran fought for, and maintained, an empire which stretched from India to Libya and from Macedonia to Ethiopia. The art and architecture of the period both reflect the diversity of the empire and proclaim a single centrally constructed theme: a harmonious world-order brought about by a benevolent and beneficent king. Following the conquests of Alexander the Great, the Persian Empire fragmented but maintained some of its infrastructures and ideologies in the new kingdoms established by Alexander's successors, in particular the Seleucid dynasts who occupied the territories of western Iran, Mesopotamia, the Levant and Asia Minor. But even as Greek influence extended into the former territories of the Achaemenid realm, at the heart of Iran a family of nobles, the Parthian dynasty, rose to threaten the growing imperial power of Rome. Finally, the mighty Sasanian dynasty ruled Iran and much of the Middle East from the third century CE onwards, proving to be a powerful foe to Late Imperial Rome and Byzantium. The rise of Islam, a new religion in Arabia, brought a sudden end to the Sasanian dynasty in the mid-600s CE.

These successive Persian dynasties left their record in the historical, linguistic and archaeological materials of the ancient world, and Edinburgh Studies in Ancient Persia has been conceived to give scholars working in these fields the opportunity to publish original research and explore new methodologies in interpreting the antique past of Iran. This series will see scholars working with bona fide Persian and other Near Eastern materials, giving access to Iranian self-perceptions and the internal workings of Persian society, placed alongside scholars assessing the perceptions of the Persianate world from the outside (predominantly through Greek and Roman authors and artefacts). The series will also explore the reception of ancient Persia (in historiography, the arts and politics) in subsequent periods, both within and outwith Iran itself.

Edinburgh Studies in Ancient Persia represents something of a watershed in better appreciation and understanding not only of the rich and complex cultural heritage of Persia, but also of the lasting significance of the Achaemenids, Parthians and Sasanians and the impact that their remarkable civilisations have had on wider Persian, Middle Eastern and world history. Written by established and up-and-coming specialists in the field, this series provides an important synergy of the latest scholarly ideas about this formative ancient world civilisation.

Lloyd Llewellyn-Jones

1 *Introduction*

Eberhard W. Sauer

Recently, Touraj Daryaee and Khodadad Rezakhani[1] observed astutely that no book on Sasanian history in English had been published between the nineteenth and the early twenty-first centuries. There have, of course, been a small number of such books in other languages, such as French, German and Russian. Monographs on ancient Persia, covering the Sasanian as well as the Parthian and Achaemenid eras, have also appeared in print, and a series of specialist studies, on specific Sasanian sites or artefacts, such as coins, are worth noting too. Over the past decade, there has been a surge of interest in Sasanian studies, and a small number of volumes devoted to the Sasanian Empire have been produced in recent years.[2] It is, however, still true that a person of medium income in Europe would easily be able to afford to buy all books dealing mainly or exclusively with matters Sasanian currently in print and would not require excessive shelving space to store them. By contrast, anybody seeking to acquire all that has been published on every aspect of Roman studies would have to be rich and require a small palace at least to house such a library. Not only have there been fairly few works on the Sasanian era, there is also a strong tendency to focus on major works of art and literary sources, sparse and mostly either written from an external perspective or centuries after the events.

It requires thus no apology for this edited work devoted to the much neglected Sasanian Empire, or for our focus being broader than textual sources and art. Neither, of course, is it our aim to go from one extreme to the other. Literary sources and works of art remain indispensable, but other strands of archaeological and environmental evidence now add much to the picture. As the title reveals, it is our aim to assess the global significance of the Sasanians, and several contributors deliberately venture even beyond the borders of the mega-empire, into the Indian Ocean, Central Asia, Arabia and the Roman world. The reach of Sasanian influence, the interrelation in peace and war between the empire and its neighbours and the comparative scale of infrastructure and construction projects cannot be appreciated from an isolationist perspective.

The ideas underpinning this edited volume are influenced by the current European Research Council-funded research project, 'Persia and its Neighbours'. It was under the auspices of the British Institute of Persian Studies, under the presidency of Vesta Sarkhosh Curtis and Ali Ansari, that an opportunity arose to pursue this project as part of a conference on 'Persia & Rum'. The first day of this conference was devoted to the topic of this volume, the second to medieval and modern studies addressing the relations between Persia and the wider world. A much larger gathering of many of the leading experts would have been attractive, but financial and logistical considerations imposed constraints. For this reason, only a small number of authorities on the Sasanian era could take part. Yet, whilst the list is selective, contributors cover an unusually wide field of specialisms. Some are participants in the 'Persia' project, others unaffiliated, some are new to Sasanian studies (the editor himself being a Romanist by training) and others senior scholars – a perfect mixture that made this conference refreshingly fruitful, with many new ideas and approaches aired for the first time. Of the fifteen speakers, or groups of speakers, twelve are included in this volume. Three more who all gave excellent presentations (Simon James on 'Martial Interactions Between the Partho-Sasanian World and Rome', Seth Priestman on 'Regional Ceramic Diversity in the Sasanian World' and Khodadad Rezakhani on 'The Economy of the Borderlands between Rome and Sasanian Iran') were unable to contribute to the proceedings, due to other important commitments. Whilst the omission of these masterly syntheses leaves gaps, a short collection of articles on a large, complex and diverse empire, lasting over 400 years, will inevitably always be selective in its coverage.

The first part of our book is devoted to surplus production, urban growth and the environment, evidently interrelated phenomena, as urban populations are dependent on farmworkers, producing enough food to feed town dwellers, and on safe supply networks. Urban growth and infrastructure are barometers of a society's economic success, stability and resourcefulness. The Sasanian era saw the foundation of several large geometric cities, with much investment in urban monuments, streets and water supply. The significance of this becomes evident if contrasted with developments in the Roman world. Here too there had been a wave of establishing new towns in earlier centuries. Sasanian geometric cities, often implanted on virgin land, date to a time when in the Roman Empire there no longer was the necessary surplus of resources and population to create new cities from scratch. Urban foundations in the Roman world between the third and seventh centuries were few in number and tended to be of smaller dimensions than their Sasanian counterparts. Notably in the late antique European west, many towns massively shrank in size. Whilst urban culture in the Eastern Roman Empire fared much better than in the empire's western half and its successor states, and Constantinople increased in size, the overall contrast in urban fortunes between late Roman and Sasanian-controlled territories is stark. In part this was facilitated by Sasanian military successes in the third century and the pragmatic decision to resettle deported communities[3] – made possible through inner stability and agricultural surplus production in Persia. And long-distance resettlement of people will only have been a small factor in what appears to be an overall growth of urban population. The 3 km^2-city of Dasht Qal'eh near modern Gonbad-e Kavus, for example, is likely to be a fifth-century foundation,[4] established at a time of peace with Rome; hence there is no obvious external group whose large-scale resettlement could account for its foundation. We may assume that most of the city's populace will have been from within imperial borders. Undoubtedly, there is much still to be learnt about Sasanian urban settlement, not just its barely explored housing and infrastructure, but also the sheer existence of some towns and cities. Circumstantial evidence suggests that some Sasanian military foundations (Ören Qala, Ultan Qalasi and Gabri Qal'eh) may already have been transformed into towns under Sasanian rule and often lasted many centuries beyond,[5] a phenomenon mirroring legionary fortresses evolving into thriving town in the early Roman Empire. Other Sasanian urban establishments will await discovery, concealed under Islamic layers in multi-period sites, and others, as has been the case with Sasanian Dasht Qal'eh, will have been wrongly assigned to earlier or later periods on the basis of shaky ceramic chronologies, postulated architectural parallels or questionable historical hypotheses.

In the light of the importance of the urban phenomenon, it is fitting that the first chapter of part I is a masterly summary of Sasanian urbanism by St John Simpson, not confined to known sites, but featuring new discoveries seen on satellite imagery. Simpson paints a vivid picture of life in Sasanian cities and the multiple trades operating alongside what may have been bazaar-like streets. Outdoor rubbish disposal led to sediments building up and in turn the need to raise indoor floors to prevent muddy water from infiltrating. The sheer number and size of cities and the dimensions of their formidable urban defences were astonishing, and all part and parcel of the integrated planning and good management that saw massive investment to safeguard urban growth and prosperity. Little wonder that many Sasanian cities, well protected by massive moat-lined walls and benefitting from urban amenities and from their location amidst fertile lands, lasted much longer than the long-lived empire itself. Here we may see a further parallel with Rome that similarly laid the foundations for many cities that proved more durable than the empire. In its highly developed urban culture, the Sasanian Empire foreshadowed the Caliphate.

How was the growing urban population fed? Several contributors address this question from a range of angles: irrigation canals increasing crop yields, site density as revealed by archaeological survey as well as tangible evidence for food. Plant remains and animal bones provide direct evidence for diet, not to mention a wide range of other activities of economic significance. Lyudmila Shumilovskikh and her co-authors offers the first ever history of Sasanian tree cultivation (arboriculture), and they also cover aspects of agriculture and pastoralism. What is special about this period of history would, of course, not be obvious if the study was confined to the Sasanian era alone. For this reason, long-term developments are analysed to reveal in what ways this epoch stands out – the same approach that, for similar reasons, is also adopted in the next chapter on animal remains. The picture, as was to be expected, is not simple and uniform across a territory as vast as that under Sasanian control. The ten sites under investigation reveal regional differences. In Fars, at the heart of the Achaemenid Empire, arboriculture, notably olive oil production, appears to have peaked under this powerful empire and the Parthians. Further north, however, several pollen profiles point to a climax in olive tree cultivation under Sasanian rule, and the same applies to walnut trees. Overall Shumilovskikh concludes that tree cultivation reached a second apogee under Sasanian rule, quite possibly the result of a political decision and in any case evidence to suggest that important products were available in greater quantities than before. Evidence for a phase of forest clearance in the late Sasanian era in the foothills of the Alborz Mountains, some 25 km east of the thriving Sasanian city of Dasht Qal'eh, provides further tantalising glimpses into the impact the empire had on its environment, extensively exploited for its natural resources.

Food production was evidently vital to feed the urban and rural population, which appears to have expanded in some parts of the empire at least, as well as the military apparatus that kept farmers and town dwellers secure. Important new evidence emerges from a study with similarly broad scope by Marjan Mashkour and her co-authors. It has long been recognised that in the north-west of the Roman Empire several domestic animal species grew in size in comparison to those of the pre-Roman Iron Age.[6] Far fewer animal bone assemblages have been studied in the Sasanian world than in the Roman west, yet Mashkour et al. make a powerful case in their pioneering study that similar developments also occurred under the rule of Rome's eastern rival. Sheep and goat, arguably the most common source of meat, grew on average in size – creating, as in imperial Rome, the right conditions for animal husbandry to flourish and to provide a growing population with animal protein. Yet, as Mashkour has already demonstrated in an earlier study, the empire tended to avoid wastage and overexploitation of its resources, with meat consumed on the Gorgan Wall mainly being from domestic animals that had reached the end of their economic usefulness. This may help to explain how large military garrisons and urban dwellers could be fed without putting undue strain on the rural population and without creating tensions in frontier societies.[7]

Large and long-lasting empires impact on the environment. This can be seen in the intensification of agriculture, arboriculture and animal husbandry. It is also evident from major construction projects that have left their imprints in the landscape up to the present day. A major study by Dan Lawrence and the late Tony Wilkinson examines the frontier landscapes of the western and northern borderlands of the Sasanian Empire. As in the case of tree cultivation, the picture is far from uniform, and we see an intensification of settlement in some areas, such as the Mil Steppe in modern Azerbaijan, and a reduction elsewhere, notably on the frontiers with Rome in Upper Mesopotamia. In places, Lawrence and Wilkinson detect possible nucleation of settlement – an important observation that demonstrates that estimating demographic developments is far from easy or straightforward. Neither settlement count nor settlement size on its own necessarily provides a reliable yardstick.

Despite such regional variations, the empire's resourcefulness as a whole is amply demonstrated by construction projects of unparalleled scale. Two investigations in particular are worth singling out, both made by graduate students under Wilkinson's supervision. The first of these is the Khandaq Shapur, a major canal to the west of the Euphrates and the heart of Sasanian Mesopotamia. This massive water channel could be dated to AD 420/570 or before and has been mapped over more than 100km by Jaafar Jotheri et al. – an impressive testimony to Sasanian hydraulic engineering. Sasanian canal construction in fertile lands facilitated transport, and boosted crop yields and population levels. Where strategically placed, such as the Khandaq Shapur, they could also prove obstacles to military opponents attempting to enter rich lands – or prove traps for those trying to escape with booty.

Similarly fascinating is the Ghilghilchay Wall in modern Azerbaijan. Its coastal and foothill section was surveyed by a multinational team in 2002. The continuation into the Caucasus, to the stronghold of Chirakh Qala high up in the mountains and beyond, had been explored previously, but not to our knowledge mapped in detail.[8] Tony Wilkinson and his student Edward East succeeded in doing so remotely, confirming that the wall indeed ran towards the prominent castle towering high over the plain and offering spectacular views over the coastal corridor – a defensive system that would not have been easy to bypass or even to approach unnoticed, not to mention that the wall continued beyond what has been mapped so far. Yet the chapter not only presents important new discoveries and a survey of relevant research, it also offers significant new insights into Sasanian strategy, arguing persuasively that there was a route system from the Sasanian fortification of Ultan Qalası on the River Araz in north-west Iran, via Ören Qala, Qala Tepe and Barda in modern Azerbaijan towards Dariali Fort in Georgia. The ability to move troops and trade goods rapidly was of vital importance in an empire as vast as the Sasanian realm – and of advantage for commerce too.

The theme of routeways is further explored by Kristen Hopper, with a focus on the Gorgan Plain, studied extensively as part of her doctoral research. Quite in contrast to imperial Rome, there are no stone-paved roads – unsurprising in a stoneless loess plain. The Gorgan Wall protecting these prosperous lands similarly employs no stone, but is built of fired bricks. Hollow ways of different periods are explored, but do not allow us on their own to map the road network that must have existed between the numerous archaeological sites across the fertile plain and beyond. In part, this may be a result of movement across flat ground only following the same corridors where obstacles had to be negotiated at fixed crossing points.

One would imagine, furthermore, that hollow ways would have filled with water in wet weather, an incentive to seek alternative routes before existing tracks were worn to sufficient depth to leave permanent traces. Whilst hollow ways traced on satellite images or the ground will represent no more than a shadow of the route network that once must have criss-crossed the plain, Hopper also explores other avenues of research. Alignments of major sites can be revealing. A possible gate in the Gorgan Wall between Forts 12 and 13 is, more or less, in alignment with a Sasanian campaign base, a mega campaign base and the city of Dasht Qal'eh, the latter perhaps the provincial capital. That the major Sasanian sites cluster in the vicinity of the region's medieval urban centre of Jurjan will not have been fortuitous and will in part be due to agricultural fertility. Hopper observes that there is also a pass across the Alborz Mountains to the south of Dasht Qal'eh that was already in use in the Sasanian era, and succeeds in shedding much new light on settlement patterns and connectivity across this frontier landscape.

As vast and varied as modern Iran is, it is easily forgotten that the Sasanian Empire covered about twice its geographic area, and considerably more than this when it reached its maximum extent in the AD 610s and 620s. Warwick Ball takes us to Sasanian sites in the territory of Afghanistan that are now not easily accessible. Formerly of the British Institute of Afghan Studies and a leading authority on Afghan archaeology, Ball makes a persuasive case that the east was of far greater importance to the Sasanians than our mainly western sources would lead us to believe. The Gorgan Wall was already remote enough not to feature in a single classical or medieval western source, quite unlike fortifications of lesser dimensions further west, yet the empire stretched another 1,500km beyond, far into the area of modern Pakistan. Modern history has taught us that Afghanistan is not easy to control militarily, and we cannot be sure to what extent any outside power was ever in control of remote regions. Yet Sasanian suzerainty already reached beyond the eastern boundaries of modern Afghanistan in the third century. After temporary setbacks, notably in the fifth century, the Sasanian state regained much ground in the sixth century. Many sites misattributed to the Kushan Empire are in fact Sasanian, and the empire has left its imprint in the area via Sasanian art, notably the Rag-e Bibi rock relief, featuring a Persian king, probably Shapur I, hunting rhinoceroses, then still found in the Indus Valley. Bactrian documents written under Sasanian rule begin to shed light on the empire from an eastern perspective. Portable objects, such as coinage, provide further evidence for Sasanian influence. A Sasanian fort is amongst the easternmost installations of its kind, although we may be sure that this is just the proverbial tip of the iceberg. Most Sasanian soldiers and officials will have been housed within existing settlements in densely populated areas. Blended in with their surroundings, such urban garrisons are archaeologically invisible. Perhaps Sasanian-era monuments which are not recognisably Sasanian are just as important in conveying why the Sasanian Empire lasted so long. Successful empires do not interfere unnecessarily with local culture. Buddhists and Nestorian Christians appear to have enjoyed, it seems, religious freedom in the cosmopolitan mega-empire's far-flung eastern provinces.

Was there indeed greater religious tolerance across the empire than the biographies of Christian martyrs and the Zoroastrian high priest Kirdir's famous rock-cut proclamations imply? Lee Patterson explores this question further, and it is also central to an important recent study by Richard Payne.[9] Whilst there were religious persecutions, notably of Christians, these were often politically motivated (and targeted at the nobility), after Christianity had become the dominant religion in the Roman Empire, as well as in Armenia and Iberia, countries on the fault lines between the Sasanian and Roman spheres of control. Other factors, such as attacks on fire temples by Christian zealots, could also trigger sanctions against those violating the *pax Sasanica* – the *modus vivendi* necessary for inner peace in the diverse religious and ethnic conglomerate under Sasanian rule. Whilst Patterson argues persuasively that the Sasanian state – far from being a loose confederacy – was based on strong, centralised royal power, commanding significant resources, such power was not normally used to stamp out religious minorities. Not only did Christianity become the mainstream religion in much of Transcaucasia, it also gained many converts elsewhere, in the empire's far-flung fringes as well at its very heart. In AD 410 a synod was held at Ctesiphon under the patronage of Yazdgerd I – at a time when in the Roman world all minority religions and cults faced persecution (just as Christian heresies did), even if the nature and intensity of anti-pagan and anti-Jewish action varied greatly over time and from place to place.[10] Suppression of minorities can destabilise states and, whilst there was occasional targeted action against troublemakers driven by faith in the Sasanian Empire, religious minorities on the whole fared much better than in monotheistic Christian Rome.

Christian Armenia, famous for its proclaimed resistance to Persian rule, features prominently in Tim Greenwood's contribution. Whilst the Armenians' claim to be allowed to follow their patrimonial Christian belief is discussed, as well as pious legacies to the church, it is legal matters that are at the heart of Greenwood's contribution. He is able to show that, in terms of Armenian law, Sasanian influence was stronger than Roman, despite the shared faith of the Transcaucasian realms and Rome. Earlier traditions and the extent of political control may account for this; the Sasanian Empire for most of the late antique era was in control of a much larger part of Armenia than Rome. Armenia was more diverse and overall under much greater oriental influence than ecclesiastical literature may imply. And this legal legacy outlived the demise of the Sasanian Empire and can still be traced in documents of the eighth and ninth centuries.

If in Armenia Sasanian rule had greater impact than commonly assumed, this should not lead us to conclude that the flow of ideas was one-directional. The next two contributions, by Pierfrancesco Callieri and Sauer et al. explore the interrelation between the Sasanian Empire and the Roman world. Callieri re-examines the famous Sasanian rock reliefs in Fars accomplished under Ardashir, and makes a persuasive case that Sasanian Persia's first king deliberately presented his dynasty as the heirs to the Achaemenid Empire, the largest and most powerful pre-medieval Near Eastern empire before and also centred on Fars. Some reliefs propagating the new Sasanian dynasty are in the immediate vicinity of Achaemenid monuments carved more than half a millennium before. This hypothesis is substantiated via careful analysis of their style, as well as of a Sasanian fire temple at Ardashir Khurrah (or Gur) near Firuzabad. Callieri's research is of significance far beyond the art of Sasanian stone carving, the reign of a single monarch or the heartland of the two empires. This is evident if we look at the question of Achaemenid traditions in Sasanian times more broadly. In our age, where academic reputation often rests on an ability to demolish earlier scholarship or prove the unreliability of textual sources, the proclaimed link between the two empires (e.g. Sasanian claims on Roman territory once under Achaemenid rule) has unsurprisingly been subjected to scrutiny and doubt. Textual evidence for the existence of a 10,000-strong Sasanian corps of 'immortals' following in the footsteps of the Achaemenids – or indeed of any Sasanian units of such numerical strength – has recently been dismissed as a western invention. Now there is clear archaeological proof for military bases that easily could have accommodated 10,000 men or more.[11] Callieri's research sets the record straight and reminds us that there is powerful material and textual evidence for Sasanian kings seeing themselves as the rightful successors to Achaemenid Iran. Yet, in their endeavour to emulate works of art and architecture that had not been produced in Fars for centuries, Callieri argues that the Sasanians took advantage of captured Roman craftsmen, collaborating with their Persian counterparts, in the wake of Ardashir's successful campaigns into Roman territory. This in no way implies inferiority; quite the contrary. Successful, and culturally diverse, mega-empires tend to learn from their conquered subjects. One only needs to remember how much Roman art and architecture owes to the Greek east.

If Sasanian royal ideology emphasised Achaemenid links, the Parthians laid the foundation for the new empire. If Roman masons made a contribution to Sasanian art in the third century, innovation and initiative grew stronger and stronger in Sasanian Persia in the centuries that followed. In the contribution of Sauer et al. we make a case not only for the 'old-fashioned' idea of the late Roman world suffering decline in capabilities containing a core of truth, but for the reverse trend prevailing amongst its major eastern rival. Our knowledge of Sasanian military infrastructure has increased massively in the early twenty-first century, due to targeted application of scientific dating of previously undated monuments and large-scale satellite survey. We now know that the late antique world's longest and most heavily guarded frontier wall was in Persia's northern frontier zone, as were various substantial barriers blocking the coastal corridors along the Caspian Sea's western and southern shores. Sasanian fortresses exceed their late Roman counterparts in size many times over, in terms of both individual examples and combined area. The Sasanian Empire built up a military infrastructure on an unparalleled scale between the late fourth and the sixth centuries and reached its territorial apogee in the early seventh century, whilst contemporary Roman fortifications were of lesser dimensions and the Western Empire suffered military annihilation. It was on the borders with the Steppes of Eurasia that we see the highest concentration of grand, purpose-built fortifications, reflecting in part the level of threat posed by the Huns, Hephthalites and Turks later – and in part that there was not the same cluster of strategic cities to shelter and protect garrisons as there was on the borders with Rome. The Sasanian Empire also pioneered the effective use of mountains as natural frontier walls, blocking passes with forts and stone walls. This substantially reduced the risk of invasion from the steppes into Transcaucasia, Mesopotamia and the Gorgan Plain and thus safeguarded the basis of the empire's economic prosperity, which in turn enabled it to keep its formidable defences well guarded.[12]

Neither Rome nor its steppe neighbours brought the Sasanian Empire to an end, no more than a generation after it had reached its greatest extent. The fatal attack came from an unexpected direction: Arabia in the south evolved into the epicentre of an expanding empire. Within less than twenty years, the Caliphate wiped out Sasanian kingship, but inherited Sasanian urbanism, engineering and institutions – owing some of its success to its Sasanian inheritance. Within a century of the emergence of Islam on the Arabian Peninsula in the early seventh century, the Caliphate reached the Atlantic, the Indus and the Caucasus. And it is Arabia where our book takes us next. Craig Morley makes a powerful case that the Sasanian Empire was much more vulnerable on its southern frontiers than history written from a western perspective tends to appreciate. And this was already the case long before the emergence of Islam. In the fourth century, according to Tabari, Shapur II faced a sea-borne Arab invasion of Fars. It was to the same king that the massive Khandaq Shapur is attributed, which protected the south-western flank of Central Mesopotamia.[13] The Arabs already then appear to have posed a serious threat to the very heart of the empire and some of its most fertile lands. This threat was not taken lightly. As early as the third century the empire expanded into the Arabian Peninsula. For much of the Sasanian era, the Persian Gulf appears to have been a Persian *mare nostrum*. Not only was there direct military investment in the Persian Gulf zone and on the approaches to Mesopotamia,[14] but the empire established alliances well beyond. Eventually even Yemen became part of the empire. Expansion and defensive infrastructure on the empire's southern frontiers were not solely designed to contain a military threat. Despite parts of Arabia not faring well economically in this period, the Indian Ocean trade in luxury goods provided highly lucrative opportunities for the Sasanian Empire. The Peninsula was both a producer of precious exports and a transhipment centre for goods from the east. This, in addition to security concerns, stimulated much interest in Arabian affairs.

The Indian Ocean trade is also at the heart of the concluding contribution by James Howard-Johnston. Yet the focus is even broader than the chapter title implies, encompassing virtually all of the known world (from a Sasanian and Roman perspective), from Western Europe and Scandinavia to China and from Central Asia to the east coast of Africa. The sea-trade between the Mediterranean world and southern Arabia, India (exporting pepper and other valuable commodities) and, to a lesser extent, territories beyond up to China (famous for its silk) had boomed ever since Rome had gained access to the Red Sea in 30 BC. In late antiquity, Sasanian merchants appear to have secured a greater share of the lucrative trade in luxury goods. Red garnets from southern India and Sri Lanka, fashionable in Europe during the Migration Period as never before, will have found their way to the west via Sasanian traders taking their share of the profits. It is, of course, often impossible to be sure whether Sasanian or Roman coins and artefacts found far beyond imperial frontiers reached their destination via direct trade or via multiple transactions and middlemen, but there is no question that the trade reached an impressive scale and that only a minute fraction of the trade goods, even those that are not perishable, has been found. Sasanian export products from South and South-East Asia have recently been compiled and discussed by Nils Ritter,[15] but Howard-Johnston makes the attractive proposition that Roman subsidies paid in gold, in support of Persian endeavours to seal off the Caucasus passes in an effort to shield both their own territories and the Roman Near East from invasions, were used for the acquisition of eastern luxury goods. Our excavations in Dariali Fort have certainly failed to reveal any evidence for coinage, let alone precious metal, having been supplied to those guarding this strategic Transcaucasian route. Like the garrison of the Gorgan Wall, the guardians of the so-called 'Caspian Gates' will have been paid in kind.

In AD 571, Sasanian Persia took over direct control of incense-producing Yemen, a feat Rome had attempted unsuccessfully under Augustus almost 600 years before. Justinian's endeavours, forty years earlier, to persuade his fellow Christians in Ethiopia and Yemen to attack Persia from the south, and to act against Persian economic interests in the Indian Ocean, had equally failed. Located at the Bab al Mandab, which all Roman merchant ships sailing from Egyptian ports into the Indian Ocean had to pass, the takeover of Yemen tightened Sasanian control of the lucrative trade. Related to this, Howard-Johnston argues convincingly, was an alliance Rome formed with the Turks and the increasing importance of overland trade across Eurasia. Silk, whilst the Roman Empire started producing its own in the sixth century, was amongst the sought-after goods from the east. The alliance between Rome and the Turks led to co-ordinated attacks on the Sasanian Empire from the AD 570s – and of course again in the early seventh century. Yet the Sasanian Empire withstood the joint assault of the major powers in the Eurasian Steppes and the Mediterranean world – no doubt a result of the strength of its northern defences and the formidable military apparatus at its disposal. And it was not just the north where the Sasanian army made its presence felt. Howard-Johnston also draws our attention to Sasanian forts – albeit on a much smaller scale than those we find in the northern borderlands – on the shores of the Indian Ocean. In addition to strongholds in the Persian Gulf, the little-known fort of Ratto Kot on an island at the mouth of the Indus will have been a strategic asset.[16] Occupied in the Islamic era and with distinct projecting towers, its architecture would be compatible with Sasanian or Islamic construction, but pottery from the earliest phase appears to suggest Sasanian origins (fourth to sixth centuries). Howard-Johnston goes far beyond shedding new light on the Indian Ocean trade, and shows convincingly how interconnected world trade and politics were in late antiquity and what a pivotal role the Sasanian Empire played in affairs of global significance.

Common themes have emerged in this volume and a strong case can be made that there is a direct link between investment in defence, irrigation and agriculture and population growth, economic wealth and a flourishing urban culture. In some parts of the Sasanian Empire we observe a significant increase in the number of sites occupied.[17] There appear to have been divergent developments in different parts of the empire. Whilst in some regions population levels may have shrunk[18] or remained stable, they appear to have reached unprecedented peaks in some territories. This went hand in hand with an efficient administrative apparatus and targeted investment in the state's key assets. As James A. Neely aptly observes,

> the Parthians, and to a much greater extent the Sasanians, were quite successful at integrating ... ethnic groups, inaugurating taxation and conscription, expanding and intensifying agriculture and water management, and competing in trade. Archaeological evidence and documents indicate that the Sasanians ... sent engineering missions into the most underdeveloped parts of their empire, and literally reshaped the land surface of large areas of the Middle East.[19]

Whilst the long survival and expansion of the empire, and archaeological evidence for large new cities, canal systems and densely occupied countryside, are a telling testimony for the empire's overall success, it is not our intention to present a one-sided picture. As already pointed out, whilst in many territories settlement density appears to have increased, in others it may have decreased. Whilst building up what appears to have been one of the strongest and most effective military machines of the premodern world, and quite possibly the strongest from the fourth to the early seventh centuries, occasional strategic errors led to Sasanian armies suffering the odd major defeat – just like those of all other long-lasting empires. Whilst the Sasanian Empire was more tolerant of minorities, such as the Christians, than commonly assumed, religious zeal thought to threaten imperial peace was suppressed. Overall, Sasanian kings pursued a significantly more tolerant religious policy than the imperial government of Christian Rome, which persecuted not only all other beliefs, but also Christian minorities.

Comparing and contrasting the Sasanian Empire to other megaempires from antiquity to modernity, most of them less enduring, sheds light on the factors that enable empires to prosper or cause them to vanish. Targeted investment in food production and urban development enabled the empire to build up a most formidable military apparatus that in turn protected these economic assets. This in its turn allowed the Sasanian Empire to safeguard its prosperity and by and large defend itself successfully for centuries against external threats – and even to expand further some 400 years after the new dynasty had gained power. In this respect it outperformed most other empires before or since. Part of the success story was its ability to learn from others as well as to foster innovation. Sasanian military and urban architecture, whilst unsurprisingly sharing some common traits with that of its neighbours, was distinctly different from earlier or contemporary Roman examples. There are no Roman frontier walls built of fired bricks and with canals running alongside them, nor are there parallels for semi-permanent campaign bases, protected by massive walls and moats, or for circular cities built from scratch. The frequent tendency in scholarship to search for western prototypes for Sasanian architecture often fails to convince, even if there is no denying that there was some flow of ideas from west to east as well as from east to west. The Sasanian system of government was quite independent too. Central power, in contrast to the Roman Empire for example, rested with one dynasty rather than shifting from the heartland to provincials. No obscure generals gained the imperial throne through revolt and civil war, destabilising and weakening the state, as happened so often in third- and fourth-century Rome.

Sasanian studies have progressed rapidly in the twenty-first century. While the state was widely seen as a rather disorganised and disunited feudal one even in the recent past, our latest evidence points to a highly organised and successful empire, whose intensified irrigation, increased food production, in places at least unprecedented population growth, flourishing urban culture and large-scale military infrastructure projects rivalled and in some respects clearly surpassed those of the western world in late antiquity.[20] Perhaps this book will form a small contribution to bringing an understudied empire into the limelight – and to rectify our western bias when studying the ancient world. And this is not just a closed chapter of history. If we move away from relativism and have the courage again to acknowledge that there were often significant imbalances of power between contemporary empires, and that 'old-fashioned' concepts of the rise and decline of states often have a core of truth – and explore the root causes of strength and weakness – we can apply the insights gained to our own time. Undoubtedly today, just as in late antiquity, there are more and less innovative societies, enjoying greater or lesser stability, success and prosperity. Relativism will blind our judgement, whilst recognising what factors caused the rise and fall of empires in the past may contribute to making the right decisions for the future.[21] (Edinburgh, May 2016).

NOTES

1. Daryaee and Rezakhani 2016: xiii.
2. These include Callieri 2014, Daryaee 2009, Harper 2006, Kennet and Luft 2008, Payne 2015, Pourshariati 2008, Sarkhosh Curtis and Stewart 2008 and Wiesehöfer and Huyse 2006.
3. Kettenhofen 1996.
4. Sauer et al. 2013: 382–406.
5. Lawrence and Wilkinson and Sauer et al., this volume.
6. Benecke 1994: 178–207.
7. Mashkour et al. 2013: 574–6; Sauer et al. 2013: 623.
8. Aliev et al. 2006. We have not been able so far to scrutinise the Russian literature thoroughly. Important is Abdullaev 1968, with a schematic map (Abdullaev 1968: 199 fig. 2). On 25 August 2012 I had an opportunity to visit this wall as well as Chirakh Qala. There was no time on this trip to search for the missing link, nor would a pedestrian survey in the area, now cluttered with petrol pumps, have been the most promising strategy to solve the riddle.
9. Payne 2015.
10. Sauer 2003 and 2014 with further sources.
11. Charles 2011, discussed in Sauer et al. 2013: 348–9, cf. 378 no. 238.
12. See Sauer et al. 2013: 619–24, cf. 290–1, 301 for a more detailed discussion of the phenomenon, contrasting this with the insecure conditions that prevailed in the unprotected Gorgan Plain in the nineteenth century.
13. See Lawrence and Wilkinson, this volume, with Fig. 5.2.
14. In addition to evidence cited by Morley, this volume, see Priestman et al. forthcoming for exciting new research that will not be pre-empted here.
15. Ritter 2010.
16. See also Potts 2006: 88.
17. See most recently Neely 2016.

18 Kennet 2007.
19 Neely 2016: 257, cf. 258–9.
20 See, for example, Payne 2014: 4–5, who rightly challenges Pourshariati 2008 and sees large-scale construction projects as evidence for central organisation.
21 We have tried to be as consistent as possible within the volume in the spelling of place names and technical terms as well as in chronological matters. The editor, whilst conscious of the fact that there is contradictory information in the sources as to the date of the birth of Jesus (retrospectively linking it to major historical figures and events), not to mention legitimate questions as to why one religion should determine the chronology of world history, believes that attempting to purge language would be a Sisyphean and unrewarding task and thus prefers sticking to the traditional BC/AD system. He has, however, left contributors the freedom to choose between this and BCE/CE, or indeed to omit AD/CE when it is obvious that a date is within the Christian era.

BIBLIOGRAPHY

Abdullaev, K. P. (1968), 'Гильгильчайская оборонительная стена и крепость Чирах-Кала', *Советская Археология,* 1968.2, pp. 196–209.

Aliev, A. A., Gadjiev, M. S., Gaither, M. G., Kohl, P. L., Magomedov, R. M. and Aliev, I. N. (2006), 'The Ghilghilchay Defensive Long Wall: New Investigations', *Ancient West & East,* 5, pp. 143–77.

Benecke, N. (1994), *Der Mensch und seine Haustiere,* Stuttgart: Theiss.

Callieri, P. (2014), *Architecture et représentations dans l'Iran Sassanide,* Studia Iranica, Cahier 50, Paris: Association pour l'Avancement des Études Iraniennes.

Charles, M. B. (2011), 'The Sasanian "Immortals"', *Iranica Antiqua,* 46, pp. 289–313.

Daryaee, T. (2009), *Sasanian Persia: The Rise and Fall of an Empire,* London and New York: I.B. Tauris.

Daryaee, T. and Rezakhani, K. (2016), *From Oxus to Euphrates: The World of Late Antique Iran,* Ancient Iran Series 1, Irvine: Jordan Center for Persian Studies and Farhang Foundation.

Harper, P. (2006), *In Search of a Cultural Identity: Monuments and Artifacts of the Sasanian Near East, 3rd–7th century* A.D., New York: Bibliotheca Persica.

Herrmann, G. (1980), *Iranische Felsreliefs E: The Sasanian Rock Reliefs at Bishapur,* 1, Iranische Denkmäler, 9, Berlin: Reimer.

Herrmann, G. (1981), *Iranische Felsreliefs F: The Sasanian Rock Reliefs at Bishapur,* 2, Iranische Denkmäler, 10, Berlin: Reimer.

Herrmann, G. (1983), *Iranische Felsreliefs G: The Sasanian Rock Reliefs at Bishapur,* 3, Iranische Denkmäler, 11, Berlin: Reimer.

Herrmann, G. (1989), 'The Sasanian Rock Reliefs at Naqsh-i Rustam', in G. Herrmann and D. N. MacKenzie, *Iranische Felsreliefs I,* Iranische Denkmäler, 13, Berlin: Reimer, pp. 9–33.

Kennet, D. (2007), 'The Decline of Eastern Arabia in the Sasanian Period', *Arabian Archaeology and Epigraphy,* 18, pp. 86–122.

Kennet, D. and Luft, P. (eds) (2008), *Current Research in Sasanian Archaeology, Art and History*, BAR International Series 1810, Oxford: Archaeopress.

Kettenhofen, E. (1996), 'Deportations II: In the Parthian and Sasanian Periods', in *Encyclopædia Iranica*, 7, Costa Mesa: Mazda, pp. 297–308.

Mashkour, M., Radu, M. and Thomas, R. (2013), 'Animal Bones', in Sauer et al. 2013, pp. 539–80.

Neely, J. A. (2016), 'Parthian and Sasanian Settlement Patterns on the Deh Luran Plain, Khuzistan Province, Southwestern Iran', *Iranica Antiqua*, 51, pp. 235–300.

Overlaet, B. (2009), 'A Roman Emperor at Bishapur and Darabgird: Uranius Antoninus and the Black Stone of Emesa', *Iranica Antiqua*, 44, pp. 461–530.

Payne, R. (2014), 'The Archaeology of Sasanian Politics', *Journal of Ancient History*, 2.2, pp. 1–13.

Payne, R. (2015), *A State of Mixture: Christians, Zoroastrians, and Iranian Political Culture in Late Antiquity*, Oakland: University of California Press.

Potts, D. T. (2006), 'Indian Ocean, I: Pre-Islamic Period', in *Encyclopædia Iranica*, 13, New York: Encyclopædia Iranica Foundation, pp. 87–91.

Pourshariati, P. (2008), *Decline and Fall of the Sasanian Empire: The Sasanian–Parthian Confederacy and the Arab Conquest of Iran*, London and New York: I.B. Tauris.

Priestman, S., Said Al-Jahwari, N., Kennet, D., Sauer, E. W., Andrews, M., Ainslie, R. Lawrence, D., MacDonald, E. and Usher-Wilson, L. S. (forthcoming), *Sasanian Military Investment on the Batinah Plain of Oman: New Discoveries at Fulayj*.

Ritter, N. C. (2010), 'Vom Euphrat zum Mekong: Maritime Kontakte zwischen Vorder- und Südostasien in vorislamischer Zeit', *Mitteilungen der Deutschen Orient-Gesellschaft zu Berlin*, 141, for 2009, pp. 143–71.

Sarkhosh Curtis, V. and Stewart, S. (eds) (2008), *The Sasanian Era: The Idea of Iran III*, London and New York: I.B. Tauris.

Sauer, E. W. (2003), *The Archaeology of Religious Hatred in the Roman and Early Medieval World*, Stroud and Charleston: Tempus.

Sauer, E. W. (2014), 'Disabling Demonic Images: Regional Diversity in Ancient Iconoclasts' Motives and Targets', in K. Kolrud and M. Prusac (eds), *Iconoclasm from Antiquity to Modernity*, Farnham and Burlington: Ashgate, pp. 15–40.

Sauer, E. W., Omrani Rekavandi, H., Wilkinson, T. J., Nokandeh, J. et al. (2013), *Persia's Imperial Power in Late Antiquity: The Great Wall of Gorgān and Frontier Landscapes of Sasanian Iran*, British Institute of Persian Studies Archaeological Monographs Series, II, Oxford: Oxbow Books.

Trümpelmann, L. (1975), *Iranische Felsreliefs B: Das Sasanidische Felsrelief von Dārāb*, Iranische Denkmäler, 6, Berlin: Reimer.

Weber, U. (2009), 'Wahrām II., König der Könige von Ērān und Anērān', *Iranica Antiqua*, 44, pp. 559–643.

Wiesehöfer, J. and Huyse, P. (eds) (2006), *Ērān und Anērān: Studien zu den Beziehungen zwischen dem Sasanidenreich und der Mittelmeerwelt*, Stuttgart: Franz Steiner.

Part I

Surplus Production, Urban Growth and the Environment

2 Sasanian Cities: Archaeological Perspectives on the Urban Economy and Built Environment of an Empire

St John Simpson

The Sasanian Empire had many large, multicultural and typically heavily defended cities. Literary sources are filled with direct or indirect references to the deportation or internal transfer of populations from one region to another, and boosting the urban population was clearly an important part of imperial economic planning, but there has been relatively little study of Sasanian urbanism. This chapter provides a timely overview by re-examining the archaeological evidence for the physical appearance and distribution of some of these urban centres, discusses their forms, and uses Google imagery to locate two previously archaeologically unrecorded cities which feature in the Arab conquest and Heraclius' campaign shortly before. It goes on to use the excavated evidence from three city sites in Iraq, Iran and Turkmenistan to illustrate the physical appearance of residential and/or commercial quarters, and concludes with some observations on the importance of the Sasanian urban economy.

INTRODUCTION

The term 'Sasanian' conjures a popular image of armoured knights, fire worshippers, courtly arts and conspicuous consumption, but a 400-year empire which stretched from Syria to Pakistan, recovered from the capture and death of one emperor on an eastern battlefield, and was one of Rome's biggest rivals and threats was not just built on exceptional kingship, feudalism and faith. Its success lay instead in effective bureaucracy and good management. Integrated planning for economic, military and civilian needs was fundamental, and without it the massive capital projects and military capabilities of the Sasanian state could not have been sustained. The huge number of mints known from marks on silver drachms implies a monetarised economy despite the fact that many of the mints are still physically unlocated. Moreover, many seals give the names of cities with which their owners were associated. The rapid movement of the Arab-led armies during the Islamic conquest was regularly punctuated by lengthy sieges and protracted negotiations with local commanders, which can be explained by the sheer number of cities and the scale of their defences.

According to the medieval Nestorian *Chronicle of Se'ert*,

> Shapur left the territories of the Romans, taking with him prisoners whom he settled in the countries of Iraq, Susiana, Persia and in the towns his father had founded. He also founded three towns and gave them names derived from his own name. One was in the land of Maisan and was called Sod Shapur [Sadh-Shapur]. The second in Persia which is still called Shapur today [Bishapur]. He rebuilt Gundeshapur which had fallen into disrepair and named it Anti-Shapur [Antioch-Shapur], a word half-Greek and half-Persian, meaning: 'You are Shapur's equal.' He constructed a third town on the banks of the Tigris called Marw Habor which is 'Akbora and its environs [Buzurg Sabur]. These towns were populated by his prisoners who were provided with lands and home to till.[1]

This is one of several ancient sources to describe the effects of Sasanian military campaigns in the Roman Empire. The sources refer to the transplanting of urban populations, give hints or direct comparisons of the new cities to their western counterparts, and show proximity to agricultural lands granted to the new citizens. Moreover the importance and interrelationship of these factors is amply illustrated by the archaeological evidence (Fig. 2.1).

> Population may have peaked on the Susiana Plain during the Parthian Period, but it was imperial Sasanian investment that radically transformed settlement and subsistence in the area. Kilometers of qanats, large new canals, and massive stone weirs were constructed to ensure and expand cultivation and to supply new urban centers. Much design work on the hydrological system was apparently done by captured Roman engineers. Extensive agricultural investment was also made in the Deh Luran area where population reached unprecedented levels.[2]

However, there has been relatively little study of the subject of Sasanian urbanism (Huff 1993). This chapter therefore provides a timely overview, with a re-examination of the archaeological evidence which is part of a wider re-evaluation of the evidence for the Sasanian economy, ranging from its agriculture and related industries[3] to other craft activities.[4]

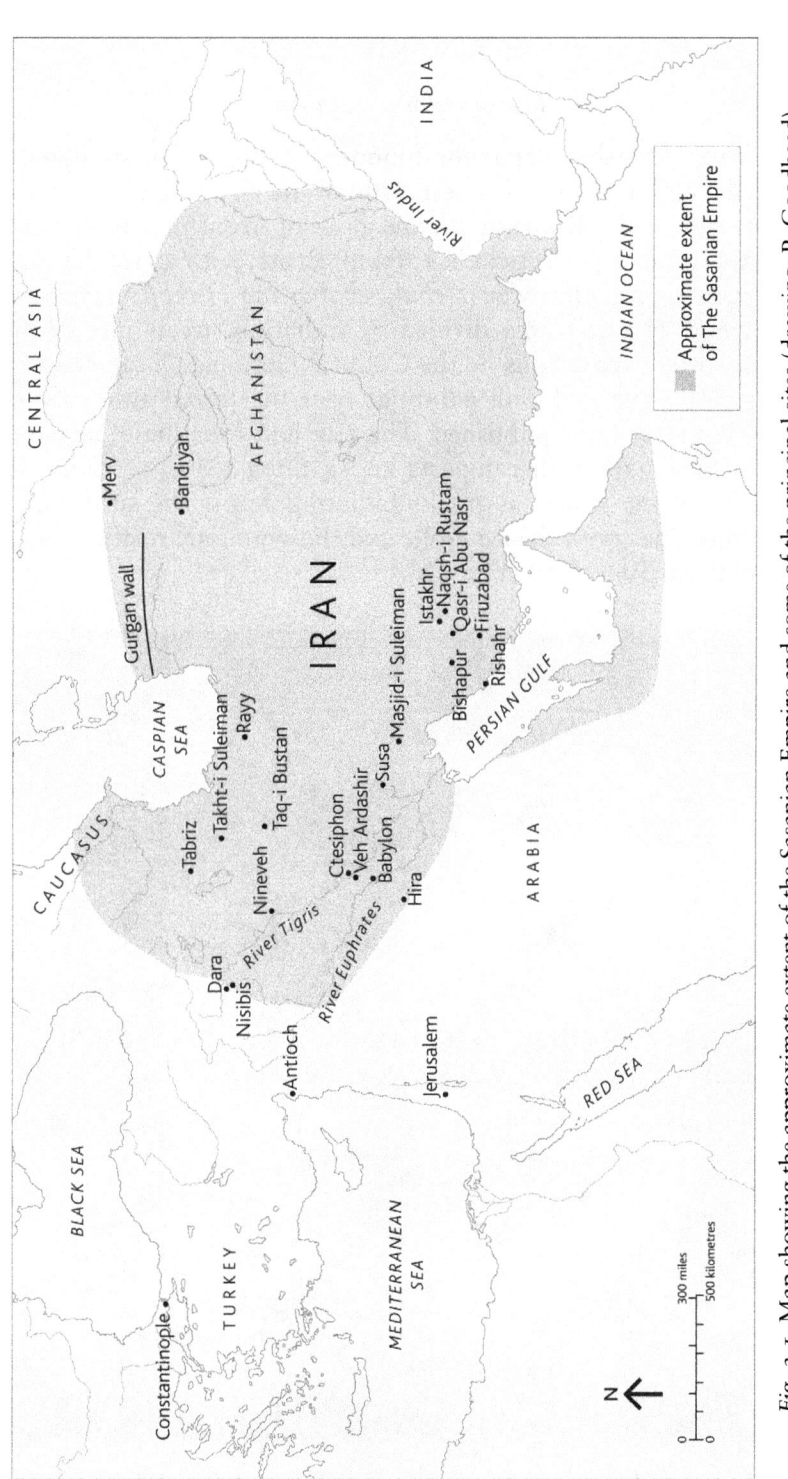

Fig. 2.1 Map showing the approximate extent of the Sasanian Empire and some of the principal sites (drawing: P. Goodhead).

NEW FOUNDATIONS

The circular exceptions

In c. 220, Ardashir Papakan, founder of the Sasanian dynasty, founded a circular city in his homeland of the Firuzabad Plain which he named Ardashir Khurrah ('divine glory of Ardashir'). It was carefully laid out in a perfect circle 1.85km across, with a circular inner area including a high tower (*tarbal*), *chahar taq* (*Takht Neshin*) and palace, and an outer area divided by radiating streets into twenty sectors.[5] Brief excavations by the Cultural Heritage Organisation of Iran in 2005 exposed wall paintings near the *tarbal* although few details have yet been published. The city had four main gates and was fortified with high ramparts and a ditch fed by a canal; the extension of the streets as tracks radiating across the surrounding plain underlines both the symbolic and the symbiotic relationship of the city to its hinterland (Fig. 2.2).[6]

Fig. 2.2 Aerial view of Ardashir Khurrah (from Google Earth, 2013).

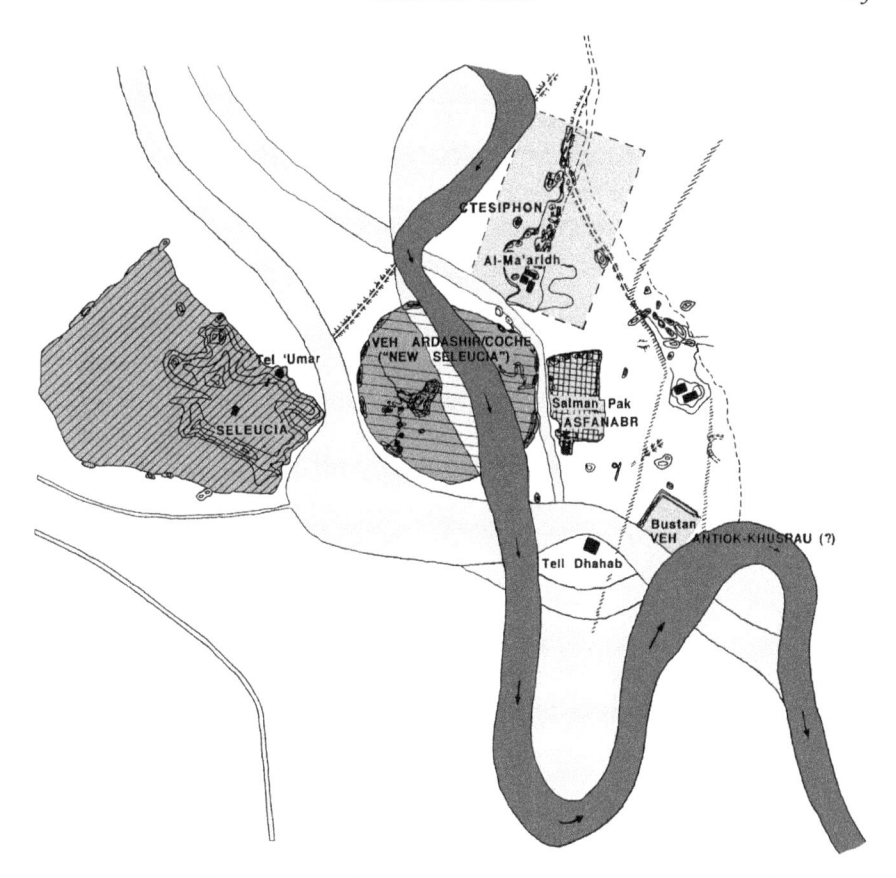

Fig. 2.3 Schematic map showing major Sasanian sites in the Ctesiphon conurbation, including the location and reconstructed extent of Ctesiphon, Veh Ardashir, Aspanabr (i.e. 'Asfanabr') and Veh-az-Antiok-Khusro, the earlier city sites of Seleucia and Valasapat, the present course of the River Tigris and the position of its palaeo-channels, and the alignment of First World War trenches following ancient canal beds (after Simpson 2015: 8, fig. 1.2).

After his defeat of Artabanus V and his adoption of the Parthian capital at Ctesiphon, Ardashir founded another – more or less circular – city on the opposite bank of the River Tigris next to the former Seleucid eastern capital of Seleucia (Fig. 2.3). This city was laid out around and on top of a small older settlement known in Aramaic as Coche, which was given the new name of Veh Ardashir ('City of Ardashir'), later Arabicised as Bahusir.[7] The old core presumably held the major public buildings, although the limited excavations at Tell Baruda, the main mound near the centre of the site, revealed only vernacular architecture.[8] The basic shape of Veh Ardashir was an irregular circle covering some 700ha. It is said to have included a fortified citadel known in Middle Persian as Garondagan and in Syriac as Aqra d'Kokhe; this was probably the seat of the mint responsible for the mint-mark 'WH' and probably corresponds to Tell Baruda. The city was heavily fortified and excavations in the southern part reveal a mudbrick wall measuring some 10m across at the base in its final phase, and elongated semi-circular or horseshoe-shaped projecting towers between straight sections 30–35m long.[9] The lowest parts of the towers and curtain walls were solid but, judging by Sasanian fortifications much better preserved at the city of Merv, may have supported a hollow curtain wall with galleries and a wall-walk.[10] The evidence from Merv that the defences were regularly reconstructed and remodelled hints too that this was also true of the (now much less well preserved) walls of Veh Ardashir. This explains the slightly different picture offered by an earlier section excavated through the western stretch of the fortifications.[11] Ammianus refers to the defences as 'blind walls',[12] perhaps an allusion to a solid rather than hollow curtain, but in any case they were strong enough to deter both Julian's army in 363 and the Arab assault in the early seventh conquest when, according to Tabari, the siege involved twenty catapults constructed by a deserting Sasanian engineer, as 'the city was protected by trenches, guards and all sorts of military gear'.[13]

The city itself was apparently divided into rectangular blocks, although the shapes of the two excavated blocks were not particularly regular, perhaps because maintaining a strictly rectilinear grid within a circular circuit was difficult. The location and number of Veh Ardashir's gates are unknown but major entrances on all sides are a reasonable assumption, to facilitate access across the river to Ctesiphon on the north, and to the Nahar Malcha on the south; equivalent gates to the east and west would have made effective use of the street grid. The main streets separating the so-called Northern and Southern blocks were slightly cambered, 7m wide and suitable for wheeled traffic, riders and large pack animals; their size implies maintenance by the municipal authorities. The preliminary reports refer to bituminised street surfaces but this is incorrect. Houses within the residential quarters appear to have been accessed via an irregular network of narrow alleys or passages suitable for pedestrians, barrows or small pack animals; the architecture is discussed in greater detail below.

A third, almost circular, city exists at Darabgird (Fig. 2.4), although the walls may date to the eighth century: the mid-tenth-century author Hamza Isfahani states the city was originally triangular but enclosed within the present walls by the Umayyad

Fig. 2.4 Aerial view of Darabgird (from Google Earth, 2012).

governor of Fars, Hajjaj ibn Yusuf.[14] The surface pottery confirms continuity of occupation as late as the twelfth century.[15] However, these circular cities appear to be the exception rather than the norm, and Whitcomb's hypothesis based on CORONA imagery that there is another circular city at Gondeshapur remains to be verified archaeologically.[16]

Variations on the rectilinear norm

Although a circular layout has military advantages and is more economical in the use of building materials, it creates challenges for the internal architecture, so it is unsurprising that most other cities were laid out on rectilinear plans. Some of these were continuations of much older centres, although their occasional renaming was probably accompanied by infrastructure schemes. The best-known examples of these are in Iran but, as we shall see, these are part of a much bigger picture.

Fig. 2.5 Aerial view of Bishapur/Bay-Shapur (from Google Earth, 2012).

In 266 following earlier victories over Roman armies, Shapur I (c. 240–72) founded a new city in Fars and named it Bay-Shapur. Better known today as Bishapur (Fig. 2.5), it measures 1.5km in length, and 1km across; it is bounded by fortifications which survive on three sides (the fourth being destroyed by the River Shapur), and appears to have been divided by major streets into 200m-square blocks with smaller intervening streets which continued to be used into the medieval period.[17]

Shapur I also founded another city in Susiana called Gondeshapur ('Military camp of Shapur'). This measured 3.1km in length and 1.5km across, is bounded on three sides by what is now a low gravel bank – perhaps representing the eroded core of a fortification originally encased in brick – and contains low scattered mounds within (Fig. 2.6). The site was described by Ghirshman as having

> practically disappeared beneath the plough, but the plan was based on a great rectangle, curiously reminiscent of a Roman military camp. The same

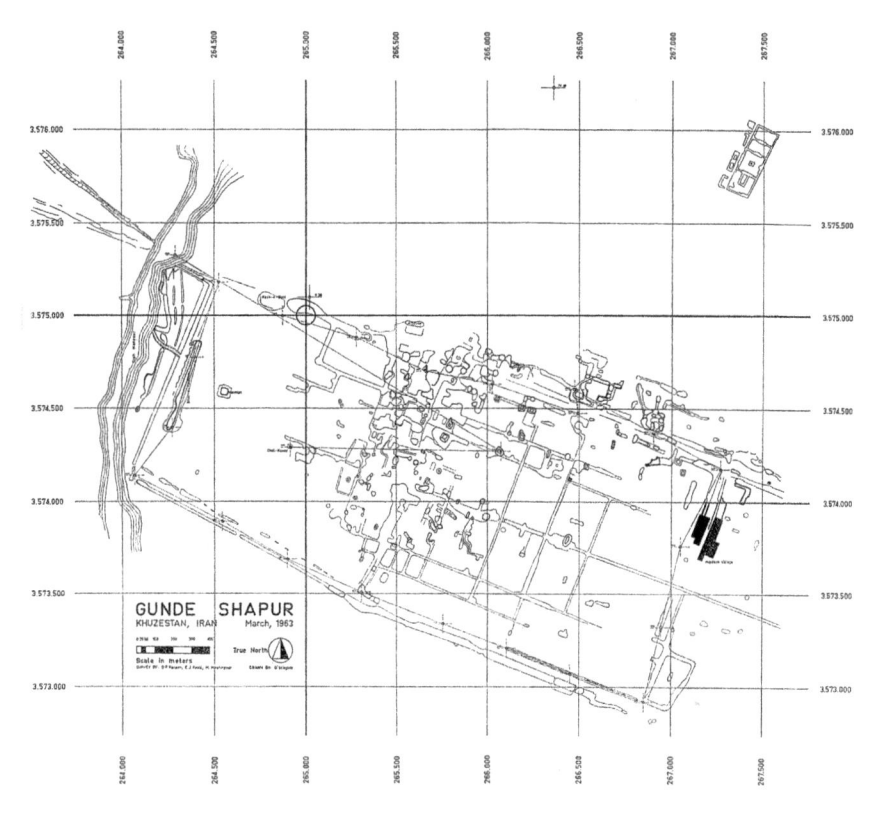

Fig. 2.6 Plan of the remains at Gondeshapur (after Adams and Hansen 1968: fig. 1).

arrangement was noticed by the writer at Eyvan-e-Karkha near Susa, where Shapur II is said to have settled his western prisoners.[18]

Ghirshman published a vertical air photograph of the latter city (Fig. 2.7), carried out a single season of excavations in 1950 and found parts of two monumental buildings, one with remains of figural wall paintings, although few details were published and their precise date is unclear.[19] In 1963 a topographic survey was carried out at Gondeshapur and four small soundings were excavated, but the results were regarded as 'uniformly unpromising'.[20] However, two important observations were made. One was that the prominent mounds in the central third of the walled area were composed of fill redeposited to support early Islamic structures, and the whereabouts and layout of Sasanian structures could not be determined from the surface as they lay below plain level. The second concerned its water supply. Soundings in the bed of the Siah Mansour, a watercourse immediately west of the city, revealed a row of ashlar masonry piers

Fig. 2.7 Aerial view of Eyvan-e Karkha (from Google Earth, 2012).

which must have originally supported a bridge, while an adjacent tunnel was part of an elaborate inverted siphon which delivered water from a canal off-take from the River Dez, passing under the Siah Mansour and into the city (Fig. 2.8).[21] The authors suggested that 'the large grid traceable within the city on the air photographs consist not so much of a rectangular arrangement of streets as a network of such tunnels'.[22] This feature explains how the engineers were able to deliver large and regular amounts of fresh water to the population; these may have been standard features of Sasanian urban planning as they recur as features within forts and the city site of Dasht Qal'eh in the Gorgan Plain.[23] Despite damage inflicted during the Iran–Iraq war and through agriculture and construction, these two city sites offer great potential in understanding the development of major Sasanian cities.

However, these are not the only two such cities of this distinctive plan. Following his survey of the Eridu–Ur region of southern Iraq in 1966, Henry Wright commented that:

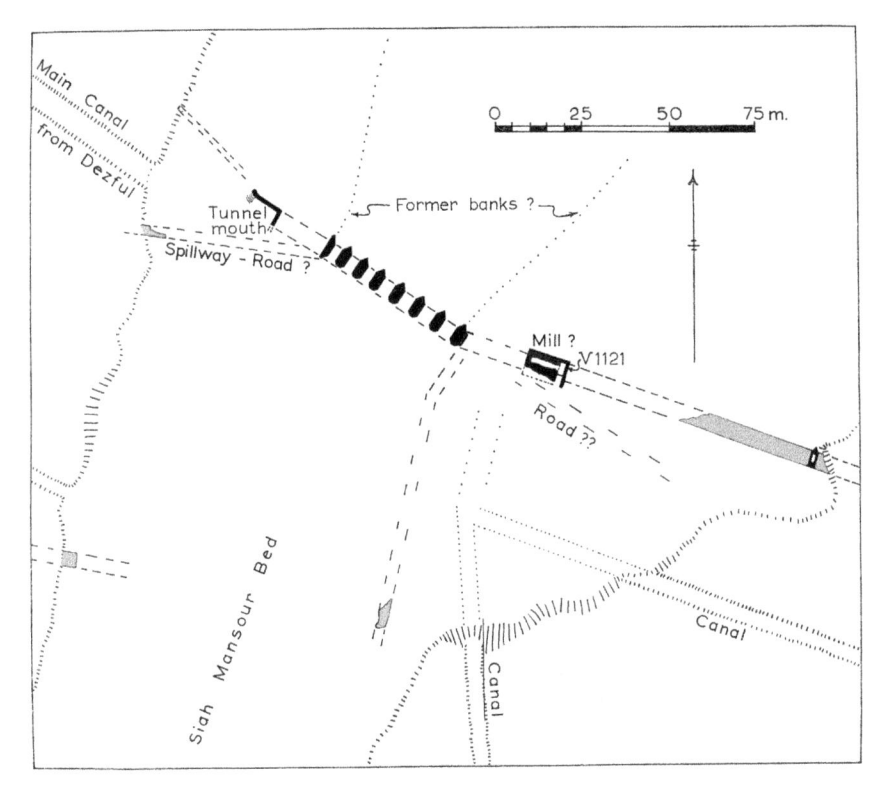

Fig. 2.8 Plan of the inverted siphon and bridge at Gondeshapur (after Adams and Hansen 1968: fig. 2).

Visible on the air photographs, which I did not see until after I returned to Baghdad, about eight kilometres west of the survey border is a roughly rectangular walled town, covering 55 hectares and divided into three parts. It is similar in plan to Jundi Shapur [i.e. Gondeshapur] and Iwan-i Karkheh [i.e. Eyvan-e-Karkha] in southwestern Iran ... and is probably a Parthian or Sasanian center. Perhaps when the present levee of the Euphrates is examined in detail we will find that EP-65 is one of a series of fortified settlements linked to this larger town, with installations such as al-Qusair being either elements in an outer line of defense or posts designed to protect routes coming from the south.[24]

Still apparently unsurveyed archaeologically, this site lies about 30km south-west of Samawah (Fig. 2.9). Nor does this appear to be the only example. Another is located near at-Taqtaqanah at the head of the Wadi al-Khirr in an oasis west of Najaf. It is rectangular, measures 1,270 × 550m across, and covers an area of about 70ha (Fig. 2.10). This site probably corresponds to the fortress of Qasr Muqatil which lay in the oasis of al-Qutqutana, and shortly before the Arab conquest was part of the desert frontier system known as the 'Uyun at-Taff, or

Fig. 2.9 Aerial view of unexcavated Sasanian new foundation south-west of Samawah (from Google Earth, 2012).

the *Khandaq* of Shapur II, re-established in the early seventh century by Khusro II.[25] The third lies midway along a major route connecting southern Kurdistan with the Hamrin Basin, and therefore commanding a major highway connecting northern Mesopotamia with the Iranian plateau and the route down the Diyala valley to Ctesiphon. This last site is known today as Eski Kifri (Fig. 2.11): it has apparently never been archaeologically surveyed but was first noted in 1820 by Claudius Rich, who collected late Sasanian stamped pottery there.[26] It is probably the site of the palace of Khusro II at Dezeridan sacked by Heraclius in late December 627, as he marched from Kirkuk to the Diyala after his victory at the battle of Nineveh.[27] A shared feature of all these sites is their carefully planned rectilinear layout with regular internal divisions and the remains of raised ridges within. However, whether these represent walls or are part of an aqueduct system like that suggested at Gondeshapur remains to be tested, and further research on these great city sites is overdue.

Fig. 2.10 Aerial view of unexcavated Sasanian new foundation at Qasr Muqatil (?) (from Google Earth, 2013).

Ctesiphon had been founded as a Parthian capital on the left bank of the Tigris, opposite Seleucia, and, by the Sasanian period at least, was surrounded by fired brick walls and a moat.[28] Located about 1.5km north of the late Sasanian royal city of Aspanabr (i.e. 'Asfanabr' on Fig. 2.3), the site corresponds to an elongated series of mounds known as al-Ma'aridh (at the southern end) and Tulul Bawi (at the northern end) which straddle the mouth of an old canal off-take of the Diyala (Fig. 2.3). This confirms a representation on the arch of Septimius Severus in Rome which indicates that the city was divided in two by a canal.[29] The line of this is still marked by a low ridge with a track running down the spine and mounds on each side, and excavations carried out in 1928/9 and 1930/1 revealed several large late Sasanian residences near the southern edge.[30]

After his sack of Antioch in 540, Khusro I founded another city said by Dinawari to be located one parasang (4–5km) south of Ctesiphon and implied by Tabari to be on the same, that is eastern, side of the

Fig. 2.11 View of unexcavated Sasanian new foundation at Dezeridan (?) (from Google Earth, 2013).

River Tigris.³¹ It was formally named Veh-az-Antiok-Khusro ('City Better than Antioch [has] Khusro [built this]') and is said to have had public baths and a hippodrome, and a street plan modelled on that of Antioch. Freedom of worship and burial was given to its Christian inhabitants. Known colloquially as Rumagan ('Town of the Greeks'), later Arabicised as ar-Rumiyya, it probably corresponds to the unexcavated site still known as Bustan Kisra ('Gardens of Khusro'), which is surrounded on two sides by the eroded remains of high rectilinear mudbrick walls, the remainder having been washed away by changes in the course of the River Tigris.³²

CONTINUITY AND THE URBAN SETTING

Adams and others have stressed the high density of Sasanian occupation, the relatively high number of large settlements and evidence for intensive and closely integrated water management systems across the Mesopotamian alluvium and south-west Iran.[33] Unfortunately, the survey quality varies across the region and very few of these sites have been recorded in detail or are closely dated: future intensive survey of some, particularly if combined with satellite imagery and geophysical survey and/or surface scraping, would be very instructive. Nevertheless, a few comments are possible on the basis of the published survey data. The most intensive surveys were conducted in the Diyala Basin and across large areas of the central alluvium between 1937 and 1975. The relative paucity of sites in the northern alluvial plains is misleading as it simply reflects the fact that sites of later periods were not fully recorded.[34] Moreover, many more sites must lie along the major levee banks of the Tigris and Euphrates. but these areas largely remain unsurveyed (Fig. 2.12). The entire region between Wasit and Basra which corresponds to the Sasanian administrative province of Ard Kaskar (Mesene) has also not yet been surveyed, but this region is known to have been important. The Sasanian precursor of Wasit was known as Kaskar and lay on the opposite (left) bank of the Tigris in the form of a roughly triangular area of mounding up to 750m across, recalling the description of Darabgird before its circumvallation in the eighth century.[35] Further south, Hansman argued that the trapezoidal walls of the 8.2 km^2 site known today as Naisan probably corresponds to the city site of Charax Spasinu, later refounded and renamed as Astarabadh Ardashir: the site lies mostly below plain level and therefore may have survived the Iran–Iraq war rather better than expected.[36]

A large number of Sasanian sites recorded on the Diyala and Nippur surveys were classified as towns (covering between four and thirty hectares), small urban centres (between thirty and a hundred hectares) and cities (more than a square km in size). Most cities have remains of fortifications and all were on either major canals or river-courses, facilitating access to transport networks as well as drinking water. The site at Medina (Tell ad-Dhiba'i) was described as square, 700m across and fortified with a wall 7m thick with possible close-set, repeating, semi-circular buttresses.[37] Ruqbat al-Mada'in was a walled pentagon where mapping of the interior revealed three areas of visible footings which appear to represent carefully planned buildings (Fig. 2.13), although the site seems to have been destroyed totally since.[38]

Other Sasanian urban centres are attested archaeologically from Iran but almost all are unexcavated. On the Damghan Plain, the extensive but heavily water-eroded ruins of the Parthian city of Hecatompylos at Shahr-e Qumis were occupied throughout

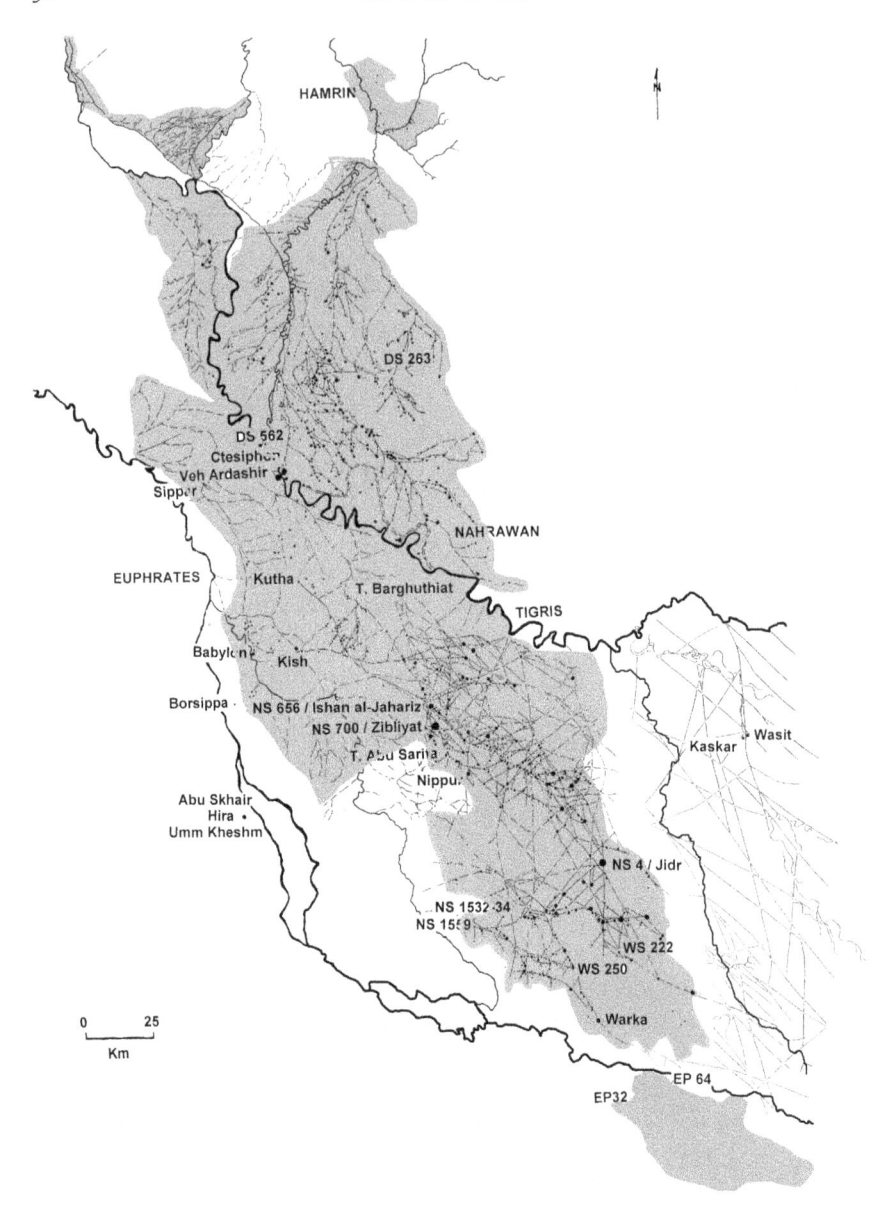

Fig. 2.12 Map of Sasanian sites and canals in central and southern Iraq, based on surface surveys and satellite imagery (after Simpson 2015: 19, fig. 1.5).

the Sasanian period according to Maurer Trinkaus, supporting Hansman's earlier conclusion that 'a recent and detailed study ... of aerial photographs covering all the Damghan Plain produced no other likely site for Sasanian Komish'.[39] Parthian, Sasanian and Islamic pottery is concentrated in different areas, suggesting that the focus

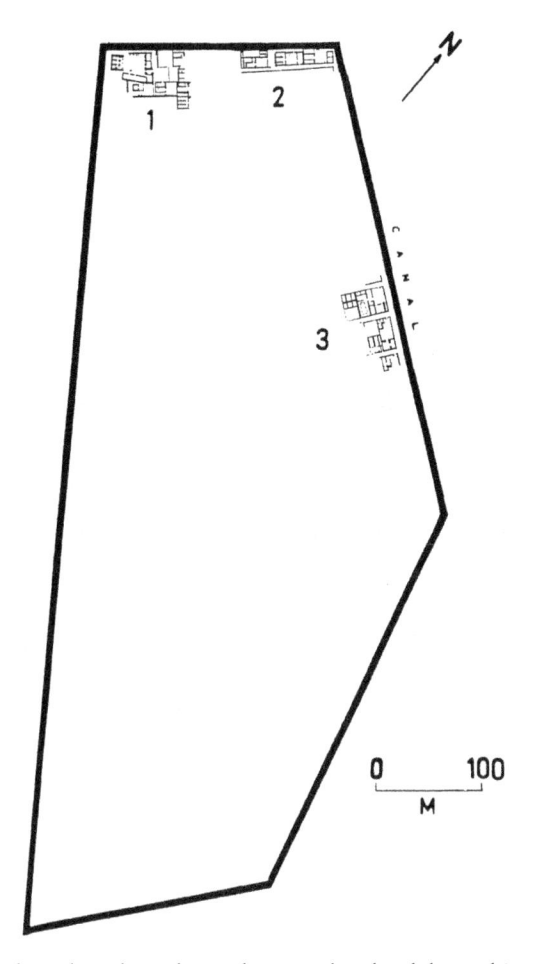

Fig. 2.13 Plan of Ruqbat al-Mada'in, showing details of the architecture visible on the surface (after Finster and Schmidt 1976: 153–57, figs 80–4).

of occupation shifted periodically, and explaining the lack of deep stratigraphy and its currently deflated condition.[40] It was also during the Sasanian period that a wall appears to have been constructed around the town of Damghan itself, some 30km to the north-east.[41] On the Gorgan Plain, the city site of Dasht Qal'eh covers an area of about 3km^2, exceeding Bishapur or Gur, and geophysical survey, followed by test excavation, proved that at least the eastern portion was divided by avenues of brick piers.[42] The main population centre on the Marv Dasht Plain was Estakhr, and Whitcomb has suggested a plausible difference between the Sasanian (and earlier) and subsequent Islamic parts of the site based on different alignments of the streets visible on air photographs; the trial excavations by the

University of Chicago in 1932 and 1934 are essentially unpublished but, with the exception of the 'West Test', were focused mostly on the later area of the site.[43] The date Shiraz was founded remains ambiguous and the nearby ruins at Qasr-e Abu Nasr probably represent its Sasanian forerunner; this site is discussed further below. In other cases, such as Isfahan, the remains of the Sasanian city attested as a mint lie buried below the modern city,[44] and the equivalent historically attested remains at Rayy and Nishapur have not been convincingly identified on the ground.[45]

EXCAVATED EVIDENCE FOR THE BUILT ENVIRONMENT

Three different city sites in central Mesopotamia, southern Iran and Central Asia offer glimpses into the internal organisation of space, patterns of circulation, water supply, storage and forms of vernacular architecture within Sasanian cities.

The most detailed evidence comes from Veh Ardashir, partly described earlier. Between 1964 and 1976, the Centro Scavi di Torino explored two areas of this city, two quarters just inside the southern walls with a smaller area on the Tell Baruda central mound (Fig. 2.3). The initial phase was characterised by wells, drains and bread ovens, but was followed by a progressive increase in settled density from the fourth to the later half of the fifth century, after which the southern portion was largely abandoned.[46] Mudbrick was the basic building material, fired brick being used more sparingly than in its precursor of Seleucia; it was limited either to areas of heavy wear, such as stairways, passages and drain linings, or the lower pivots of solid doors. House floors were usually well compacted, perhaps because of the combined effect of frequent water sprinkling to reduce the dust from sweeping and trampling. Some of the domestic rooms contained small oval hearths sunk 15–20cm below floor level, and similar features were noted in domestic architecture at Merv. Walls were plastered with finer clay but surviving architectural decoration is scarce, partly because the walls were regularly cut down before rebuilding on a similar alignment. This also partly reflects the constraints of a heavily built up environment with little opportunity to extend properties, and is a feature of any urban setting. The excavated houses often possessed a small open courtyard inside the door or entrance lobby (Fig. 2.14). In one case, additional fireplaces and probable bread ovens were found in the courtyard, while in others there were low benches or pads for wooden posts which would

Fig. 2.14 Plan of the excavated area at Veh Ardashir (after Simpson 2015: 10).

have originally supported a light superstructure and offered partial shade.⁴⁷ The courtyards also acted as light and air wells for adjacent rooms and generally functioned as private open spaces at the heart of the household; there are references in the Babylonian Talmud to these being places where ovens and grinding stones might be kept, animals held overnight, chickens reared, clothes washed and manure stored as a source of fuel.⁴⁸ The same source refers to how they might be shared between households but it is not surprising to find disputes over visual trespass, particularly if one property passed into different ownership, or over the dripping of water from one person's roof into the neighbouring courtyard.⁴⁹ The relevance of the excavated findings to many other passages in the Babylonian Talmud is a subject explored by the author in greater detail elsewhere.⁵⁰

Most buildings in Veh Ardashir were probably flat-roofed and single storey. However, the plan of one large house on the northwest corner of the Northern block shows a staircase leading either to an upper storey or to the roof, in three phases next to the vaulted reception room (*iwan*) and in another above the entrance lobby. Two larger houses had an *iwan* facing the courtyard entrance: these lacked fixed furniture and were doubtless furnished with carpets or rugs and cushions instead. Similar *iwans* are a feature of the larger houses excavated at Qasr-e Abu Nasr and al-Ma'aridh as well as on a much larger scale at Aspanabr (notably the Taq-e Kisra) and Takht-e Suleiman.

The two residential blocks excavated at Veh Ardashir are thought to consist largely of houses with shops along the street frontages in the southern portion (Area 1) and houses and workshops for making glassware and metal furniture elements in the northern (Area 2). The mixture of functions within a given quarter illustrates a case in the Babylonian Talmud which refers to the fire risk caused by the proximity of a blacksmith to other properties.⁵¹ Another passage refers to tailors, tanners, teachers and craftsmen operating within a single neighbourhood.⁵² Moreover, the eighth book of the Middle Persian compendium known as the *Denkard* states that 'every trade had its own series of shops in the bazaar', and this practical arrangement is likely to have been a very ancient tradition.⁵³ The city therefore probably resembled the traditional concept of a Middle Eastern *suq* rather than a classical definition of segregated functions in different *insulae*. The nearby open areas within the southern defences may have housed temporary markets, perhaps for agricultural produce and combining the sale of locally manufactured items with those brought in from outside the city. Alternatively, it is possible that these markets were situated along the main roads, as is still the normal practice in large premodern cities such as Fez, but in either case they have left no tangible remains, nor would they be likely to. The existence of temporary markets is hinted at within the Bavli and other sources as they refer to the open display of turnips,[54] the transport of 'kegs' of wine,[55] and complaints over the presence of untethered goats.[56] Moreover, Bishop Georgios of Izla, a converted Iranian noble, was crucified in a straw or hay market in the city in 615 and buried in a monastery of St Sergios in the nearby settlement of Mavrakta.[57]

The second case study is Qasr-e Abu Nasr, near Shiraz. Excavations there between 1932 and 1935 focused on the citadel, fortifications and raised western portion (now destroyed by modern housing), leaving the intervening urban core largely uninvestigated.[58] The citadel was densely packed with large courtyard houses, a main street running along the centre and smaller side streets running in parallel. It was approached through a single narrow gateway below a massive bastion which puzzled the excavators and was given the rather misleading description of a 'podium' in the final report (Fig. 2.15). The vernacular architecture was constructed of mudbrick on stone footings, and a number of the houses possessed wells and storage jars, suggesting that households were largely self-sufficient in terms of water supply but foodstuffs were hoarded.

The last Sasanian city site to be considered here is Merv (Fig. 2.16). This was founded in the Achaemenid period but refounded as a much larger city during the third century BC. It remained continuously occupied for the next millennium and the essentially rectangular layout of the Seleucid foundation remained unchanged, as the positions of the main gates effectively fossilised the orientation of the major arteries.[59] Soviet excavations revealed part of a residential quarter immediately inside the north gate, termed by them the 'millers' quarter' because of the large number of storage jars and grinding stones. Properties were regularly rebuilt on the same alignments, explaining the excavators' inability to distinguish the doorways. Two other areas of housing were excavated between 1992 and 2000, including part of a late Sasanian residential complex on the citadel and part of a residential quarter in the lower city.[60] The latter was, like Veh Ardashir, characterised by mudbrick houses rebuilt repeatedly on the same alignments with alleys and streets providing sufficient access for pedestrians, barrows and pack animals, but not large forms of wheeled transport. Interiors were kept scrupulously clean, refuse was deposited externally or dumped

Fig. 2.15 Multi-phase plan of the excavated architecture on the citadel of Qasr-e Abu Nasr (after Whitcomb 1985: fig. 30).

elsewhere and streets were periodically resurfaced, with solid pavements added and maintained either side of open channels used as drains. Rebuilding streets in this manner meant that adjoining householders were obliged to raise their outer thresholds regularly and periodically infill rooms behind in order to prevent them from becoming too far below the street level, and to reconstruct walls on the same alignments. This is a typical feature of modern as well as ancient mudbrick architecture, yet has not always been recognised in previous excavations: it has important implications for understanding site formation processes and the degree of redeposition of finds; and it underlines the need to combine careful stratigraphic excavation with stripping of the wall plaster in order to match the horizontal and vertical stratigraphy.[61]

Fig. 2.16 Oblique aerial view of Merv looking north: the Sasanian city site is on the right with its citadel at the top; the site on the left is its medieval successor (from Google Earth, 2009).

CONCLUSION

The Sasanian Empire was built on an urban economy and had many large multicultural cities. Literary sources are filled with direct or indirect references to the deportation or internal transfer of populations from one region to another, and boosting the urban population was clearly an important part of imperial economic planning. The size and forms of these urban centres varied. Only two, both founded by Ardashir I, are circular; the rest are rectilinear. Most show signs of fortification and careful planning, and an elaborate system of water supply is proven in the case of one. The sizes of the population are difficult to estimate reliably, but must have been very substantial and these urban centres must have been economic powerhouses of industry and culture, and helped generate revenues through poll tax as well as produce. They were sustained by, and integrated into, a highly complex pattern of local and long-distance trade and agriculture. Although the scale of trade is more difficult to quantify, archaeological surveys confirm the massive scale of investment by the state in agricultural works and water engineering which not only sustained year-round harvests but also created new lines of communication and means of transport.[62] Moreover, canals and rivers doubled as linear water barriers which could be monitored and defended at key crossings. The Gorgan project has demonstrated how Sasanian military planners of the fifth century built a linear barrier which respected the course of the River Gorgan behind, and in front drew water into a ditch which was not only defensive but also facilitated brick-making as well as domestic water supply.[63] Similar integrated planning must lie behind the construction of the *Khandaq Shapur* and is implicit in the accounts of campaigns by Julian, Heraclius and the Arab armies. The location and fortification of many Sasanian cities, particularly new foundations, must be viewed in this light, and future study could be directed at the role of integrated central planning teams encompassing the needs of the government functions of war, internal security, agriculture and urban planning.

The success or otherwise of Sasanian urban planning can be gauged by how long these cities were occupied. In some cases there is insufficient evidence to show how long they continued after the Islamic conquest, but many, including Bishapur, Estakhr, Merv and some of the older Mesopotamian towns such as Nippur and Nineveh, certainly continued to thrive for several centuries, and were only gradually abandoned as their populations drifted into other nearby centres of power and patronage. The level and social impact of this continuity have been underestimated, and the widespread earlier correlation of the rise and fall of Sasanian society with political events or the alleged fragility of its agricultural economy is simply not supported by the archaeological evidence.

NOTES

1 Lieu 1986: 478.
2 Johnson 1987: 291.
3 Simpson 2014a; 2015.
4 See for example Simpson 2014b.
5 Huff 1974: 157–9.
6 Huff 1974: 159.
7 El-Ali 1968–9: 433–4.
8 Venco Ricciardi 1973–4; 1977.
9 Negro Ponzi 1967: 45–7, figs 20–2.
10 Zavyalov 2007: 322–4.

11 Sarre and Herzfeld 1920: vol. II, 54; Reuther 1931.
12 Ammianus Marcellinus 24.4.
13 Tabari 1.2428 (trans. Juynboll 1989: 9).
14 Huff 1996.
15 Morgan 2003: 333.
16 Whitcomb 2003–4: 92–3.
17 Salles 1939–42: 93, pl. XVII; Ghirshman et al. 1956; Amiri, Genito et al. 2013.
18 Ghirshman 1978: 320.
19 Ghirshman 1952: 11–12; 1978: 179.
20 Adams and Hansen 1968; 1972: 301.
21 Sauer et al. 2013: fig. 12:13.
22 Adams and Hansen 1972: 301.
23 Sauer et al. 2013: 235–6, 312–18, 387.
24 Wright 1981: 335.
25 Cf. Morony 1982: 28, fig. 7.
26 Rich 1836: vol. I, 20; cf. Simpson 2013.
27 Kaegi 2003: 171; cf. Sarre and Herzfeld 1920: vol. II, 88; Greatrex and Lieu 2002: 214–15.
28 Gregory of Nazianzus *Or.*, 5.10 P.G. 36.676 B/C.
29 Gullini 1966: 33.
30 Kröger 1982: 80–136, figs 41, 47, 49.
31 El-Ali 1968–9: 431.
32 Reuther 1938: 574.
33 Adams 1962; 1965: 69–83; 1972: 188; 1981: 200–14; Gibson 1972: 51–2; Jacobsen and Adams 1958; Wenke 1975–6; 1987: 255.
34 Adams 1972: 183.
35 Cf. Safar 1945: fig. 2.
36 Hansman 1984.
37 Adams and Nissen 1972: 62, 222, site 64.
38 Adams and Nissen 1972: 62; Finster and Schmidt 1976: 151–63, pls 52–3.
39 Maurer Trinkaus 1986: 30; Hansman 1968: 138–9.
40 Cf. Gye et al. 1969: 34–5; Hansman and Stronach 1970.
41 Adle 1993.
42 Sauer et al. 2013: 382–406.
43 Whitcomb 1979.
44 CAIS 2010.
45 Keall 1979; Rante, Collinet et al. 2013; Rante 2015.
46 Cavallero 1966; Negro Ponzi 1966; Venco Ricciardi 1968–9; Venco Ricciardi and Negro Ponzi 1985.
47 Cavallero 1966: 66–7, pl. VI = level S, room 22, pl. VII = level I, room 20.
48 For example Bava Basra 57a–b.
49 Bava Basra 6a, 59a–b, 60a; citations from the Babylonian Talmud are taken from the Schottenstein edition.
50 Simpson 2015.
51 Bava Basra 26a.
52 Bava Basra 21b.
53 Tafazzoli 1974: 192.
54 Bava Kama 20a.

55 Bava Metzia 83a.
56 Bava Kama 23b.
57 Fiey 1961.
58 Whitcomb 1985.
59 Simpson 2008a: 71.
60 Simpson 2008b.
61 Simpson 2008a.
62 Simpson 2014a; 2015.
63 Sauer et al. 2013.

BIBLIOGRAPHY

Adams, R. M. (1962), 'Agriculture and Urban Life in Early Southwestern Iran', *Science*, 136.3511, pp. 109–22.
Adams, R. M. (1965), *Land Behind Baghdad: A History of Settlement on the Diyala Plains*, Chicago: University of Chicago Press.
Adams, R. M. (1972), 'Settlement and Irrigation Patterns in Ancient Akkad', in M. Gibson (ed.), *The City and Area of Kish*, Coconut Grove: Field Research Projects, pp. 182–208.
Adams, R. M. (1981), *Heartland of Cities: Surveys of Ancient Settlement and Land Use on the Central Floodplain of the Euphrates*, Chicago: University of Chicago Press.
Adams, R. M. (2005), 'Intensified Large-Scale Irrigation as an Aspect of Imperial Policy: Strategies of Statecraft on the Late Sasanian Mesopotamian Plain', in J. Marcus and C. Stanish (eds), *Agricultural Strategies*, Cotsen Advanced Seminars, 2, Los Angeles: Cotsen Institute of Archaeology, University of California, pp. 17–37.
Adams, R. M. and Hansen, D. P. (1968), 'Archaeological Reconnaissance and Soundings in Jundî Shâhpûr', *Ars Orientalis*, 7, pp. 53–70, plus folding figure.
Adams, R. M. and Hansen, D. P. (1972), 'Soundings at Gunde Shapur', in *The Memorial Volume of the Vth International Congress of Iranian Art and Archaeology, Tehran–Isfahan–Shiraz, 11th–18th April 1968*, Tehran: Ministry of Culture and Arts, vol. I, pp. 300–2.
Adams, R. M. and Nissen, H. J. (1972), *The Uruk Countryside: The Natural Setting of Urban Societies*, Chicago: University of Chicago Press.
Adle, S. (1993), 'Damghan', in *Encyclopædia Iranica*, 6, New York: Encyclopædia Iranica Foundation, pp. 632–8.
Amiri, M., Genito, B. et al. (2013), 'Bīšāpūr and its Territory (Fars, Iran)', *Newsletter di Archeologia CISA*, 4, pp. 1–45.
CAIS (2010), 'Archaeologists Excavating Sasanian Esfahan', 2 August, <http://www.cais-soas.com/News/2010/august2010/02-08.htm>.
Cavallero, M. (1966), 'The Excavations at Choche (Presumed Ctesiphon) – Area 2', *Mesopotamia*, 1, pp. 63–81, figs 16–25, pls V–X.
El-Ali, S. A. (1968–9), 'Al-Madā'in and its surrounding area in Arabic literary sources', *Mesopotamia*, 3.4, pp. 417–39.
Fiey, J.-M. (1961), 'Les saints Serge de l'Iraq', *Analecta Bollandiana*, 79, pp. 102–14.
Fiey, J.-M. (1967), 'Topography of al-Mada'in (Seleucia–Ctesiphon area)', *Sumer*, 23, pp. 3–38.

Finster, B. and Schmidt, J. (1976), 'Sasanidische u. Frühislamische Ruinen im Iraq', *Baghdader Mitteilungen*, 8, pp. 1–169, pls 1–79.

Ghirshman, R. (1952), *Cinq Campagnes de Fouilles a Suse (1946–1951)*, Mémoires de la mission archéologique en Iran, Rapports Préliminaires, I, Paris: Presses Universitaires de France.

Ghirshman, R. (1978), *Iran from the Earliest Times to the Islamic Conquest*, Harmondsworth: Penguin (reprint).

Ghirshman, R. et al. (1956), *Bichapour*, Musée du Louvre, Département des Antiquités Orientales, série archéologique, vols VI–VII, Paris: Paul Geuthner.

Gibson, M. (ed.) (1972), *The City and Area of Kish*, Coconut Grove: Field Research Projects.

Greatrex, G. and Lieu, S. N. C. (2002), *The Roman Eastern Frontier and the Persian Wars. Part II: AD 363–630. A Narrative Sourcebook*, New York: Routledge.

Gullini, G. (1966), 'Problems of an Excavation in Northern Babylonia', *Mesopotamia*, 1, pp. 7–38.

Gye, D. H., Beauchamp, R., Durie, I. and Wilkinson, G. (1969), *Report of the Cambridge Expedition to Komis 1968*, n.p.: privately printed.

Hansman, J. (1968), 'The Problems of Qūmis', *Journal of the Royal Asiatic Society*, 1968, pp. 111–39, pls I–IV.

Hansman, J. (1984), 'The Land of Meshan', *Iran*, 22, pp. 161–6.

Hansman, J. and Stronach, D. (1970), 'Excavations at Shahr-ī Qūmis, 1967', *Journal of the Royal Asiatic Society*, 1970, pp. 29–62, pls I–IX.

Huff, D. (1974), 'An Archaeological Survey in the Area of Fīrūzābād, Fārs, in 1972', in *Proceedings of the IInd Annual Symposium on Archaeological Research in Iran (Muzeh-e Irān-e Bāstān, Tehran, Iran, 29th October–1st November 1973)*, Tehran: Iranian Center for Archaeological Research, pp. 155–79.

Huff, D. (1993), 'Architecture sassanide', in B. Overlaet (ed.), *Splendeur des Sassanides : L'empire perse entre Rome et la Chine (224–642)*, Brussels: Musées Royaux d'Art et d'Histoire, pp. 45–61.

Huff, D. (1996), 'Dārāb. ii. History and Archaeology', in *Encyclopædia Iranica*, 7, Costa Mesa: Mazda, pp. 5–7.

Jacobsen, T. and Adams, R. M. (1958), 'Salt and Silt in Ancient Mesopotamian Agriculture', *Science*, 128.3334, pp. 1251–8.

Johnson, G. A. (1987), 'Nine Thousand Years of Social Change in Western Iran', in F. Hole (ed.), *The Archaeology of Western Iran: Settlement and Society from Prehistory to the Islamic Conquest*, Smithsonian Series in Archaeological Inquiry, Washington, DC: Smithsonian Institution Press, pp. 283–91.

Juynboll, G. H. A. (trans.) (1989), *The History of al-Ṭabarī XIII: The Conquest of Iraq, Southwestern Persia, and Egypt*, New York: State University of New York Press.

Kaegi, W. E. (2003), *Heraclius, Emperor of Byzantium*, Cambridge: Cambridge University Press.

Keall, E. J. (1979), 'The Topography and Architecture of Mediaeval Rayy', in *Akten des VII International Kongresses fur iranische Kunst und Archäologie, München, 7.–10. September 1976*, Berlin: Archaeologische Mitteilungen aus Iran, Ergänzungsband, 6, pp. 537–44.

Kröger, J. (1982), *Sasanidischer Stuckdekor: Ein Beitrag zum Reliefdekor aus*

Stuck in sasanidischer und frühislamischer Zeit nach den Ausgrabungen von 1928/9 und 1931/2 in der sasanidischen Metropole Ktesiphon (Iraq) und unter besonderer Berücksichtigung der Stuckfunde vom Tahti-Sulaiman (Iran), aus Nizamabad (Iran) sowie zahlreicher anderer Fundorte, Mainz am Rhein: Von Zabern.

Lieu, S. N. C. (1986), 'Captives, Refugees and Exiles: A Study of Cross-Frontier Civilian Movements and Contacts Between Rome and Persia from Valerian to Jovian', in P. Freeman and D. Kennedy (eds), *The Defence of the Roman and Byzantine East: Proceedings of a Colloquium Held at the University of Sheffield in April 1986*, BAR International Series 297 (2 vols), British Institute of Archaeology at Ankara, Monograph 8, Oxford: British Archaeological Reports, pp. 475–505.

Maurer Trinkaus, K. (1986), 'Pottery from the Damghan Plain, Iran: Chronology and Variability from the Parthian to the Early Islamic Periods', *Studia Iranica*, 15.1, pp. 23–88.

Morgan, P. (2003), 'Some Remarks on a Preliminary Survey in Eastern Fars', *Iran*, 41, pp. 323–38.

Morony, M. G. (1982), 'Continuity and Change in the Administrative Geography of Late Sasanian and Early Islamic al-'Irāq', *Iran*, 20, pp. 1–49.

Negro Ponzi, M. M. (1966), 'Area 1', *Mesopotamia*, 1, pp. 81–8, pls XI–XIV.

Negro Ponzi, M. M. (1967), 'The Excavations at Choche Area 1', *Mesopotamia*, 2, pp. 41–8, figs 18–23.

Rante, R. (2015), *Rayy: From Its Origins to the Mongol Invasion. An Archaeological and Historiographical Study*, Leiden and Boston: Brill.

Rante, R., Collinet, A. et al. (2013), *Nishapur Revisited: Stratigraphy and Ceramics of the Qohandez*, Oxford: Oxbow Books.

Reuther, O. (1931), *Die Ausgrabungen der deutschen Ktesiphon-Expedition im Winter 1928-9*, Berlin: Islamische Kunstabteilung der Staatlichen Museen.

Reuther, O. (1938), 'Sasanian Architecture: History', in A. U. Pope (ed.), *A Survey of Persian Art*, Oxford: Oxford University Press, vol. I, pp. 493–578, vol. IV, pls 146–53.

Rich, C. J. (1836), *Narrative of a Residence in Koordistan and on the Site of Ancient Nineveh with a Journal down the Tigris to Bagdad and an Account of a Visit to Shiraz and Persepolis* (2 vols), London: no publisher.

Safar, F. (1945), *Wasit: The Sixth Season's Excavations*, Cairo: Institut Français d'Archéologie Orientale and Directorate General of Antiquities, Iraq.

Salles, G. (1939–42), 'Nouveaux documents sur les fouilles de Châour: IVme et Vme campagnes', *Revue des Arts Asiatiques*, 13, pp. 93–100, pls XVII–XXIII.

Sarre, F. and Herzfeld, E. (1920), *Archäologische Reise im Euphrat- und Tigris-Gebiet* (4 vols), Berlin: Reimer.

Sauer, E. W., Omrani Rekavandi, H., Wilkinson, T. J., Nokandeh, J. et al. (2013), *Persia's Imperial Power in Late Antiquity: The Great Wall of Gorgan and Frontier Landscapes of Sasanian Iran*, British Institute of Persian Studies Archaeological Monograph Series, II, Oxford: Oxbow Books.

Simpson, St J. (2008a), 'Suburb or Slum? Excavations at Merv (Turkmenistan) and Observations on Stratigraphy, Refuse and Material Culture in a Sasanian City', in D. Kennet and P. Luft (eds), *Current Research in Sasanian Archaeology, Art and History: Proceedings of a Conference Held at Durham*

University, November 3rd and 4th, 2001, BAR International Series 1810, Oxford: Archaeopress, pp. 65–78.
Simpson, St J. (2008b), 'Ancient Merv: Archaeological Insights into the Economy of the City During the Sasanian Period (3rd–7th centuries AD)', in *The Turkmen Land as a Centre of Ancient Cultures and Civilizations*, Ashgabat: Ministry of Culture and TV and Radio Broadcasting of Turkmenistan, pp. 247–56.
Simpson, St J. (2013), 'Rams, Stags and Crosses from Sasanian Iraq: Elements of a Shared Visual Vocabulary from Late Antiquity', in A. Peruzzetto, F. Dorna Metzger and L. Dirven (eds), *Animals, Gods and Men from East to West: Papers on Archaeology and History in Honour of Roberta Venco Ricciardi*, BAR International Series 2516, Oxford: Archaeopress, pp. 103–17.
Simpson, St J. (2014a), 'Merv, an Archaeological Case-Study from the North-Eastern Frontier of the Sasanian Empire', *Journal of Ancient History*, 2.2, pp. 116–43.
Simpson, St J. (2014b), 'Sasanian Glass: An Overview', in D. Keller, J. Price and C. Jackson (eds), *Neighbours and Successors of Rome: Traditions of Glass Production and Use in Europe and the Middle East in the Later First Millennium AD*, Oxford: Oxbow Books, pp. 200–31.
Simpson, St J. (2015), 'The Land Behind Ctesiphon: The Archaeology of Babylonia During the Period of the Babylonian Talmud', in M. J. Geller (ed.), *The Archaeology and Material Culture of the Babylonian Talmud*, Leiden and Boston: Brill, pp. 6–38.
Tafazzoli, A. (1974), 'A List of Trades and Crafts in the Sassanian Period', *Archaeologische Mitteilungen aus Iran*, n.s. 7, pp. 191–6.
Venco Ricciardi, R. (1968–9), 'The Excavations at Choche: Seasons 1966, 1967 and 1968', *Mesopotamia*, 3.4, pp. 57–68, figs 56–80, pls VIII–X.
Venco Ricciardi, R. (1973–4), 'Trial Trench at Tell Baruda (Choche)', *Mesopotamia*, 8.9, pp. 15–20, figs 11–16.
Venco Ricciardi, R. (1977), 'Trial Trench at Tell Baruda, Choche (1975)', *Mesopotamia*, 12, pp. 11–14.
Venco Ricciardi, R. and Negro Ponzi Mancini, M. M. (1985), 'Coche', in E. Quarentelli (ed.), *The Land Between Two Rivers: Twenty Years of Italian Archaeology in the Middle East. The Treasures of Mesopotamia*, Turin: Il Quadrante, pp. 100–10.
Wenke, R. J. (1975–6), 'Imperial Investment and Agricultural Development in Parthian and Sassanian Khuzestan: 150 B.C. to A.D. 640', *Mesopotamia*, 9.11, pp. 31–221.
Wenke, R. J. (1987), 'Western Iran in the Partho-Sasanian Period: The Imperial Transformation', in F. Hole (ed.), *The Archaeology of Western Iran: Settlement and Society from Prehistory to the Islamic Conquest*, Smithsonian Series in Archaeological Inquiry, Washington, DC: Smithsonian Institution Press, pp. 251–81.
Whitcomb, D. S. (1979), 'The City of *Istakhr* and the Marvdasht Plain', in *Akten des VII International Kongresses für iranische Kunst und Archäologie, München, 7.–10. September 1976*, Berlin: Archaeologische Mitteilungen aus Iran, Ergänzungsband 6, pp. 363–70.
Whitcomb, D. S. (1985), *Before the Roses and Nightingales: Excavations at Qasr-i Abu Nasr, Old Shiraz*, New York: Metropolitan Museum of Art.

Whitcomb, D. S. (2003–4), 'Iranian Cities of the Sasanian and Early Islamic Periods', in *The Oriental Institute Annual Report*, 2003/04, pp. 91–4.

Wright, H. T. (1981), 'The Southern Margins of Sumer: Archaeological Survey of the Area of Eridu and Ur', in R. M. Adams, *Heartland of Cities: Surveys of Ancient Settlement and Land Use on the Central Floodplain of the Euphrates*, Chicago: University of Chicago Press, pp. 295–345.

Zavyalov, V. A. (2007), 'The Fortifications of the City of Gyaur Kala, Merv', in J. Cribb and G. Herrmann (eds), *After Alexander: Central Asia before Islam*, London: British Academy, pp. 313–29.

3 Palaeoecological Insights into Agri-Horti-Cultural and Pastoral Practices Before, During and After the Sasanian Empire

Lyudmila Shumilovskikh, Morteza Djamali, Valérie Andrieu-Ponel, Philippe Ponel, Jacques-Louis de Beaulieu, Abdolmajid Naderi-Beni and Eberhard W. Sauer

Pollen data obtained from radiocarbon-dated sediments of several peat bogs and lakes located in different parts of Iran and surrounding areas have recently provided invaluable new information on agricultural practices during the Persian empires, from the Achaemenids to the Sasanians. A review of the published and unpublished data has revealed distinct phases of intensified tree cultivation and pastoral activities during this era.

INTRODUCTION

The Sasanian Empire was one of the largest empires in the late antique world (Fig. 3.1). Recent archaeological fieldwork has shed much new light on major investment in military infrastructure, urban growth and large-scale irrigation systems. Feeding an increased urban population as well as military personnel and the large workforce needed for these infrastructure projects required surplus food production. Until recently, little has been known about the cultivation of domestic plants and trees within the territory of this vast mega-empire. The latest research on this much-neglected and very important factor for the Sasanian Empire's resourcefulness is the subject of this chapter. It deliberately does not examine this 400-year period in isolation, but compares and contrasts it with developments before and after, as this is the only way to establish what was special about this particular period.

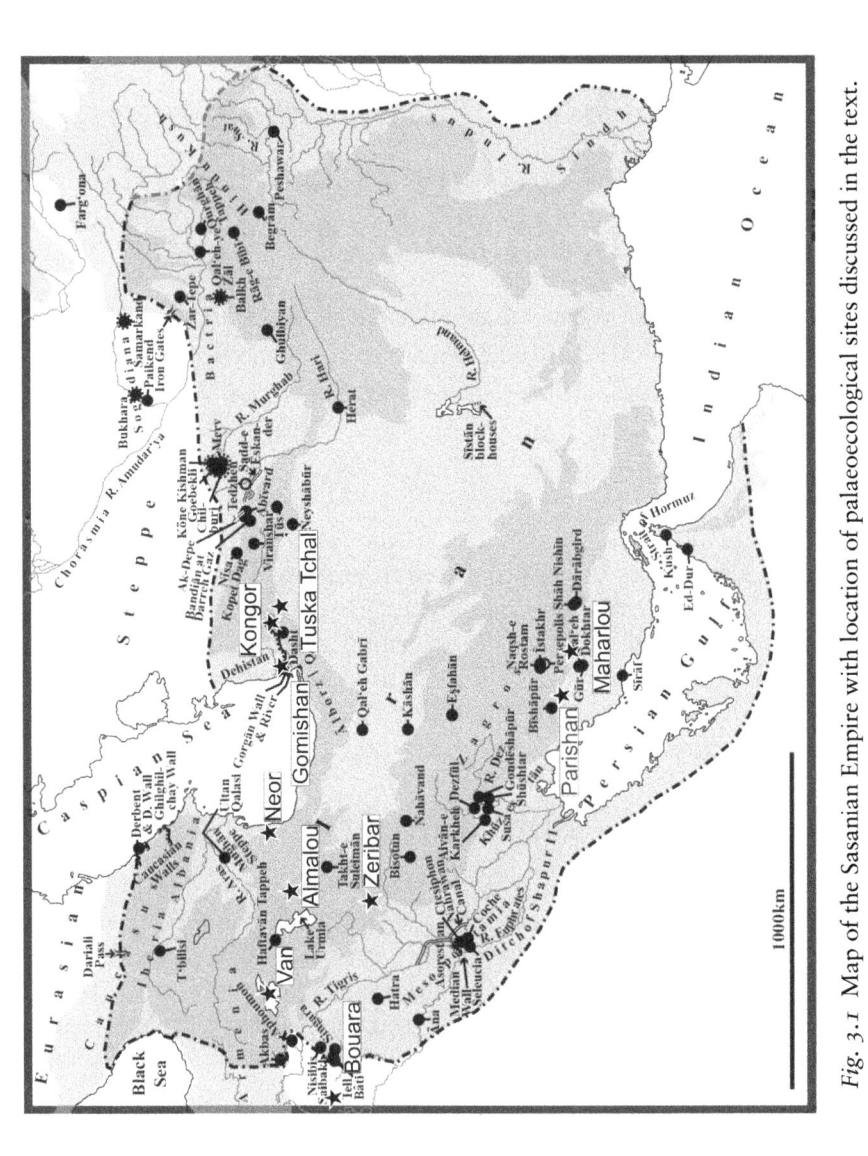

Fig. 3.1 Map of the Sasanian Empire with location of palaeoecological sites discussed in the text.

Table 3.1 List of sites. (^{14}C refers to the number of radiocarbon samples unless the chronology is based on varve dating.)

Name	Sediment	Lat, N	Long, E	Alt, m	^{14}C	Reference
Almalou	lake	37°39'55"	46°37'55"	2,491	8	Djamali et al. 2009a
Bouara	salt marsh	35°14'0"	41°11'0"	210	1	Gremmen and Bottema 1991
Gomishan	lagoon	37°09'56"	54°03'23"	2	10	Leroy et al. 2013
Kongor	peat	37°21'21"	55°23'27"	93	9	Shumilovskikh et al. 2016
Maharlou	lake	29°28'38"	52°45'35"	1,455	4	Djamali et al. 2009b
Neor A	lake	38°0'54"	48°34'18"	2,481	3	Ponel et al. 2013
Parishan	lake	29°30'50"	51°48'08"	823	3	Djamali et al. 2016
Tuska Tchal	peat	37°11'38"	55°31'40"	1,037	6	De Beaulieu et al., work in preparation
Van	lake	38°30'0"	43°0'0"	1,645	varves	Van Zeist and Woldring 1978
Zeribar	lake	35°32'0"	46°7'0"	1,288	5	Van Zeist 1967

The territory once controlled by Sasanian Persia displays great variety in climate, topography, landforms and vegetation, which imply differences in agro-pastoral activities across the whole territory. In order to reconstruct anthropogenic influences on vegetation, we have evaluated available pollen, coprophilous fungal spores and insect records from a wide range of sites within the Sasanian Empire (see Table 3.1 for a list of sites).

PALAEOECOLOGICAL RECORDS

We have compiled published and unpublished data as well as records from the European Pollen Database (www.europeanpollendatabase. net). Altogether, there are ten sites with pollen records, three with fungal spores and two with insects (Table 3.1). Except for the Zeribar record, they cover all or part of the Sasanian era. Sites are located in different biogeographical zones and different altitudes. Specific macro- and microclimatic, pedological and land-use conditions will have played an important role in cultivation. To understand these factors better, we will first provide a short description of every site in the context of biogeographical and floristic factors and its location within the Sasanian Empire.

The Caspian Sea Coast and the Hyrcanian Forests in the Alborz Mountains

The Alborz Mountains, south of the Caspian Sea, range in altitude from c. 2,000 to 4,000m, their highest peak reaching c. 5,600m. Such considerable height presents a physical barrier to moisture transport from the Caspian Sea, resulting in considerable orographic precipitation on the northern slopes of the mountains and dry conditions over the southern slopes due to the rain-shadow effect. There is a west–east gradient in precipitation patterns with >2,000mm/year in the west and <600mm/year, with droughts of up to three months, in the east, and this is also reflected in vegetation patterns.[1]

1 *Lake Neor*. Neor (2,481m a.s.l. [above sea level]) is a freshwater lake of tectonic origin located on a high-altitude plateau (c. 2,480m) in the Talysch Mountains (western part of the Alborz). The lake itself is about 4,000m long and 1,000m wide. The vegetation surrounding Lake Neor shows evidence of strong grazing activity, notably the presence of many ruderal plants including *Rumex*, *Plantago* etc. Beyond the lake margin, the slopes of mountain ranges are covered by an Irano-Turanian thorn-cushion montane steppe vegetation, dominated by *Onobrychis cornuta* – *Astragalus* spp. – *Acantholimon* – *Agropyron* communities, and *Festuca heterophyllum* – *Trifolium montana* communities. The core Neor A, taken from the northern peaty border of the lake and dated via three radiocarbon samples, covers the last 6,500 years and was studied for pollen and insects (Fig. 3.2).[2]

2 *Gomishan Lagoon*. To the west of Gomishan (-23/-27m a.s.l.), at the south-eastern corner of the Caspian Sea, is a lagoon. The lagoon is surrounded by lowland halophilous vegetation dominated by *Halocneum strobilaceum*, *Aeluropus littoralis*, *Puccunellia distans*, *Tamarix ramosissimum*, *Suaeda maritima* and *Salsola rigida*. The area is used for cultivation of winter barley and wheat. The core TM (27.70m long) covers the whole Holocene with a hiatus between 7,200 and 3,500 cal. BP (calibrated years before present, i.e. 1950), corresponding to the low stand of the Caspian Sea (Fig. 3.3).[3]

3 *Lake Kongor*. Kongor (93m a.s.l.) is a temporary lake located in the eastern part of the Gorgan Plain between the River Gorgan and

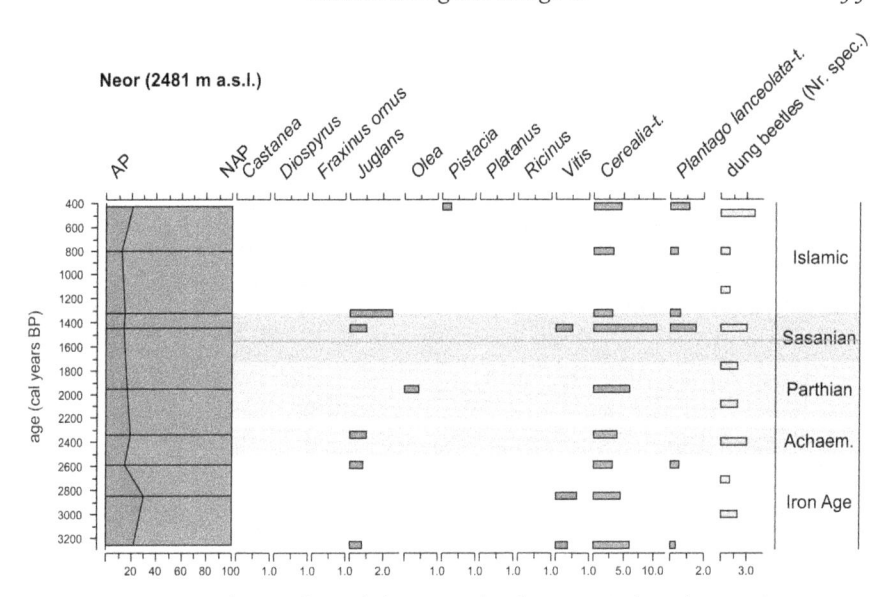

Fig. 3.2 Palaeoecological diagram of Lake Neor (selected curves).

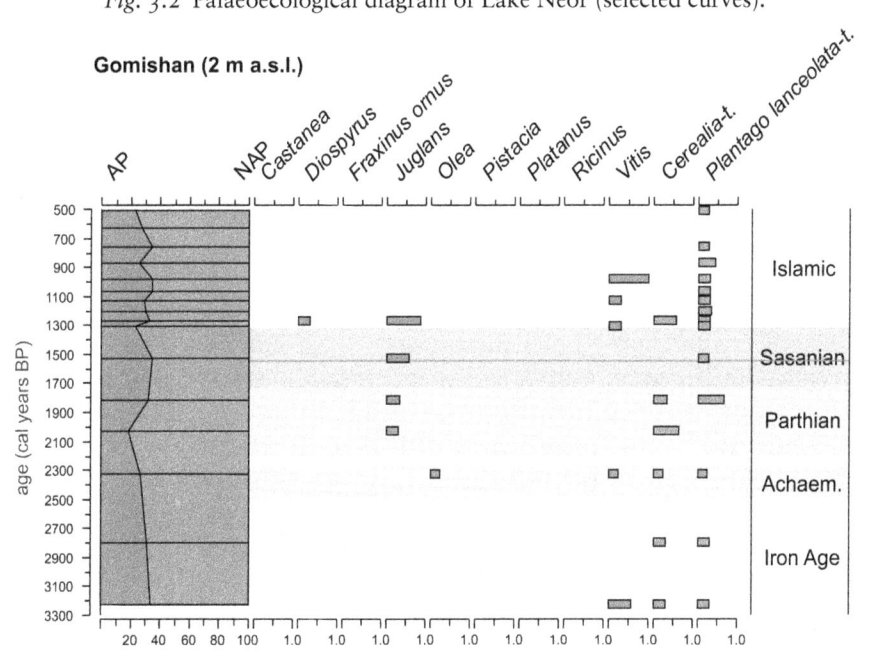

Fig. 3.3 Palaeoecological diagram of Gomishan Lagoon (selected curves).

the Alborz Mountains. The natural vegetation is steppe, but the area is intensively exploited for agriculture, with wheat and soya beans being the main crops, and for pasture. The site is not connected to any significant stream and is fed by groundwater and direct

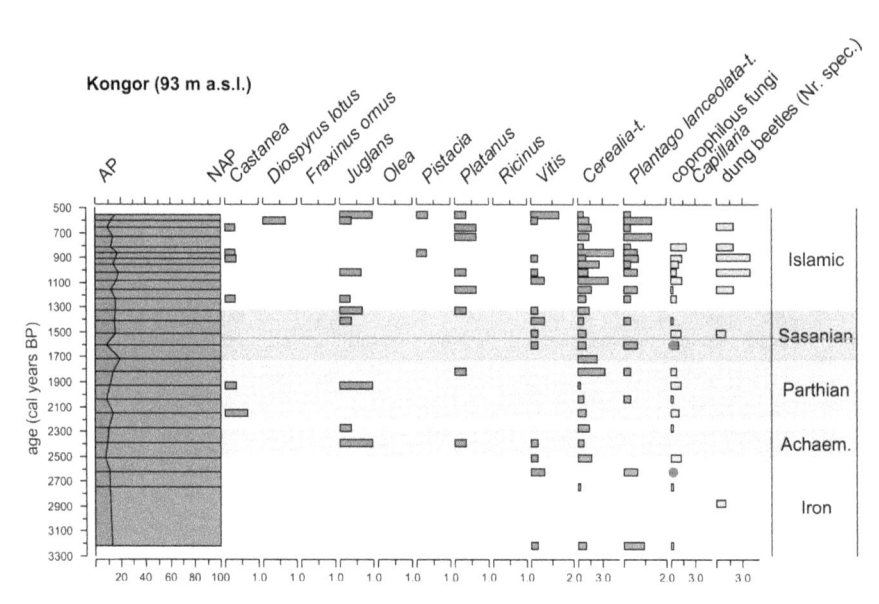

Fig. 3.4 Palaeoecological diagram of Lake Kongor (selected curves).

precipitation. Therefore, the sedimentary profile reflects the local environment. Kongor is situated c. 20km east of the city of Dasht Qal'eh, a regional urban centre during the Sasanian period. For the purpose of this chapter we discuss pollen, coprophilous fungal spores and insects (Fig. 3.4).[4]

4 *Tuska Tchal peat bog*. Tuska Tchal (1,037m a.s.l.) is a peat bog located in the heart of the eastern Alborz Mountains. The wetland is located between cultivated lands (mainly *Nicotiana*) and the Hyrcanian Forest dominated by *Quercus castaneifolia* and *Carpinus betulus*. The latter has been mostly completely cleared close to villages for agricultural and pastoral purposes. There are no known archaeological remains of settlements of the Sasanian era in the immediate vicinity. The core was dated via six radiocarbon samples and studied for pollen and fungal spores (Fig. 3.5).[5]

Taurus and Zagros Mountains

5 *Lake Almalou*. Almalou (2,491m a.s.l.) is a small lake located within a volcanic crater near Lake Urmia. Natural upland vegetation around the lake is an Irano-Turanian montane *Artemisia* steppe with species of *Astragalus, Centaurea, Cousinia, Eryngium, Gypsophila, Scabiosa, Trifolium, Hypericum* and Poaceae. Due to overgrazing,

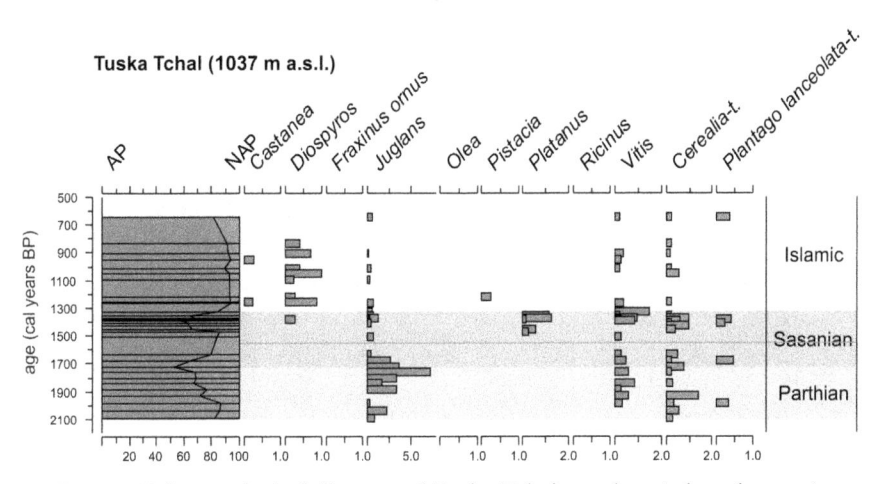

Fig. 3.5 Palaeoecological diagram of Tuska Tchal peat bog (selected curves).

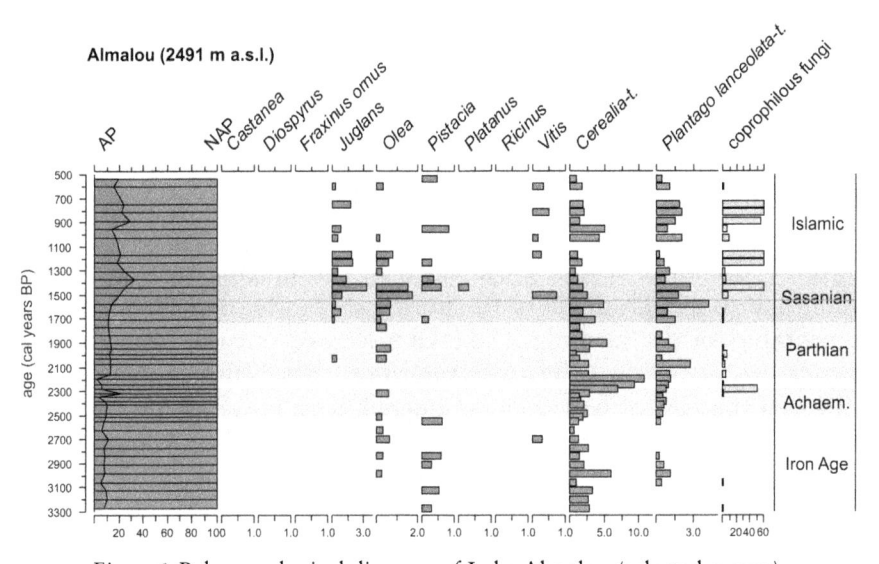

Fig. 3.6 Palaeoecological diagram of Lake Almalou (selected curves).

the local vegetation is now, however, dominated by *Chondrilla*, *Euphorbia*, *Malva*, *Taraxacum*, *Xerantheum* and *Verbascum*. The sediment core was dated with eight radiocarbon samples and studied for pollen (Fig. 3.6).[6]

6 *Lake Van* (1,650m a.s.l.). Van is a highland deep lake situated in the eastern Taurus Mountains, and its slopes are covered by Irano-Turanian montane steppe and oak steppe-forests. The water is extremely alkaline, and the lake is very poor in plant and animal species (Fig. 3.7).[7]

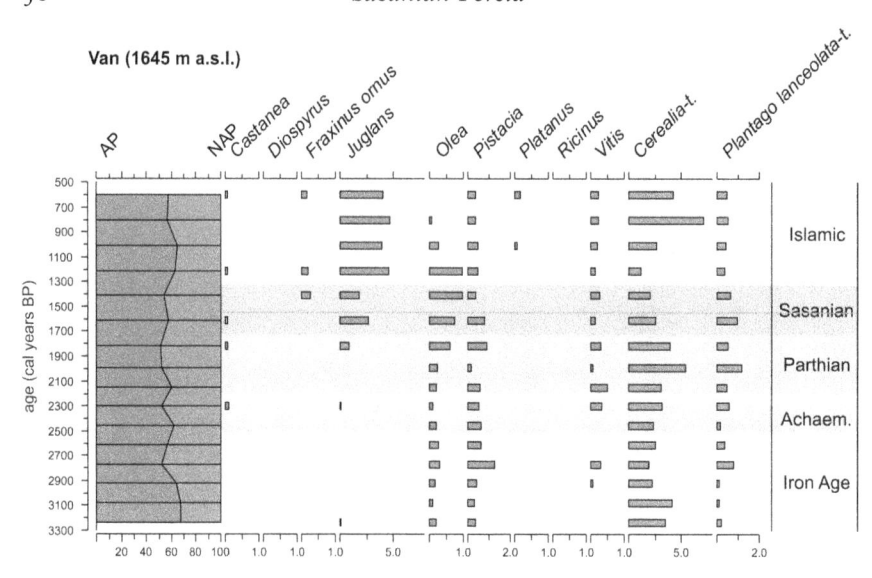

Fig. 3.7 Palaeoecological diagram of Lake Van (selected curves).

7 *Lake Bouara.* Bouara (210m a.s.l.) is a shallow salt lake located in the steppe in Syria, dominated by *Artemisia sieberi* (former *herba-albae*) and, in places, by *Halocnemum strobilaceum, Seidlitzia rosmarinus, Suaeda baccata, S. vermiculata* and *Aeluropus* sp.[8] Nowadays the natural vegetation is strongly affected by overgrazing and deforestation, due to a high demand for firewood, as the area of Bouara is unsuitable for dry farming. The lake is located outside Sasanian territory, except for the brief period in the early seventh century when much of the Levant had been conquered. It is, however, rather close to Sasanian frontiers and has therefore been included in our study, as it forms an interesting comparative example. The core, of 4.32m length, was radiocarbon-dated via one sample and studied for pollen (Fig. 3.8).[9]

8 *Lake Zeribar.* Zeribar (1,300m a.s.l.) is situated in an inter-montane valley in the Zagros Mountains within an oak–pistachio woodland belt.[10] The lake is c. 4.5km long and c. 2km wide. The core Zeribar 63-J of 25m length was radiocarbon-dated via five samples, showing that it covers the late Pleistocene and the Holocene (Fig. 3.9).[11]

9 *Lake Parishan.* Parishan (823m a.s.l.) is a freshwater to brackish water lake in south-western Iran. The lake is located between three main vegetation zones: (1) *Ziziphus spina-christi* shrubland with *Pistacia, Ficus carica* and *Populus*; (2) *Amygdalus scoparia* shrubland with *Fraxinus, Pistacia atlantica, Ficus carica* and *Crataegus*;

Palaeoecological Insights

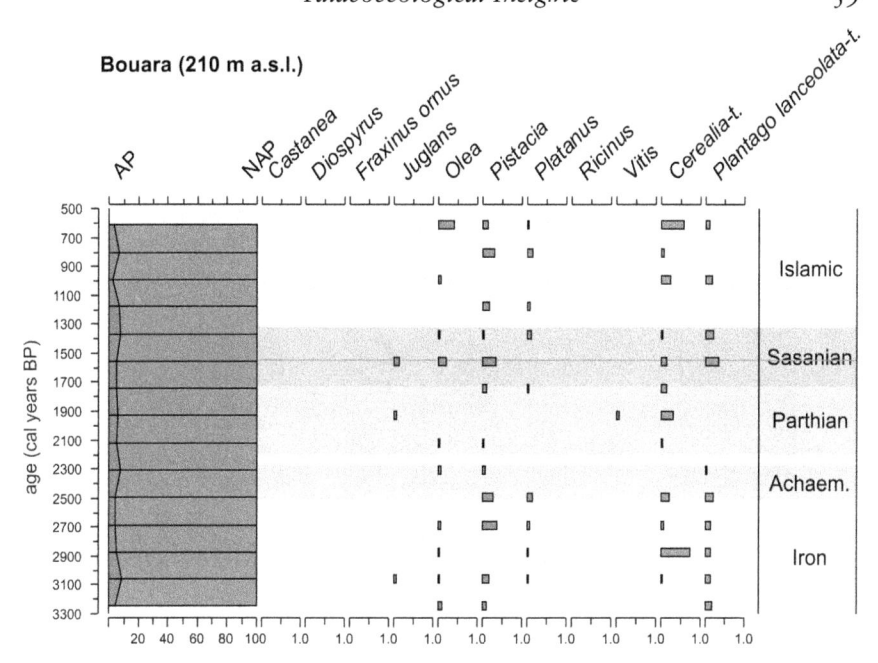

Fig. 3.8 Palaeoecological diagram of Lake Bouara (selected curves).

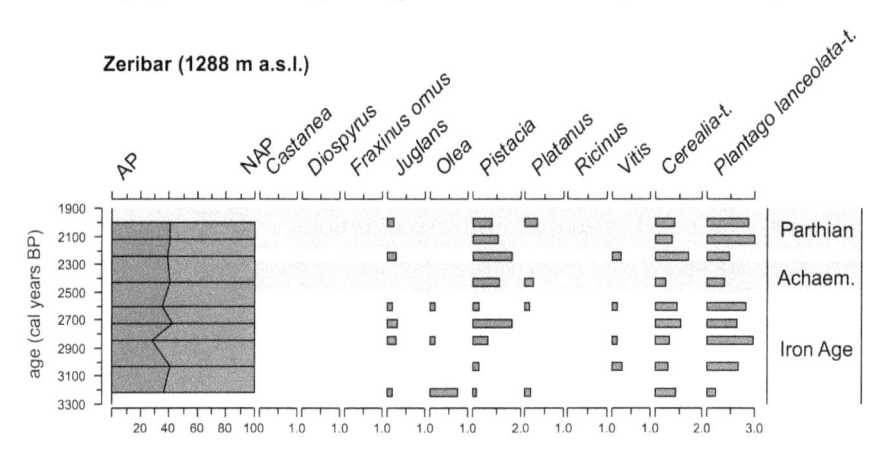

Fig. 3.9 Palaeoecological diagram of Lake Zeribar (selected curves).

and (3) *Quercus brantii* open woodlands with *Pistacia*, *Amygdalus* and *Cerasus*. The local vegetation is represented by marshland communities with *Phragmites*, *Typha* and *Scirpus*. The sediment core from the centre of the lake was studied palynologically in order to reconstruct the vegetation history (Fig. 3.10).[12]

10 *Lake Maharlou*. Maharlou (1,455m a.s.l.) is a large, shallow, hypersaline lake in south-western Iran. The lake is located within

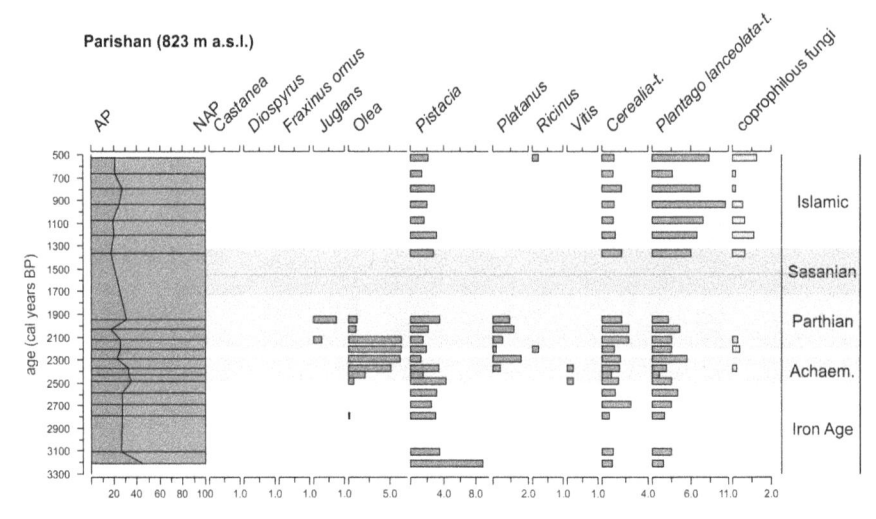

Fig. 3.10 Palaeoecological diagram of Lake Parishan (selected curves).

the *Pistacio–Amygdalus* shrub zone in the Zagros Mountains.[13] To the south and east, this vegetation is replaced by *Quercus brantii* woodlands and shrublands, with *Cerasus microcarpa*, *Ficus carica*, *Rhamnus persica*, *Artemisia*, *Astragalus*, *Cousinia*, *Capparis*, *Convolvulus*, *Ephedra* and other herbs. The local vegetation is dominated by halophytes such as *Salicornia* and *Halopelis*. Lake Maharlou is located very close to the Achaemenid capital Persepolis, as well as to several important Sasanian sites (Fig. 3.1). A sediment core from the lake was radiocarbon-dated and a palynological study was carried out (Fig. 3.11).[14]

TREES, SHRUBS, CEREALS AND PASTURE INDICATORS

***Castanea sativa* Mill. (sweet chestnut)** is intensively exploited for its nuts, used for human or animal consumption, as well as for managed coppicing and pollarding stands. Today, its main distribution area is in the northern Mediterranean, the Pontic Mountains and the Caucasus, but it can be found also in temperate regions of western and central Europe. In Iran, Browicz reports the presence of two small populations in the western Hyrcanian Forest in Gilan Province.[15] The place of origin and domestication history of the sweet chestnut are, however, unclear. Northern Asia Minor (Turkey) and the Caucasus region seem to be the place of initial domestication of the tree.[16] Charred remains are known from Bronze Age

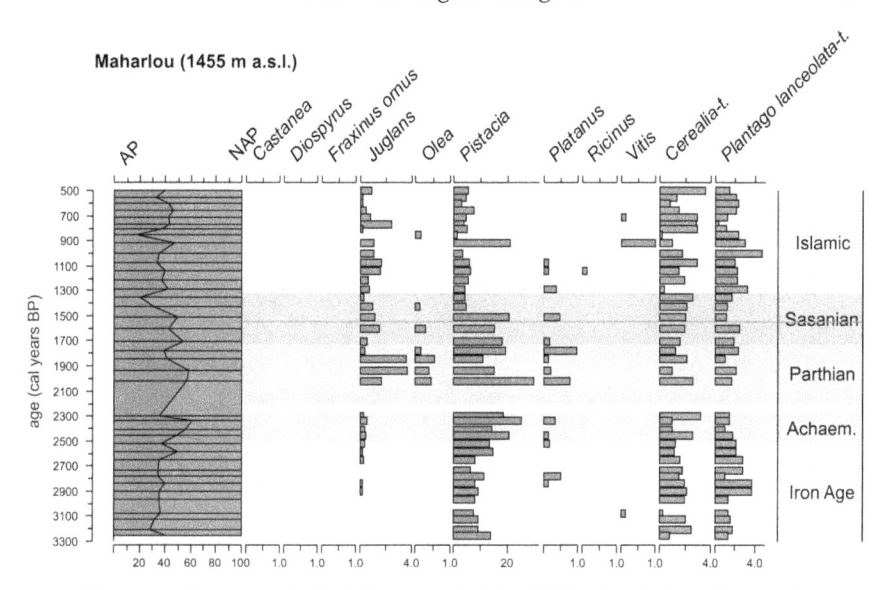

Fig. 3.11 Palaeoecological diagram of Lake Maharlou (selected curves).

and Iron Age settlements in Europe and increase in quantity from the Roman era onwards.[17] As far as the Sasanian Empire is concerned, sweet chestnut pollen from the Parthian and Islamic periods has been found in peat bogs in the eastern Alborz (Kongor and Tuska Tchal). Records from Lake Van point to the first appearance of *Castanea* in the Achaemenid era, but on a very limited scale. Whether this tree, today no longer present in the eastern Hyrcanian Forest of Iran, was cultivated in the northern part of the Persian Empires remains unknown, as the very low and irregular occurrence of chestnut pollen at all sites studied can be explained by long-distance windborne transport from the Pontic Mountains and the Caucasus.

Distributed across the Hyrcanian Forest of the Alborz Mountains, ***Diospyros lotus* L. (ebony tree)** is cultivated in the Euxino-Hyrcanian regions, because of its delicious fruits. Its natural origin in the Middle East has long been questioned and its presence has been attributed to introduction by caravans coming from eastern Asia.[18] Although the tree may form pure forest stands in lowland Hyrcanian and Euxinian regions, felling has commonly been practised to collect its edible fruits more easily. Thus, whereas the decrease in *Diospyrus* pollen is not necessarily indicative of its cutting because of the lack of human interest in its wood, the increase in its pollen does indicate its cultivation. *Diospyrus* pollen was found on wetland sites studied in the eastern Alborz (Gomishan, Kongor and Tuska Tchal).

Cultivation started in the late Sasanian era, but did not reach its climax until the Islamic period.

Fraxinus ornus L. (**manna ash**) was of particular importance for arboriculture during the so-called 'Beyşehir occupation phase' (3535–2185 BP) in Bronze Age Anatolia.[19] It grows naturally in Mediterranean broadleaved montane forest, and as an insect-pollinated plant has a low occurrence in pollen spectra.[20] Manna trees were cultivated for their sweetish exudate, manna, extracted from the bark by incision. Within the territory of the Sasanian Empire, pollen of *Fraxinus ornus* is documented only in the vicinity of Lake Van in the late Sasanian and Islamic periods, perhaps cultivated here, because it does not grow naturally in this region.

Juglans regia L. (**common or Persian walnut**) is a tree traditionally cultivated in the Old World, used for its oil-rich nuts and beautiful hard timber. It grows in the temperate deciduous forests of the Balkans, Pontus Mountains, Caucasus, Iranian Plateau, Central Asia and Tien Shan. In the Caucasus, the presence of *Juglans* pollen and botanical macroremains goes back to the Eocene, whereas *Juglans regia* pollen is documented from the middle Miocene, and macroremains in the Eopleistocene.[21] Palynological investigations reveal that during the Pleistocene ice ages, *Juglans* survived in several refuge zones in southern Europe and the Pontus Mountains,[22] the Caucasus, China and the Himalayas. The exact place of origin and the time of *Juglans* domestication are still unknown.[23] Whilst wild thick-shell walnut finds are known from Mesolithic, Neolithic and Bronze Age sites in Europe and Asia,[24] remains of thin-shell domesticated walnut have been found at Roman sites. Palynological data reveal walnut cultivation during the Beyşehir occupation phase (3600 cal. BP) in western Anatolia (van Zeist and Bottema 1991) and its spread at around 2000 cal. BP in northern Anatolia[25] and in Kyrgyzstan,[26] coinciding with the spread of Persian, Greek and Roman civilisations. In the territory of Sasanian Persia (Fig. 3.1), with the exception of the Zeribar record, which shows *Juglans* already present during the Iron Age, walnut pollen appears at several sites under the Achaemenids (Kongor, Maharlou, Neor A) and spreads further during the Parthian era (Almalou, Bouara, Gomishan, Parishan, Tuska Tchal and Van). Walnut cultivation had evidently been already widespread prior to the Sasanian period, but several sites reveal maximum percentages of *Juglans* under Sasanian rule (Almalou, Neor A, Tuska Tchal and Van), suggesting an intensification of walnut cultivation in the northern Zagros as well as in the western and eastern Alborz Mountains. The presence of walnut trees in the latter region in the Sasanian era is not in doubt. The charcoal assemblage in a brick kiln excavated next to the Tammisheh Wall, in the piedmont area, was strongly dominated by *Juglans* – walnut branches, it seems, being the kiln's main source of fuel.[27]

Nowadays, **Olea europaea L. (olive)** cultivation epitomises typical human-made Mediterranean landscapes. Its oil-rich fruits are used for oil production, eating and cooking. The olive, together with the grapevine, fig and date palm, belongs to the oldest group of trees cultivated in the Old World since the Bronze Age.[28] Olives grow in the typical Mediterranean climate. It is therefore not surprising that, within the territory of Sasanian Empire, *Olea* pollen occurs at sites in the Mediterranean zone, but is absent in the vicinity of the sites reported here (Neor, Gomishan, Kongor and Tuska Tchal). In the northern Zagros (Van, Bouara, Zeribar and Almalou), *Olea* is present at all the sites examined, strong evidence for a long tradition of olive cultivation or the presence of natural olive trees in this area. It reaches, however, its climax during the Sasanian Empire, suggesting the intensification of olive cultivation. In the southern Zagros (Parishan and Maharlou), by contrast, *Olea* has a distinctive start in the late Iron Age, reaching its maxima during the Achaemenid and Parthian Empires, whilst decreasing subsequently under Sasanian rule.

Pistacia vera **L. (pistachio)** is very popular for its tasty, oil-rich nuts. As a typical Mediterranean tree, pistachio is very drought resistant, growing naturally in the semi-arid steppe-forest vegetation belt and cultivated in Iran, south-east Turkey, and Central and South-West Asia.[29] Possibly pistachio was used in Central Asia (Uzbekistan and Iran) in the Neolithic and Bronze Age. However, there is no concrete evidence of actual cultivation until the classical period.[30] Pollen of *Pistacia* can be identified to genus and includes several species of naturally growing and cultivated trees widely distributed in the Middle East. For example, pollen of *Pistacia* varies between 1 per cent and 15 per cent in the Maharlou record, showing the dominance of pistachio shrubs in the natural vegetation. During the Achaemenid, Parthian and Sasanian eras, as well as parts of the Islamic period, *Pistacia* pollen reaches up to 30 per cent in this record, suggesting cultivation. Pollen profiles from Parishan, Van, Zeribar, Almalou and Bouara, by contrast, do not show peaks for *Pistacia* corresponding to human occupation periods, and thus might represent natural pollen spectra. Profiles from the Alborz Mountains indicate the presence of *Pistacia* pollen since Islamic times, suggesting introduction by humans. In the western part of the Gorgan Plain, however, charcoal from *Pistacia* has been found at two Sasanian sites: at the Bansaran Fort, near the Tammisheh Wall, and in Qal'eh Kharabeh,[31] probably evidence for cultivation and pistachio consumption.

Platanus orientalis L. (**plane tree**) is planted in towns and villages not for its fruits but for its shade. It grows naturally along river valleys in the north-eastern Mediterranean region (Balkans, Crete and the Aegean Islands). However, its place of origin and domestication remains unknown.[32] Palynological research indicates that its main spread occurred since the Greek and Roman eras.[33] At Bouara and Zeribar, it is represented in all periods, suggesting the plant's natural occurrence there. Distinct peaks in the Sasanian era in the eastern Alborz (Tuska Tchal) and during all the Persian Empires, from the Achaemenids to the Sasanians, in the southern Zagros (Parishan and Maharlou) suggest cultivation. On the Gorgan Plain (Kongor), *Platanus* occurs since the Achaemenids too, slightly increasing during the Islamic period. Under Sasanian rule, its presence is suggested by possible finds of *Platanus* charcoal in archaeological excavations in Fort 4 and, during the Sasanian or Islamic periods, in a canal at Qal'eh Kharabeh. However, the charcoal of *Platanus* is difficult to distinguish from that of *Fagus*.[34]

Ricinus communis L. (**castor oil plant**) is used for oil production, employed as fuel or for medicinal purposes. It may have started being cultivated in subtropical regions of Africa, possibly by the ancient Egyptians.[35] Pollen of *Ricinus* is documented only in the Almalou and Urmia pollen records[36] since the seventeenth century, with occasional statistically insignificant values in southern Zagros (unpublished data from Lake Parishan and Maharlou).

Vitis vinifera L. (**grapevine**) has a long history of domestication and cultivation, going back to the sixth millennium BC. This plant spread much further, however, during the early Bronze Age, around the third millennium BC.[37] Pollen of *Vitis* is easy to identify on the genus level but not on that of the species. In the European–Mediterranean region, the *Vitis* pollen type includes two species, *Vitis vinifera* and *Vitis sylvestris*, which also grow in the native vegetation in riparian gallery forests. The grapevine is underrepresented in pollen rain; therefore even low percentages can indicate abundant growth of the plant. In the diagrams under consideration (Figs 3.2, 3.3, 3.4, 3.6, 3.7, 3.9 and 3.11), grapevine pollen is already present during the Iron Age. Its geographic distribution is, however, very irregular with strong variations from site to site. In the Sasanian era, *Vitis* occurs along the Alborz (Neor, Kongor and Tuska Tchal) and the northern Zagros (Almalou and Van), and it continues to be grown on the Gorgan Plain during the Islamic period (at Kongor and Gomishan).

Cereals have, of course, been an essential staple crop in food production in the Near East since the Neolithic Revolution. Unfortunately, pollen of the *Cerealia* type includes, besides cereals, many wild grass species (possibly ancestors of cultivated plants), as well as other grass genera.[38] Additionally, domesticated grasses release less pollen than wild grasses, due to their self-fertilisation, which makes it difficult to detect their presence even close to the field.[39] Therefore, *Cerealia*-type curves in pollen diagrams should be treated with caution and, if possible, in comparison with archaeobotanical findings from archaeological excavations close to the sites. With a general presence of the *Cerealia* type throughout all records, those from Neor, Tuska Tchal and Almalou show distinctive maxima of the type during the Sasanian era and especially the late Sasanian era, although records from Kongor, Tuska Tchal, Almalou, Van and Parishan already indicate an increase of cereal cultivation under the Parthians. Pollen profiles from Kongor, Van and Almalou support an increase in cereal production during the Islamic period.

Pastoral indicators, which are very useful in reconstructions of pastoral activities in Central Europe,[40] are as hard to explore in the Near East as *Cerealia*-type pollen. For the purposes of this chapter, we took *Plantago lanceolata*-type pollen,[41] coprophilous fungal spores and dung beetles as indicators of increased pastoral activities.

Coprophilous fungi grow on dung and are used as indicators of animal presence. With an ability to grow on different kind of decaying organic matter, some genera prefer dung as a substrate (*Sporormiella, Sordaria, Podospora*) and can be considered as strictly coprophilous, whilst other genera are more flexible (*Cercophora, Chaetomium, Delitschia*) and are defined as fimicolous.[42] Spores of coprophilous fungi are frequently used in palaeoecological studies as a proof of the presence of animals close to the site[43] or of pasture pressure.[44] For the purpose of this chapter, we investigate spores of strictly coprophilous fungi. In all three records (Kongor, Almalou and Parishan), spores rise in numbers mainly after the demise of the Sasanian Empire, perhaps as a result of increased pastoral activities around the sites after the collapse of Sasanian rule.

Dung-associated beetles are useful indicators for the presence of animals close to a site. For example, at Neor (Fig. 3.12)[45] two important genera of coprophagous Coleoptera are present throughout the sequence, *Onthophagus* and *Aphodius*. Both taxa feed on the dung of big mammals. The adults of *Onthophagus* lay eggs in burrows

Fig. 3.12 Example of pastoralism on the Neor plateau: (a) landscapes around the lake (photo P. Ponel); (b) *Gymnopleurus* sp., a dung beetle species swarming on human faeces in the Zagros Mountains (photo P. Ponel).

excavated in the substratum below the dung, whereas *Aphodius* species live during larval and adult stages inside the mass of excrement itself. Both genera are represented by hundreds of species in the Palaearctic region. *Cercyon* is a Hydrophilidae genus mainly associated with dung and decaying plant debris. *Oxytelus* and *Platysthetus* prey upon small Arthropods such as Diptera larvae and mites that in turn feed on excrement. At Neor, coprophagous and coprophilous Coleoptera suggest that dung was present throughout the sequence, and indicate the regular presence of herbivores of medium and large size, wild and/or domestic. At Kongor too, coprophagous beetles suggest that the site was visited by large mammals, possibly domestic cattle.[46] Dung beetles are scarce from the Iron Age to the Sasanian period, but much more abundant during the Islamic era, indicating increased pasture pressure.

Changes in the **forest cover** can be deduced from percentages of arboreal pollen (AP). Especially in naturally forested areas, tree clearance by humans can be easily recognised in the pollen records, as it is in the case of Tuska Tchal. It reveals two distinctive phases of settlement during the Parthian and late Sasanian periods. In naturally open landscapes, AP values can decrease, through cutting firewood, or increase during active settlements phases as a result of arboriculture. A good example of the latter phenomenon is provided by the Maharlou and Almalou pollen records, where *Juglans*, *Olea*, *Pistacia* and *Platanus* clearly contribute to a general increase of AP.[47]

AGRICULTURAL AND PASTORAL ACTIVITIES IN THE SASANIAN EMPIRE

The time resolution of the pollen records analysed varies greatly, notably as the number of radiocarbon dates used for establishment of the age-depth models may be large or small. One thus has to be very cautious in making estimates of the time scales involved. For the Sasanian period, there are only four records (Tuska Tchal, Kongor, Almalou and Maharlou) with five to ten palynological samples, allowing us to follow changes in vegetation during the intervals. All other records have only one or two samples.

Palynological records allow us to trace human activity in the Middle East especially in the late Holocene. For example, the Beyşehir occupation phase saw an increased anthropogenic impact on vegetation in south-west Turkey, characterised by deforestation, enhanced pastoral activities and cultivation of trees and shrubs such as *Fraxinus ornus*, *Juglans*, *Castanea*, *Olea* and *Vitis*.[48] Within the territory of the Sasanian Empire, the pollen of several trees and shrubs, such as *Juglans*, *Vitis*, *Olea*, *Platanus* and *Pistacia*, is present in some pollen diagrams at least since the Iron Age. Some trees and shrubs, such as *Castanea* and *Ricinus*, first occur under the Achaemenids, whereas *Fraxinus ornus* and *Diospyrus* appear first in the Sasanian era. In general, low amounts of pollen in the sediment examined make it difficult to make a case for tree cultivation close to the site. The pollen might belong to wild trees or be transported by wind over long distances, like that of *Olea*, or belong to the local vegetation, like *Pistacia* in the Zagros Mountains or *Diospyrus* in the Hyrcanian Forest.

In general, the distribution of arboricultural activities in the area under investigation shows similarities, as well as differences, across the empire, in part determined by natural conditions. For instance, *Juglans* and *Vitis* were apparently used and most probably cultivated in all the regions examined. *Diospyrus* and *Castanea* naturally belong to the Ponto-Hyrcanian vegetation, and occur only at sites in the northern regions of the empire. Mediterranean *Olea* and *Pistacia* are typical features of the western and southern parts of the empire, whereas *Fraxinus ornus* is documented only in the west (Van). A typical representative of African flora, *Ricinus*, is known from Almalou and Urmia since the seventeenth century, with a possible presence in the southern zone (Parishan and Maharlou) since antiquity.

During the Achaemenid era, tree and shrub cultivation reached its apogee in Fars, and there is evidence that walnut, olive, grapevine and plane were grown, among others. While walnut was intensively cultivated in the Lake Maharlou catchment area[49] (the Shiraz Plain), it was some 100km further west, in the Lake Parishan area,[50] that olive trees were similarly intensively cultivated, suggesting most probably some sort of state control of agricultural practices in the centre of the empire. *Juglans* also occurs in the south-eastern Caspian Sea region since the Achaemenids (Kongor). The collapse of the Achaemenid Empire at about 330 BC was possibly accompanied by a reduction in arboricultural practices in Fars. During the late Parthian Empire, there are visible phases of walnut, pistachio, plane and olive cultivation in Fars (Maharlou). In the eastern Alborz Mountains too (at Tuska Tchal and Gomishan) walnut and grape were planted, suggesting that cultivation spread to the north-east of the empire.

Large-scale arboriculture reached its second apogee under the Sasanian Empire. An intensification of walnut cultivation appears to have occurred in the northern regions of the empire: Taurus (Van), the northern Zagros Mountains (Almalou), and the western and eastern Alborz (Gomishan, Kongor and Tuska Tchal). The intensification in the late Sasanian era may have been the result of a political decision on investment in agriculture. In Fars (Maharlou), walnut, olive and plane decreased, suggesting a general reduction of arboriculture in this region, possibly the result of a drier climate.

High-resolution records from Tuska Tchal provide new insights into settlement activity in the eastern Hyrcanian Forest. During the late Parthian to early Sasanian period farmers cleared the forest and used the space for walnut, grape and cereal plantations. At some stage between the early and late Sasanian era, the settlement was abandoned, so the forest could regenerate. During the late Sasanian period, a second phase of occupation occurred, which went hand in hand with deforestation and with reduced walnut but increased grape, cereal and plane cultivation. After the end of Sasanian rule, settlement activity decreased and arboricultural practices changed, with an increase of *Diospyrus* and some continuation of *Castanea*, walnut and grape cultivation.

After the collapse of the Sasanian Empire, arboriculture lost widely in importance, whilst pastoral activities appear to have increased in scale, notably in Fars, the northern Zagros and western Alborz, suggesting a possible switch to nomado-pastoralism. But this decrease was far from uniform across the territory of the former empire, so that for example, on the Gorgan Plain (at Kongor and Gomishan) walnut, grape, plane, chestnut and pistachio were still cultivated, interestingly accompanied by an increase in cereal production, despite pastoral pressure. In the Taurus (Van), olive cultivation decreased, whilst walnut production appears to have risen in scale.

CONCLUSION

Progress in irrigation techniques and socio-political stability in the interior, during both the Achaemenid and Sasanian Empires, were the key factors boosting agricultural prosperity on the Iranian Plateau and surrounding lands. Agricultural practices seem to have been more intensive in the Fars area under the Achaemenids than under the Sasanians. Such activities were, instead, intensified in northern Persia, suggesting a particular socio-political and economic development of this region under the Sasanian Empire. It is important to note that, despite a wide variety of divergent trends for individual domestic plants, food production on the whole may well have peaked under these two major empires. Further botanical records from other areas within the former territory of the Persian Empires may potentially shed more light on the socio-economic organisation inside the imperial borders.

NOTES

1 Djamali et al. 2011.
2 Ponel et al. 2013.
3 Leroy et al. 2013.
4 Shumilovskikh et al. 2016.
5 De Beaulieu et al., work in preparation.
6 Djamali et al. 2009a.
7 Van Zeist and Woldring 1978.
8 Zohary 1973.
9 Gremmen and Bottema 1991.
10 Van Zeist and Bottema 1991.
11 Van Zeist 1967; Van Zeist and Bottema 1977.
12 Djamali et al. 2016.
13 Zohary 1973.
14 Djamali et al. 2009b.
15 Browicz 1982.
16 Zohary and Hopf 1994.
17 Zohary et al. 2012.
18 Browicz 1982.
19 Van Zeist and Bottema 1991.
20 Van Zeist and Bottema 1991.
21 Shatilova et al. 2011.
22 Shumilovskikh et al. 2014.
23 Zohary et al. 2012.
24 Zohary et al. 2012.
25 Shumilovskikh et al. 2012.
26 Beer et al. 2008.
27 Poole and Gale 2013.
28 Zohary et al. 2012.
29 Zohary et al. 2012.
30 Zohary et al. 2012.
31 Poole and Gale 2013.
32 Browicz 1982.
33 Van Zeist and Bottema 1991.
34 Poole and Gale 2013.
35 Djamali et al. 2010.
36 Bottema 1986.
37 Zohary et al. 2012.
38 Van Zeist and Bottema 1991; Beug 2004.
39 Bottema 1992; Zohary et al. 2012.
40 E.g. Behre 1990.
41 Behre 1990; van Zeist and Bottema 1991; Beer et al. 2008.

42 Krug et al. 2004.
43 E.g. van Geel et al. 2003; Graf and Chmura 2006.
44 Lehmkuhl et al. 2011.
45 Ponel et al. 2013.
46 Shumilovskikh et al. 2016.
47 Djamali et al. 2009a; 2009b.
48 Van Zeist and Bottema 1991.
49 Djamali et al. 2009b.
50 Djamali et al. 2016.

BIBLIOGRAPHY

Beer, R., Kaiser, F., Schmidt, K., Ammann, B., Carraro, G., Grisa, E. and Tinner, W. (2008), 'Vegetation History of the Walnut Forests in Kyrgyzstan (Central Asia): Natural or Anthropogenic Origin',? *Quaternary Science Reviews*, 27, pp. 621–32.

Behre, K.-E. (1990), 'Some Reflections on Anthropogenic Indicators and the Record of Prehistoric Occupation Phases in Pollen Diagrams from the Near East', in S. Bottema, G. Entjes-Nieborg and W. van Zeist (eds), *Man's Role in the Shaping of the Eastern Mediterranean Landscape*, Rotterdam: Brookfield, pp. 219–30.

Beug, H.-J. (2004), *Leitfaden der Pollenbestimmung*, Munich: Friedrich Pfeil.

Bottema, S. (1986), 'A Late Quaternary Pollen Diagram from Lake Urmia (Northwestern Iran)', *Review of Palaeobotany and Palynology*, 47, pp. 241–62.

Bottema, S. (1992), 'Prehistoric cereal Gathering and Farming in the Near East: The Pollen Evidence', *Review of Palaeobotany and Palynology*, 73, pp. 21–33.

Browicz, K. (1982), *Chorology of Trees and Shrubs in South-West Asia and Adjacent Regions*, vol. 1, Warsaw: Polish Scientific Publishers.

Djamali, M., de Beaulieu, J.-L., Miller, N., Andrieu-Ponel, V., Berberian, M., Gandouin, E., Lahijani, H., Ponel, P., Salimian, M. and Guiter, F. (2009a), 'A late Holocene Pollen Record from Lake Almalou in NW Iran: Evidence for Changing Land-Use In Relation to Some Historical Events During the Last 3700 Years', *Journal of Archaeological Science*, 36, pp. 1346–75.

Djamali, M., de Beaulieu, J.-L., Miller, N. F., Andrieu-Ponel, V., Lak, R., Sadeddin, M., Akhani, H. and Fazeli, H. (2009b), 'Vegetation History of the SE Section of Zagros Mountains During the Last Five Millennia: A Pollen Record from the Maharlou Lake, Fars Province, Iran', *Vegetation History and Archaeobotany*, 18, pp. 123–36.

Djamali, M., Miller, N. F., Ramezani, E., Akhani, H., Andrieu-Ponel, V., de Beaulieu, J.-L., Berberian, M., Guibal, F., Lahijani, H., Lak, R. and Ponel, P. (2010), 'Notes on the Arboricultural and Agricultural Practices in Ancient Iran Based on New Pollen Evidence', *Paléorient*, 36.2, pp. 175–88.

Djamali, M., Akhani, H., Khoshravesh, R., Andrieu-Ponel, V., Ponel, P. and Brewer, S. (2011), 'Application of the Global Bioclimatic Classification to Iran: Implications for Understanding the Modern Vegetation and Biogeography', *Ecologia Mediterranea*, 37.1, pp. 91–114.

Djamali, M., Jones, M. D., Migliore, J., Balatti, S., Fader, M., Contreras, D., Gondet, S., Hosseini, Z., Lahijani, H., Naderi, A., Shumilovskikh, L. S.,

Tengberg, M. and Weeks, L. (2016), 'Olive Cultivation in the Heart of the Persian Achaemenid Empire: New Insights to Agricultural Practices and Environmental Changes Reflected in a Late Holocene Pollen Record from Lake Parishan, SW Iran', *Vegetation History and Archaeobotany*, 25.3, pp. 255–69.

Graf, M.-T. and Chmura, G. L. (2006), 'Development of Modern Analogues for Natural, Mowed and Grazed Grasslands Using Pollen Assemblages and Coprophilous Fungi', *Review of Palaeobotany and Palynology*, 141, pp. 139–49.

Gremmen, W. H. E. and Bottema, S. (1991), 'Palynological Investigations in the Syrian Gazira', in H. Kühne, A. Mahmoud and W. Röllig (eds), *Berichte der Ausgrabung Tall Šeh Hamad und Daten zur Umweltrekonstruktionen der assyrischen Stadt Dur-Katlimmu*, Berlin: Reimer, pp. 105–16.

Krug, J. C., Benny, G. L. and Keller, H. W. (2004), 'Coprophilous Fungi', in G. M. Mueller, G. F. Bills and M. S. Foster (eds), *Biodiversity of Fungi: Inventory and Monitoring Methods*, London: Editora Elsevier Academic, pp. 467–98.

Lehmkuhl, F., Hilgers, A., Fries, S., Hülle, D., Schlütz, F., Shumilovskikh, L., Felauer, T. and Protze, J. (2011), 'Holocene Geomorphological Processes and Soil Development as Indicator for Environmental Change Around Karakorum, Upper Orkhon Valley (Central Mongolia)' *Catena*, 87.1, pp. 31–44.

Leroy, S. A. G., Kakroodi, A. A., Kroonenberg, S., Lahijani, H. K., Alimohammadian, H. and Nigarov, A. (2013), 'Holocene Vegetation History and Sea Level Changes in the SE corner of the Caspian Sea: Relevance to SW Asia Climate', *Quaternary Science Reviews*, 70, pp. 28–47.

Ponel, P., Andrieu-Ponel, V., Djamali, M., Lahijani, H., Leydet, M. and Mashkour, M. (2013), 'Fossil Beetles as Possible Evidence for Transhumance During the Middle and Late Holocene in the High Mountains of Talysch (Talesh) in NW Iran?', *Environmental Archaeology*, 18, pp. 201–10.

Poole, I. and Gale, R. (2013), 'Charcoal', in E. Sauer et al., *Persia's Imperial Power in Late Antiquity: The Great Wall of Gorgan and Frontier Landscapes of Sasanian Iran*, Oxford: Oxbow Books, pp. 581–90.

Shatilova, I., Mchedlishvili, N., Rukhadze, L. and Kvavadze, E. (2011), *The History of the Flora and Vegetation of Georgia*, Tbilisi: Georgian National Museum.

Shumilovskikh, L. S., Tarasov, P., Arz, H. W., Fleitmann, D., Marret, F., Nowaczyk, N., Plessen, B., Schlütz, F. and Behling, H. (2012), 'Vegetation and Environmental Dynamics in the Southern Black Sea Region since 18 kyr BP Derived from the Marine Core 22-GC3', *Palaeogeography, Palaeoclimatology, Palaeoecology*, 337–8, pp. 177–93.

Shumilovskikh, L. S., Fleitmann, D., Nowaczyk, N. R., Behling, H., Marret, F., Wegwerth, A. and Arz, H. (2014), 'Orbital- and Millennial-Scale Environmental Changes Between 64 and 20 ka BP Recorded in Black Sea Sediments', *Climate of the Past*, 10, pp. 939–54.

Shumilovskikh, L. S., Hopper, K., Djamali, M., Ponel, P., Demory, F., Rostek, F., Tachikawa, K., Bittmann, F., Golyeva, A., Guibal, F., Talon, B., Wang, L. C., Nezamabadi, M., Bard, E., Lahijani, H., Nokandeh, J., Omrani Rekavandi, H., de Beaulieu, J.-L., Sauer, E. and Andrieu-Ponel, V. (2016), 'Landscape Evolution and Agro-Sylvo-Pastoral Activities on the Gorgan Plain (NE Iran) in the Last 6000 Years', *Holocene*, 26.10, pp. 1676–91.

Van Geel, B., Buurman, J., Brinkkemper, O., Schelvis, J., Aptroot, A., van Reenen, G. and Hakbijl, T. (2003), 'Environmental Reconstruction of a Roman Period Settlement Site in Uitgeest (The Netherlands), with Special Reference to Coprophilous Fungi', *Journal of Archaeological Science*, 30, pp. 873–83.

Van Zeist, W. (1967), 'Late Quaternary Vegetation History of Western Iran', *Review of Palaeobotany and Palynology*, 2, pp. 301–11.

Van Zeist, W. and Bottema, S. (1977), 'Palynological Investigations in Western Iran', *Palaeohistoria*, 19, pp. 19–85.

Van Zeist, W. and Bottema, S. (1991), *Late Quaternary Vegetation of the Near East*, Wiesbaden: Reichert.

Van Zeist, W. and Woldring, H. (1978), 'A Postglacial Pollen Diagram from Lake Van in East Anatolia', *Review of Palaeobotany and Palynology*, 26, pp. 249–76.

Zohary, D. (1973), *Geobotanical Foundations of the Middle East*, Stuttgart: Gustav Fischer, Amsterdam: Zeitlinger.

Zohary, D. and Hopf, M. (1994), *Domestication of Plants in the Old World*, Oxford: Clarendon Press.

Zohary, D., Hopf, M. and Weiss, E. (2012), *Domestication of Plants in the Old World*, 4th edn, Oxford: Oxford University Press.

4 Animal Exploitation and Subsistence on the Borders of the Sasanian Empire: From the Gorgan Wall (Iran) to the Gates of the Alans (Georgia)

Marjan Mashkour, Roya Khazaeli, Homa Fathi, Sarieh Amiri, Delphine Decruyenaere, Azadeh Mohaseb, Hossein Davoudi, Shiva Sheikhi and Eberhard W. Sauer

This chapter is based on our recent investigations into the subsistence economy at a military fort in the northern Caucasus (in modern Georgia), in comparison with sites along the Gorgan Wall in the north-east of Iran. The latter include forts and settlements in the hinterland. These studies highlight the diversity of animal consumption during the Sasanian era, influenced by the environmental setting of the sites, general agro-pastoral practices in the study regions and different cultural traditions. In all cases, however, herded animals (sheep/goats and cattle) provided most of the animal protein, complemented by the exploitation of other resources such as poultry, fish and wild birds. The huge quantity of animal remains from Dariali Fort in Georgia and the other Sasanian-era sites presented here shed new light on animal exploitation at the frontiers of one of antiquity's largest empires and provide a solid foundation for future archaeozoological studies in this part of the ancient world.

INTRODUCTION

The relationship between humans and animals can be approached from various angles and is of major significance for our understanding of past societies. Archaeozoology provides crucial information in this regard, and the study of animal remains from historical sites sheds light on socio-economic interaction, the environment, food production, trade and exchange and beliefs. While bioarchaeological studies (archaeozoology and archaeobotany) of historical periods are well established in European and American archaeology, they still remain extremely deficient in South-West Asia. Bioarchaeological studies are applied unevenly across chronological periods, and for historical periods the main focus has been on the classical world. This tendency is, however, changing in the wake of growing integration of scientific disciplines into historical archaeology.

Recent excavations in Iran and in Georgia, within the framework of the European Research Council 'Persia and its Neighbours' project, have provided the opportunity to study faunal assemblages from two regions located at the frontiers of the Sasanian world[1] (Fig. 4.1). In the north-east of Iran the excavation of several sites on the Gorgan Plain, along the 195km Gorgan Wall, has provided valuable information on animal exploitation in various social contexts. Four sites have yielded significant Sasanian-era bone assemblages studied to date: Dasht Qal'eh, an urban centre; Qal'eh Kharabeh, a temporary military campaign base; and Bansaran and Fort 4, forts on the Tammisheh and Gorgan Walls. In the far north-west of the empire, recent excavations in the Dariali Gorge, in northern Georgia and on the Russian border, were focused on Dariali Fort (popularly known as Tamara's Fort), a further Sasanian military stronghold.

In both regions fortifications were erected against the invasions of nomadic groups, but these sites are located in very different environmental settings. The Gorgan Plain north of the Alborz Mountains is lush and green, in contrast to the northern part of the plain towards modern Turkmenistan, which is steppe land and semi-arid. In the east, the alluvial Gorgan Plain reaches an altitude of 300–400m, but it is below sea level in the west. The River Gorgan flows through the plain from east to west, and the Gorgan Wall north of the river protects the entire river valley and the most fertile parts of the plain. Dariali Fort is located in an entirely different environmental setting at an altitude of c. 1,380m, where the cold, wet climate for more than eight months of the year poses major problems for subsistence and sustainable herding.

Besides environmental and geographical factors, it seems likely that religion had a significant impact on the subsistence economy too. Zoroastrianism was the dominant religion in the Sasanian Empire, and there were also many Christians, notably in Transcaucasia, for whom the consumption of boar and pig was permitted, contrary to the prohibition imposed by Judaism and later Islam.

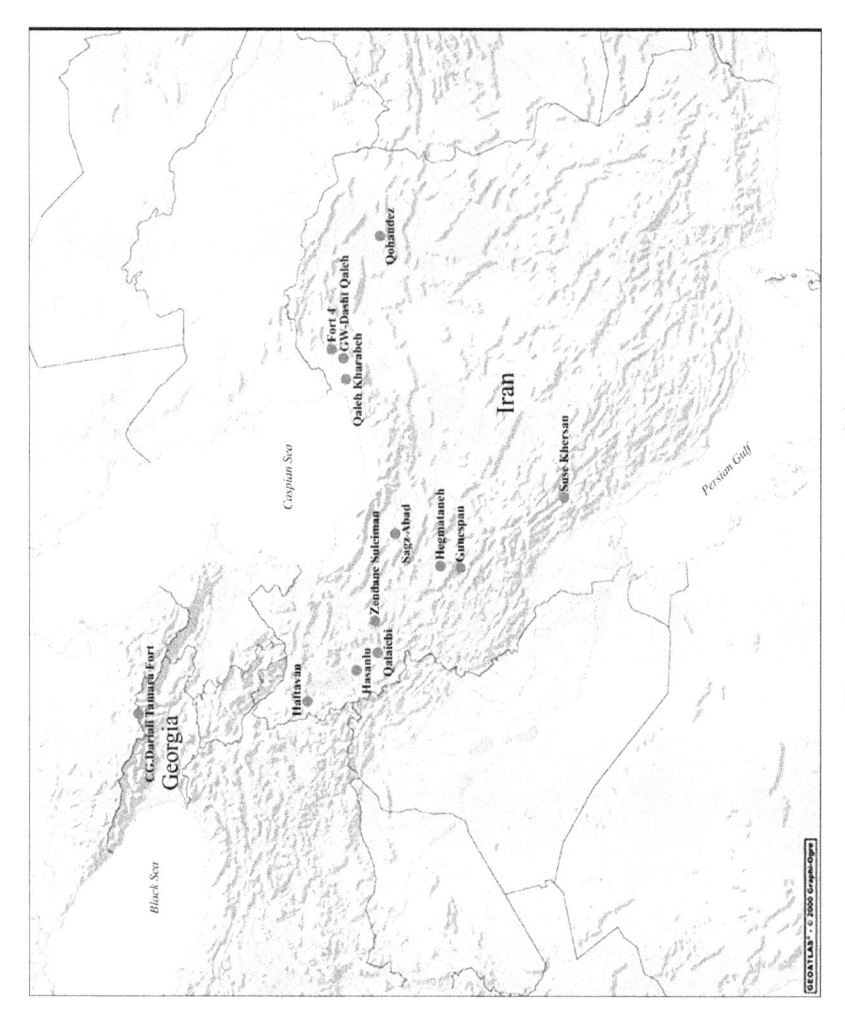

Fig. 4.1 Location map with key sites.

Although many Sasanian sites have been excavated within the empire and in neighbouring territories, the number of archaeozoological assemblages of this period studied to date is rather small. Moreover, the material available to date originates from a wide range of different contexts, such as towns, villages, palaces, military bases, temples etc., so that it is difficult to tell to what extent differences are best explained by geography as opposed to site type. Consequently it is still too early to present a coherent picture of animal exploitation within the Sasanian Empire during the four centuries before the advent of Islam. Current archaeological studies in Iran and in the sphere of the Sasanian world, namely in the southern part of the Persian Gulf, the United Arab Emirates and Oman, Central Asia and the Caucasus, have the potential to increase significantly the number of animal bone assemblages of the Sasanian era. Two sites are particularly promising. One is Tole Qal'eh Seyfabad (TQS), located in south-western Fars and near the major Sasanian city of Bishapur, an important administrative, economic and commercial centre.[2] The other site is the Fulayj Fort near Saham on the Batinah Plain of the Sultanate of Oman.[3] Both of these sites have provided a considerable amount of bioarchaeological material that is currently under study.

In this chapter we will focus on the material coming from Iran and the northern extensions of the Sasanian Empire. Our objective is to describe briefly the main characteristics of the subsistence economy at the newly excavated site of Dariali Fort, investigated between 2013 and 2016. We will examine how animals were exploited during the Sasanian period across a large geographic space under the domination of a centralised power, but inhabited by various ethnic and religious groups.

ANIMAL EXPLOITATION ON THE GORGAN WALL

The faunal material from the Gorgan Plain available to date is limited in quantity (c. 4,000 bone fragments), but is from well-dated Sasanian contexts, belonging to the fifth to seventh centuries AD, from Qal'eh Kharabeh, Fort 4 and Dasht Qal'eh. The first is located in the west of the Gorgan Plain and quite close to the Caspian Sea, the other two much further inland in the east. The faunal material shows clear influence from environmental factors, notably the availability of aquatic resources in proximity to Qal'eh Kharabeh. This is expressed by the presence of a variety of migratory water bird and fish remains.⁴ Fort 4 and Dasht Qal'eh, by contrast, two sites in the eastern part of the plain, have inland characteristics, with an emphasis on the consumption of domestic herbivores and domestic fowl. In this less lush inland region, flocks of sheep and herds of goats probably needed to migrate between the plain and the altitudinal zones in various seasons.

Sheep and goats are the main species represented at the sites on the Gorgan Plain explored in the course of this project, as well as at the majority of settlements on the Iranian Plateau. Bovines were also an important source of meat and dairy products for the inhabitants of this region. One of the highlights of the Gorgan Wall archaeozoological studies was the discovery of water buffalo remains, confirmed by DNA analyses and attested for the first time in Iran, although iconographic evidence exists from as early as the third millennium BC in Mesopotamia.⁵

Besides these animals exploited for meat and dairy products, pack animals were also important components of everyday life, and camel and equid bones were found among the assemblages. Wild mammals were also hunted, as shown by a small quantity of red deer, gazelle and boar bones. Boar and red deer hunting also features, of course, in Sasanian art.⁶

Fish remains are quite common. They were found at Dasht Qal'eh and Qal'eh Kharabeh. Interestingly, they are absent from Fort 4, although it is not very far from the River Gorgan. The study of fish remains indicates that some anadromous species were captured, such as sturgeon and shad, and freshwater fish, such as southern Caspian roach, roach vobla, carp and pike-perch.⁷ In the near future new information will be available from Fort 2, a military site located further east on the wall.

DARIALI FORT

The faunal remains from Dariali Fort were studied by a team of five archaeozoologists in 2014 and 2015. The animal bone assemblage from this stronghold is unique in the whole north Caucasian region because it represents a long chronological sequence from the Sasanian to the premodern period, with medieval material strongly represented. Trench F is the largest and most thoroughly investigated trench on the fort so far and is located just inside the western walls. It has provided the bulk of the faunal remains of the Dariali Gorge excavations. The chronology and phasing of this trench have been established via an extensive series of radiocarbon dates and pottery analysis.[8] The material from Trench F has been subdivided into five phases. Phase 3 belongs to the Sasanian period, from the late fourth to the seventh century. Phase 4 (seventh century) is from the transition of the Sasanian era to the Middle Ages. Phases 5, 6 and 7 are post-Sasanian: phase 5 runs from the late seventh or eighth to the late tenth century; phase 6 encompasses the first half of the second millennium, notably the fourteenth century; and phase 7 is post-medieval. (Phase 1 is geological and phase 2, pre-Sasanian, is absent from Trench F and so far only represented by a minute assemblage from another trench.)

The cold climate in this part of modern Georgia has created favourable conditions for bone preservation. This has resulted in the recovery of 739kg of animal bones. Up to now, almost 50,000 bone remains, representing approximately 400kg, have been studied, with a taxonomic identification rate of almost 70 per cent, a very high percentage in comparison to most archaeological sites. A significant number of bones was found embedded in Sasanian-era (phase 3) deposits, but a much greater quantity was deliberately discarded by the inhabitants of the fort in the early Middle Ages (phase 5), forming a large pile covering the earlier deposits of phases 3 and 4 and protecting bones from post-depositional fragmentation. Many bones recovered from Trench F show various signs of human activities such as chopping or butchering, and bones were also used for other purposes such as games, as evidenced by the presence of knucklebones, or tools.

ANIMAL EXPLOITATION AT DARIALI FORT

The faunal remains recovered from Trench F belong to a 1,600-year sequence (late fourth century to modern). Whilst the emphasis in this chapter is on those from the Sasanian era, what is special about the fort's late antique occupation is best appreciated in comparison with subsequent phases. Tables 4.1a and 4.1b show the taxonomic distribution of the remains using fragment counts and weight for phases 3 to 7. More than 35,000 bone fragments (more than 380kg) of were studied, out of which more than 23,000 (287kg) were identified. The bulk of the identified remains belong to caprines: sheep (*Ovis aries*) and goat (*Capra hircus*). Cattle (*Bos taurus*) were also an important source of food for the inhabitants of the fort, second only to sheep and goat, and the bone weight of cattle, which also provides an idea of relative meat weight, shows that their contribution to diet was even more important.

Table 4.1a Trench F on Dariali Fort. Taxonomic distribution of bone fragments.

Taxa	Phase 3			Phase 4		Phase 5			Phase 6		Phase 7	Grand total
	3	3,4	3,5	4	4,5	5	5,6	5,7	6	6,7		
Capra hircus	52	4	18	21	13	768	16	20	23	37	15	983
Wild Capra				1		1			2		3	7
Ovis aries	68	17	28	42	31	1021	22	19	106	22	21	1397
cf. Ovis orientalis						5						5
Caprini	742	193	326	332	372	13054	363	312	905	360	257	17216
Bos taurus	61	12	21	23	62	2336	43	59	249	85	97	3048
Sus scrofa	7		2	4		22		2	1	3	1	42
Rupicapra/Capreolus				1		5						6
Equus caballus	1											1
Equidae	8			1		33			1		1	44
Ursus arctos						5					1	6
Felis catus						1						1
Vulpes sp.			3			2			1			6
Meles meles						1						1
Canidae			1			1						2
Carnivores						6	1					7

Lepus europaeus	3							2	2	2		7
Testudo sp.	1	1										1
Gallus gallus						14						14
Aves	3	4	11	4	15	295	2	2	12	2		350
Fish	1	1			3	30			7			42
Molluscs	1		1									1
Total identified taxa	943	231	411	429	496	17607	448	414	1307	509	396	23187
Large mammals	109	23	116	109	58	3034	74	87	96	246	147	4099
Medium mammals	1					1	1	1				3
Small mammals				9		246	3					258
Small ruminants	189	34	59	138	135	4578	56	1	208	153	109	5660
Unidentified	25	28	4	11	117	1304	48	38	392	31		1998
Total unidentified taxa	324	85	179	267	310	9162	182	127	696	430	256	12018
Grand total	1267	316	590	696	806	26769	630	541	2003	939	652	35205

'Phase 3,5' refers to an assemblage that belongs to phase 3, 4 or 5. Similarly, all other phases featuring more than one number refer to the earliest and latest possible phase.

Table 4.1b Trench F on Dariali Fort. Taxonomic distribution by bone weight (in grams).

Taxa	Phase 3			Phase 4				Phase 5			Phase 6			Phase 7	Grand total
	3	3,4	3,5	4	4,5	5		5,6	5,7		6	6,7			
Capra hircus	835.8	102.2	179.5	433.6	159.9	10830		278.3	284		529	469.1		256	14315.4
Wild Capra				26.1		19					15			101	161.1
Ovis aries	925.3	226.6	363	779.9	646.9	19020.4		203	290		1634.8	302.4		336.1	24728.4
cf. Ovis orientalis						460.6									460.6
Caprini	5118.4	1065.8	1850.8	2728.8	2920	99236.4		1715.9	1855		6571.9	2527.8		2617.1	128207.9
Bos taurus	1650	373.9	482.8	675.35	2452.6	91227.8		1451.6	1912		8097.3	2120.4		3883.8	114327.6
Sus scrofa	167.4		25.4	59.4		437.3			18		23	54		2	786.5
Rupicapra/Capreolus				14.8		77.5									92.3
Equus caballus	601														601.0
Equidae	328.4			109.9		1427.9					11.1			42	1919.3
Ursus arctos						8.6								0	8.6
Felis catus						0									0.0
Vulpes sp.			8			5					3				16.0
Meles meles						6.5									6.5
Canidae			2.5			8									10.5
Carnivores						1.9		5							6.9

Lepus europaeus						11.6						
Testudo sp.							3					
Gallus gallus						42						
Aves	6.1	11.5	17.8	10.1	18.9	499.4	5.8	5	28.3	1.1		604.0
Fish	0.9	1.7			4.3	49.5			9.6			66.0
Molluscs			0.3									0.3
Total identified taxa	9633.3	1781.7	2930.1	4837.95	6202.6	223369.4	3662.6	4364	16923	5474.8	7238	286375
Large mammals	1634.4	286.6	1799.1	2121.2	897.5	54033.8	1030.2	1357	1238.4	3505.4	2230	70133.6
Medium mammals	23						43	13				79.0
Small mammals				28.4		815	4.3					847.7
Small ruminants	498.8	64.9	113.9	395.1	372.2	13811.2	200.4	5	641.7	378.5	368	16849.7
Unidentified	124.4	34	6	41.3	292.5	4293.7	127	96	933	233		6180.9
Total unidentified taxa	13017.7	2180.4	4903.1	7618.15	7788	298898.3	5081.3	5858	19811.1	9646.8	9880	94090.9
Grand total	22651	3962.1	7833.2	12456.1	13990.6	522267.7	8743.9	10222	36734.1	15121.6	17118	380466.4

Hunting was practised by the inhabitants of Dariali Fort, but does not appear to have been an important source of meat. A few bones could be attributed to wild caprines, because of their unusual size and the fact that they can be morphologically distinguished from other remains. Three different species are present in Georgia, including two Caucasian turs (*Capra caucasica* and *Capra cylindricornis*) that are endemic to the Greater Caucasus Range, where they inhabit altitudes between 2,000 and 4,000m, and also *Capra aegagrus*. We cannot distinguish these species on the basis of the skeletal elements present at the site. As for the large sheep specimens, they may belong to *Ovis orientalis gmelini*, but we remain cautious about the firm allocation of these caprine bones to wild species. Six bone fragments were attributed to rupicapra (*Rupicapra rupicapra* or *Capreolus capreolus*). The specimens tentatively allocated to these small ruminants are poorly represented amongst the faunal remains from Dariali Fort, and whilst they may have been present, the case is not proven beyond doubt. Whilst there is no certain evidence for wild *capra* or *rupicapra* in phase 3, one specimen belongs to phase 4, at the transition from the Sasanian era to the Middle Ages. Finally, fewer than fifty remains of suids (*Sus scrofa*) were present on the site (from all phases, but including certain Sasanian-era examples) and we are completing analysis for their allocation to wild or domesticates.

Other mammals

It is generally difficult to address the question of which animals were actually consumed when all faunal remains are found together and the context by itself does not allow an interpretation. We have categorised some as non-consumed only because of the lack of clear evidence of their consumption, such as burning or cut marks. This is the case of equids, for which we identified forty-five bones, of which one could be attributed with certainty to the horse (*Equus caballus*), although most of the other remains are generally of the size of large equids. The third phalanx of a horse (*Equus caballus*)[9] with a radiocarbon date of AD 401–538, at 95.4 per cent confidence, was found just a few centimetres above the bedrock, next to a late antique fort wall and below samples likely to date to the early fifth century. Some of the equid bones are currently being analysed genetically, and we will soon have more information on the possible presence of hybrids (between donkey and horse) that could be expected in this kind of environment.

Several bones of carnivores were also found amongst the faunal remains from Trench F. Dogs (*Canis familiaris*) and cats (*Felis catus*) were probably companion animals. Wild carnivores were also present, indicating occasional hunting of fox (*Vulpes sp.*), badger (*Meles meles*) and bear (*Ursus arctos*). A few hare (*Lepus europaeus*) bones are worth noting. Interestingly, however, none of these species is so far represented in a certain Sasanian context. As their number in the much more sizeable early medieval assemblage (phase 5) is small, it is hard to be sure whether this is mere coincidence or points to hunting not normally being practised prior to the Middle Ages.

Poultry and fish

Besides the three main species, sheep/goat and cattle, chicken (*Gallus gallus*) was also consumed, but there is no evidence for it so far from phase 3. Freshwater fish remains, probably cyprinids, are also present and currently under study.

THE EVOLUTION OF THE SUBSISTENCE ECONOMY DURING THE SASANIAN PERIOD

Figures 4.2a and 4.2b show the distribution of major groups of animals in various phases, although some contexts could not be precisely allocated to a single phase. The Sasanian era covers phase 3 and probably parts of phase 4. No major change appears to have occurred between these phases, caprines being the main group of domesticates exploited and sheep seemingly preferred to goat. Cattle provided the second-most important source of meat. An analysis of the exploitation of dairy products will be possible once the kill-off pattern has been established by the end of the excavation project. In phase 5, however, animal exploitation changed, and the proportion of cattle increased significantly.

The bovid population of Dariali Fort

Metric analysis of animal bones and bone fragments is used for their taxonomic distinction and also for an indication of morphological modification within a species over time and space. This allows us to gain insights into the variability of animal populations in the past. The good preservation of these bone assemblages in general has allowed us to record a significant number of measurements. We used the measurement codes published by Angela von den Driesch.[10]

Trench F: NISP (n= 23,117)

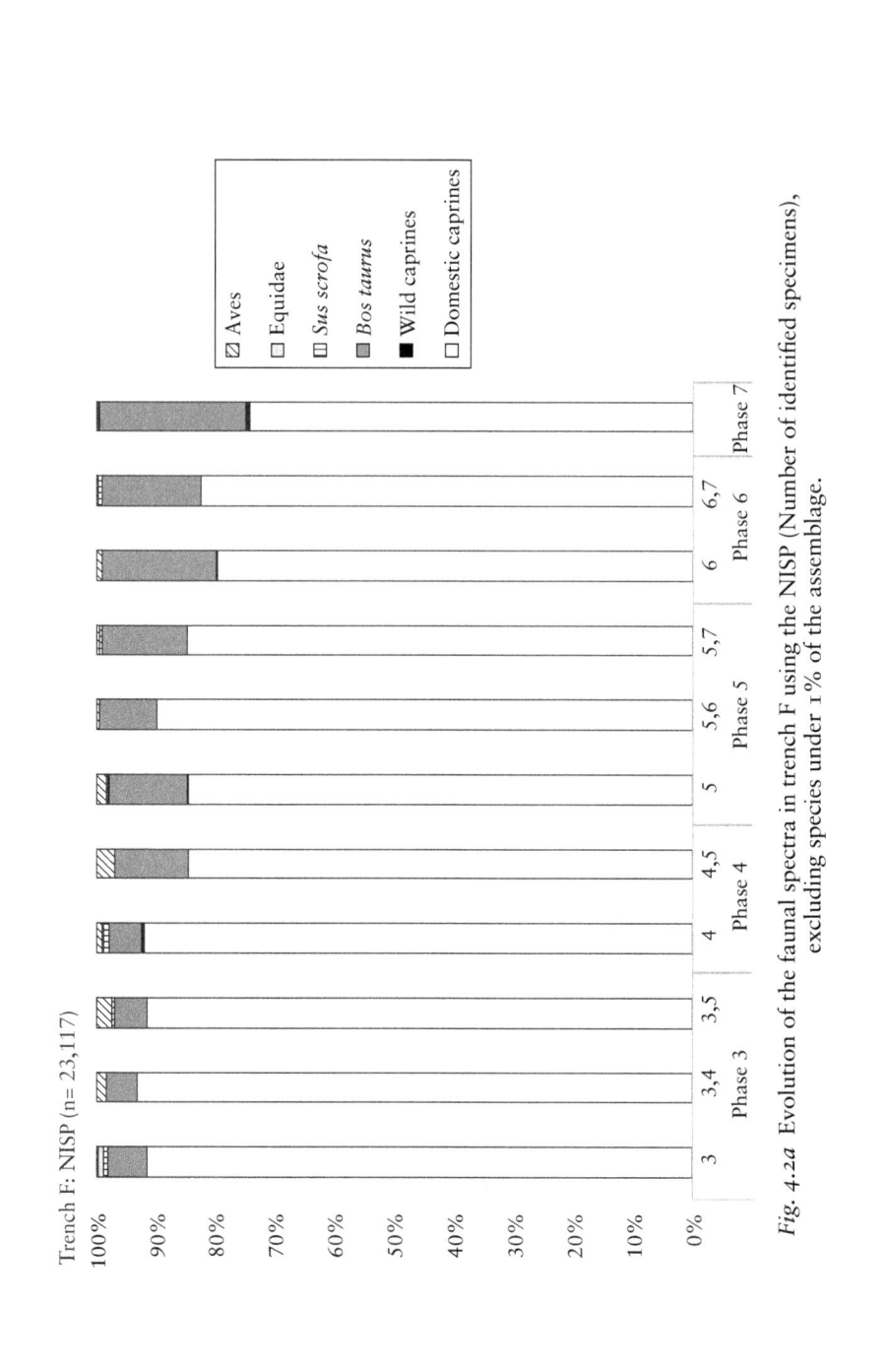

Fig. 4.2a Evolution of the faunal spectra in trench F using the NISP (Number of identified specimens), excluding species under 1% of the assemblage.

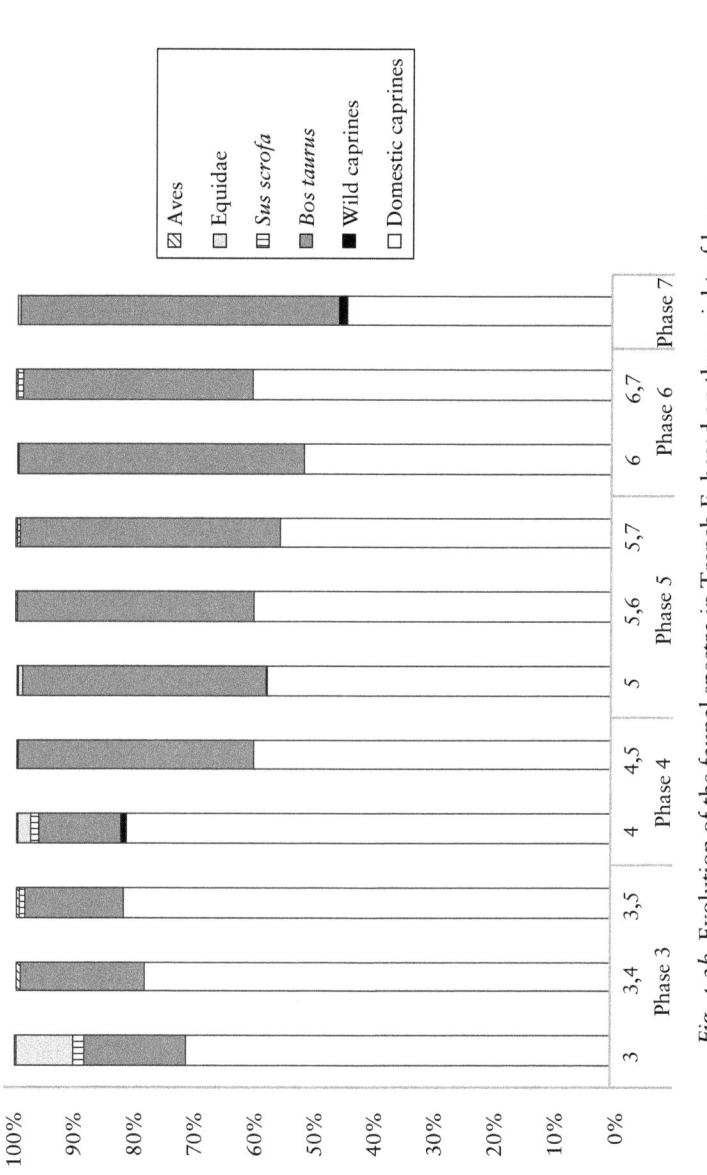

Fig. 4.2b Evolution of the faunal spectra in Trench F, based on the weight of bones, excluding species under 1% of the assemblage.

The logarithmic method for statistical analysis of an assemblage provides a useful way to compare sites. Because of a scale difference within different measurements of a bone, for example the length and the breadth, all measurements are converted to logarithms to diminish the effect of these scale differences. The 'Size Index Method' was developed by Hans-Peter Uerpmann[11] and simplified by Richard Meadow.[12] The basic idea is to relate every find measurement to the respective measurement of a known and preferably recent individual – the so called 'Standard' – and to use the distance from the standard (S) as an indication (= Index) of the size of the unknown individual (X) from which the find was derived, and the ratio (of the standard to the archaeological specimen), which is expressed by this calculation: $LSI = \log X - \log S$. For the sheep and goat standard, we used measurements of wild sheep and goats published by H. P. and M. Uerpmann.[13]

Here we present the results of the LSI analysis for *Ovis*, *Capra* and *Bos* in Dariali Fort, compared to other contemporaneous, earlier and later sites (Figs 4.3, 4.4 and 4.5). For sheep and goat, the remains datable to the Sasanian period (indicated as 'CG Dariali Fort (late 4th–7th c. AD)')[14] were compared to the modern populations from two localities in Iran: Ziyaran in the north of the Qazvin area and Bakhtiyari in the middle of the Zagros region[15] (Figs 4.3 and 4.4). Moreover, in the archaeological material we selected all the available sites for which we could access the data. The earliest sites are from the Iron Age of northern Iran (Sagzabad,[16] Hasanlu,[17] Haftavan Tepe[18] and Gunespan[19]). Assemblages from ancient periods (from Mannean to Sasanian) were also available from some sites that are represented in the LSI graphs, including Qalaichi Bukan, Zendan-e Suleiman,[20] Haftavan Tepe,[21] Hasanlu[22] and Hegmataneh.[23] We also compared the measurements from Dariali Fort to sites on the Gorgan Wall and in its hinterland (Dasht Qal'eh, Qal'eh Kharabeh and Fort 4[24]) when possible. Finally, we included Islamic assemblages (Haftavan,[25] Suse Khersan,[26] Qohandez[27]), in order to evaluate possible changes in the size of the animals in post-Sasanian times.

Comparison of the average size of sheep populations shows that sheep in the Sasanian era were generally larger than those of earlier periods. The contrast is particularly striking when comparing Sasanian and Iron Age sheep (Fig. 4.3). Dariali Fort and the Gorgan Wall (GW) sites are close in size, except for Qal'eh Kharabeh, although this may be a bias due to the low number of bones available for measurement from this site. The physical size of sheep from Dariali Fort and the Gorgan Wall sites falls within

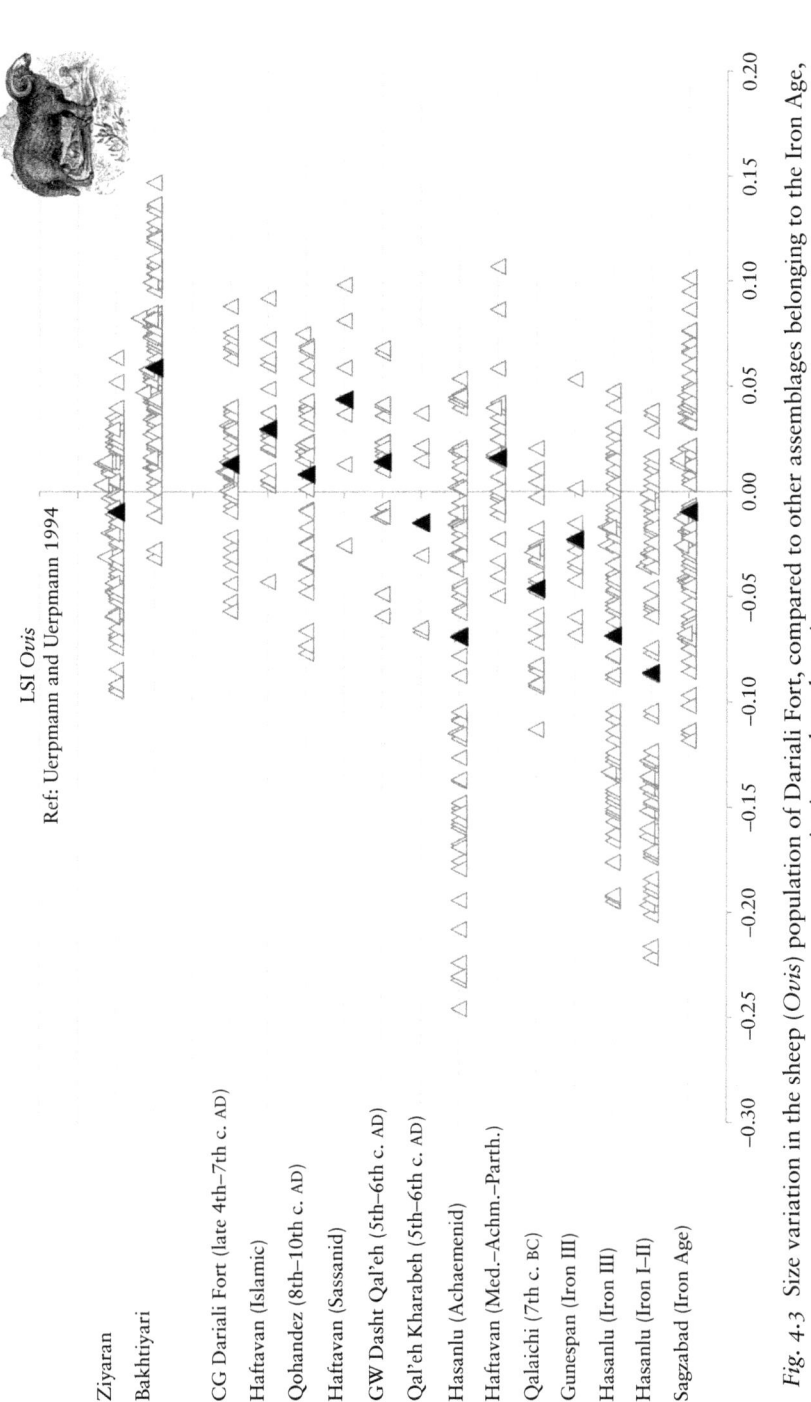

Fig. 4.3 Size variation in the sheep (*Ovis*) population of Dariali Fort, compared to other assemblages belonging to the Iron Age, antiquity and modern times.

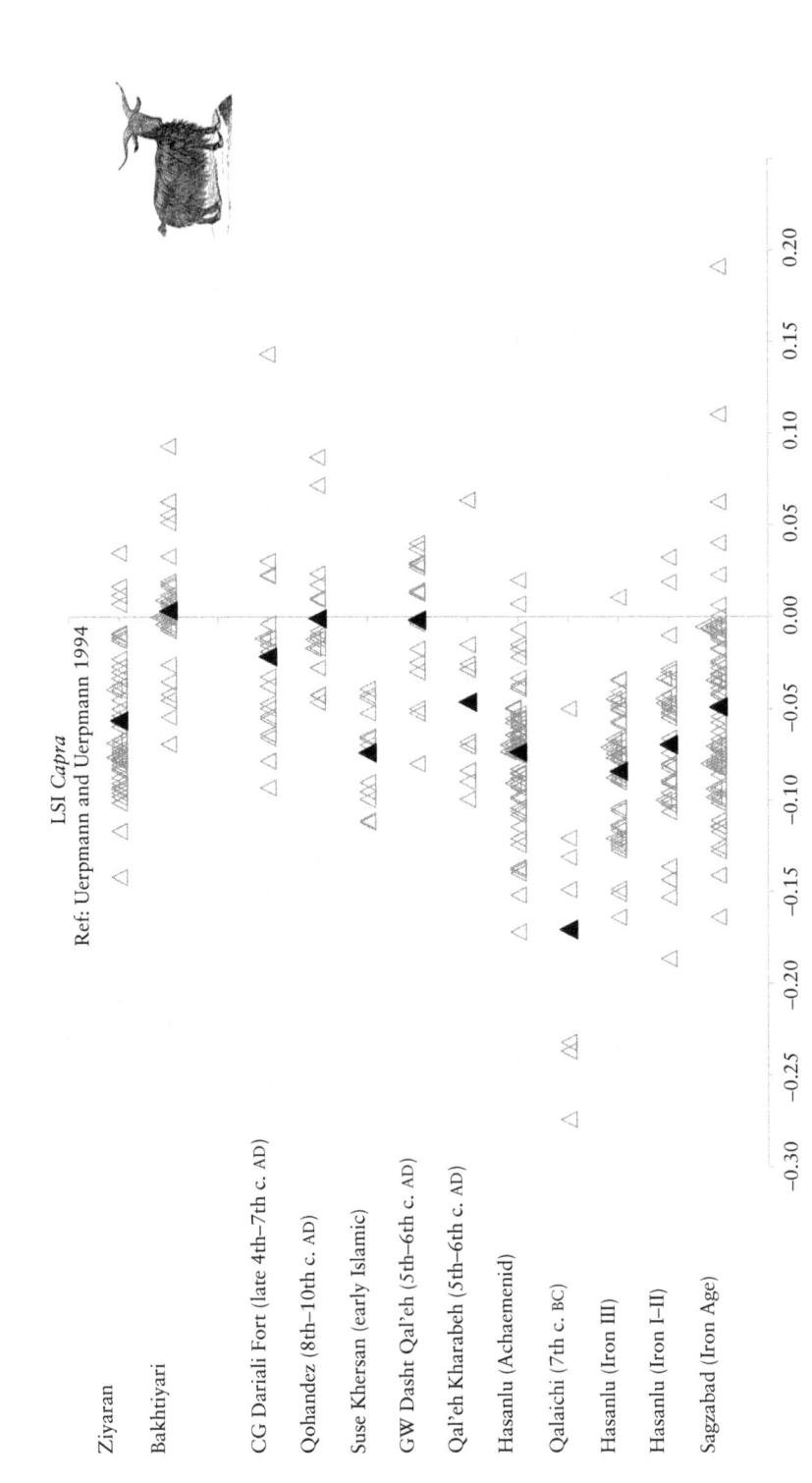

Fig. 4.4 Size variation in the goat (*Capra*) populations at Dariali Fort, compared to other assemblages belonging to the Iron Age, antiquity and modern times.

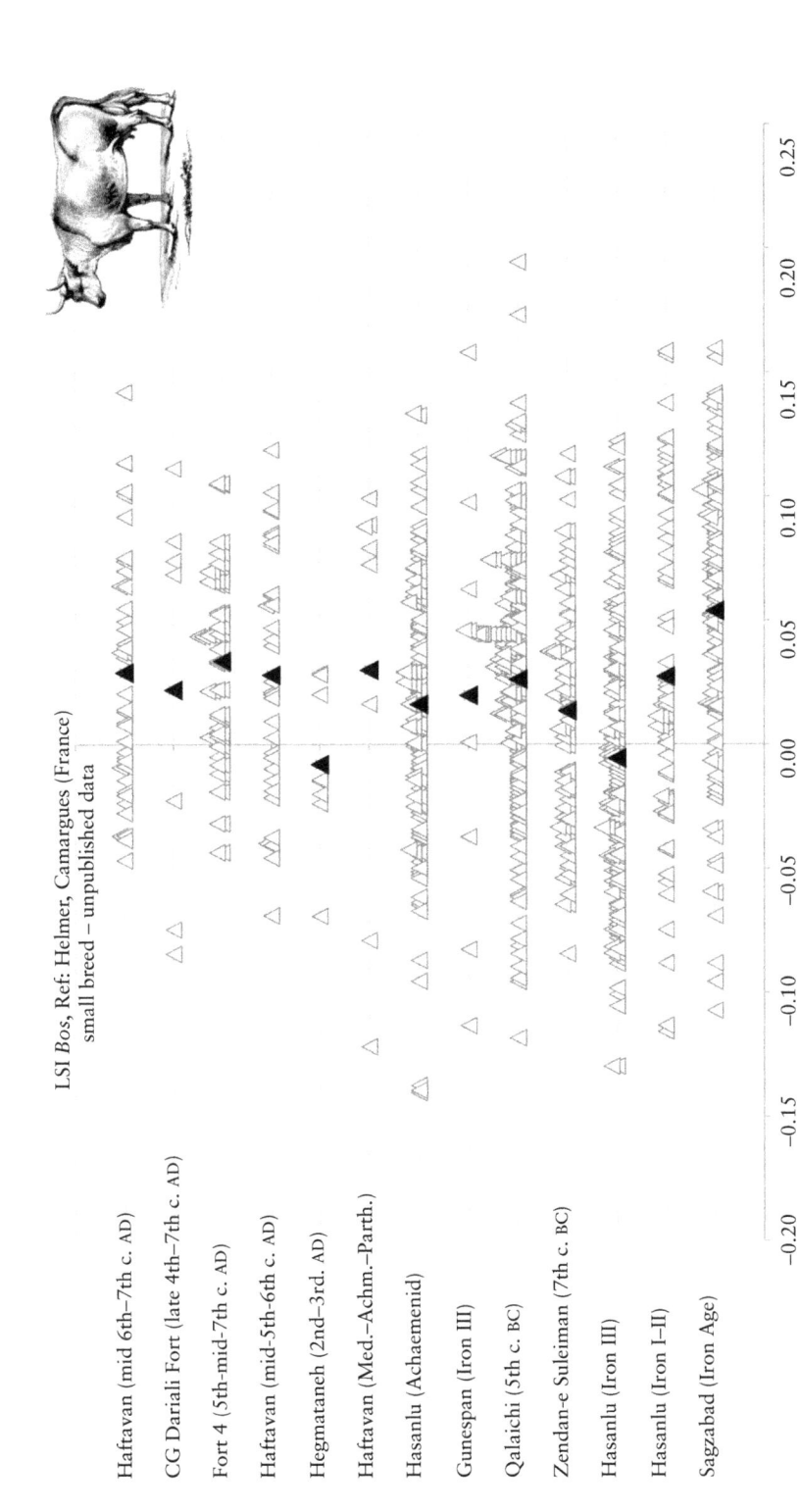

Fig. 4.5 Size variation in the cattle (*Bos*) population at Dariali Fort, compared to other assemblages belonging to the Iron Age, antiquity and modern times.

the range of the modern parallels provided by the populations of Ziyaran and Bakhtiyari.

For goats (Fig. 4.4), we observe the same general trend. Dariali Fort is intermediate between the two modern collections and also the Gorgan Wall sites, the latter displaying similar size variations to the modern assemblages. In general, it is worth noting that the goat populations of the Sasanian, medieval and modern eras are larger on average than populations from the Iron Age to the Achaemenid period.

Finally, cattle assemblages (Fig. 4.5) are very uniform all over the sequence and do not show major differences.

CONCLUSION

The study presented here is a first attempt to analyse the available archaeozoological data from the Sasanian era in comparison to other sites from the Iron Age to the Islamic period. Considering the number of assemblages in each chronological category, distributed over a large geographic area, it is difficult to discern consistent patterns. What is clear, however, is that the environment had a significant impact on the diversity of faunal exploitation. The difference between Qalʻeh Kharabeh, close to the Caspian Sea, and those sites in the Gorgan Plain at greater distance from the shore, for example, is striking. The same observations apply to Dariali Fort, located in a harsh environment far from the sea. Here too, the main animal resources seem to come from domesticates as being more readily available. The contribution of wild mammals is very low, even if wild bovids might have been available in the surrounding area.

Analysis of the metric data of the faunal assemblages, despite their relative scarcity, nevertheless shows noteworthy variations in the size of sheep and goats within the geographical territories and periods under investigation, indicating that there was a fair degree of variability within the pastoral system across the region. Interestingly, this observation is not valid for cattle, which appear to show a more homogeneous pattern, even if we lack relevant assemblages from the Islamic period. One reason for this may be due to the more mobile character of sheep and goat herding compared to cattle herding. These hypotheses need to be re-examined in the future, as more data become available.

Our research, rather than showing similarities, demonstrates the diversity of animal exploitation at the edges of the Sasanian Empire, while the basis of the animal food economy at least in these specific contexts relies on the three main domesticates: sheep, goats and cattle, while curiously pig was largely absent from the diet, and hunting was practised on a small scale only.

NOTES

1. Sauer et al. 2013; 2015.
2. Ghasemi et al. in press.
3. Priestman et al. 2015.
4. Mashkour 2013; Radu 2013.
5. Uepmann 1987.
6. Ghirshman 1962.
7. Radu 2013.
8. Eberhard Sauer and Seth Priestman pers. comm.
9. Find 1065 from context F.127.
10. Driesch 1976.
11. Uerpmann 1979: 174ff.
12. Meadow 1999.
13. Uerpmann and Uerpmann 1994.
14. CG stands for Caucasian Gates, one of the ancient names for Dariali Gorge.
15. Mashkour and Mohaseb, unpublished data.
16. Mashkour 2001; 2002.
17. Davoudi in prep.
18. Mohaseb Karimlou 2012; Mohaseb and Mashkour in press.
19. Amiri et al. 2014b.
20. Nezamabadi et al 2011.
21. Mohaseb Karimlou 2012; Mohaseb and Mashkour in press.
22. Davoudi in prep.
23. Mashkour et al. 2013.
24. Mashkour 2013.
25. Mohaseb Karimlou 2012; Mohaseb and Mashkour in press.
26. Amiri et al. 2014a.
27. Khazaeli 2014.

BIBLIOGRAPHY

Amiri, S., Mashkour, M., Mohaseb, F. A. and Ghasemi P. (2014a), 'Preliminary Report of the Faunal Remains from Tepe Suse (Chahar Mahal-e Bakhtiyari), Iran', unpublished report ICAR-ICHHTO (in Persian).

Amiri, S., Mashkour, M., Mohaseb, F. A. and Naseri, R. (2014b), 'A Glance into the Subsistence Economy of Gunespan (Hamedan, Iran) during the Bronze Age and Median Periods' (in Persian), in M. H Azizi Kharanaghi, M. Kkanipour and R. Naseri (eds), *Proceedings of the International Conference of Young Archaeologists*, Tehran: University of Tehran, pp. 597–626.

Davoudi, H. (in prep.), 'Subsistence Economy of Iron Age Societies in North-Western Iran Based on Archaeozoological Studies – the Case of Tepe Hasanlu', PhD thesis, Tarbiyat Modares University.

Driesch, A. von den (1976), *A Guide to the Measurement of Animal Bones from Archaeological Sites*, Peabody Museum Bulletin 1, Cambridge: Harvard University Press.

Ghasemi, P., Noruzi, R., and Rezaei, A. (in press), 'The First Season of Excavations at the Sasanian Site of Tole Qaleh Seyfabad (TQS), South-West Iran: Preliminary Report', in St J. Simpson (ed.), *Studies in Sasanian Archaeology: Settlement, Environment and Material Culture*, Oxford: Archaeopress.

Ghirshman, R. (1962), *Iran: Parthians and Sassanians*, London: Thames and Hudson.

Khazaeli, R. (2014), 'The Subsistence Economy of the Old Nishapur from the Formation of the City through the Parthian up to the Mongol Period', MA thesis, Department of Archaeology, University of Tehran (in Persian).

Mashkour, M. (2001), 'Chasse et élevage du Néolithique à l'Âge du Fer dans la plaine de Qazvin (Iran): Étude archéozoologique des sites de Zagheh, Qabrestan et Sagzabad', PhD thesis, Université Paris 1 Panthéon-Sorbonne.

Mashkour, M. (2002), 'Chasse et élevage au nord du Plateau central iranien entre le Néolithique et l'Âge du Fer', *Paléorient*, 28.1, pp. 27–42.

Mashkour, M. (2013), 'Animal Exploitation During the Iron Age to Achaemenid, Sasanian and Early Islamic Periods Along the Gorgan Wall', in Sauer et al. 2013, pp. 548–80.

Mashkour, M., Sheikhi Seno, S. and Hozhabri, A. (2013), 'Hegmataneh Faunal Remains: A Brief Insight into the Parthian Archaeozoology', in A. Hozhabri (ed.), *The Archaeology of Hamadan*, Tehran: ICHHTO, pp. 27–42.

Meadow, R. H. (1999), 'The Use of Size Index Scaling Techniques for Research on Archaeozoological Collections from the Middle East', in C. Becker, H. Manhart, J. Peters and J. Schibler (eds), *Historia Animalium ex Ossibus: Beiträge zur Paläoanatomie, Archäologie, Ägyptologie, Ethnologie und Geschichte der Tiermedizin. Festschrift für Angela Von den Driesch.*, Rahden: Marie Leidorf, pp. 285–300.

Mohaseb, A. F. and Mashkour, M. (in press), 'Animal Exploitation from the Bronze Age to the Early Islamic Period in Haftavan Tepe (Western Azerbaijan–Iran)', in M. Mashkour and M. J. Beech (eds), *Archaeozoology of the Near East 9: Proceedings of the 2008 Al Ain-Abu Dhabi conference*, Oxford: Oxbow Books.

Mohaseb Karimlou, F. (2012), 'Exploitation des animaux de l'Âge du Bronze au début de la période Islamique dans le nord-ouest de l'Iran: L'étude archéozoologique de Haftavan Tepe', PhD thesis, Université Paris 1 Panthéon-Sorbonne.

Nezamabadi, M., Mashkour, M. and Kargar, B. (2011), 'Mannaean Faunal Remains from Tepe Qalaichi, Northwestern Iran (9th–7th BC)', *Journal of Iranian Archaeology*, 2, pp. 33–40.

Priestman, S., Al-Jahwari, N. S., Kennet, D., Sauer, E., Andrews, M., Ainslie, R., Lawrence, D., MacDonald, E. and Usher-Wilson, L. S. (2015), 'Sasanian Military Investment on the Batinah Plain of Oman: New Discoveries at Fulayj', unpublished report.

Radu, V. (2013), 'Fish Consumption on the Gorgān Plain in Antiquity', in Sauer et al. 2013, pp. 539–46.

Sauer, E. W., Omrani Rekavandi, H., Wilkinson, T. J., Nokandeh, J. et al. (2013), *Persia's Imperial Power in Late Antiquity: The Great Wall of Gorgān and Frontier Landscapes of Sasanian Iran*, British Institute of Persian Studies Archaeological Monographs Series II, Oxford: Oxbow Books.

Sauer, E. W., Pitskhelauri, K., Hopper, K., Tiliakou, A., Pickard, C., Lawrence, D., Diana, A., Kranioti, E. and Shupe, C. (2015), 'Northern Outpost of the Caliphate: Maintaining Military Forces in a Hostile Environment (the Dariali Gorge in the Central Caucasus in Georgia)', *Antiquity*, 89, pp. 885–904.

Uerpmann, H.-P., (1979), *Probleme der Neolithisierung des Mittelmeerraums. Beihefte zum Tübinger Atlas des Vorderen Orients*, Reihe B, No. 28, Wiesbaden: Reichert.

Uerpmann, H.-P., (1987), *The Ancient Distribution of Ungulate Mammals in the Middle East: Fauna and Archaeological Sites in Southwest Asia and Northeast Africa*, Wiesbaden: Reichert.

Uerpmann, M. and Uerpmann, H.-P. (1994), 'Animal Bone Finds from Excavation 520 at Qala'at al Bahrain', in F. Højlund and H. H. Andersen (eds), *Qala'at al Bahrain. Vol. I: The Northern City Wall and the Islamic Fortress*, Carlsberg Foundation's Gulf Project, Aarhus: Aarhus University Press, pp. 417–44.

Part II
Frontiers and Frontier Landscapes

5 The Northern and Western Borderlands of the Sasanian Empire: Contextualising the Roman/Byzantine and Sasanian Frontier

Dan Lawrence and Tony J. Wilkinson

This chapter investigates the archaeological landscapes of the frontiers of the Sasanian Empire. Drawing on evidence from current and archived archaeological surveys, in combination with high-resolution remote sensing datasets such as CORONA spy photography, we compare the organisation of settlements and defensive structures of the Sasanian frontier zones in response to a variety of external pressures. These varied from the Roman Empire in the west to less centralised entities, including nomadic groups, in the southwest and north-east. Following a general discussion of the multiple manifestations of Sasanian frontiers drawn from southern Mesopotamia (Iraq), northern Syria and north-eastern Iran, the main focus of the chapter is on the complex frontier landscape of the southern Caucasus, particularly the area of modern Azerbaijan, Georgia and Daghestan. We discuss the role of linear barriers, including the Gorgan Wall in north-eastern Iran and the Ghilghilchay and Derbent Walls in the Caucasus, irrigation systems, and alignments of fortifications and settlements in shaping their local landscapes. By placing the archaeological remains of the Sasanian Empire in a wider context we are able to examine the relationships between military installations, settlement patterns, infrastructure and geographical features such as mountain ranges and rivers. Comparing the different case studies allows us to conclude with some general statements on the nature of Sasanian power in the frontier territories of the empire.

INTRODUCTION

As a large territorial entity, the Sasanian Empire encompassed a variety of geographical, environmental and socio-cultural zones. Even within the northern and western reaches discussed here, the empire included the high mountain ranges of the Taurus, Caucasus and eastern Anatolia, the fertile dry farming plains of much of northern Mesopotamia and Gorgan, heavily irrigated southern Mesopotamia and steppe and desert regions in various guises (Fig. 5.1). Threats to Sasanian power were similarly diverse, from the agrarian might of the Roman Empire in the west to smaller local 'states', client kingdoms and decentralised nomadic groups in the north and north-east. This diversity had a profound impact on the organisation and character of the frontier regions at the edges of imperial control. In this chapter we make use of data acquired as part of the recent upsurge in interest in Sasanian frontiers across the study region,[1] as well as satellite imagery and textual information, to examine the structure and function of the frontier zones in different areas.

Before embarking on this analysis, it is necessary to characterise briefly our approach to frontiers. Early discussions of frontiers and borderlands focused on a judicial understanding of boundaries as the result of legal agreements or treaties between states.[2] However, during the late nineteenth and early twentieth century ideas relating to natural boundaries began to emerge, particularly through the work of German geographers such as Friedrich Ratzel.[3] Combining Social Darwinism with a biological understanding of the state as an organic system capable of growth, it was possible to justify the imperial expansionism of western states during this period as a result of inherent strengths and weaknesses in national character. In Britain, Lord Curzon[4] made a distinction between 'natural' and 'artificial' frontiers, arguing that physical barriers such as mountains, deserts, large bodies of water and rivers could become important as both conceptually significant and easily defensible boundaries, but that in the absence of such features frontiers could involve manmade structures such as linear barriers or areas of depopulated land. This framework has had a profound effect on ancient frontier studies. For example, in a recent study of the frontiers of the Roman world, David Breeze[5] defined seven different types of frontier: (1) linear barriers; 2) river frontiers; (3) desert frontiers; (4) mountain frontiers; (5) sea frontiers; (6) forests, marshes and swamps; and (7) the frontier in depth.

In opposition to the ideas of Ratzel and others, scholars such as

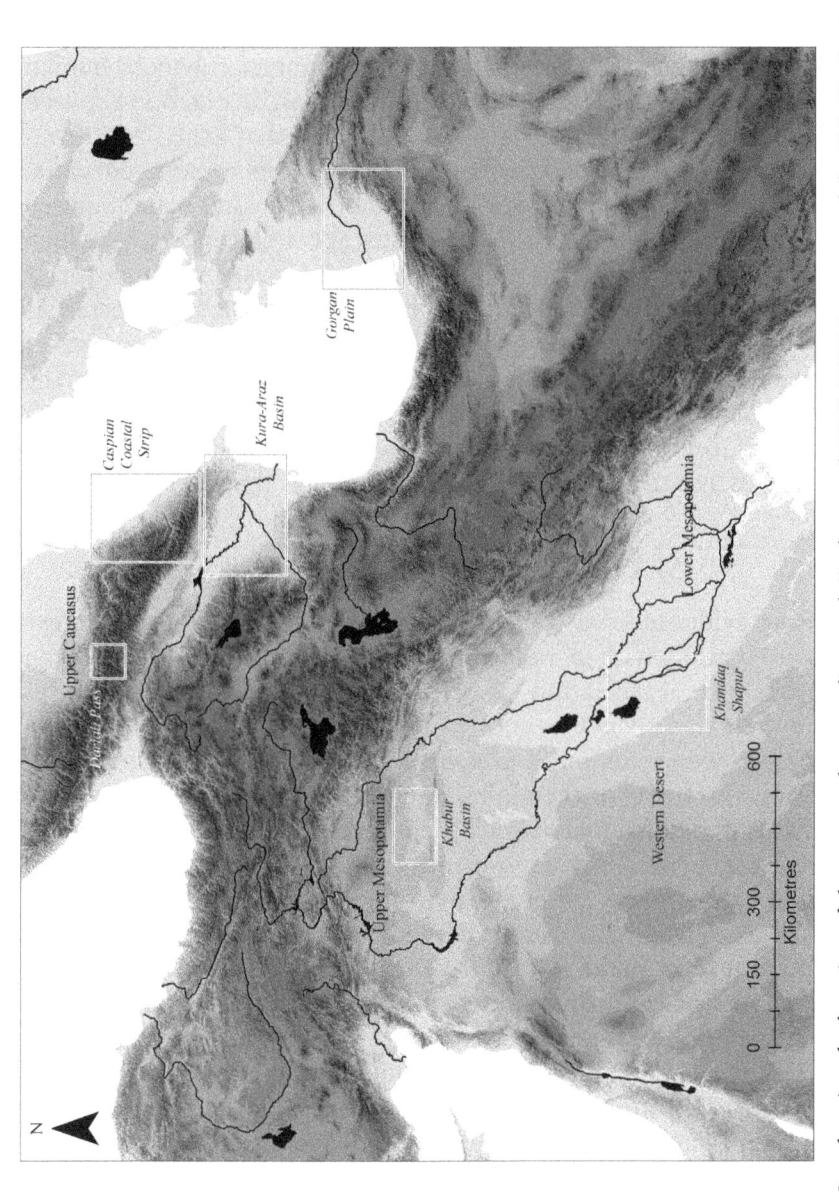

Fig. 5.1 Map showing the location of the case study areas discussed. Background SRTM DEM courtesy of the U.S. Geological Survey.

Febvre[6] argued for a more contextual approach, focusing on the particular history of the frontier in question and the different actors involved; 'in reality it is not by beginning with the frontier itself that it can be studied ... it is by starting with the State'.[7] Although frontiers may form zones of exclusion or control, such a focus reminds us that they can also be areas of intense cultural encounters, enhanced human activity and growth.[8] Rather than drawing a sharp distinction between natural and artificial frontiers we would argue that analyses of frontier regions need to consider the complex interplay between social and geographic factors, especially at the broad spatial scale required to understand imperial processes. Landscape archaeology, by which we mean the investigation of the cultural landscape through time,[9] provides an ideal lens through which to examine these processes. In this chapter we draw on a variety of case studies of discrete regions to compare the archaeological landscapes of the Sasanian frontiers in the northern and western borderlands of the empire. Such an approach allows us to contextualise the archaeological remains within their landscapes and to bring out broader geographical patterns.

MATERIALS AND METHODS

Utilising evidence from current and archived archaeological surveys in combination with a range of remote sensing datasets, we can compare the organisation of settlement and defensive structures of the Sasanian frontier zones in response to a variety of internal factors, as well as external pressures. Because of their capability of covering vast areas of the globe, satellite images are ideal for topics such as imperial frontiers which themselves cover very large regions. These images can allow us to identify similar features, such as fortification types, in very different environments and landscape settings, as well as providing wider landscape context for such features. In this chapter we make use of recently acquired Landsat 8 multispectral imagery and Digital Elevation Models (DEMs) derived from the Shuttle Radar Topography Mission (SRTM) alongside declassified CORONA spy photography acquired in the 1960s. The value of the CORONA imagery when applied to Near Eastern landscapes has been discussed extensively elsewhere[10] and has proved extremely effective for identifying and mapping Sasanian features in several of the regions considered here.[11] Nevertheless, it is not possible to cover the entire western and northern blocks of the Sasanian Empire; therefore the following key examples should be seen as sample areas within a greater whole.

Before discussing the study areas in detail, it is worth noting some general limitations of the evidence available. The most important of these is the problem of dating. This is particularly acute in relation to discoveries made through satellite imagery, since without ground-truthing (visiting sites on the ground) it is almost impossible to assign settlements and features definitively to specific periods. Even on the ground, features such as canals, earthworks and routeways which are not commonly associated with relevant material culture (in the Near East during the Sasanian period this almost exclusively means ceramics) are very difficult to date except through association with sites, excavation, or the use of radiometric techniques such as radiocarbon or Optically Stimulated Luminescence (OSL). Finally, the precision of dating available through ceramic periodisation is itself reliant on excavation data, and on the quantity and quality of relevant sequences within a given region.[12] For the Sasanian period this is compounded by the relative paucity of ceramic types visible throughout the empire, at least in comparison to the Roman world, which make secure local sequences even more important and results in different levels of precision across the region. In the Gorgan Plain, for example, excavations at several sites have allowed the survey team to distinguish Sasanian-period ceramics fairly clearly, and in some cases to subdivide the Sasanian period even further into early, middle and late periods.[13] On the other side of the Caspian in the Mil Plain of Azerbaijan, however, ceramic sequences for the historic periods are far less clear, such that some sites can only be dated to a period encompassing the Parthian, Sasanian and early Islamic periods, covering perhaps as long as 800 years. Recent work at Ultan Qalası on the southern side of the River Araz in Iran has provided an important, though small, assemblage for the late Sasanian period,[14] but applying this to the collections from the survey has proved challenging. In northern Syria, and to some extent southern Mesopotamia, the problem is distinguishing between Sasanian and early Islamic ceramics, meaning some sites must be assigned to a period sometime between the end of the third century (note already within the historically attested Sasanian imperial period) and the end of the eighth century.[15] This is not to say that we cannot make statements about the nature of the Sasanian landscape at particular times, only that we need to be aware of local chronological issues when doing so.

GEOGRAPHICAL CASE STUDIES
Western Iraq

The 'breadbasket' of the Sasanian Empire was situated within Khuzestan in Iran and the Mesopotamian plains of southern Iraq.[16] A series of massive irrigation canals and associated distribution systems was deployed in this region to raise agricultural yields and ensure a consistent level of production for taxation by the Sasanian state. At the same time, both urban and rural settlement rose in comparison to earlier periods[17] and the Sasanian capital, Ctesiphon, was located on the Tigris to the south of modern Baghdad. Given its importance to the Sasanian Empire, it is easy to forget that this region was located in close proximity to a major frontier, the western desert. Beyond the limits of irrigation-fed agriculture, the western desert stretched between the Mesopotamian plains in the east and the Jordan Valley in the west, an area populated by highly mobile tribal groups who negotiated a series of complex and shifting alliances with the Roman and Sasanian states.[18] Although no formal frontier between the two zones has been defined, early travellers and some scholars of the late antique world[19] have recognised the presence of a distinct earthwork roughly corresponding to the western limits of the alluvial plain. This feature is known as the Jari Sa'deh or Khandaq Shapur (Trench of Shapur) and is variously described as a sub-surface trench, an upstanding linear mound and a canal by western travellers to the region. In fact it may have been all three, with the upcast from the trench excavation forming a mound on one or both sides. The feature was first described by the Danish explorer Carsten Niebuhr in the eighteenth century and parts of it were mapped during surveys by several British naval officers in the mid-nineteenth, when it was thought to extend from Hit in the north to Basra in the south.[20] Although heavily truncated by later development, analysis of high-resolution satellite imagery has allowed us to trace the feature for over 100km from just south of Fallujah in the north to Najaf (Fig. 5.2).[21] A radiocarbon sample taken from one of the levees still upstanding provides a date between AD 420 and 570,[22] firmly in the late Sasanian period. This mapping has revealed the highly judicious use made of the local topography, even in this apparently flat and featureless landscape. The trench follows the eastern edge of the Al-Khir alluvial fan, a subtle topographic rise which prevents irrigation canals from extending further into the desert; indeed, even today modern, mechanised irrigation systems have not extended any further than the line of the Khandaq in this area.

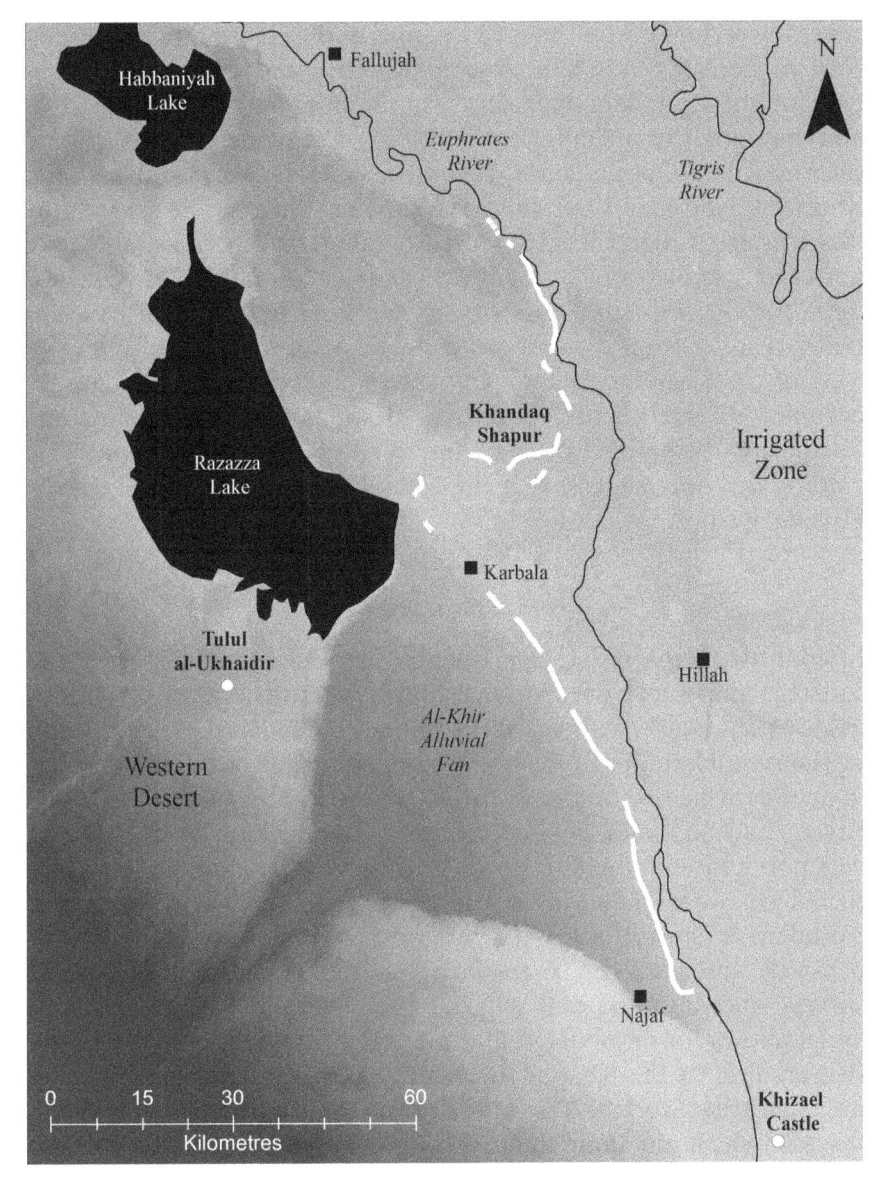

Fig. 5.2 Map of the Khandaq Shapur region. Black squares are modern towns, white circles are ancient sites and white lines represent sections of the Khandaq Shapur. Background SRTM DEM courtesy of the U.S. Geological Survey.

Beyond the Khandaq, a series of pre-Islamic ruins suggest an extension of the frontier zone into the desert. These so-called desert castles, perhaps best interpreted as residential forts, have been extensively mapped in southern Syria, Jordan, Palestine and Iraq and are generally related to the Umayyad period in the eighth century.[23] Sites such as Tulul al-Ukhaidir, close to Karbala and only some 50km west of the Khandaq (Fig. 5.2), are likely to be Sasanian in date and may point to a similar earlier form of settlement. Smaller forts such as Ruda, Qusair South, Nuqrat as-Salman, Dab' and perhaps Khizael Castle may have operated as way stations.[24] It seems that this scatter of desert castles served a range of functions, and it is not clear whether any of them operated as formal defensive structures for the western limits of the empire. However, we can say that a distinct form of settlement, the desert castle, is visible to the west of the Khandaq Shapur and stands in contrast to the densely occupied irrigated landscape in the Mesopotamian plains. In combination with the landscape setting at the limits of irrigation agriculture, this does suggest that the Khandaq functioned as a genuine boundary feature.

Eastern Syria

In contrast to the irrigated plains and dry steppe landscape of the southern alluvium, Upper Mesopotamia represents a relatively homogeneous landscape with sufficient rainfall to undertake dry farming agriculture. Here the Roman and Sasanian states faced one another in an area which, with the exceptions of the Euphrates and the Tigris Rivers, had no major physical features. The location of the frontier was not static for the duration of the period in question, and fluctuated eastwards and westwards between these two major rivers. Sasanian settlement across Upper Mesopotamia has been comprehensively discussed by Simpson,[25] but the publication of several surveys since his important article, especially in the Khabur region in Syria, allows for an updated interpretation. The border between the two empires in the Khabur included a no-man's land inhabited by nomadic tribes such as the Tayy.[26] Trade and movement across the frontier, which ran along the River Jaghjagh, was controlled through urban centres such as Nisibis to the north and Dara slightly further west (Fig. 5.3).[27] Control of these cities was therefore extremely important, as evidenced by Shapur II's redistribution of populations, including nobility, from southern Iran to Nisibis in the fourth century AD[28] and the massive investment in fortifications at Nisibis after its capture by the Sasanians in AD 363.[29] However, recent archaeological surveys in the vicinity of Tell Brak,[30] Tell Hamoukar[31] and Tell Beydar[32] allow for a reassessment of the 'empty' sector of the Khabur Basin (Fig. 5.3). In contrast to the picture provided by the textual

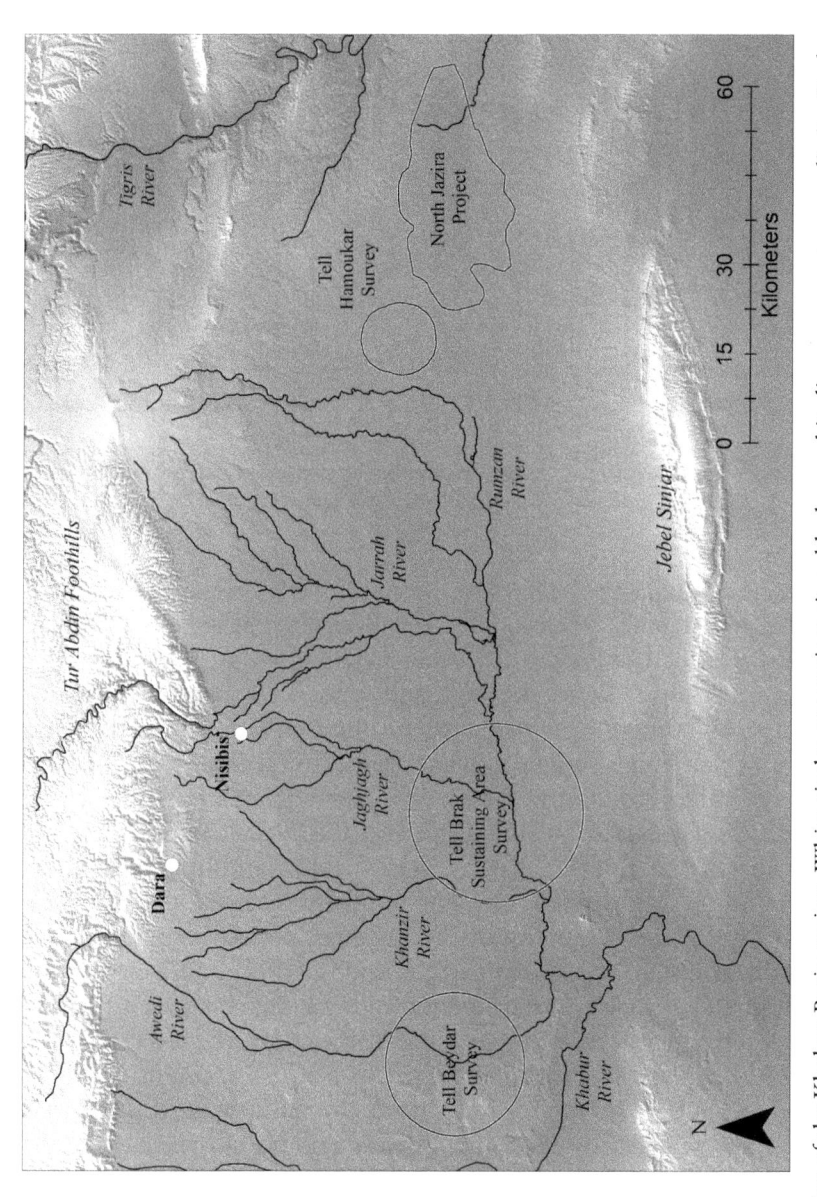

Fig. 5.3 Map of the Khabur Basin region. White circles are ancient sites, black on white lines represent survey limits. Background SRTM DEM courtesy of the U.S. Geological Survey.

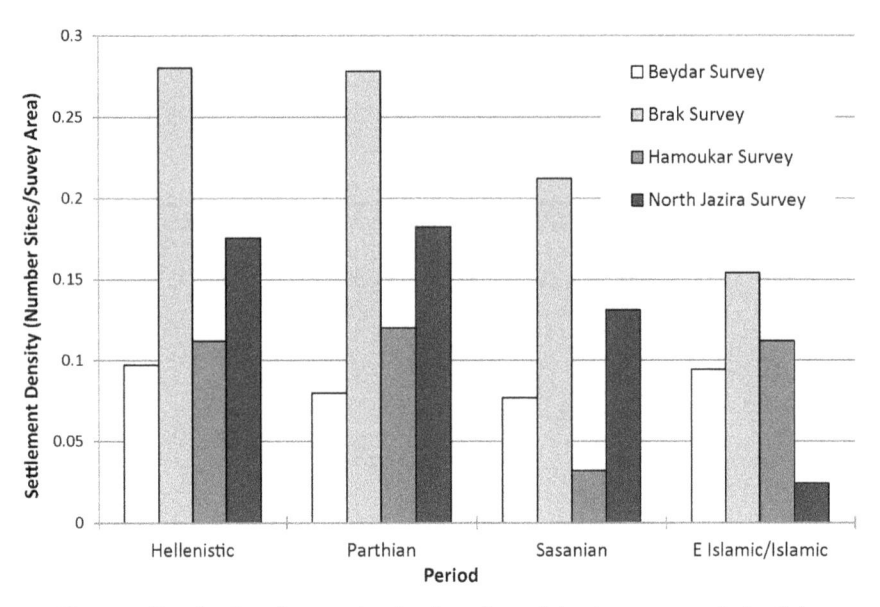

Fig. 5.4 Graph of settlement density (number of sites/survey area in km²) by survey across the Khabur Basin (arranged west to east).

sources, Sasanian (probably late Sasanian) occupation appears to have been reasonably dense. The Tell Brak Sustaining Area Survey (TBSAS) recorded 106 sites of Sasanian date in an area of just under 500km² on either side of the Jaghjagh, only a slight drop in settlement density compared with the preceding Parthian and Hellenistic periods, which had 139 and 140 sites respectively (Fig. 5.4). In addition, a possible crossing point on the Jaghjagh has been identified between the Castellum at Tell Brak and the site of Saibakh on the other side of the river.[33] In the 125km² Tell Hamoukar Survey to the east of the Jaghjagh, settlement numbers declined from sixteen sites to four at the beginning of the Sasanian period before expanding again in the late Sasanian/early Islamic period. Interestingly, the decline into the early Sasanian period may be the result of a process of nucleation, with three large villages replacing the earlier, more dispersed settlement. This may be interpreted as a defensive move perhaps related to greater threat from nomadic groups, although none of the villages seems to have been walled. On the other side of the Jaghjagh, to the west of the possible frontier zone, the Tell Beydar Survey (TBS) also shows a strong continuity of settlement, with 34 Hellenistic, 28 Parthian and 27 Sasanian/early Islamic sites. Although the precise dating of many of these sites is problematic, there is good evidence from the surveys for a dense network of small to medium-sized sites across the Khabur Basin during the Roman–Sasanian period, with the highest density of settlement located on the River Jaghjagh, supposedly the frontier itself (Fig. 5.4). Quite how autonomous this network of rural settlement was in relation to the powerful urban centres which are the focus of the classical sources must be the object of further study, but the near-continuous nature of settlement suggests a high level of interaction between different groups. At the very least, this was a very different sort of frontier from that further south.

The southern Caucasus

Recent survey and remote sensing work in the southern Caucasus by a variety of local and foreign teams allows us to reconstruct this frontier at a regional scale. Here the mountain chain of the Upper Caucasus forms a long linear obstacle between the Caspian and Black Seas, with a narrow strip of land on the Caspian side and several mountain passes in the central part of the range offering the only viable crossing points. Although this was undoubtedly a formidable 'natural frontier', in order to function effectively it had to be supplemented at strategic points. This is most obvious along the Caspian coast, where several linear barriers, large forts and fortified urban sites were constructed (Fig. 5.5). From north to south, these include the World Heritage Site at Derbent in Daghestan, with a fortress and parallel set of walls within the modern city and a 42km mountain section to the west,[34] the 125ha fort of Torpakh Qala, the Ghilghilchay Wall and Chirakh Qala in modern Azerbaijan[35] and the Beshbarmak Fort and possible wall further south. All of these features appear to have been constructed during the fifth–sixth centuries AD, with an initial construction of a mudbrick wall at Derbent followed by the Ghilghilchay Wall and later a reorganisation of the Derbent defences, now built in stone.[36]

There is insufficient space to discuss each of these in detail here (for overviews see the papers cited) but some general patterns in the organisation of the linear barriers and forts are worth mentioning. Both the Derbent and Ghilghilchay Walls make use of local topographic features to enhance their defensive capacities (Fig. 5.5). Derbent is located at the narrowest point of the coastal strip, where a long spur of raised land extends to within 4km of the Caspian Sea. The major stone walls linking the fortress of Narynqala, situated on the end of this spur, to the coast could therefore be relatively short, reducing the amount of manpower and materials needed and

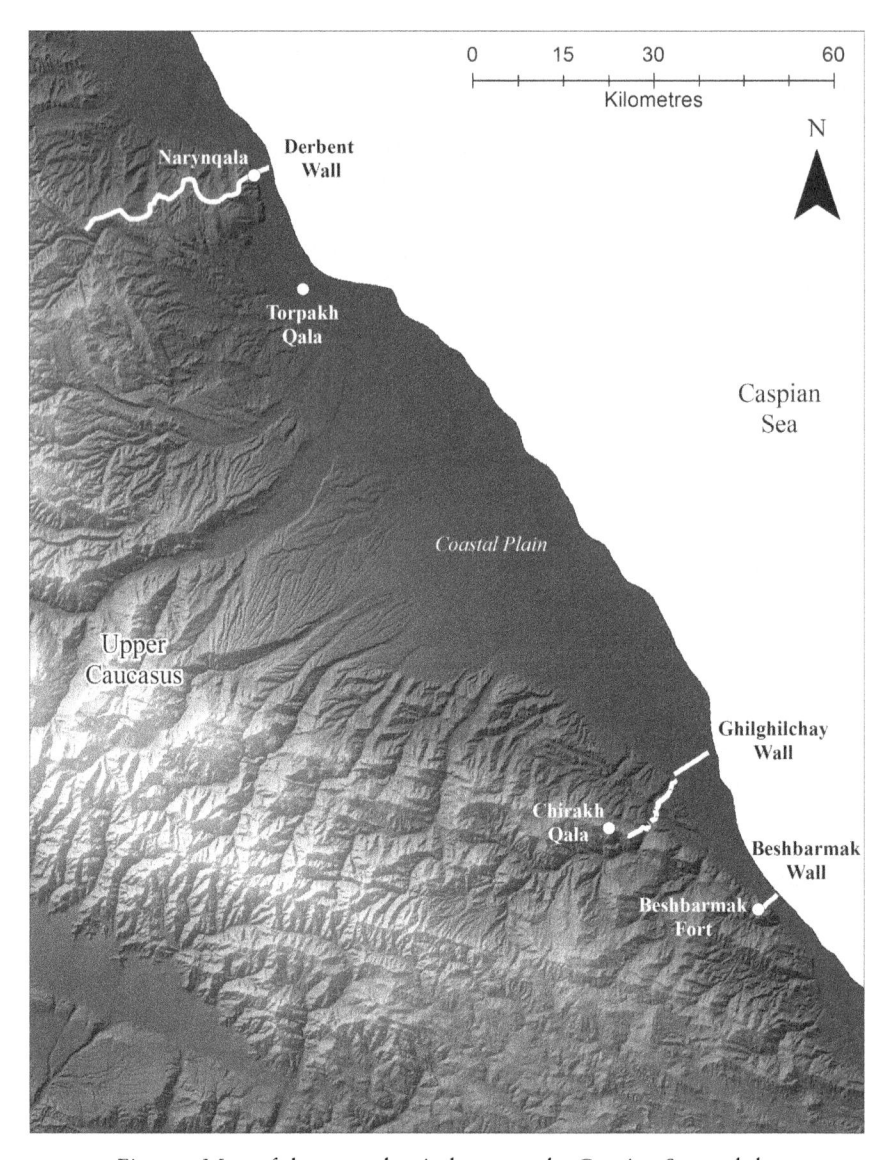

Fig. 5.5 Map of the coastal strip between the Caspian Sea and the Upper Caucasus. White circles are ancient sites and white lines represent linear barriers. Background SRTM DEM courtesy of the U.S. Geological Survey.

allowing for a fairly rapid period of construction. Nevertheless, the walls within Derbent represent a substantial investment, standing at between 18 and 20m in height and including 100 round towers. Much less is known about the 42km mountain section further inland, of which there is no trace on either the CORONA or modern

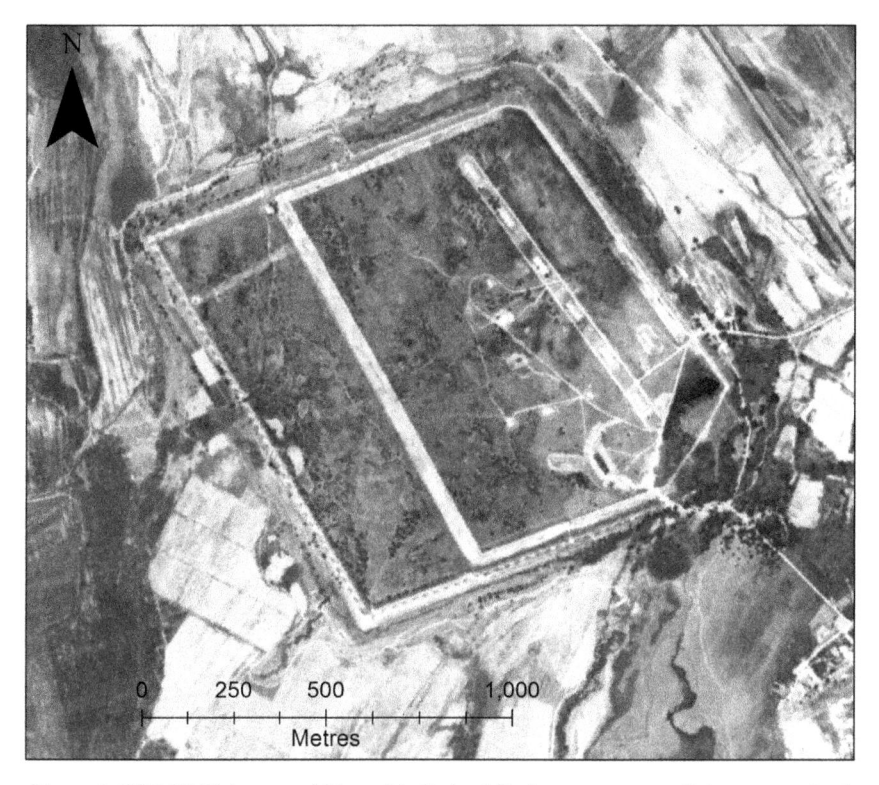

Fig. 5.6 CORONA image of Torpakh Qala. Mission 1110–1057DA111 acquired 24 May 1970, reproduced courtesy of the U.S. Geological Survey.

high-resolution imagery, but it was certainly a single rather than a double wall with around forty forts along its length.[37] To the south of Derbent the coastal strip widens significantly, and here we find the major Sasanian site of Torpakh Qala, a walled rectangular site of 125ha with regularly spaced towers along its walls and an external ditch. Torpakh Qala closely resembles the 'mega-campaign base' at Qal'eh Pol Gonbad in the Gorgan Plain, as well as Qal'eh Gabri close to Varamin in the Tehran Plain (Figs 5.6 and 5.7).[38] The position of the site, some 20km to the south of the Derbent defences in an area of flat, fertile land, may be related to the need to provision a large number of troops. Given Sauer's estimate for campaign bases of around 40ha to hold 10,000 horsemen,[39] we might expect the mega-campaign bases to accommodate 30,000 individuals, likely to have been a substantial drain on local resources.

The Ghilghilchay Wall makes similar use of local topography and is again situated at a point where the mountains lie close to the Caspian. Drawing on fieldwork undertaken by a joint

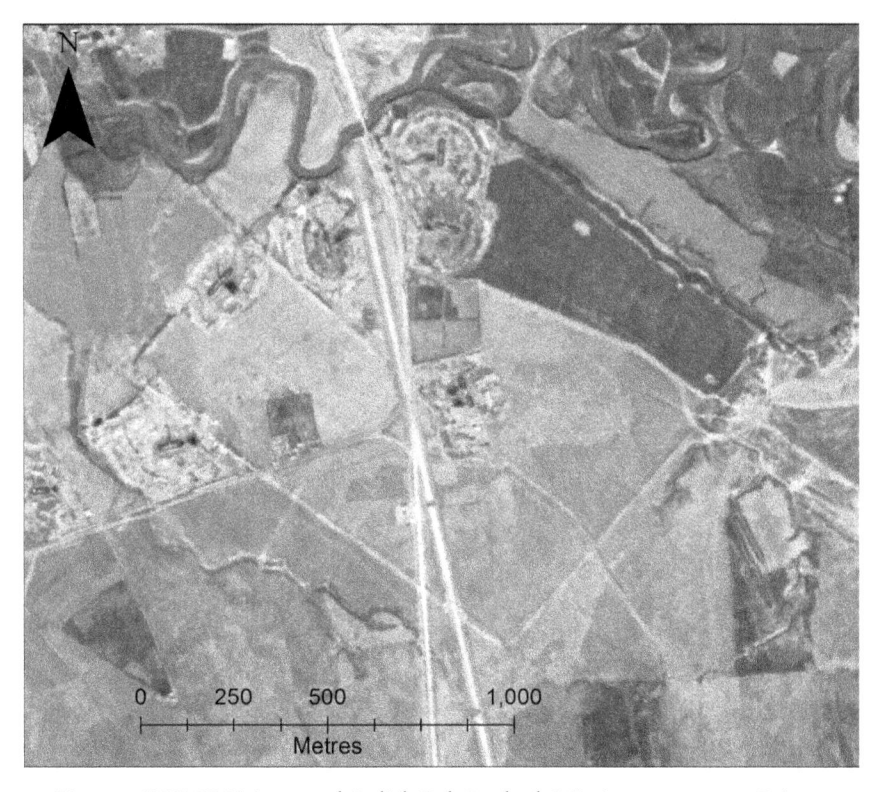

Fig. 5.7 CORONA image of Qal'eh Pol Gonbad. Mission 1103–2218DA035 acquired 7 May 1968, reproduced courtesy of the U.S. Geological Survey.

Azerbaijani–Daghestani–American team,[40] we have used CORONA satellite imagery to examine the extant remains of the wall as it was visible during the late 1960s. The remote sensing analysis has revealed several previously undocumented sections of the wall, most of which had been destroyed by industrial and agricultural development by the time of the surveys in the early 2000s, as well as a new fortification structure in the mountain section (Fig. 5.8). The wall extends at least 27km inland from the coast and includes an 8km section in the plain ending at the Yenikend Fortress, a 10km piedmont section which runs parallel to the River Ghilghilchay, and a section in the mountains (≥9km), running to the stronghold of Chirakh Qala or beyond. The plain and piedmont sections of the wall were constructed from mudbrick and reach 7m in height in places, with a ditch on the northern side visible in the plain section, perhaps a source for the mudbricks used in its construction,[41] and clear use of the steep-sided River Ghilghilchay as an extra barrier in the piedmont section. The mountain section was not investigated by

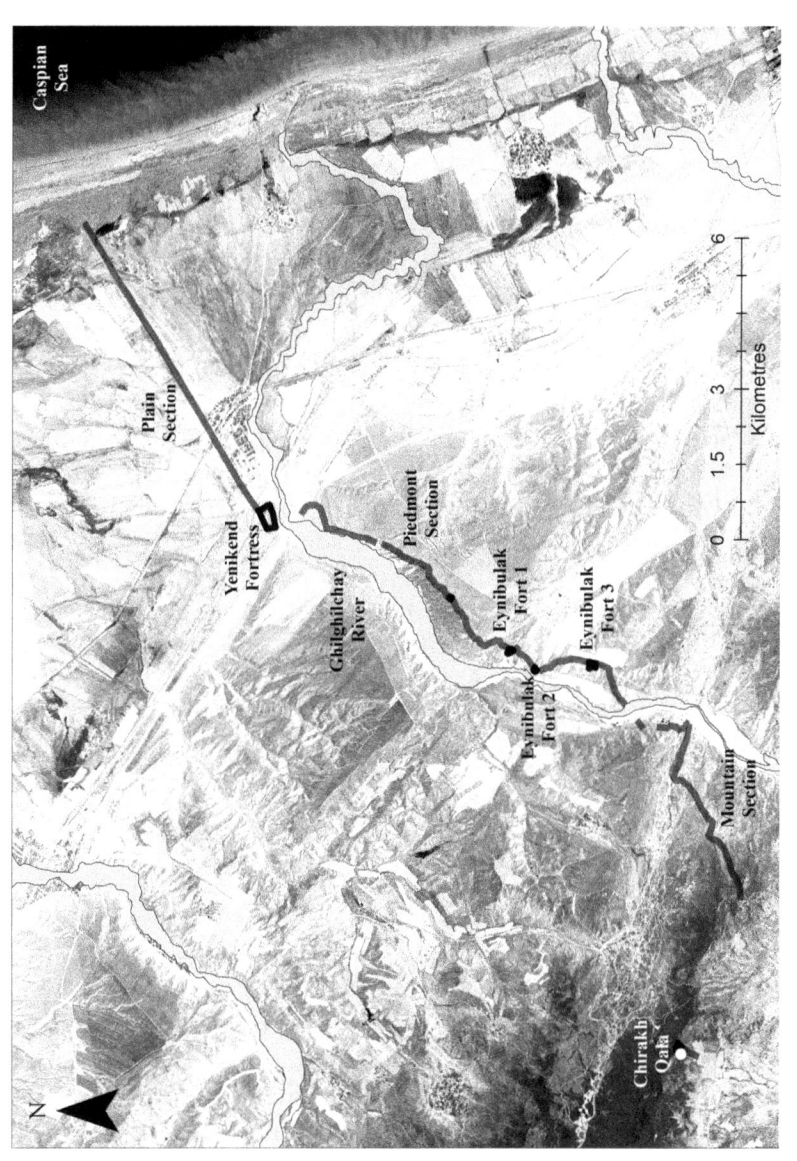

Fig. 5.8 Map of the Ghilghilchay Wall sections and fortifications. Background CORONA Mission 1110–1057DA111 acquired 24 May 1970, reproduced courtesy of the U.S. Geological Survey.

Aliev and his team but, given the similarity in size and morphology visible on the CORONA imagery, is likely to follow similar construction techniques and date to the same period. Unlike the fortifications further north, there are no obvious campaign base sites in the vicinity of the Ghilghilchay Wall. However, the size of the forts incorporated within the wall itself is much larger, with Yenikend Fortress at the edge of the plain covering approximately 9ha, while Chirakh Qala and the three smaller sites in the piedmont section add an extra two or three hectares of potential settled area. It is possible that the wider coastal strip in this area could accommodate a greater number of troops in the immediate vicinity of the wall itself.

Alongside the Caspian coastal strip, the Dariali Pass, also known as the Caspian Gates, in modern Georgia was the main route for hostile forces seeking to cross the Upper Caucasus during the ancient and medieval periods, and is still a major routeway today.[42] This narrow gorge was controlled by several small forts, the most important of which, Dariali Fort, has been securely dated to the Sasanian period.[43] Again, the landscape setting is clearly of the utmost importance here, with the fort situated at one of the narrowest points in the gorge, with areas of open land to the south available for cultivation to feed any potential garrison. There is also evidence for terracing and landscape management dating back to at least the tenth century, and potentially much earlier.[44]

To the south of the Upper Caucasus, the plains of the Kura and Araz River valleys provide ample evidence for significant Sasanian presence and capital investment. To the south of the River Araz, recent survey and excavation work has revealed several Sasanian sites and fortifications, many of which were directly associated with large-scale irrigation canals.[45] The most impressive of these is Ultan Qalası, a 70ha settlement comprising a rectangular fortified complex, a substantial lower town and an associated canal system.[46] Further north on the Mil Steppe in Azerbaijan, a similar configuration is visible at Ören Qala, ancient Beylaqan, which was excavated by a Soviet team in the 1950s and 1960s.[47] Survey transects undertaken as part of the Mil Steppe Survey by the first author and colleagues recovered Sasanian ceramics similar to the Ultan Qalası assemblage across a vast area, suggesting the settlement could have been as large as 300ha. Continuing north, layers described as late antique have been recovered from Nargiz Tepe, a site of unknown, but probably large, size very close to the disputed Nagorno Karabakh region, and at the 25ha site of Qala Tepe, both of which have been excavated by Professor Tevekkul Aliyev. Recent work by a team from

Oxford University at Barda has confirmed the Sasanian occupation suggested by textual sources. There is also some textual evidence that the major Islamic site at Shemkir was occupied during the Sasanian period, as the city was described as ancient at the time of the Arab conquest by Baladhuri in the ninth century, although excavations have so far only recovered remains dating back to the eighth century.[48] Of these, Ören Qala, Qala Tepe and Shemkir all include substantial fortifications. Unfortunately our interpretation of all of the sites in modern Azerbaijan is hampered by significant occupation layers postdating the Sasanian period, especially during the medieval period at Ören Qala, Qala Tepe and Shemkir, but even continuing to the present day at Barda,[49] which means dating individual features such as city walls requires excavation. The alignment of these sites is suspiciously linear, and follows the edge of the plain as it runs along the Karabakh Hills (Fig. 5.9). It is possible that they formed nodes on a road network which may have extended as far as the Dariali Gorge in the north.

In addition to the urban centres, evidence from the Mil Plain Survey suggests a rise in rural settlement during the Sasanian period. It should be stressed that our interpretation of the ceramic chronology in this region is at best provisional and much more excavation is required to firm up the sequence. However, our preliminary findings indicate peaks in site numbers during the Iron Age, Sasanian and medieval periods, interspersed with periods of near abandonment of the region. This mirrors the cycles of settlement seen in the Mughan Steppe, although here a mid-twentieth-century irrigation system and the short duration of the survey meant that recovery of small rural sites was much more limited.[50] The Sasanian sites in the Mil Steppe are small and fairly evenly distributed along the larger streams running down from the Nagorno Karabakh range, with a particular concentration close to the site of Ören Qala. Taken together, the new evidence from the Mil Plain survey and Oxford project suggests we can extend Alizadeh's argument[51] for significant investment in infrastructure during the late Sasanian period along the Araz much further north, where a similar pattern of the foundation of large urban centres and the construction of canals and forts is visible. The settlement evidence from the Mil Plain may also support Alizadeh's proposal for large-scale resettlement of local nomadic groups and population transfer from central parts of the empire to frontier zones.

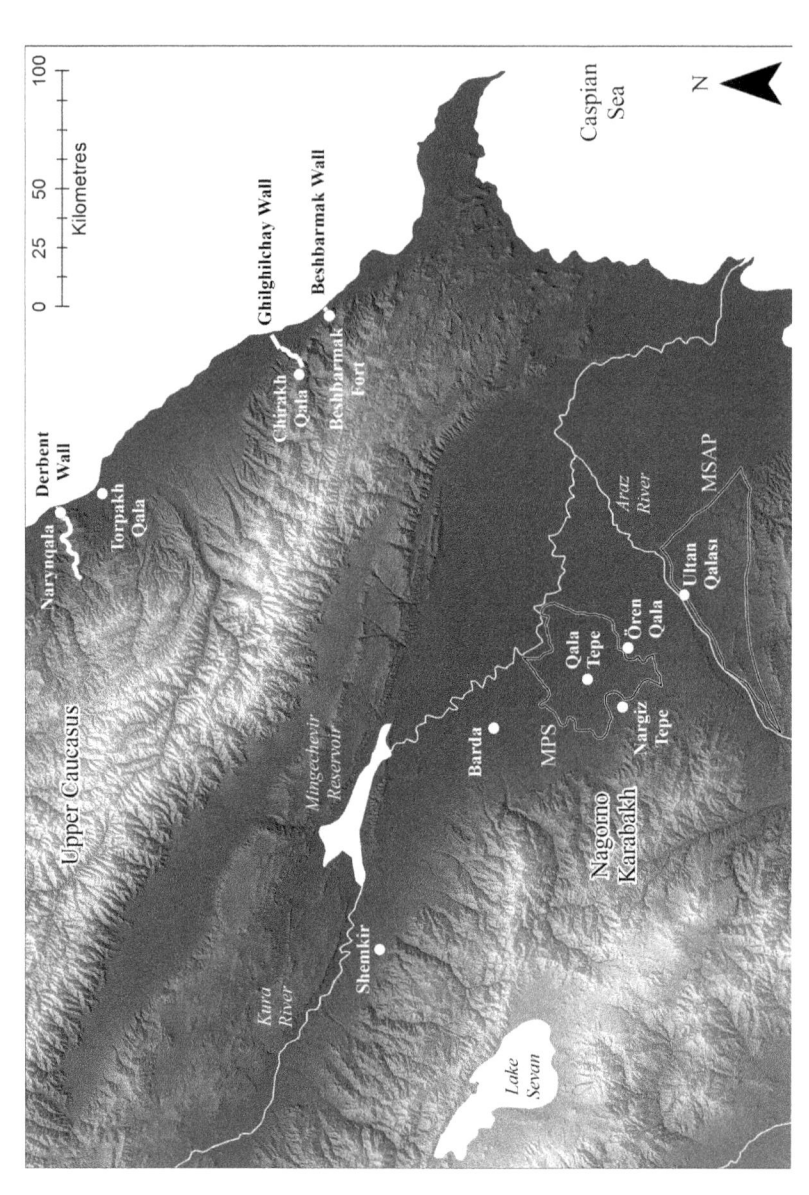

Fig. 5.9 Map of the southern Caucasus region (excluding the Dariali Pass). Background SRTM DEM courtesy of the U.S. Geological Survey.

The Gorgan Plain

The Gorgan Plain has been extensively discussed, both in this volume[52] and elsewhere,[53] and here we will confine ourselves to a brief summary of major relevant aspects. The plain extends from the foothills of the Alborz and Kopet Dag Mountain ranges to the dry steppes of modern Turkmenistan, with rainfall decreasing from south to north from 600mm to 200mm per annum in a little over 60km, and is bisected by the River Gorgan, which flows roughly east to west into the Caspian Sea. During the Sasanian period the Gorgan Wall was constructed, a 195km-long fired brick barrier running across the plain and up into the Kopet Dag, with over thirty forts and a ditch on the northern side.[54] Water was supplied to the ditch via a complex system of feeder canals and aqueducts. Further Sasanian fortification in the region occurred to the south-west, where the Tammisheh Wall runs almost north to south at a narrow point between the Alborz and the Caspian coast. In the plain itself, to the south of the Gorgan Wall, a series of large fortified structures, described as campaign bases by Sauer,[55] was constructed, including the aforementioned Qalʻeh Pol Gonbad, Qalʻeh Kharabeh, Qalʻeh Daland and Qalʻeh Gug A, as well as the 300ha urban centre of Dasht Qalʻeh. All of these constructions can be more or less securely dated to the fifth century during a period of peace with the Eastern Roman Empire.[56]

A striking aspect of the Gorgan Plain settlement pattern is the relative paucity of landscape investment of a non-military nature. Two major irrigation canals discovered during the survey by Wilkinson and colleagues cannot have functioned later than the Parthian period, judging by the associated sites,[57] and those clearly related to Sasanian features all either fed the ditch on the north side of the wall or supplied the campaign bases, such as Qalʻeh Kharabeh. The plain to the south of the wall probably received sufficient levels of rainfall to conduct rain-fed agriculture at this time, especially closer to the Alborz Mountains, but this was also the case in the Mughan and Mil Steppes where, as we have seen, substantial canals were put in place. Part of the reason for this absence may relate to later landscape destruction in the more fertile areas of the plain to the south of the wall, but numerous qanat mounds are visible on the CORONA imagery and we would therefore expect some traces of similar canal features to survive. Ongoing analysis of the surveys carried out in the plain suggests a drop in rural settlement during the Sasanian period,[58] precisely the opposite of what we might expect if increasing agricultural yields through dry farming was a primary aim. We might, therefore, characterise the Gorgan Plain frontier as a relatively militarised zone, especially in comparison with the situation in the southern Caucasus.

DISCUSSION

This brief discussion of key case studies from the northern and western parts of the Sasanian Empire reveals the multiple manifestations of frontiers in this region, as well as the intimate relationship between military installations, urban and rural settlement and local geography. The Sasanians were adept at co-opting aspects of the physical landscape into local and regional defensive strategies, as in the southern Caucasus, but were also capable of recognising the limits of rain-fed agriculture or irrigable land and making strategic decisions accordingly, as in the Gorgan Plain and southern Iraq. Comparing the frontier zones allows us to make some general statements about Sasanian frontier strategies.

Three of the four case studies discussed included linear barriers of one sort or another, and they represent a significant aspect of Sasanian frontier policy, at least from the fifth century onwards. The placement of these barriers seems to be a function of both the local and regional landscape and the type of threat faced. It is tempting to see long walls as a response to a particular kind of enemy, namely semi-nomadic or nomadic groups with a tribal or confederate social organisation. The northern walls on the Gorgan Plain and the coastal strip on the other side of the Caspian conform to this pattern, designed to defend against the Hephthalites and subsequently the Khazar Khaganate respectively, both political organisations comprised of people of the Central Asian Steppe. The Khandaq Shapur can now also be added to this model, as it was probably constructed as a defence against the various Arab tribal groups present in the western desert of Iraq and Jordan. The absence of similar features in north Syria, where the Sasanians faced an enemy of similar strength and military organisation to themselves in the Eastern Roman Empire, lends support to this argument.

Contrary to what one might expect, all of the linear barriers conform to what Breeze has called the frontier in depth,[59] and may be interpreted as creating arenas of combat, enclosed areas 'for trapping, engaging and defeating enemy forces'.[60] This is most clearly visible in the southern Caucasus, where almost 120km separate the

Derbent Wall from the Ghilghilchay Wall, with the Beshbarmak Fort a further 30km south along the Caspian coastal strip. The opposite side of this arena may have been created by the fortified urban centres running along the edge of the Nagorno Karabakh, and the string of fortified sites along the River Araz suggests this may have formed the southern edge.[61] In the Gorgan Plain a similar arena may have been created between the Gorgan and Tammisheh Walls and the Alborz Mountains, but, as Hopper shows in her chapter, Sasanian interest also projected further north. In southern Iraq a series of fortifications extended far beyond the Khandaq Shapur out into the desert, while the dense network of irrigation canals to the east in Mesopotamia proper would have hampered movement significantly and have been argued to act as further defensive features.[62]

Alongside linear barriers, the frontier zones received a significant amount of capital investment through the founding or renewal of urban centres and the construction of large-scale irrigation systems, as well as increases in rural population.[63] However, this investment was not uniform, even in areas with fairly similar environmental conditions. How, then, should we make sense of the variable nature of Sasanian frontier landscapes across the northern and western borderlands? A useful concept here is the network empire, first proposed by Liverani in relation to the Neo-Assyrian Empire[64] and recently expanded upon by Monica Smith.[65] Smith sees the Sasanian Empire itself as a network, with urban centres and forts acting as nodes, and canals and linear barriers as connecting corridors. A notable absence from Smith's model is the rural landscape outside of the irrigated zones, in part a product of the lack of evidence available at the time. For Liverani, rural settlement is a key aspect of the model. He contrasts network empires with territorial ones, arguing that in some cases the development of imperial power should be understood not through the metaphor of an oil stain expanding outwards but through that of 'a network whose mesh thickens',[66] whereby increased control of territory is manifested in colonisation and a move away from urban and military nodes into occupation of the wider landscape. We can transpose Liverani's temporal model to the geographical differences between the case studies discussed above, bringing in landscape investment as a further variable. In the Mil and Mughan Steppes and southern Iraq (as well as the Merv Oasis),[67] canal systems were put in place, cities expanded, and preliminary evidence indicates rural settlement rose, suggesting a high degree of territorial control. This investment occurred behind substantial defensive systems in the Upper Caucasus and Caspian strip and the edge of the Western Desert respectively. By contrast in the Gorgan Plain, almost all of the canal systems appear to have been of a military nature. Although irrigation may not have been required for agriculture in the southern part of the Gorgan Plain, it would certainly have increased both productivity and reliability of yield. The northern part of the plain (immediately south of the wall) receives a similar level of rainfall to the Mil Steppe close to Ören Qala. Rural settlement probably fell, and the extent of urban expansion is as yet unclear: Dasht Qal'eh represents a major city built from scratch, but may not have been the only Sasanian urban foundation, to judge by recent fieldwork.[68] Here the network metaphor is more suitable and the landscape appears to have been far more militarised. In eastern Syria rural settlement also declined slightly and there is no secure evidence for irrigation dating to the Sasanian period.[69] The fact that 60 per cent of the Sasanian settlements in the Brak region were also occupied in the preceding Parthian period suggests that the new empire had limited impact on settlement patterns. In the densely settled landscapes along the Roman frontier, it seems controlling and fortifying large urban sites such as Nisibis was of greater importance to elites than raising tax revenues in the wider landscape. Again, a network model of empire works well here, with urban centres acting as nodal installations 'embedded in a native ... world'.[70]

CONCLUSION

These are exciting times for the archaeology of the Sasanian Empire. Surveys and excavations alongside remote sensing work across the northern and western frontiers are bringing new data to light which have the potential to affect our understanding profoundly. However, our theoretical models for making sense of this wealth of information have not kept pace with our ability to generate it. The sheer size of empires, and the variability in landscape types which commonly results, means that issues of scale are a key hurdle to overcome. Frontiers and frontier installations by their nature operate at a variety of scales, utilising and impacting upon the local environment, but also functioning as part of wider regional and even imperial level systems. As we hope to have shown in this chapter, it is vital to integrate these different scales of analysis in order to understand the multiple manifestations of frontier landscapes visible in the archaeological record.

NOTES

1. See Daryaee 2016 for discussion of the history of Sasanian research.
2. Brandell 2006.
3. Ratzel 1897.
4. Curzon 1907.
5. Breeze 2011.
6. Febvre 1962.
7. Febvre 1962 quoted in Brandell 2006.
8. Turchin 2006.
9. Wilkinson 2003.
10. Hritz 2014; Casana et al. 2013.
11. Alizadeh and Ur 2007; Wilkinson et al. 2013.
12. Lawrence, Bradbury and Dunford 2012.
13. Priestman 2013; Wilkinson et al. 2013.
14. Alizadeh 2011.
15. Ur 2010; see also Wells 2015.
16. Adams 2006.
17. Adams 1965; 1981.
18. See Morley, this volume.
19. Howard-Johnston 2012.
20. Ooghe 2007.
21. Much of this work was undertaken by Jaafar Jotheri as part of his PhD thesis at Durham University. A detailed discussion of the feature and its landscape will be published in a future article.
22. Jotheri et al. 2016.
23. Finster and Schmidt 1976.
24. Finster and Schmidt 2005; Howard-Johnston 2012.
25. Simpson 1996.
26. Simpson 1996: 88.
27. See also Comfort 2008.
28. Morony 1976.
29. Howard-Johnston 2012.
30. Wright et al. 2006–7.
31. Ur 2010.
32. Ur and Wilkinson 2008.
33. See discussion in Hopper, this volume.
34. Gadjiev 2008; 2009.
35. Aliev et al. 2006.
36. Aliev et al. 2006.
37. Howard-Johnston 2012.
38. Sauer et al. 2013: 321–2, 358–60, 372; Sauer et al., this volume.
39. Sauer et al. 2013: 347–9, 365–71.
40. Aliev et al. 2006. A detailed discussion of the results of our remote sensing work, predominantly undertaken by Edward K. East, will be published in a future article.
41. Aliev et al. 2006.
42. Sauer et al. 2015.
43. See Sauer et al., this volume.

44 Lisa Snape-Kennedy pers. comm., January 2016.
45 Alizadeh and Ur 2007; Alizadeh 2014.
46 Alizadeh 2011.
47 Ahmadov 1997.
48 Dostiyev 2012.
49 This situation is rather different from that in the sites in the Mughan Steppe, where no glazed ceramics associated with Islamic periods were recovered on the surface. The contrast between the Mil and Mughan Steppes during the Islamic period is worth exploring but is beyond the scope of this chapter.
50 Alizadeh and Ur 2007.
51 Alizadeh 2014.
52 See Hopper and Sauer et al., this volume.
53 Most recently, and comprehensively, Sauer et al. 2013.
54 Sauer et al. 2013.
55 Sauer et al. 2013: 303–81.
56 Sauer et al. 2013: 593–629. A date in the early sixth century is compatible with the radiocarbon dates as well, but more difficult to reconcile with the sources.
57 Wilkinson et al. 2013.
58 Kristen Hopper pers. comm., February 2016. This will be discussed further in Hopper's forthcoming PhD thesis.
59 Breeze 2011.
60 Howard-Johnston 2012.
61 At the Rome conference, James Howard-Johnston suggested that the River Kura may have formed the southern barrier of this arena. However, no relevant sites are known in this area and extensive analysis of satellite imagery in the region has yielded no likely candidates for Sasanian fortifications, settlements or other features. Still, the Kura has a far more active channel than the Araz, evidenced by the numerous palaeochannels visible on the CORONA imagery, meaning sites situated in close proximity to the floodplain may have been eroded away.
62 Howard-Johnston 2012.
63 Alizadeh 2014.
64 Liverani 1988.
65 Smith 2005; 2007. For a rather different use of this concept see Glatz 2009.
66 Liverani 1988.
67 Simpson 2014.
68 See Sauer et al., this volume.
69 Although see Ur 2010: 123 for information on a canal system in the vicinity of Nisibis itself. Ur provisionally dates this to the Islamic period on the basis of associated sites.
70 Liverani 1988.

BIBLIOGRAPHY

Adams, R. M. (1965), *Land Behind Baghdad: A History of Settlement on the Diyala Plains*, Chicago: University of Chicago Press.
Adams, R. M. (1981), *Heartland of Cities: Surveys of Ancient Settlement and*

Land Use on the Central Floodplain of the Euphrates, Chicago: University of Chicago Press.
Adams, R. M. (2006), 'Intensified Large-Scale Irrigation as an Aspect of Imperial Policy: Strategies Of Statecraft on the Late Sasanian Mesopotamian Plain', in J. Marcus and C. Stanish (eds), *Agricultural Strategies*, Los Angeles: Cotsen Institute of Archaeology, pp. 17–37.
Ahmadov, Q. (1997), *Qadim Beylaqan*, Baku: Azerbaijan Dovlat Nashriyati.
Aliev, A. A., Gadjiev, M. S., Gaither, M. G., Kohl, P. L., Magomedov, R. M. and Aliev, I. N. (2006), 'The Ghilghilchay Defensive Long Wall: New Investigations', *Ancient West & East*, 5, pp. 143–77.
Alizadeh, K. (2011), 'Ultan Qalası: A Fortified Site in the Sasanian Borderlands (Mughan Steppe, Iranian Azerbaijan)', *Iran*, 49, pp. 55–77.
Alizadeh, K. (2014), 'Borderland Projects of the Sasanian Empire: Intersection of Domestic and Foreign Policies', *Journal of Ancient History*, 2.2, pp. 93–115.
Alizadeh, K. and Ur, J. (2007), 'Formation and Destruction of Pastoral and Irrigation Landscapes on the Mughan Steppe, North-Western Iran', *Antiquity*, 81, pp. 148–60.
Brandell, I. (2006), 'Introduction', in I. Brandell (ed.), *State Frontiers: Borders and Boundaries in the Middle East*, New York: I.B. Tauris, pp. 1–32
Breeze, D. (2011), *The Frontiers of Imperial Rome*, Barnsley: Pen and Sword Military.
Casana, J., Cothren, J. and Kalayci, T. (2013), 'Swords into Ploughshares: Archaeological Applications of CORONA Satellite Imagery in the Near East', *Internet Archaeology*, 32.
Comfort, A. (2008), 'Euphratesia, Osrhoene and Mesopotamia from AD 363 to 602', PhD thesis, University of Exeter.
Curzon, Lord. (1907), *Frontiers*, Oxford: Oxford University Press.
Daryaee, T. (2016), 'The Limits of Sasanian History: Between Iranian, Islamic and Late Antique Studies', *Iranian Studies*, 49.2, pp. 193–203.
Dostiyev, T. (2012), 'Medieval Shamkir in Light of Archaeological Excavations', *IRS Heritage*, 4.11, pp. 36–43.
Febvre, L. (1962), *Pour une histoire à part entière*, Paris: SEVPEN.
Finster, B. and Schmidt, J. (1976), *Sasanidische und Frühislamische Ruinen im Iraq*, Baghdader Mitteilungen, 8, Berlin: Mann.
Finster, B. and Schmidt, J. (2005), 'The Origin of "Desert Castles": Qasr Bani Muqatil, Near Karbala, Iraq', *Antiquity*, 79, pp. 339–49.
Gadjiev, M. (2008), 'On the Construction Date of the Derbend Fortification Complex', *Iran and the Caucasus*, 12.2, pp. 1–15.
Gadjiev, M. (2009), 'On the Interpretation of Derbent's Mason Marks', in J. Evans Pim, S. A. Yatsenko and O. Perrin (eds), *Traditional Marking Systems: A Preliminary Survey*, Dover: Dunkling Books, pp. 147–78.
Glatz, C. (2009), 'Empire as Network: Spheres of Material Interaction in Late Bronze Age Anatolia', *Journal of Anthropological Archaeology*, 28.2, pp. 127–41
Howard-Johnston, J. (2012), 'The Late Sasanian Army', in T. Bernheimer and A. Silverstein (eds), *Late Antiquity: Eastern Perspectives*, Oxford: Oxbow Books, pp. 87–127.
Hritz, C. (2014), 'Contributions of GIS and Satellite-Based Remote Sensing

to Landscape Archaeology in the Middle East', *Journal of Archaeological Research*, 22, pp. 229–76.

Jotheri, J., Allen, M. B. and Wilkinson, T. J. (2016), 'Holocene Avulsions of the Euphrates River in the Najaf Area of Western Mesopotamia: Impacts on Human Settlement Patterns', *Geoarchaeology*, 31, pp. 175–93.

Lawrence, D., Bradbury, J. and Dunford, R. (2012), 'Chronology, Uncertainty and GIS: A Methodology for Characterising and Understanding Landscapes of the Ancient Near East', in W. Bebermeier, R. Hebenstreit, E. Kaiser and J. Krause (eds), *Landscape Archaeology: Proceedings of the International Conference held in Berlin, 6th–8th June 2012*, Berlin: Excellence Cluster Topoi, pp. 353–9.

Liverani, M. (1988), 'The Growth of the Assyrian Empire in the Habur/Middle Euphrates Area: A New Paradigm', *State Archives of Assyria Bulletin*, II.2, pp. 81–98.

Morony, M. G. (1976), 'The Effects of the Muslim Conquest on the Persian Population of Iraq', *Iran*, 14, pp. 41–59.

Oates, D. and Oates, J. (1959), 'Ain Sinu: A Roman Frontier Post in Northern Iraq', *Iraq*, 21, pp. 207–42.

Ooghe, B. (2007), 'Off the Beaten Track: Travellers, Maps, and the Landscapes of Ottoman Mesopotamia', PhD thesis, Ghent University.

Priestman, S. (2013), 'Sasanian Ceramics from the Gorgan Wall and Other Sites on the Gorgan Plain', in Sauer et al. 2013, pp. 447–534.

Ratzel, R. (1897), *Politische Geographie: Oder, Die Geographie der Staaten, des Verkehres und des Krieges*, Berlin: Oldenbourg

Sauer, E. W., Omrani Rekavandi, H., Wilkinson, T. J., Nokandeh, J. et al. (2013), *Persia's Imperial Power in Late Antiquity: The Great Wall of Gorgān and the Frontier Landscapes of Sasanian Iran*, British Institute of Persian Studies Archaeological Monograph Series, II, Oxford: Oxbow Books.

Sauer, E. W., Pitskhelauri, K., Hopper, K., Tiliakou, A., Pickard, C., Lawrence, D., Diana, A., Kranioti, E. and Shupe, C. (2015), 'Northern Outpost of the Caliphate: Maintaining Military Forces in a Hostile Environment (the Dariali Gorge in the Central Caucasus in Georgia)', *Antiquity*, 89, pp. 885–904.

Simpson, St J. (1996), 'From Tekrit to the Jaghjagh: Sasanian sites, Settlement Patterns and Material Culture in Northern Mesopotamia', in K. Bartl and S. R. Hauser (eds), *Continuity and Change in Northern Mesopotamia from the Hellenistic to the Early Islamic Period*, Berlin: Reimer, pp. 87–126.

Simpson, St J. (2014), 'Merv, an Archaeological Case-Study from the Northeastern Frontier of the Sasanian Empire', *Journal of Ancient History*, 2.2, pp. 1–28.

Smith, M. L. (2005), 'Networks, Territories, and the Cartography of Ancient States', *Annals of the Association of American Geographers*, 95.4, pp. 832–49.

Smith, M. L. (2007), 'Territories, Corridors, and Networks: A Biological Model for the Premodern State', *Complexity*, 12.4, pp. 28–35.

Turchin, P. (2006), *War and Peace and War: The Life Cycles of Imperial Nations*, New York: Pi Press.

Ur, J. (2010), *Urbanism and Cultural Landscapes in Northeastern Syria: The Tell Hamoukar Survey, 1999–2001*, Oriental Institute Publications, 137, Chicago: Oriental Institute of the University of Chicago.

Ur, J. and Wilkinson, T. J. (2008), 'Settlement and Economic Landscapes of

Tell Beydar and its Hinterland', in M. Lebeau and A. Suleiman (eds), *Beydar Studies*, Turnhout: Brepols, pp. 305–27.
Wells, R. (2015), 'Settlement in the Diyala and Southern Mesopotamis: A Reassessment of Robert McCormick Adams' Sasanian and Early Islamic Ceramic "Type-Fossils"', MA dissertation, Durham University.
Wilkinson, T. J. (2003), *Archaeological Landscapes of the Near East*, Tucson: University of Arizona Press.
Wilkinson, T. J., Omrani Rekavandi, H., Hopper, K., Priestman, S., Roustaei, K. and Galiatsatos, N. (2013), 'The Landscapes of the Gorgān Wall', in Sauer et al. 2013, pp. 24–132.
Wright, H. T., Rupley, E. S. A., Ur, J., Oates, J. and Ganem, E. (2006–7), 'Preliminary Report on the 2002 and 2003 Seasons of the Tell Brak Sustaining Area Survey', *Les Annales Archéologiques Arabes Syriennes*, 49–50, pp. 7–21.

6 Connectivity on a Sasanian frontier: Route Systems in the Gorgan Plain of North-East Iran

Kristen Hopper

Using examples from several different regions of the Sasanian Empire, this chapter will look at the archaeological evidence for connectivity in frontier zones. Though a number of geographically diverse cases will be considered, I will focus on the evidence for local, regional and interregional networks in the Gorgan Plain of north-east Iran. We currently know very little about Sasanian-period routes through this landscape. Itineraries exist from antique- through Islamic-period textual sources, but the routes that they describe are often difficult to identify in the archaeological record. European travellers of the nineteenth century provide more detailed accounts, but the routes they describe reflect the political and economic landscape of a much later period. However, this information, combined with archaeological evidence for both earlier- and later-period routes, can be compared to archaeological settlement data for the Sasanian period to suggest potential pathways of movement. This approach will highlight how cultural, political and economic networks in this region (including both routes and boundaries) have changed through time.

FRONTIERS AND CONNECTIVITY

Frontiers are often drawn as simplistic linear borders, which fail to represent their dynamic nature. In reality they are comprised of multiple, and often overlapping, military, cultural or economic boundaries that can range along a continuum between physical barriers and conceptual boundaries; this makes them important zones of cultural contact where identities and political and social affiliations are formed and reformed at different scales and through time.[1]

Recent work on the northern and western frontiers of the Sasanian Empire has deepened our understanding of military boundaries in these borderlands, where the Sasanian Empire appears to have excelled at utilising and augmenting natural features, or constructing elaborate defensive systems to limit or constrain movement.[2] However, these military frontiers often represent only one element within a complex frontier zone. In order to develop a more nuanced understanding of an empire's interactions with communities within and beyond its frontiers, we also need to explore evidence (or lack therefore) for the cultural and economic boundaries that existed alongside these military barriers, as well as evidence for the changing nature of these frontiers through time.

Empires, it can be argued, are perhaps best portrayed as a series of networks operating at different scales; these networks are made up of nodes of investment connected by routes for communication and transport.[3] Frontiers are one of these nodes, as well as, in some cases, connectors themselves.[4] As well as existing at different scales, these networks also change through time as physical and ideological frontiers, levels of imperial control and many other factors change.[5] Therefore one way in which to explore the dynamic and changing nature of frontiers is through an investigation of the archaeological evidence for diachronic networks within these landscapes at different scales. This chapter will discuss the types of archaeological evidence that we find for connectivity on several geographically dispersed frontiers of the Sasanian Empire before exploring, in detail, the archaeological evidence for local and regional pathways of movement and interregional connectivity in the Gorgan Plain (see Figs 6.1 and 6.2). Starting with the period contemporary with the use of the Gorgan Wall, I will also draw on evidence for earlier and later period networks to develop a broad understanding of how connectivity, and by extension cultural, political and economic boundaries, changed through time.

ARCHAEOLOGICAL EVIDENCE FOR ROUTE SYSTEMS IN FRONTIER ZONES

The most obvious evidence for ancient route systems is the physical manifestation of the routes themselves. In some cases, the restrictions of topography allow us to identify major routes through the landscape more easily. For example, the Dariali Gorge, straddling the border between modern Georgia and Russia, has been a key route through the Caucasus Mountains since antiquity; historical sources

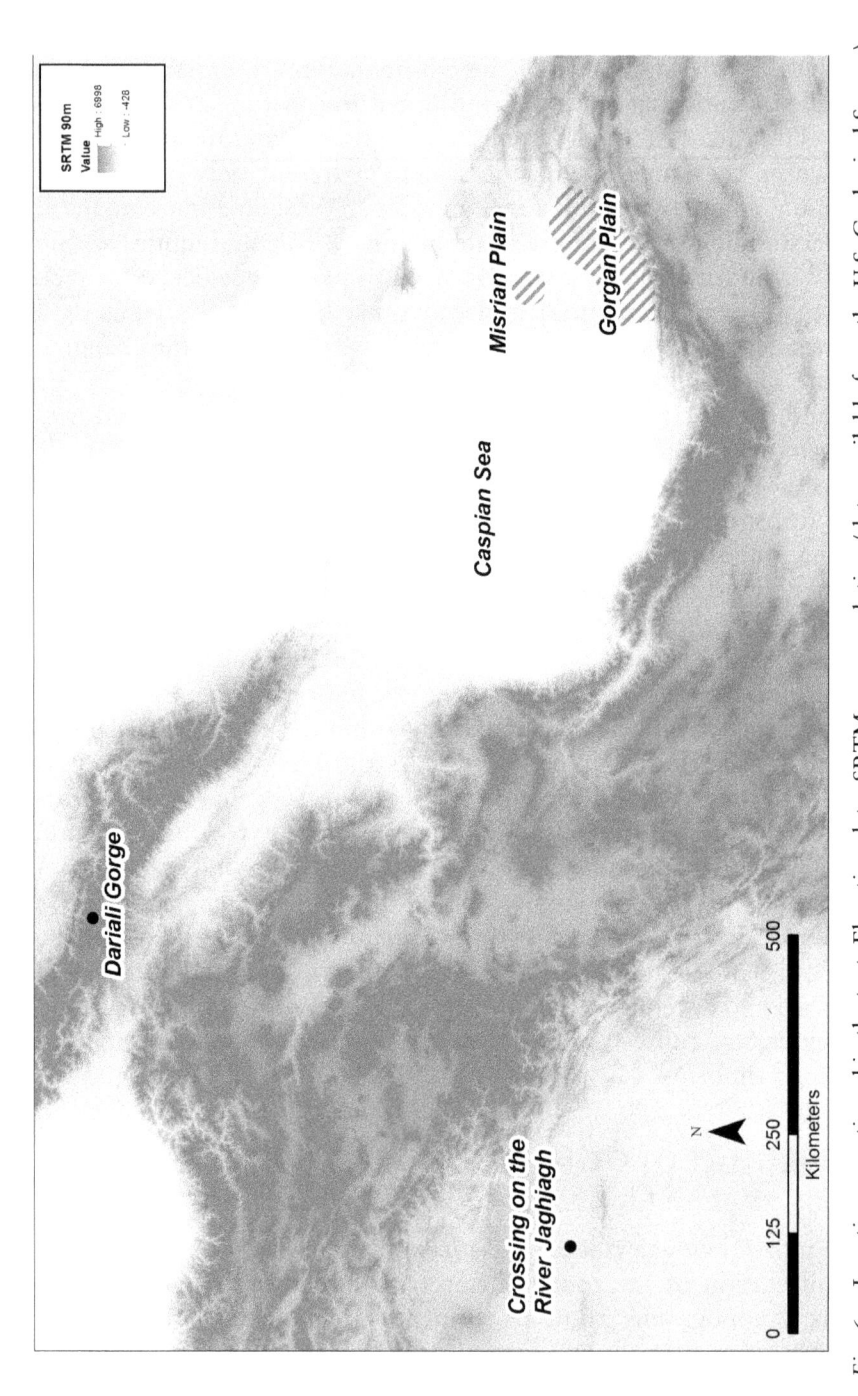

Fig. 6.1 Locations mentioned in the text. Elevation data: SRTM 90m resolution (data available from the U.S. Geological Survey).

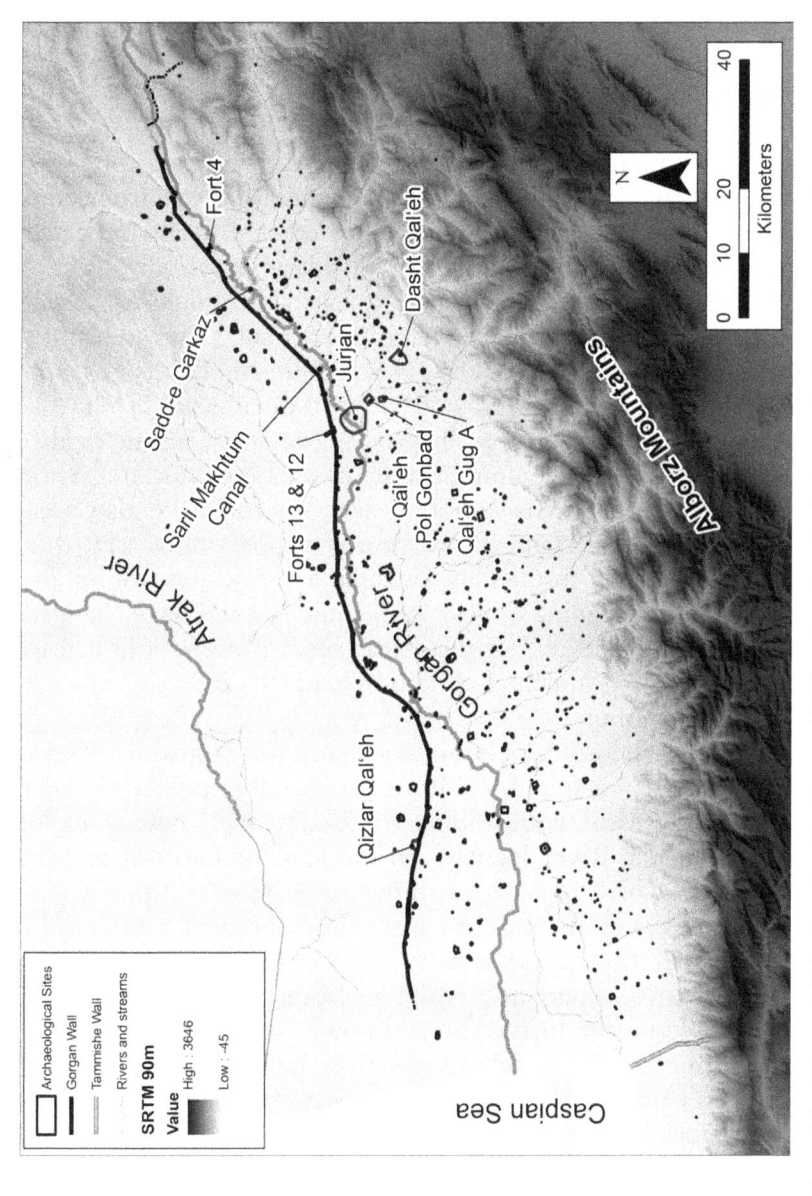

Fig. 6.2 Map of the Gorgan Plain showing the Gorgan Wall and archaeological sites of all periods mapped on CORONA imagery. Sites and features mentioned in the text are marked. Elevation data: SRTM 90m resolution (data available from the U.S. Geological Survey).

and current archaeological investigations indicate that control of this pass, via fortifications such as Dariali Fort, appears to have been important to local kingdoms and foreign powers, including the Sasanian Empire from the third century AD.[6] While many local routes exist within the landscape, regional routes that would ensure the expedient movement of people and goods are constrained by topography.

Direct evidence for local routes can be found in the form of hollow ways. Hollow ways are depressed linear features that represent ancient roads, tracks or droveways often radiating out from, and sometimes connecting, archaeological sites created by the repeated movement of people and animals over considerable periods of time.[7] In the Near East, these features are most clearly identifiable on aerial photographs and satellite imagery, and in particular on the historical images taken from the CORONA satellite in the 1960s and 1970s.[8] While many hollow ways have been documented in northern Mesopotamia, and relate to Bronze Age activity,[9] instances also exist in Khuzestan, where some examples can be associated with late Sasanian sites.[10] Extensive hollow way systems have also been mapped in the Gorgan Plain, and while many appear to be related to late Iron Age through to possibly Parthian activity, they are important for our understanding of how local route systems have changed through time. The survival of these features, however, is linked to factors such as environmental conditions and the intensity of later settlement and land use.[11]

On frontiers where linear boundaries such as long-walls, rivers, canals or ditches are found, evidence for crossing points of these features can represent nodes along route systems.[12] For example, a ford crossing the River Jaghjagh in the Khabur Basin of eastern Syria, a region which formed a frontier zone between the Roman/Byzantine and Sasanian Empires, may represent such a node in a postulated late antique route system.[13] Interestingly, at certain times the river may have demarcated a military frontier.[14] Of further interest are two rectilinear fortifications, known as the Castellum and Saibakh, sitting on either side of the river near the ford. Limited ceramic finds from the Castellum (on the west bank)[15] and architectural similarities between Saibakh (on the east bank) and forts on the Gorgan Wall may suggest that the former was Roman and the latter Sasanian.[16] However, in this dynamic and changing frontier zone these affiliations will have changed through time, as suggested, for example, by the density of (probably) late Sasanian occupation on both sides of the river.[17] The maintenance of the ford through time (possibly from the fourth millennium BC onwards), however, suggests that cultural and economic links are likely to have transcended actual or perceived military or political boundaries.

THE GORGAN WALL AND THE SASANIAN LANDSCAPE

The Gorgan Plain is defined by the arc of the Alborz Mountains in the south and east, the lower River Atrak in the north and the Caspian Sea in the west. To the south, the Alborz Mountains rise dramatically from the nearly flat plain to over 3000m in height. The lush vegetation of the Alborz Mountains and the piedmont zone give way to a vast plain, with increasing aridity as one moves north. The long-term settlement history of the region seems to reflect maximum settlement density and investment in agriculture in areas immediately north of the Alborz foothills, diminishing gradually in intensity as one moves towards the River Gorgan, which dissects the plain from east to west.[18] Historical and ethnographic accounts from the Islamic period to the early twentieth century indicate a corresponding increase in mobile pastoralism as an important part of subsistence strategies moving from south to north towards and beyond the River Gorgan.[19] However, land-use practices appear to have been in flux over the long term, resulting in periods of significant investment in agriculture in the steppe north of the River Gorgan (see Fig. 6.2).[20]

Within this complex landscape palimpsest we can identify several 'signature landscapes', that is, dominant settlement and land-use patterns associated with the economic, political and social situation of a particular period and reflecting adaptations to a specific environmental zone.[21] In the southern part of the Gorgan Plain (i.e. roughly from the region of the River Gorgan to the Alborz foothills) the most robust archaeological landscape signature is that of the mid- to late Sasanian period (c. later fifth to seventh centuries), characterised by defensive features such as the Gorgan Wall, numerous rectilinear fortified sites, and large-scale water management features such as canals.[22] It is likely that accompanying the landscape transformations detailed above, there may have been a similar level of investment in a network for the transport of people and goods within and beyond the empire. While the landscape signature contemporary to the Gorgan Wall may only represent a relatively short period within the life of the empire, because of the robust nature of the features involved in that landscape signature it is likely that evidence for imperial route systems would be more obvious.

Routes within and beyond the Gorgan Plain are mentioned in texts from the antique through to the Islamic periods.[23] There is, however, often very little physical evidence for the routes themselves. Maps and descriptions of the region by nineteenth-century European travellers are more specific, but of course reflect an anachronistic political and cultural landscape.[24] However, using this information in combination with archaeological evidence gathered from field survey and the remote sensing of satellite imagery can help us to reconstruct potential route systems of the Sasanian era.

MOVING ACROSS THE FRONTIER

While not impassable, the Alborz Mountains form a significant barrier to movement; traffic between the Gorgan Plain and the Iranian Plateau, both today and in the past, is restricted through a few defiles.[25] North of the Alborz Mountains, however, the wide, flat Gorgan Plain presents few natural limitations to movement. Prior to the building of the Gorgan Wall, the main obstacle would have been the River Gorgan, which may have been difficult to cross at certain times of year. Le Strange,[26] citing the Islamic geographer Mustawfi (fourteenth century AD), states that 'throughout its course the stream was deep, almost unfordable, so that travellers were often drowned in crossing it; and in flood-time its waters were carried off by channels and used up in irrigation, though much always ran to waste', indicating the abundance of water that flowed in the winter and spring months. In summer the river may have been far lower, making crossing much easier.[27] Howard-Johnston has suggested, that the River Gorgan did not have the same capacity to act as a defensive barrier as rivers such as the Euphrates or Tigris, and this may be true for part of the year.[28] Travel accounts from the nineteenth century AD mention fords and small boats being utilised for the crossing of people and animals,[29] and it is likely that fords similar to the one near the Castellum and Saibakh in the Khabur could be found at numerous points along the river. The identification of premodern bridges or fords is hampered by the highly active nature of the river. Besides the seasonal flooding, erosion of the loess soils along the river banks is common while the many palaeochannels and relict meanders visible on the CORONA imagery and in the field, particularly in the western plain, provide evidence for channel changes at multiple scales.[30] However, bridges spanning the river are known in Jurjan from the Islamic period.[31]

The Gorgan Wall, however, provided a much more reliable barrier to traffic. It would also have channelled movement across the frontier through controllable crossings. Following the course of the river, the wall, built several kilometres to the north, secured the river's resources both for supplying the water-filled ditch on the north side and potentially for irrigating the lands to the south. After the construction of the wall, routes crossing the frontier would have had to negotiate not only crossing the river but also crossing the wall and ditch, probably through well-monitored gates. The Gates of Sul, mentioned by Tabari in the ninth century but in reference to supposed events in the later fifth century, may possibly refer to a gate on the Gorgan Plain. Bosworth suggests the gate controlled traffic coming from the north and travelling through Dehistan (south-west Turkmenistan), through Gorgan and eventually onto the Iranian Plateau.[32] More specifically, it is possible that these gates may refer to a gate in the Gorgan Wall as recently proposed.[33]

The clearest feature that survives on the CORONA imagery is the wall ditch, not the wall itself, and therefore locating gaps or gates in the wall is difficult. However, it is possible that features such as canals or forts that are numerous along the wall's length may also have served as gates or crossing points. At least five canals supplying the Gorgan Wall ditch have been clearly identified on CORONA satellite imagery and in field survey.[34] Besides canals being conduits of movement in their own right, routes along them are also well known in the ancient and modern Middle East.[35] All of the known examples of wall-ditch feeder canals are located in the eastern end of the plain. Gaps in the wall to accommodate these canals, such as where the Sarli Makhtum canal flows into the wall ditch, could have provided access through the wall if a bridge over the ditch were constructed.[36] The Chai Qushan-e Kuchek canal also connects to the wall ditch, and furthermore is fed by an elaborate system involving the transport of water along the Kal-e Garkaz canal and along an earthen aqueduct called the Sadd-e Garkaz, which then may have spanned the River Gorgan via a bridge.[37] Whether or not crossing both the river and wall was achievable along this alignment is open to speculation. However, canals that meet the wall ditch near forts (such as at the Band-e Vali Canal, or the possible canal feature west of Fort 4)[38] might be far more plausible candidates as crossings when the wall was active, for the purposes of security and taxation.

The other likely locations of crossing points of the wall are the forts which line it. The presence of troops at these locations would have provided the opportunity to inspect goods, collect duties and monitor movement. Gates were detected on the wall side of Fort 4 through geophysical survey; this gate was linked by a central road to a gate on the opposite side of the fort.[39] It is debatable, however, whether public access would have been permitted through the fort, and whether anyone other than the soldiers occupying the structure would have passed through. Crossing points in the wall could also have been located near forts. Two possibilities stand out for the location of such features. One is at the site of Qizlar Qal'eh, a prominent qal'eh (here a morphological category indicating an archaeological mound with a dish-shaped interior indicating fortification) that exists as part of a much larger settlement complex known as Qarniareq Qal'eh. Surface survey and associated archaeological features indicate that this complex set of mounds may originally have been occupied in the Iron Age and later incorporated into the defences associated with the Gorgan Wall during the Sasanian period.[40]

However, the most obvious location for a possible gate is the closely spaced Forts 12 and 13 (see Fig. 6.3). With only c. 200m separating them, they create an ideal corridor for monitoring traffic crossing the wall. Fort 12 appears to contain barrack blocks like many of the forts along the wall.[41] Fort 13, however, differs in its internal morphology, and topographical features are present including, in the north-west corner, a much older tappeh. Low archaeological mounds north and immediately south of Fort 13 may also be part of an earlier site complex. Architectural differences noted in excavations of Fort 13 by M. Y. Kiani (i.e. brick alignment and wall thickness) may suggest a different or supplementary purpose for this structure.[42] However, as many of the forts have not been excavated we lack a sufficient comparative sample to draw too many conclusions from these facts alone. In the next section, the discussion will draw on the available regional and interregional settlement data, including an analysis of historical satellite imagery, to explore whether the last of these proposed crossing points represents a node within a larger interregional network.

AN INTERREGIONAL ROUTE IN THE EASTERN GORGAN PLAIN: REMOTE SENSING OF HOLLOW WAYS

Maps based on aerial photographs and historical CORONA satellite imagery were examined both north and south of Forts 12 and 13 for evidence of ancient tracks, or hollow ways, leading

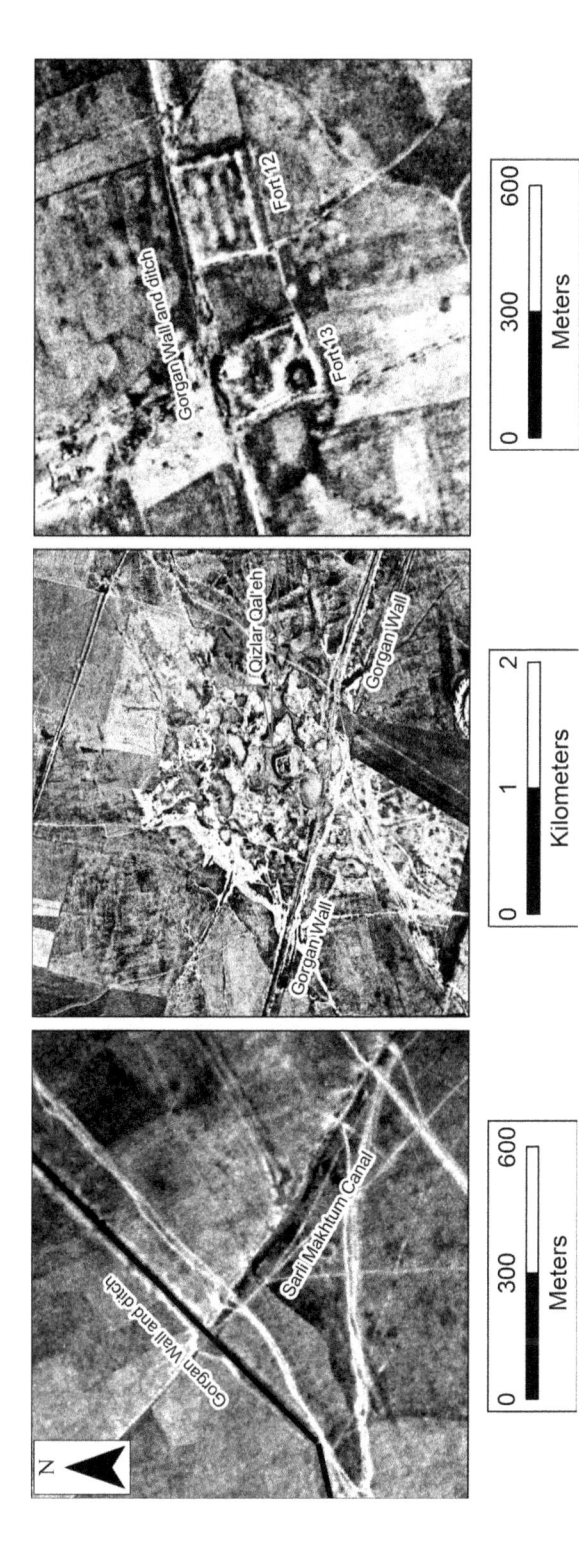

Fig. 6.3 Possible crossing points of the Gorgan Wall. The Sarli Makhtum canal flowing through a gap in the wall into the ditch on its northern side (left); Qizlar Qal'eh, an earlier site incorporated into the Gorgan Wall (centre); and Forts 12 and 13 on the Gorgan Wall (right) on the CORONA imagery. CORONA images from 6 October 1969 (data available from the U.S. Geological Survey).

towards or beyond these forts (see Fig. 6.4). The maps of M. Y. Kiani, themselves based on aerial photographs, seemed to indicate several routes or tracks in this vicinity.[43] Many of these correlated to modern roads and tracks, also visible on the CORONA images, that led towards or away from the modern city of Gonbad-e Kavus. Besides being oriented on the modern city, these features also appear to dictate modern field boundaries. These are in contrast, both in signature and alignment, to a series of dark hollow-way-like features c. 10–20m wide. Different alignments and visible stratigraphic relationships between some of the hollow ways suggest that not all of these features were in use at one time. Several groupings can be commented on.

1. A curving, dark, linear depression is obvious leading from/to the west side of Fort 13 and might be related to occupation at the fort or the earlier site on this location. No relationship between this and other hollow ways can be established.
2. Two faint hollow ways run south-west to north-east roughly towards the possible gate but fade out between 800m tand 1km before reaching them. These are cut by feature (3).
3. This group appears to branch out from a point along the possible outer wall of the ruins of the town of Jurjan, an important early Islamic period centre; this site is also a possible candidate for the Sasanian capital of the same name, though any trace of an earlier city at this site has yet to be found.[44] Two of these tracks lead towards Fort 13. All appear to fade out between c. 1km and 600m before the wall. It can be assumed that these features are probably contemporary with occupation at Jurjan.
4. Another two hollow ways run from Jurjan towards the wall west of the forts. Before meeting the wall one of these hollow ways is joined by two other tracks coming from an unknown point to the south, and together they appear to traverse the wall ditch. As there would be little reason for these tracks to converge if the wall or ditch, even in a ruined state, did not pose some sort of obstacle, these tracks must be contemporary with or later than the wall. No clear stratigraphic relationship can be established between this hollow way and the wall ditch on the CORONA image, although the hollow way does appear to continue beyond the wall to the north. However, the location where the hollow way meets the wall seems an unlikely candidate for a crossing point while the wall was in use because of the lack of other features in the area.

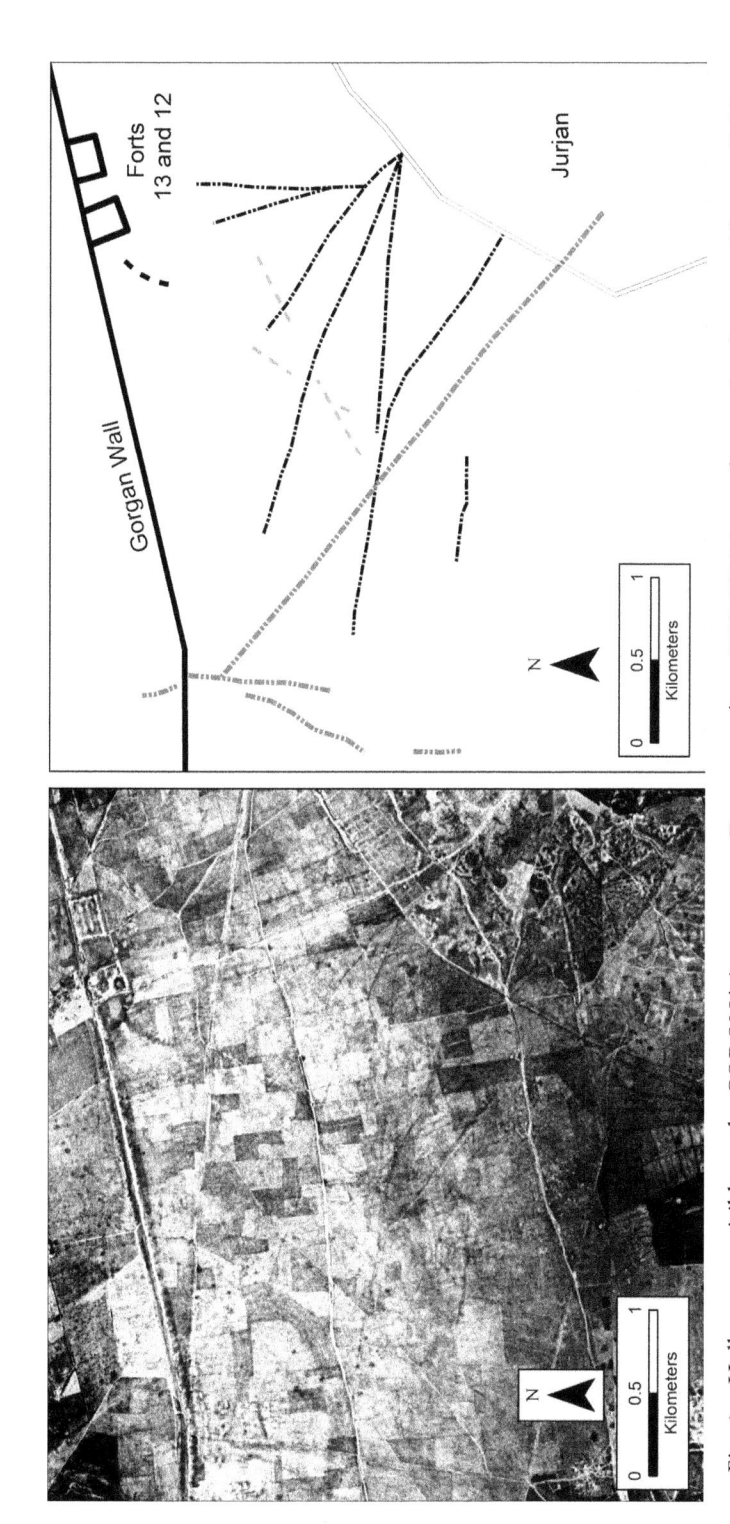

Fig. 6.4 Hollow ways visible on the CORONA imagery near Forts 12 and 13. CORONA image from 6 October 1969 (data available from the U.S. Geological Survey).

While this appears to have been a high traffic area in the past, it is difficult to say whether any of this activity was associated with the active period of the wall.

SETTLEMENT DATA

While routes immediately south of these proposed gates cannot be dated more precisely through the evidence available from remote sensing, widening our view to take into consideration the broader mid- to late Sasanian settlement pattern in the region is instructive. Archaeological survey and excavation have revealed several roughly contemporary sites south and south-east of Forts 12 and 13 and Jurjan. These include two large square fortifications (Qal'eh Gug A and Qal'eh Pol Gonbad, the former of which has been confidently dated by ceramic assessment to the mid-Sasanian period).[45] Another c. 10km further to the south-east sits the large urban settlement of Dasht Qal'eh. This c. 338ha site is enclosed within ramparts and has a prominent mound in its south-east corner. Ceramics from the site indicate prehistoric, Sasanian and early Islamic occupation.[46] Radiocarbon dates from contexts interpreted as signalling the construction of the ditch and ramparts suggest a date similar to the construction of the Gorgan Wall for the site in its urban form.[47] These sites form an intriguing alignment of possible gates, fortifications and an urban centre (see Fig. 6.5).

Furthermore, continuing to follow the trajectory of this alignment to the south leads to the entrance of one of the most easily traversed passages across the Alborz Mountains that connects the Gorgan Plain to the Great Khorasan Road that ran from Mesopotamia to Central Asia.[48] Abbasi also notes the presence of a Sasanian-period site several kilometres into the pass (from the direction of the plain).[49] No evidence is currently available on the ceramics from the site, but it presents an intriguing possibility for another node in this route system.

Dasht Qal'eh (possibly a more convincing candidate for Sasanian Jurjan, but certainly another significant Sasanian city) would therefore have sat in a strategic position for communicating with the plateau to the south and the steppes to the north. People and goods coming from the north could be monitored and taxed, and one or both of the large fortifications to the south could have provided further security. Equally, if we assume that Qal'eh Gug A and Qal'eh Pol-Gonbad were bases for campaigns against the Hephthalites,[50]

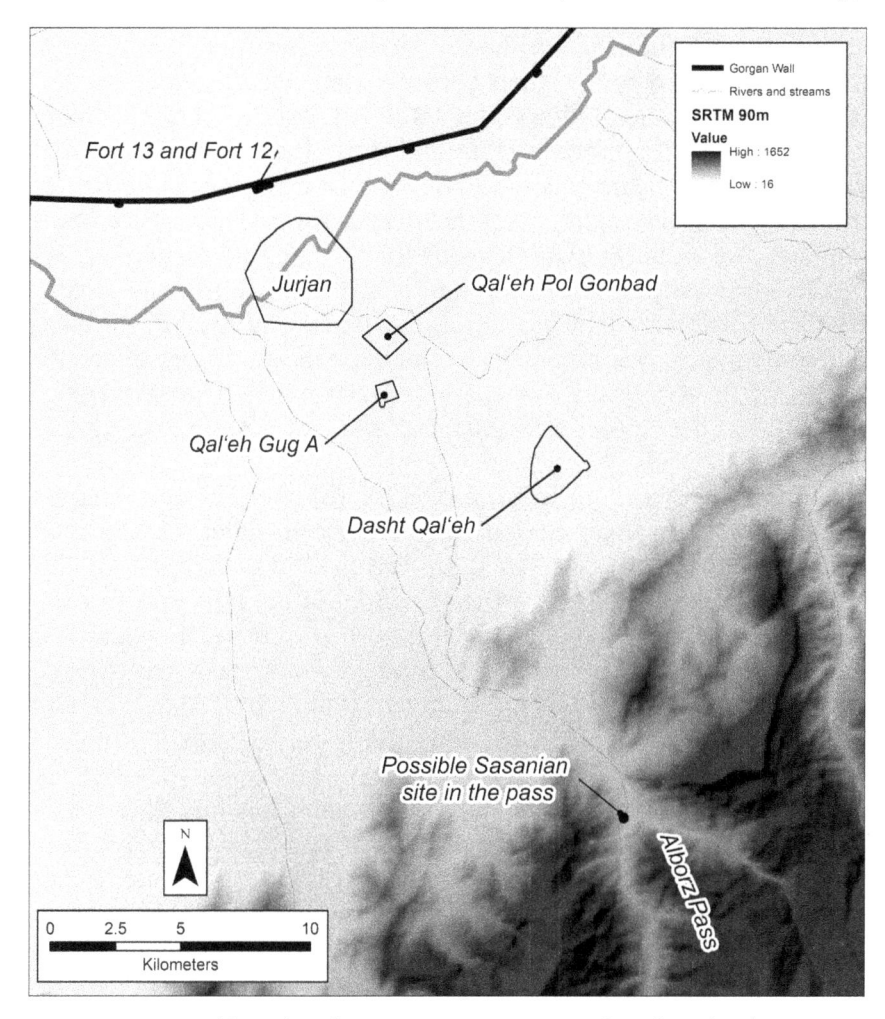

Fig. 6.5 A possible mid- to late Sasanian route system based on the alignment of forts, campaign bases, urban sites (Sauer et al. 2013; Wilkinson et al. 2013: 102–45) and a mountain pass. Note the location of a possible Sasanian site in the pass (Abbasi 2011: 217–18). Elevation data: SRTM 90m resolution (data available from the U.S. Geological Survey).

then their location on a main route north would make strategic sense. Taken together, the archaeological data draw a convincing picture of an interregional route system at an imperial scale connecting the Iranian Plateau, the Gorgan Plain and perhaps the regions north of it.

But what evidence do we have for a continuation of this level of investment in a route system to the north through Dehistan and on to Khwarezm? Textual sources suggest that Sasanian, or more aptly imperial, influence in these regions (either direct or indirect) may have waxed and waned through time on the basis of economic benefits and military threats.[51] Analysis of ceramics from excavations on the Gorgan Plain and those from survey and excavations of sites in the Misrian Plain (Dehistan), c. 100km north of the Gorgan Wall, suggests similarities in forms between the two regions, and possibly with Khwarezm throughout various points in the Sasanian period.[52] The complete publication of the ceramics from Sasanian-period sites in the Misrian Plain is still awaited, but some material comparable to the mid- to late Sasanian assemblages of the Gorgan Plain contemporary with or subsequent to the wall has been noted from the sites of Ortadepeslik and Khanly Depe.[53]

Similarities in the material culture of the Gorgan and Misrian Plains in the Sasanian period may suggest a significant level of cultural connectivity between these regions.[54] The strength of this connectivity, however, is likely to be found in the longevity of local traditions (dating back to the Iron Age)[55] as opposed to consistent imperial involvement. However, at times, it would have made strategic sense for the Sasanian Empire to invest directly in Dehistan, and perhaps by extension stations along the route towards it from the south.[56]

The level of investment in a route system beyond the wall in the Sasanian period is not currently known. Settlement data from archaeological survey indicate that there was little settlement immediately north of the wall that can be obviously attributed to the mid- to late Sasanian period.[57] No clear evidence for a road or hollow way leading from our proposed gate can be seen on the CORONA imagery. However, beyond the core settled area, tracks would not be confined to set paths through cultivated fields and the flat topography would not have limited movement to particular corridors. Further remote sensing of the satellite imagery farther north may reveal features associated with routes through this region such as stations, cisterns and wells, as documented in early travellers' accounts.[58] Cursory examination of the limited survey data and CORONA imagery already suggests intriguing possibilities for nodes in this network south of the River Atrak.[59] However, only future fieldwork can help us to date these features with accuracy.

LOCAL PATHWAYS OF MOVEMENT AND REGIONAL CONNECTIVITY: A DIACHRONIC VIEW

Thus far, this chapter has been focused on building a picture of an interregional network contemporary with the mid- to late Sasanian period. The available evidence can also be used to elaborate on local pathways of movement and suggest ways in which networks may have changed though time.

Evidence for local networks prior to the construction of the Gorgan Wall can be found in abundance to the north of the River Gorgan in the eastern end of the plain. Here, the lack of intensive later land use (until the twentieth century) has resulted in well-preserved hollow way systems radiating out from almost all of the archaeological sites that have been identified through field survey or remote sensing (see Fig. 6.6 for an example). Ceramic evidence suggests that many of these sites were occupied primarily between the later Iron Age and Parthian periods.[60] In several instances hollow ways appear to connect these sites, further strengthening the argument for contemporaneity at some point during their occupation.[61] These hollow ways represent local networks through which people and animals could travel to fields, water sources (such as the River Gorgan) or perhaps pastures beyond the limits of cultivation around a site. Equally, some can be seen to represent a regional network facilitating movement between sites and across the plain.

These networks appear to have been no longer in use by the time the Gorgan Wall was built. Hollow ways radiating out from the site of GWS-25 in the eastern steppe north of the River Gorgan, for example, are clearly cut by the Gorgan Wall ditch (see Fig. 6.6). GWS-25, and its neighbouring sites such as GWS-26 and GWS-27, all possibly linked through hollow ways, were probably occupied at the same time at some point between the late Iron Age and Parthian periods, after which the latter two (and by extension the use of these routes) were abandoned. At GWS-25, however, there is possible evidence for early Sasanian occupation, suggesting that some of these pathways of movement may have continued to be used.[62] As such, the pattern of settlement characteristic of the mid- to late Sasanian period, in which almost all occupation is concentrated in the southern part of the plain, may have been a gradual process. We know that by the fourth century, Sasanian emperors were already campaigning against nomadic groups north of the Gorgan Plain,[63] and this threat could have been a contributing factor in formalising the

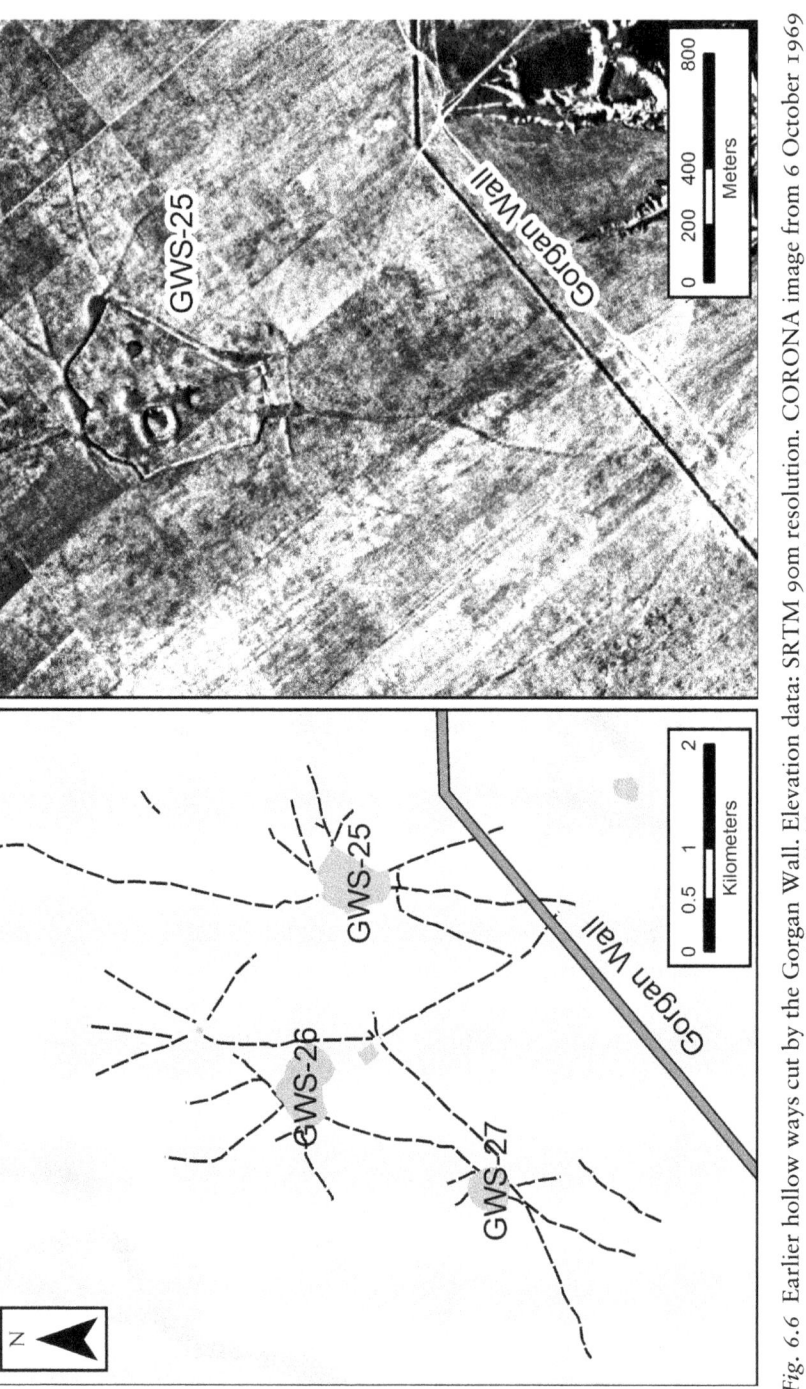

Fig. 6.6 Earlier hollow ways cut by the Gorgan Wall. Elevation data: SRTM 90m resolution. CORONA image from 6 October 1969 (data available from the U.S. Geological Survey).

Sasanian settlement pattern that solidified after the wall was built. Clearly the construction of the wall would have altered connectivity on the plain by cutting across local routes that may have been in use for several centuries prior.

As our understanding of the early Sasanian period on the Gorgan Plain is sketchy at best, it is difficult to say whether any kind of formal military frontier existed, and how it might have affected movement on a regional scale. If a military frontier did exist it may have been more permeable, perhaps consisting of an arrangement of sites and fortifications like the *Limes Arabicus* of the Roman/Byzantine Empire; this system would allow for tabs to be kept on seasonal movements of mobile pastoral groups, but would not exclude trade or the daily movement of herds.[64] It is also difficult to say, without further chronological refinement, at what level movement through the Gorgan Wall was regulated from the period of its construction through to the end of the Sasanian period. Periods of more cordial political relations with the Hephthalites or the need to send troops elsewhere could have reduced the number of persons active along the wall,[65] though crossing points may still have been used to collect tolls on goods moving into and out of the empire.

What is clear, however, is that while the wall was actively in use from the fifth/sixth to seventh centuries, small- and medium-scale movement on a regular basis would probably have been restricted to the southern half of the plain. The wall would have constituted a considerable barrier to movement at all but a few tightly controlled crossings, making daily movements towards the northern part of the plain, perhaps in search of pasture, less likely. However, the exploitation of various herd animals is clear in the faunal remains recovered from mid- to late Sasanian sites on the plain, suggesting that alternative patterns of local movement must have developed while the wall was in use.[66]

CONCLUSION

The scale of imperial investment in the landscapes of the Gorgan Plain in the mid- to late Sasanian period makes it easier to identify nodes within large-scale networks. However, it is clear that an immense amount of work still needs to be done in order to understand the different spatial and temporal manifestations of local and imperial networks on this and other Sasanian frontiers. It is hoped with further work we can refine our understanding of the chronological developments during the Sasanian period. What is likely is that a physical boundary like the wall would have substantially changed the way in which people moved around the plain, and beyond it. However, even physical boundaries are not completely restrictive, and economic, cultural and social networks often cross them.[67] The available evidence suggests that military boundaries did not consistently match the limits of political or economic influence, or indeed the cultural connectivity evident between the Gorgan Plain and communities to the north over the long term.

NOTES

1. Eaton 2005: 52; Elton 1996; Glatz and Matthews 2005; Lattimore 1951; Lightfoot and Martinez 1995: 472; Parker 2002; Rodseth and Parker 2005: 12; Smith 2005.
2. See Lawrence and Wilkinson, this volume; Nokandeh et al. 2006; Omrani Rekavandi et al. 2007; 2008; Sauer et al. 2013.
3. Liverani 1988: 85–6; Smith 2005.
4. See next section.
5. See Smith 2005.
6. Sauer et al. 2015; fig. 6.1
7. Wilkinson 1990; 2003: 111–17.
8. Casana 2013; Ur 2003; 2010; Wilkinson 2003.
9. Ur 2003; Wilkinson et al. 2010.
10. Casana 2013: 7–10.
11. Wilkinson 2003: 41–3.
12. Equally, alignments of sites, and landscape features, as well as linear boundaries, can also be interpreted as corridors of movement (Parker 2002: 373; Smith 2005). Lawrence and Wilkinson (this volume) have presented a convincing argument for a potential Sasanian route system following a line of fortified sites that form nodes in a larger imperial network in the Caucasus.
13. Green 2001: 46–9; Oates and Oates 1990: 230, fig. 62; Simpson 1996: 90; fig. 6.1.
14. Simpson 1996: 90.
15. Oates and Oates 1990: 227; Ur et al. 2011: 15.
16. Sauer et al. 2013: 235–37.
17. See Lawrence and Wilkinson, this volume.
18. Abbasi 2011; Arne 1945; Wilkinson et al. 2013; Shiomi 1976; 1978.
19. Bode 1848; Bosworth 1989b; Hopper and Omrani Rekavandi in press; Irons 1969; 1974; Muraviev 1871; Okazaki 1968; Vámbéry 1864; Yate 1900: 256–60.
20. Wilkinson et al. 2013: 93.
21. Wilkinson 2003: 9.
22. Wilkinson et al. 2013: 100–2.
23. Collins 2001: 291; Le Strange 1905: 380; Schoff 1914: 8–9.
24. See Baker 1876; Muraviev 1871; Napier and Ahmad 1876; Marvin 1881; Vámbéry 1864: 80–1.

25 Fisher 1968: 38.
26 Le Strange 1905: 376–7.
27 Muraviev 1871: 12.
28 Howard-Johnston 2012: 100.
29 Muraviev 1871: 12; O'Donovan 1882: 291.
30 Wilkinson et al. 2013: 30–2, fig. 3.7.
31 Kiani 1982: fig. 1; Collins 2001: 291; Le Strange 1905: 377, citing Ibn Hawkal.
32 Bosworth 1989a: 113 no. 290.
33 Sauer et al. 2013: 4.
34 Wilkinson et al. 2013: 72–80.
35 Smith 2005: 841; Wilkinson et al. 2013: 80.
36 Wilkinson et al. 2013: 76; see fig. 6.3.
37 Wilkinson et al. 2013: 73–6; Sauer et al. 2013: 637–8, 640.
38 Wilkinson et al. 2013: 79–80
39 Sauer et al. 2013: 184.
40 Kiani 1982: fig. 8a; Wilkinson et al. 2013: 124; see fig. 6.3.
41 See Sauer et al. 2013: 232; Sauer et al. in press.
42 Kiani 1982: 17, 43; Sauer et al. 2013: 20 no. 12; 174, 234.
43 Kiani 1982.
44 Kiani 1984; Sauer et al. 2013: 360.
45 Wilkinson et al. 2013: 124.
46 Priestman 2013: 523.
47 Sauer et al. 2013: 401–2.
48 Le Strange 1905: 9, map X; Marvin 1881: map 2; Napier and Ahmad 1876: 111.
49 Abbasi 2011: 217–18.
50 See Sauer et al. 2013: 309–11.
51 Bivar 1983: 210–15; Frye 1983: 129; Helms et al. 2002; Lecomte 1999: 145–7; 2007: 306–7; Nerazik and Bulgakov 1996: 208–9.
52 Boucharlat and Lecomte 1987: 113, 119; Lecomte 1999: 162; 2007: 304; Priestman 2013: 529–30.
53 Priestman 2013: 529–30.
54 Lecomte 2007: 304.
55 See Cleuziou 1985: 175–9; Lecomte 1999: 138.
56 See Lecomte 2007: 307. Lecomte, for example, has suggested, on the basis of textual references and site layout, that the site of Ulu Kizylli in the Misrian Plain may in fact have originated as the Sasanian city of Shahrestan-e Yazdegird founded by Yazdegird II, as a base from which to campaign against the Hephthalites in the fifth century. Of course, only further archaeological explorations will be able to confirm or refute this.
57 Wilkinson et al. 2013: 103.
58 Marvin 1881: 38, Vámbéry 1864: 83.
59 Morgan 1895; Kiani 1982: figs 30–1.
60 Wilkinson et al. 2013: 99–100.
61 Wilkinson et al. 2013: 45–8.
62 Wilkinson et al. 2013: 119
63 Bivar 1983: 211; Litivinsky 1996: 138.

64 Fisher 2004; Mayerson 1986: 71, 1989. Lecomte (2009: 301, 310–11), believing the Gorgan Wall to be originally a Parthian construction, reused in the Sasanian period, has suggested a *limes*-style second line of defence existed behind the wall within the plain. While the dating of the wall has now been confirmed as Sasanian, it is possible that a *limes*-style arrangement may have predated the wall, or indeed existed behind it.
65 Sauer et al. 2013: 214–15.
66 Mashkour 2013 and this volume.
67 Lightfoot and Martinez 1995: 482.

BIBLIOGRAPHY

Abbasi, G. (2011), *Final Report of the Archaeological Excavations at Narges Tappeh, Gorgān Plain, Iran* (in Persian), Tehran: Ganjineh Naqshe Jahan; Gorgan: Golestan Cultural and Heritage Organization and Golestan Higher Education Institute.

Arne, T. J. (1945), *Excavations at Shah Tepe, Iran*, Stockholm: Elanders Boktryckeri Aktiebolag Göteborg.

Baker, V. (1876), *Clouds in the East: Travels and Adventures on the Perso-Turkman Frontier*, London: Chatton and Windus.

Bivar, A. D. H. (1983), 'The History of Eastern Iran', in E. Yarshater (ed.), *The Cambridge History of Iran: The Seleucid, Parthian and Sasanian Periods*, Cambridge: Cambridge University Press, 3.1, pp. 180–231.

Bode, C. A. de. (1848), 'On the Yamud and Goklan Tribes of Turkomania', *Journal of the Ethnological Society of London*, 1, pp. 60–78.

Bosworth, C. E. (trans.) (1989a), *The History of al-Ṭabarī V: The Sāsānids, the Byzantines, the Lakhmids, and Yemen*, New York: State University of New York Press.

Bosworth, C. E. (trans.) (1989b), *The History of al-Ṭabarī XXX: The Abbāsid Caliphate in Equilibrium: The Caliphates of Mūsā al-Hādī and Hārūn al-Rashīd A.D. 785–809/A.H. 169–193*, New York: State University of New York Press.

Boucharlat, R. and Lecomte, O. (1987), *Fouilles de Tureng Tepe. 1 : Les périodes sassanides et islamiques*, Paris: Editions Recherche sur les Civilisations.

Casana, J. (2013), 'Radial Route Systems and Agro-Pastoral Strategies in the Fertile Crescent: New Discoveries from Western Syria and Southwestern Iran', *Journal of Anthropological Archaeology*, 32.2, pp. 257–73.

Cleuziou, S. (1985), 'L'Age du Fer a Tureng Tepe (Iran) et ses relations avec l'Asie centrale', in *L'archéologie de la Bactriane Ancienne: Actes du colloque franco-sovietique, Dushanbe (U.R.S.S.), 27 octobre–3 novembre 1982*, Paris: Editions du CNRS, pp. 175–201.

Collins, B. (trans.) (2001), *The Best Divisions for Knowledge of the Regions by Al-Muqaddasi*, Reading: Garnet.

Eaton, R. (2005), 'Three Overlapping Frontiers in Early Modern Bengal: Religious, Agrarian, Imperial', in L. Rodseth and B. Parker (eds), *Untaming the Frontier in Anthropology, Archaeology, and History*, Tucson: University of Arizona Press, pp. 52–82.

Elton, H. (1996), *Frontiers of the Roman Empire*, Bloomington: Indiana University Press.
Fisher, G. (2004), 'A New Perspective on Rome's Desert Frontier', *Bulletin of the American Schools of Oriental Research*, 336, pp. 49–60.
Fisher, W. B. (1968), 'Physical Geography', in W. B. Fisher (ed.), *The Cambridge History of Iran*, Cambridge: Cambridge University Press, pp. 1–110.
Frye, R. N. (1983), 'The Political History of Iran under the Sasanians', in E. Yarshater (ed.), *The Cambridge History of Iran: The Seleucid, Parthian and Sasanian Periods*, 3.1, Cambridge: Cambridge University Press, pp. 116–80.
Glatz, C. and Matthews, R. (2005), 'Anthropology of a Frontier Zone: Hittite–Kaska Relations in Late Bronze Age North-Central Anatolia', *Bulletin of the American Schools of Oriental Research*, 339, pp. 47–65.
Green, W. A. (2001), 'Area JF (Jaghjagh Ford)', in G. Emberling and H. McDonald, 'Excavations at Tell Brak 2000: Preliminary Report', *Iraq*, 63, pp. 46–9.
Helms, S. W., Yagodin, V. N., Betts, A. V. G., Khozhaniyazov, G. and Negus, M. (2002), 'The Karakalpak–Australian Excavations in Ancient Chorasmia: The Northern Frontier of the "Civilised World"', *Ancient Near Eastern Studies*, 39, pp. 3–44.
Hopper, K. and Omrani Rekavandi, H. (in press), 'Investigating Mobile Pastoralist Landscapes in North East Iran: The Contribution of Remote Sensing', in D. Lawrence, M. Altaweel and G. Philip (eds), *New Agendas in Remote Sensing and Landscape Archaeology: Studies in Honor of Tony J. Wilkinson*, Chicago: Oriental Institute of the University of Chicago.
Howard-Johnston, J. (2012), 'The Late Sasanian Army', in T. Bernheimer and A. Silverstein (eds), *Late Antiquity: Eastern Perspectives*, Oxford: Gibb Memorial Trust, pp. 87–127.
Irons, W. (1969), 'The Turkmen of Iran: A Brief Research Report', *Iranian Studies*, 2.1, pp. 27–38.
Irons, W. (1974), 'Nomadism as a Political Adaptation: The Case of the Yomut Turkmen', *American Ethnologist*, 1.4, pp. 635–58.
Kiani, M. Y. (1982), *Parthian Sites in Hyrcania: The Gurgan Plain*, Berlin: Reimer.
Kiani, M. Y. (1984), *The Islamic City of Gurgan*, Berlin: Reimer.
Lattimore, O. (1951), *Inner Asian Frontiers of China*, New York: American Geographical Society.
Lecomte, O. (1999), 'Vehrkana and Dehistan: Late Farming Communities of South-West Turkmenistan from the Iron Age to the Islamic Period', *Parthica: Incontri di culture nel mondo antico*, 1, pp. 135–70.
Lecomte, O. (2007), 'Gorgān and Dehistan: The North-East Frontier of the Iranian Empire', in J. Cribb and G. Herrmann (eds), *Proceedings of the British Academy: After Alexander: Central Asia Before Islam*, Oxford: Oxford University Press, pp. 295–312.
Lecomte, O. (2009), 'Origine des cultures agricoles du Dehistan (Sud-Ouest Turkmenistan)', in M. Mouton and M. Al-Dbiyat (eds), *Stratégies d'acquisition de l'eau et société au Moyen-Orient depuis l'antiquité*, Paris: Institut Français du Proche-Orient, pp. 69–77.
Le Strange, G. (1905), *The Lands of the Eastern Caliphate: Mesopotamia,*

Persia, and Central Asia, from the Moslem Conquest to the Time of Timur, Cambridge: Cambridge University Press.

Lightfoot, K. G. and Martinez, A. (1995), 'Frontiers and Boundaries in Archaeological Perspective', *Annual Review of Anthropology*, 24, pp. 471–92.

Litivinsky, B. A. (1996), 'The Hepthalite Empire', in B. A. Litivinksy (ed.), *History of Civilizations of Central Asia. Vol. III: The Crossroads of Civilizations: A.D. 250–750*, Paris: UNESCO, pp. 135–62.

Liverani, M. (1988), 'The Growth of the Assyrian Empire in the Habur/Middle Euphrates Area: A New Paradigm', *State Archives of Assyria Bulletin* 2.2, pp. 81–98.

Marvin, C. (1881), *Merv, the Queen of the World; and the Scourge of the Man-Stealing Turcomans*, London: W.H. Allen.

Mashkour, M. (2013), 'Animal Bones', in Sauer et al. 2013, pp. 539–80.

Mayerson, P. (1986), 'The Saracens and the *Limes*', *Bulletin of the American Schools of Oriental Research*, 262, pp. 35–47.

Mayerson, P. (1989), 'Saracens and Romans: Micro–Macro Relationships', *Bulletin of the American Schools of Oriental Research*, 274, pp. 71–9.

Morgan, J. de (1895), *Mission scientifique en Perse: Cartes*, Paris: E. Leroux.

Muraviev, N. (1871), *Journey to Khiva Through the Turcoman Country, 1819–20*, trans. from Russian by P. Strahl and from German by W. S. A. Lockhart, Calcutta: Foreign Department Press.

Napier, G. C. and Ahmad, K. S. (1876), 'Extracts from a Diary of a Tour in Khorassan, and Notes on the Eastern Alburz Tract; with Notes on the Yomut Tribe', *Journal of the Royal Geographical Society of London*, 46, pp. 62–171.

Nerazik, E. E. and Bulgakov, P. G. (1996), 'Khwarizm', in B. A. Litivinksy (ed.), *History of Civilizations of Central Asia. Vol. III: The Crossroads of Civilizations: A.D. 250–750*, Paris: UNESCO, pp. 207–32.

Nokandeh, J., Sauer, E. W., Omrani Rekavandi, H., Wilkinson, T., Abbasi, G. A., Schwenniger, J.-L., Mahmoudi, M., Parker, D., Fattahi, M., Usher-Wilson, L. S., Ershadi, M., Ratcliffe, J. and Gale, R. (2006), 'Linear Barriers of Northern Iran: The Great Wall of Gorgān and the Wall of Tammishe', *Iran*, 44, pp. 121–73.

O'Donovan, E. (1882), *The Merv Oasis: Travels and Adventures East of the Caspian During the Years 1979–80–81*, New York: G.P. Putnam's Sons.

Oates, D. and Oates, J. (1990), 'Aspects of Hellenistic and Roman Settlement in the Khabur Basin', in P. Matthiae, M. van Loon and H. Weiss (eds), *Resurrecting the Past: A Joint Tribute to Adnan Bounni*, Leiden: Nederlands Instituut voor het Nabije Oosten, pp. 227–48.

Okazaki, S. (1968), *The Development of Large-Scale Farming in Iran: The Case of the Province of Gorgān*, Tokyo: Institute of Asian Economic Affairs.

Omrani Rekavandi, H., Sauer, E. W., Wilkinson, T,., Safari Tamak, E., Ainslie, R., Mahmoudi, M., Griffiths, S., Ershadi, M., Jansen Van Rensburg, J., Fattahi, M., Ratcliffe, J., Nokandeh, J., Nazifi, A., Thomas, R., Gale, R. and Hoffmann, B. (2007), 'An Imperial Frontier of the Sasanian Empire: Further Fieldwork at the Great Wall of Gorgān', *Iran*, 45, pp. 95–136.

Omrani Rekavandi, H. O., Sauer, E. W., Wilkinson, T., Abbasi, G. A., Priestman, S., Safari Tamak, E., Ainslie, R., Mahmoudi, M., Galiatsatos, N., Roustai, K., Jansen Van Rensburg, J., Ershadi, M., MacDonald, E., Fattahi, M., Oatley, C., Shabani, B., Ratcliffe, J. and Usher-Wilson, L. S. (2008), 'Sasanian Walls,

Hinterland Fortresses and Abandoned Ancient Irrigated Landscapes: The 2007 Season on the Great Wall of Gorgān and the Wall of Tammishe', *Iran*, 46, pp. 151–78.

Parker, B. J. (2002), 'At the Edge of Empire: Conceptualizing Assyria's Anatolian Frontier ca. 700 BC', *Journal of Anthropological Archaeology*, 21.3, pp. 371–95.

Priestman, S. (2013), 'Sasanian Ceramics from the Gorgān Wall and Other Sites on the Gorgān Plain', in Sauer et al. 2013, pp. 447–534.

Rodseth, L. and Parker, B. (2005), *Untaming the Frontier in Anthropology, Archaeology, and History*, Tucson: University of Arizona Press.

Sauer, E. W., Omrani Rekavandi, H. and Nokandeh, J. (in press), 'The Gorgan Wall's Garrison Revealed via Satellite Search', in D. Lawrence, M. Altaweel and G. Philip (eds), *New Agendas in Remote Sensing and Landscape Archaeology: Studies in Honor of Tony J. Wilkinson*, Chicago: Oriental Institute of the University of Chicago.

Sauer, E. W., Omrani Rekavandi, H., Wilkinson, T. J., Nokandeh, J. et al. (2013), *Persia's Imperial Power in Late Antiquity: The Great Wall of Gorgān and Frontier Landscapes of Sasanian Iran*, British Institute of Persian Studies Archaeological Monographs Series, II, Oxford: Oxbow Books.

Sauer, E. W., Pitskhelauri, K., Hopper, K., Tiliakou, A., Pickard, C., Lawrence, D., Diana, A., Kranioti, E. and Shupe, C. (2015), 'Northern Outpost of the Caliphate: Maintaining Military Forces in a Hostile Environment (the Dariali Gorge in the Central Caucasus in Georgia)', *Antiquity*, 89, pp. 885–904.

Schoff, W. H. (trans.) (1914), *Parthian Stations by Isidore of Charax: An Account of the Overland Trade Route Between the Levant and India in the First Century B.C.*, Philadelphia: Commercial Museum.

Shiomi, H. (1976), *Archaeological Map of the Gorgān Plain: Iran No. 1*, Hiroshima University Scientific Expedition to Iran, Hiroshima: Denshi Insatsu.

Shiomi, H. (1978), *Archaeological Map of the Gorgān Plain: Iran No. 2*, Hiroshima University Scientific Expedition to Iran, Hiroshima: Denshi Insatsu.

Simpson, St J. (1996), 'From Tekrit to the Jaghjagh: Sasanian Sites, Settlement Patterns and Material Culture in Northern Mesopotamia', in K. Bartl and S. R. Hauser (eds), *Continuity and Change in Northern Mesopotamia from the Hellenistic to the Early Islamic Period*, Berlin: Reimer, pp. 87–126.

Smith, M. (2005), 'Networks, Territories, and the Cartography of Ancient States', *Annals of the Association of American Geographers*, 95.4, pp. 832–49.

Ur, J. A. (2003), 'CORONA Satellite Photography and Ancient Road Networks: A Northern Mesopotamian Case Study', *Antiquity*, 77, pp. 102–15.

Ur, J. A. (2010), *Urbanism and Cultural Landscapes in Northeastern Syria: The Tell Hamoukar Survey, 1999–2001*, Oriental Institute Publications, 137, Chicago: Oriental Institute of the University of Chicago.

Ur, J. A., Karsgaard, P. and Oates, J. (2011), 'The Spatial Dimensions of Early Mesopotamian Urbanism: The Tell Brak Suburban Survey, 2003–2006', *Iraq*, 73, pp. 1–19.

Vámbéry, A. (1864), *Travels in Central Asia*, London: John Murray.

Wilkinson, T. J. (1990), 'The Development of Settlement in the North Jazira between the 7th and 1st Millennia BC', *Iraq*, 52, pp. 49–62

Wilkinson, T. J. (2003), *Archaeological Landscapes of the Near East*, Tucson: University of Arizona Press.

Wilkinson, T. J., French, C., Ur, J. A. and Semple, M. (2010), 'The Geoarchaeology of Route Systems in Northern Syria', *Geoarchaeology*, 25.6, pp. 745–71.

Wilkinson, T. J., Omrani Rekavandi, H., Hopper, K., Priestman, S., Roustaei, K. and Galiatsatos, N. (2013), 'The Landscapes of the Gorgān Wall', in Sauer et al. 2013, pp. 24–132.

Yate, C. E. (1900), *Khurasan and Sistan*, Edinburgh: Blackwood.

7 The Sasanian Empire and the East: A Summary of the Evidence and its Implications for Rome

Warwick Ball

Sasanian studies in the past have focused mainly on its western regions, with its well-known remains from Azerbaijan through to Mesopotamia and Fars, and its relationship with the Roman Empire to the west. However, more recent discoveries in the east have emphasised the equal importance of these more neglected regions: the investigations of the Gorgan Wall, new fire temple complexes at Bandiyan and Sarakhs, the Bactrian documents, the Ghulbiyan painting and the rock relief of Shapur at Rag-e Bibi to name just some. This chapter will offer an overview of the Sasanian material evidence, mainly in Afghanistan, as well as the traces of Sasanian influences in art and archaeology further east. We will then attempt to identify the Sasanian presence in the archaeological record in Afghanistan and tie this to some of the documentary and literary evidence. In the light of this evidence it is then possible to reassess the Sasanian Empire, its focus and its attitudes to the west.

INTRODUCTION

Maps of the Sasanian Empire frequently emphasise its western half: see, for example, Figure 7.1.[1] The western half is the location of many of the best-known Sasanian monuments: Takht-e Sulaiman, Paikuli, Ctesiphon, Qasr-e Shirin and Taq-e Bustan, for example. Our historical sources for the Sasanians furthermore are predominantly western, mainly the Greek and Latin sources.[2] Most of all, so much of Iranian history is viewed in terms of conflict with the West: the Graeco-Persian wars, the invasion of Alexander of Macedon, and the conflicts of the Romans[3] with the Parthians and Sasanians.[4]

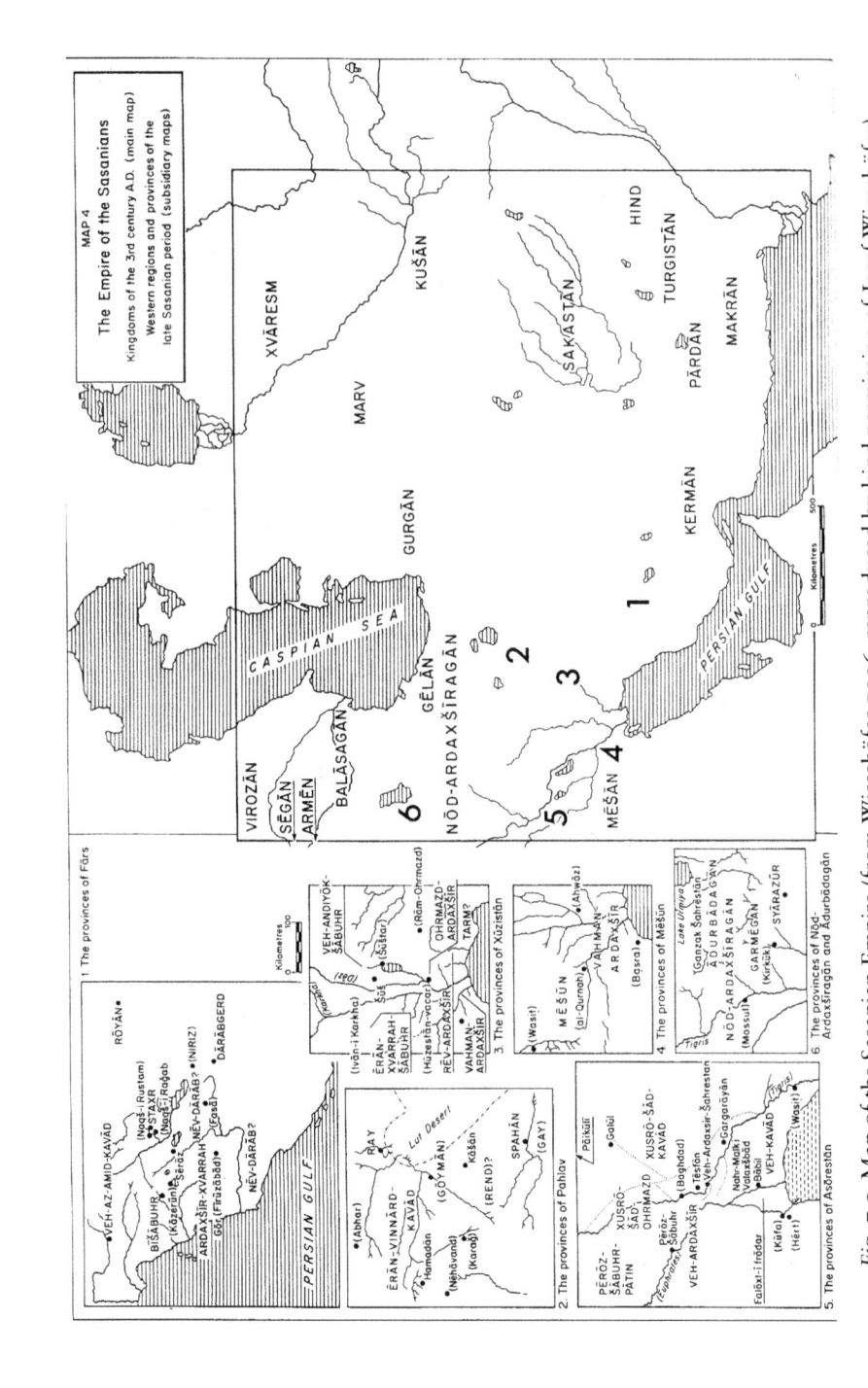

Fig. 7.1 Map of the Sasanian Empire (from Wiesehöfer 1996, reproduced by kind permission of Josef Wiesehöfer).

Does such a view reflect a true picture of the Sasanian Empire from within? Compare, for example, the number of Sasanian sites in Afghanistan shown in Figure 7.2 with those in the western half shown in Figure 7.1.[5] Of course, such a comparison is not necessarily a valid one: Figure 7.2 supposedly depicts *all* Sasanian-period archaeological sites recorded in Afghanistan, so a better comparison might be those recorded in, say, surveys of the Diyala Plain or the North Jazira.[6] Figure 7.2 in addition might not necessarily reflect Sasanian political control, merely settlement corresponding to the Sasanian period. But it does nonetheless reflect a considerable body of evidence for the eastern parts of the empire that is frequently overlooked. For the Sasanians looked to the east as much as to the west – as well as to the north and to the sea routes. In the following pages we will summarise briefly some of this evidence.

NEW DISCOVERIES IN THE EAST

A number of recent dramatic discoveries in the eastern half of the Sasanian Empire have shifted attention to its hitherto neglected half. One of the most important has been the Gorgan Wall to the east of the Caspian. Although hardly a 'recent discovery' – its existence had been known for centuries – recent investigations have re-dated it to the Sasanian period, in the process revealing it to be one of the most formidable defensive systems of the ancient world.[7] This is discussed elsewhere in this volume, but it is graphic confirmation of the importance that the Sasanians attached to their eastern (or at least north-eastern) defences.

The most important discoveries of Sasanian religious architecture in recent years have also been in the north-eastern borderlands. These have been the excavations of two Sasanian fire temple complexes, one at Bandiyan near Darrehgaz just to the south of the Iran–Turkmenistan border, and the other at Mele Hairam in the Sarakhs oasis just to the north of the border.[8] Both are probably the most complete Sasanian fire temples hitherto documented, Bandiyan in particular consisting of an elaborate complex and associated *dakhma*, the only such association known from antiquity, 'of exceptional importance ... [that has] opened a new chapter in the religious architecture of the Sasanian period', in the words of the excavator.[9] Both also preserve elaborate decoration, forming a major contribution to the corpus of Sasanian architectural decoration generally. Viewed against the background of the increasing documentation of Central Asian fire cult complexes in the Iron and

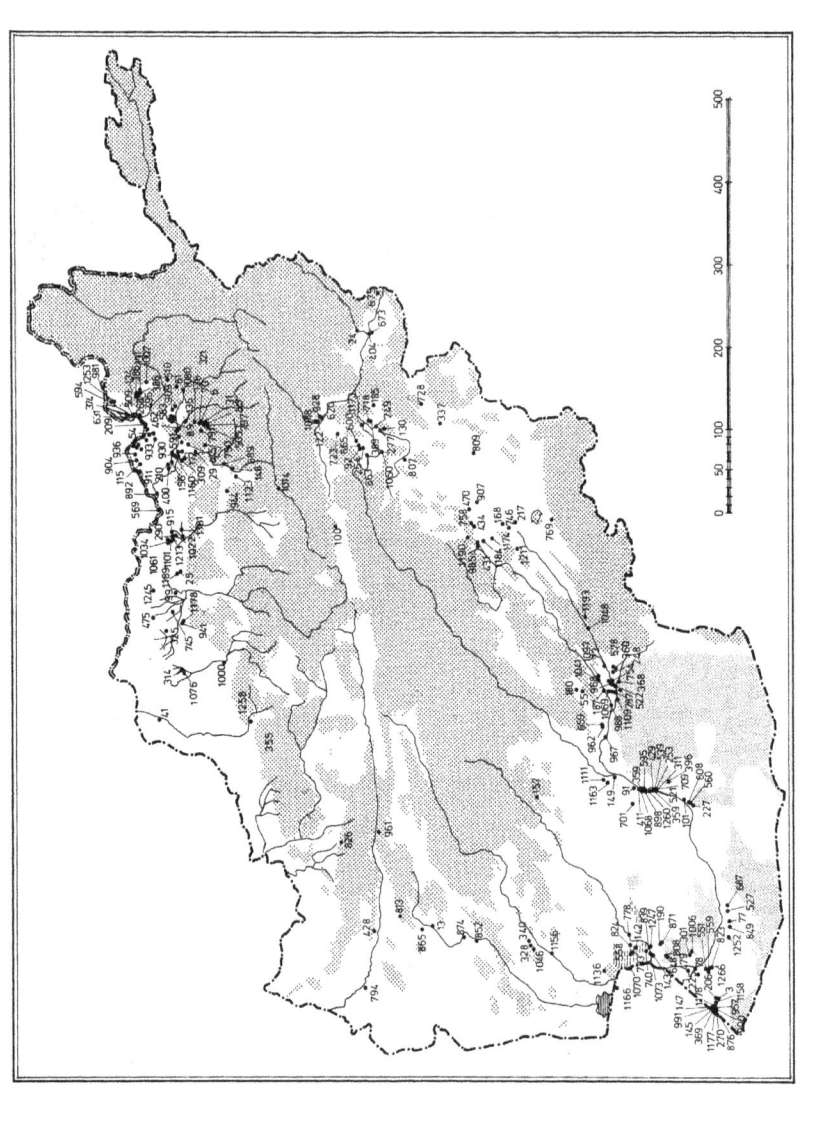

Fig. 7.2 Map of early Sasanian sites in Afghanistan, third to fourth century (from Ball 1982).

Bronze Ages,[10] these discoveries have added considerably to the reorientation of Iranian pre-Islamic religion to the east. Religious aspects are discussed further below.

Without doubt the most intriguing Sasanian 'discovery' never discovered concerns a nineteenth-century description of a 'Sasanian' rock relief in the mountains of north-western Afghanistan to the south of Sar-e Pol. This was described by a former Napoleonic officer turned soldier of fortune, General J. P. Ferrier, who travelled through Iran and Afghanistan in the 1840s with the aim of seeking employment at the court of Ranjit Singh of Panjab (as indeed several other ex-Napoleonic officers did, not to mention a motley collection of other larger-than-life adventurers of all nationalities). His description, the English translation of which was published by John Murray in 1857, is worth quoting in full:

> On the most elevated point I remarked an enormous block of rock, turned to the sun, on the smooth surface of which were sculptured several figures and inscriptions. The former were in a group; one represented a king on his throne administering justice before his assembled court; a warrior stretched on the ground in chains had been executed, as the monarch's attitude and extended right arm appeared to indicate, by his order; another captive, liberated from his chains, has fallen at the prince's knee, and with terror depicted on his countenance seems to implore his mercy. The Arab inscription, which I could not read, seemed to me much more recent than the bas-relief, and appears to have replaced another which once existed a little higher up, where a hollowed part of the rock indicates that it had been cut or scraped to efface something.[11]

Naturally, such an extraordinary description of an apparent 'Sasanian' rock relief so far to the east of all other Sasanian reliefs in the west and south of Iran aroused considerable excitement and has since attracted a number of efforts at rediscovery. The first of these were by members of the Afghan Boundary Commission in the 1880s from British India. Although military intelligence was the prime concern of the Commission, antiquities were of considerable interest to individual members, but despite producing the most complete record of all aspects of routes, geography and antiquities of north-western Afghanistan ever made, no trace of the relief was ever found.[12]

Renewed interest in – and perhaps indirect confirmation of – the Ferrier relief was prompted by the discovery of Roman coins, mainly of Gordian III, in the bazaar of Sar-e Pol in the early 1930s by the director of the French archaeological mission in Afghanistan, Carl Hackin. The prostrate figure of a Roman emperor depicted in the Sasanian reliefs at Bishapur has been interpreted as Gordian III, killed while on campaign in the east against the Sasanians, which tallies with Ferrier's description of a prostrate figure; his description of the kneeling captive therefore would correspond to that of Emperor Philip I depicted in the Bishapur and Naqsh-e Rostam reliefs. Subsequent searches for the relief, however, still failed to find it: by an Italian mission in the 1940s, by André Maricq in the 1950s (who did discover the Minaret of Jam), by Andrea Bruno in the 1960s, by David Bivar in the 1960s, and several efforts by Jonathan Lee in the 1970s.[13]

Was the relief therefore a figment of Ferrier's imagination? This seems unlikely. Elsewhere Ferrier proved himself a reliable and accurate observer, and his description of the relief rings true. However, a short while later in his travels, Ferrier was captured and imprisoned in Girishk, when the relevant part of his diary was lost. Much of his account, therefore, had to be reconstructed from memory. In the ensuing reconstruction, might he have confused Sar-e Pol in Afghanistan with Sar-e Pol (-e Zuhab) in Iran, near the present Iraq–Iran border, where there is a rock relief? Ferrier did pass through here earlier in his travels. The Sar-e Pol relief is Lullubi of the late third millennium, but it does depict a (standing) king, a prostrate captive and two kneeling captives (Fig. 7.3). This, conflated with Sasanian reliefs elsewhere in Iran, could transmogrify into his description above: the Bishapur relief of Shapur, for example (Bishapur (I)), depicts a prostrate figure on the ground (usually interpreted as Emperor Gordian III) and a captive kneeling in supplication before Shapur (interpreted as Emperor Philip the Arab, or occasionally as Valerian); the scene is repeated at Naqsh-e Rostam, although without a prostrate figure – although here Shapur is extending his right arm, as in Ferrier's description. Neither has the monarch enthroned, but another of the Bishapur reliefs does. However, Ferrier visited neither Bishapur nor Naqsh-e Rostam, so could not have seen any of these reliefs.[14]

Then, in 1978, the last-named investigator above to search for the relief, Jonathan Lee, discovered further indirect evidence for its existence – and in the process made one of the most important discoveries in Sasanian archaeology. This was a large painting in a rock shelter not far from the purported location of Ferrier's relief, depicting thirteen figures, including a crowned monarch seated on a throne (Figs 7.4 and 7.5). The painting is without doubt Sasanian, dated to the fourth–early fifth century.[15] While still not Ferrier's relief, it does prove beyond any doubt that major works of Sasanian pictorial art do after all exist in a region far to the east of where such works would normally be expected, and that Ferrier's relief might still yet be found (indeed, Lee did find local reports of its existence).[16] More

Fig. 7.3 A case of mistaken location: the Sar-e Pol relief in Iran confused with Sar-e Pol in Afghanistan? (after Herzfeld 1941).

important, Ghulbiyan is the most complete example of Sasanian painting to have survived. Sasanian palaces were known from historical sources to have been extensively decorated with paintings, but none have survived. This makes Ghulbiyan one of the most important works of Sasanian art in existence.

Ferrier's purported relief still defies discovery, but astonishingly a major Sasanian rock relief was recently discovered in Afghanistan – and again, the discovery was made by Jonathan Lee. This was nowhere near (and nowhere like) the Ferrier relief, but – even more astonishingly – lay only a few kilometres off Afghanistan's main north–south arterial road. It also lay only 5km to the south

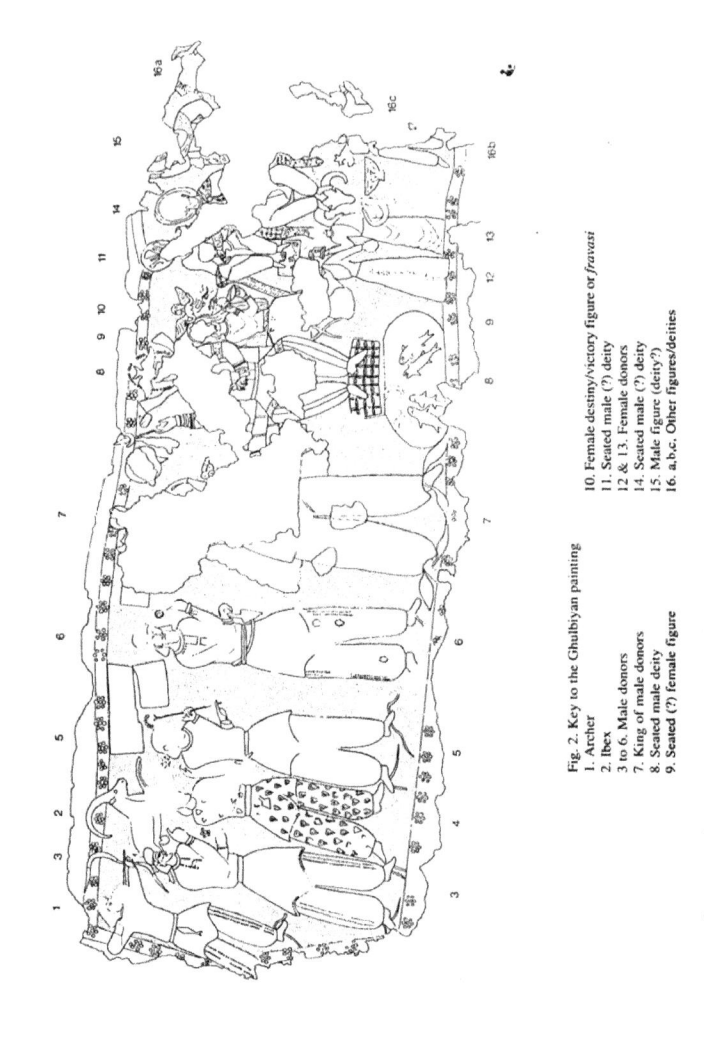

Fig. 2. Key to the Ghulbiyan painting
1. Archer
2. Ibex
3 to 6. Male donors
7. King of male donors
8. Seated male deity
9. Seated (?) female figure
10. Female destiny/victory figure or *fravashi*
11. Seated male (?) deity
12 & 13. Female donors
14. Seated male (?) deity
15. Male figure (deity?)
16. a,b,c. Other figures/deities

Fig. 7.4 Interpretive drawing by Anne Searight of the Ghulbiyan painting (after Grenet and Lee 1998, reproduced by kind permission of the authors).

Fig. 7.5 The Ghulbiyan painting (copyright© J. L. Lee 2006; by kind permission, all rights reserved).

of Surkh Kotal, one of the most important archaeological sites in Afghanistan, which had been extensively investigated by archaeologists between 1952 and 1963. This is the Sasanian rock relief of Rag-e Bibi, whose existence was never suspected and which was first investigated by Lee in 2003. Although much damaged, it is a scene depicting a Sasanian emperor, probably Shapur I, so dated to the middle decades of the third century. Shapur is depicted hunting rhinoceros, hence commemorating the Sasanian advance to the Indus (where there were rhinoceroses). It also depicts a captive Kushan, presumably a Kushan king, and so marks the Sasanian conquest of the Kushan Empire. In this way it recalls Shapur's other more famous triumphalist reliefs at Naqsh-e Rostam and – most especially – at Bishapur, depicting captive (or slain) Roman emperors. However, unlike the captive Roman prisoners of war depicted in, for example, the famous Bishapur (III) relief, the captive Kushans at Rag-e Bibi are depicted still bearing their arms. In the words of Frantz Grenet, 'Taken together, the message addressed to the Kushans is one of reconciliation rather than of humiliation' (Fig. 7.6).[17]

It was erected here presumably because of its proximity to Surkh Kotal, and so conveys another message. Surkh Kotal was a major Kushan dynastic shrine celebrating its kings, probably founded by Kanishka himself. It included a fire temple complex, of obvious Zoroastrian affinities, but also included other religious elements

Fig. 7.6 The Rag-e Bibi relief (copyright © J. L. Lee 2004; by kind permission, all rights reserved).

forming a cult focused on the person of the emperor, apparently intended to symbolise the unity of different regions of the empire and the cultural tolerance of the Kushans. A kilometre to the south-east of Surkh Kotal is the site of Kohna Masjid, excavated as part of the Surkh Kotal excavations. It consists of some massive mudbrick fortifications on top of a hill dating from the Sasanian period (Fig. 7.7).[18] This and the Shapur relief therefore might well have been part of the same complex. Thus, the association of the Rag-e Bibi relief with such visible remains of a former major dynasty is the same triumphalist association as Shapur's victory relief at Naqsh-e Rostam.

Another major recent discovery in eastern Afghanistan has added considerably to our knowledge of the Sasanian period in the region. This is the discovery of the Bactrian documents, a corpus of some 150 documents on wood, cloth and leather that started appearing in the Peshawar bazaar and the international art markets in the 1990s and 2000s, but are now mainly in a private collection in London. The Bactrian language is the Middle Persian language of the eastern Parthian and Sasanian Empire, written in a cursive derived form of the Greek alphabet. The origin of the documents has been identified as north-eastern Afghanistan, and they cover the period of Sasanian rule in the region (albeit with Hephthalite interruptions: see below) from the fourth century to the early years of the Arab conquest. They

Fig. 7.7 The Sasanian fort of Kohna Masjid at Surkh Kotal.

include Buddhist texts as well as legal and economic documents, many in the form of letters that still remained sealed, altogether comprising one of the most important corpuses of information for the Sasanian period.[19]

THE EVIDENCE FROM EXCAVATIONS

The *Archaeological Gazetteer of Afghanistan* identifies some 267 sites of the early period of Sasanian rule (c. mid-third to second half of the fourth century), probably a conservative estimate (Fig. 7.2). A similar number exists for the period of the Sasanian reconquest (c. 560–615) as well as the Hephthalite interregnum.[20] Yet the actual evidence for Sasanian rule in Afghanistan remains difficult to pinpoint in the archaeological record. Unless there is direct epigraphic or numismatic evidence (and the latter can be unreliable, due to the longevity of coins), most of these dates are based on ceramics. The ceramics are very imprecise, with most of those described for the period under discussion broadly as 'Kushan-Sasanian' and 'Hephthalo-Turk', or even merely 'Kushano-Turk', covering effectively all of the first millennium AD. This is largely due to the prevalence of the ubiquitous 'spiral-burnished wares', a highly distinctive and popular style that continued with minor variations from the mid-first millennium BC until the Arab conquest. This is found almost solely in the eastern half of the country, east of a line roughly from Balkh to Kandahar;[21] however, this is mainly a reflection of where most archaeological and ceramic studies have been carried out: there have been few in western Afghanistan.

At the excavations of Kandahar, the preponderance of the spiral-burnished wares in the Sasanian period was noted as displaying very little variation from those of the Indo-Parthian preceding it, hence making it difficult to identify a 'Sasanian' period. Bowls from both periods were virtually the same, and the highly distinctive chalices continued throughout.[22] A Sasanian cemetery was excavated, identified by the Sasanian silver coins placed in the cadavers' mouths ('Charon's obol'). However, on analysis these coins were identified as sixth-century Hephthalite imitations of the coins of Kavad I.[23] A study of the pre-Islamic coins in the Kandahar Museum revealed only 13 Sasanian coins, compared to 111 Kushan. The ratio was hardly better in the Herat Museum: 14 Sasanian and 24 Kushan.[24] Other Sasanian-period burials were excavated nearby at Deh Morasi Ghundai, although these were intrusive into the earlier Bronze Age settlement (the main object of the excavations) and dated by the problematic spiral-burnished wares noted above, and so contribute little to our knowledge of the Sasanian period in Afghanistan.[25]

To some extent the Sasanian period in Afghanistan is clouded by the most conspicuous art that characterises the period: Gandharan art. The story of the rediscovery of Gandharan art since the nineteenth century is a sad tale of despoliation of sites, looting and accidental discoveries. By far the majority of objects in museum collections are divorced from their contexts, with very few from controlled excavations. Consequently, it is impossible to date much of the sculpture closer than first-century BC to sixth-century AD, and chronology is the biggest problem that continues to plague the study of Gandharan art. Most is divorced from both its sculptural and archaeological contexts, as well as the broader social and historical contexts that might provide us with the information to fill the many gaps in its evolution. Gandharan art and the academic questions which surround it, perhaps more than most other art styles, are a victim of the art's own intrinsic collectability and value.[26]

Part of the problem lies with the close association of Gandharan art – and Buddhist art generally – with the Kushans. This has resulted in Sasanian studies in Afghanistan being overshadowed by the excess of attention given to the Kushan period preceding it, when eastern Afghanistan was the centre of a major empire. This is perhaps a correct emphasis, given the importance of the Kushans, but it has

Fig. 7.8 The Sasanian-period Buddhist stupa-monastery complex of Guldara.

nonetheless led to the neglect of the Sasanians, who ruled in parts of Afghanistan as long as or longer than the Kushans. The greater attraction of Kushan studies has even led to many of Afghanistan's major monuments being commonly misattributed to the Kushan period rather than the Sasanian: the major third–fourth-century Buddhist stupa-monastery complex of Guldara, for example, one of the few monuments dated precisely to the Sasanian period, is one of many such misattributions (Fig. 7.8).[27] (Conversely, I know of few studies of Sasanian architecture that include Guldara and similar Sasanian-period monuments in eastern Afghanistan: 'Kushanocentricism' has its Iranian counterpart.) Many such 'Kushan' sites might well be Sasanian once the chronology of Gandharan art and architecture becomes more accurate.

Most sites of the Sasanian period are almost invariably continuations of previous periods – and often continue into subsequent – so the specifically Sasanian elements are difficult to isolate: there have been no excavations in Afghanistan aimed specifically at the Sasanians. A sounding at the early Islamic fortress of Ahangaran in western Afghanistan did reveal a corpus of Sasanian-period ceramics, one of the few corpuses from an excavated context, and a survey of the large polygonal fortress of Dasht-e Archi in northern Afghanistan revealed pottery dating solely to the Sasanian period, without earlier or later material to obscure the picture.[28] But the only part of Afghanistan where a Sasanian-period assemblage seems to have been successfully differentiated from those before and after is in Sistan in the south-west.[29]

In sum, we know from our historical sources that the Sasanian Empire extended into Afghanistan, ruling directly or by proxy for a considerable period in most parts (see below). However, Sasanian studies in Afghanistan are at best elusive, at worse overlooked. With discoveries such as the Ghulbiyan fresco and Rag-e Bibi, Sasanian studies in Afghanistan are now thrust more centre stage.

EAST OF THE IMPERIAL FRONTIERS

A Sasanian maritime supremacy in the western Indian Ocean has been long (if not widely) acknowledged, with ports throughout the Persian Gulf and outposts in south Arabia and the mouth of the Indus. There have also been arguments for possible colonies on the East African coast and Ceylon, and even mercantile colonies as far as the South China Sea.[30] Of more interest here are the traces of the Sasanians stretching into Central Asia and China, of which the following can only be the briefest summary.

Ghulbiyan might be the only substantial work of Sasanian painting to have survived within Sasanian territory. But the influence of Sasanian painting has been acknowledged in a huge amount of art that has survived throughout Central Asia and into China. In Afghanistan itself, the late Buddhist cave paintings of the Turk period of the seventh–eighth centuries at Bamiyan, Dukhtar-e Nushirvan and Kakrak are clearly derived from Sasanian art.[31] In Central Asia the Sasanian influence is primarily seen in the art of the Sogdians, an Iranian people whose wall paintings have survived so spectacularly at Afrasiab and Panjikent (Fig. 7.9). Scenes that appear to anticipate the Iranian epic genre (discussed further below) have also been recognised in the wall paintings of Panjikent. Further east, Sasanian influence is recognised in the Buddhist cave paintings of Qizil in Xinjiang, particularly in details of the costume depicted on the figures of the donors (who are thought to be Sogdian; Fig. 7.10). Indeed, it is in the textile arts of Inner Asia that the influence of Sasanian painting is most apparent.[32] Sasanian textile designs were not only a popular motif in the textiles themselves, but also resurfaced in wall paintings and ceramics, the reliquary from Kucha being a particularly famous example (Fig. 7.11).[33] The popularity of Sasanian – or at least Partho-Sasanian – modes of dress is seen in the art of Dura-Europos and Palmyra, and its durability in the east is seen in the

Fig. 7.9 Sogdian wall painting from Panjikent, now in the Hermitage, St Petersburg.

Fig. 7.10 Donors from Cave 8 at the Buddhist cave paintings at Qizil in Xinjiang.

Fig. 7.11 Detail of the Kucha reliquary (after Bussagli 1978).

main form of national dress in Afghanistan and Pakistan today (e.g. see the style of dress depicted on the Sasanian reliefs, almost identical to the modern male mode of dress – the *kamiz-o shalwar* – in Afghanistan and Pakistan: Fig. 7.12).

Many other Sasanian, Sasanian-imitation and Sasanian-derived objects spread throughout Eurasia: glass, metal, stone and other objects. Sasanian imported glass vessels as well as local imitations have been found in tombs in Xinjiang and Ningxia. Particularly distinctive have been the Sasanian silver vessels – bowls, plates, ewers – that have been found as widely distributed as Ningxia, south Siberia and northern Russia (Figs 7.13, 7.14 and 7.15). The distribution of such glass and metal objects over such a vast area is evidence not so much of Sasanian trade as of the admiration in which Sasanian works of art were held, valued and imitated for their intrinsic worth. Indirect influence of Sasanian – or at least Iranian – influence in western China is also seen on stone funerary couches, some of which depict Zoroastrian scenes, probably evidence of Sogdian merchant colonies rather than Sasanian (although there is evidence of Sasanian merchant colonies in China as well).[34]

Fig. 7.12 Sasanian-derived dress in modern Kandahar.

Indeed, religion played an important part in the diffusion of Sasanian influence through Asia. The strength and longevity of Iranian religion – both Zoroastrianism and its offshoot Manichaeism – were far greater in the eastern parts of the empire than the western: indeed, Manichaeism travelled deep into China, where it lasted until modern times. In writing of Iranians east of the Pamirs, R. E. Emmerick postulates that 'The remarkable diffusion of Iranians throughout Central Asia and into China was clearly due to two courses: their love of trade and their desire to propagate their own religion.'[35]

Not only Zoroastrianism and Manichaeism, but also – surprisingly – Christianity spread into China through the Sasanian medium. The Nestorians, persecuted by the Orthodox Church in Constantinople, found refuge in the Sasanian Empire, where they established the Church of the East under Sasanian patronage as a counterpart to the Orthodox Church of the West. Although there was occasional persecution by the Sasanians as well, the Church of the East not only flourished but became the very first world church, spreading from the Sasanian Empire to India, Central Asia and as far as China.[36]

Fig. 7.13 Sasanian silver ewer from Ningxia, now in the Yinchuan Museum. Compare with Fig. 7.14.

Fig. 7.14 Sasanian silver ewer from Perm in northern Russia, now in the Hermitage.

Fig. 7.15 Sasanian-derived gold and silver plate of the ninth–tenth century in the Museum of the Institute of Archaeology in Akademgorodok.

THE LITERARY AND HISTORICAL TRADITION

Throughout Iranian history, it was the eastern frontiers and the nomadic threats that mattered most. The Sakas invaded twice, via Sistan and via the Karakoram; the Parthians arrived from the north; and the Kushans, Hephthalites and Turks invaded from the north-east, coming ultimately from the Chinese borderlands. In this context the threats from the west and south are comparatively minor, Macedonian and Arab invasions notwithstanding. Roman sources make much of Sasanian claims on the eastern provinces of the Roman Empire being a Sasanian demand for the 'return' of historic Iranian (i.e. Achaemenid) provinces, but there is no evidence for such a claim in Sasanian sources. Indeed, Sasanian sources (such as they are) give a very different picture.

Shapur in his Naqsh-e Rostam testament lists Gorgan, Margiana,

Aria, Abarshahr, Kerman, Sakastan, Turgistan, Makran, Sind, Kushanshahr and all the lands as far as Peshawar and the borders of Kashgaria, Sogdia and Chach as the eastern parts of the Sasanian Empire. In both the Naqsh-e Rostam and Paikuli testament, Narseh (who later succeeded Shapur) is named as king of Hind. Kartir's inscription at Naqsh-e Rajab refers to Buddhists, which at that time meant eastern Afghanistan.[37] Sasanian proclamations routinely emphasise 'Eran and Aneran' or 'non-Iran', where 'Eran' refers to all the land of the Iranians stretching into Afghanistan and Central Asia, and 'Aneran' the non-Iranian lands of the Near East that were conquered from the Romans. In other words, the east was an integral part of Iran, the west was not. 'For the Sasanians, Kushanshahr belonged to Iran while the Roman Empire belonged to "non-Iran", and we can see now that they were keen to mark the difference', as Grenet remarks in concluding his commentary on the Rag-e Bibi relief.[38]

The Sasanian historical tradition, as reflected (if not exactly recorded) in Ferdowsi's tenth–eleventh-century great epic, the *Shahnama*, is overwhelmingly concerned with the east: Turan, the lands beyond the Oxus, Kabulistan, Zabulistan, Sistan, the occasional foray into Mazanderan. Rum – the west – was quite simply of lesser concern. Much of the *Shahnama* – the Rostam cycle of legends in particular – is thought to derive from a Sistan historical tradition. Although the bulk of the *Shahnama* supposedly reflects pre-Sasanian and mythical history, Yarshater emphasises its Sasanian elements, reflecting Sasianian ideals, self-views and identity. Indeed, he emphasises that 'Some of the episodes between Iran and Turan appear to be modelled on the battles which took place on the eastern frontiers of Iran during and after the reign of Pērōz.' There were fantastic feats and expeditions by Shapur II, Narseh, Bahram V and Khusro I into China and India. On the other hand, 'The history of the relations between Iran and Rome and their wars during the reigns of the early Sasanian kings is often cursory, rhetorical and laden with fiction and whimsical tales.'[39] The eleventh-century *Garshaspnama* of Asadi Tusi, also reflecting Sasanian tradition, is even more concerned with the east.[40]

Even an epic that might be viewed as ultimately related to the Iranian epic tradition, Shota Rustaveli's great thirteenth-century Georgian epic *Knight in the Panther's Skin*, uses India and China for its canvas more than countries to the west, despite the prevailing Greek Orthodox Christian climate of Rustaveli's and Queen Tamara's era when it was written. Similarly, that huge compendium of stories, fables and myths that are collected as the *Arabian Nights* is concerned more with lands further to the east than the west: the Sinbad cycle, for example. While even more fictional than the *Shahnama*, many of its stories are ancient, Sasanian and older, and reflect Sasanian literary tradition.[41]

The Zoroastrian religious literary tradition is of course concerned wholly with Central Asia and the east, and the eastern origins of Zoroastrianism, together with its close associations with the Sasanians, are well enough known not to require emphasising here. Another Sasanian religious literary tradition concerns the prophet Mani's journey to Turan – the geographically located Turan in Makran, rather than the legendary Turan of the *Shahnama* – not to mention his incorporation of Buddhism and other eastern religious elements.

The actual history of the Sasanian east can be summarised briefly.[42] In the third century the Kushan Empire in Afghanistan collapsed at the hands of the Sasanians. From then until the second half of the fourth century the region was ruled on behalf of the Sasanians by governors known as 'Kushanshahs', although there are many problems with the chronology. The dynasty is known only by their Sasanian-style coins, minted at Balkh, which presumably was the capital. A Kushanshah revolt in 293 was suppressed by Bahram II. Between 350 and 358, during the time of Shapur II, there was a massive invasion by a Hun group known as the Chionites or Hephthalites, which occupied the eastern parts of the Sasanian Empire. In 457 Peroz overthrew his brother Hormizd III with the aid of the Hephthalites, but he later perished in a war against them. The Hephthalite wars of the fifth century (mainly under Peroz) were among the greatest wars fought by the Sasanians. The Hephthalite kingdom – mainly eastern Afghanistan – was established at Sasanian expense in about 400 and various Hunnic states lasted there until about 560, when eastern Afghanistan was finally brought back into the empire by Khusro I (although Hunnic elements lasted in southern Afghanistan as the Zunbils of Zabul into the early Islamic period). The Sasanian reoccupation, however, was short-lived, as the period soon after sees the arrival of the Turks in Central Asia.

The final century of the Sasanian era was dominated by wars with the Romans, particularly during the time of Khusro I Anushirvan and Justinian and again during the time of Khusro II Parviz and Heraclius. Indeed, this latter part has been rightly described by James Howard-Johnston as 'the last great war of antiquity'.[43] But even Khusro II Parviz' war with the west had a dramatic effect on the east. Khusro II's initial campaigns against the Roman Empire had the direct effect of thinning Iran's eastern defences. This prompted the Kagan of the Western Turk Empire of Central Asia to invade in 616, broadening the war into Central Asia – and beyond. The Turks advanced as far as Rayy in northern Iran and, in response, Khusro II sent a hastily assembled force of Armenians (who might otherwise have been pro-Roman) under Smbat Bagratuni to his eastern border. The Turk Kagan died, however, and his successor turned away from Iran when faced with this unexpected new resistance from the Armenians, and focused his attentions further east, where the Kagan of the Eastern Turks, Shih-pi (609–19), was instrumental in eventually bringing about the end of the Sui Dynasty of China and establishing the new Tang as its successor in 618. These were the beginnings of medieval Chinese civilisation.[44]

Chinese history adds several more unexpected footnotes to Iranian history. For it was China that witnessed the swansong of the Sasanian dynasty. Following the Arab invasion and the extinction of Sasanian Iran, members of the deposed Sasanian royal family fled eastward to the Tang court, where they were awarded asylum. They are thus depicted among the life-size statues attending the Tang emperor at the vast mausoleum of Emperor Gaozong at Qianling (Fig. 7.16).[45] Indeed, in the early eighth century China came very near to being ruled by an Iranian dynasty, when a major rebellion was led by the Sogdian An Lushan which almost toppled the infant Tang Dynasty.[46]

Fig. 7.16 Delegates to the Tang court at the vast Tang necropolis at Qianling.

Finally, it must be noted that following the Arab conquest the centre of gravity of Iranian culture moved east: to Sistan, Khurasan and Transoxiana, with the emergence of the new dynasties of the Saffarids, the Tahirids and above all the Samanids. In the end it was Turkish-dominated Ghazna that saw a renaissance of Iranian civilisation, rather than Arab-dominated Baghdad.

CONCLUSION

What are the implications of the evidence from the east for Rome? Pinning down evidence for an actual Sasanian presence – and even a broad Sasanian period – in the eastern fringes of its empire has proved elusive. However, some of the most important discoveries in Sasanian archaeology in recent times have been in the eastern half. Unexpected though these discoveries might have been, they make the undoubted spread of Sasanian cultural influence throughout the east more explicable, influence that lasted long after the collapse of the dynasty itself. Wars in the west against the Romans were undoubtedly of great importance to the Sasanians, but the Hephthalite wars of the fifth century (mainly under Peroz) were probably the greatest wars of the Sasanians. Such a gigantic undertaking as the construction of the Gorgan Wall is mute testament to this, a defensive system that the investigators themselves emphasise was one of the greatest defensive systems of antiquity.

Viewed against this background, therefore, the answer to the question 'What light does the evidence from the east shed on Sasanian–Roman relations?' must be that the Empire of Rome and the west generally meant far less to the Sasanians than our Roman sources imply.

NOTES

1 Wiesehöfer 1996: 152 – although this in no way implies criticism of this excellent work. However, see also for example the maps in Herrmann 1976: 10 and Frye 1983: 122–3, although again this does not imply western bias in either work, Frye's chapter in the *Cambridge History* in particular being followed immediately by three on the east (Bivar 1983; Zeimal 1983; Emmerick 1983).
2 Even such works as Wiesehöfer 1996 and Daryaee 2009, which make a deliberate attempt to turn away from the classical sources, are still heavily dependent upon them. Daryaee's book overall is an excellent study of the Sasanians. But despite claims to be writing an Iranocentric history of Sasanian Iran, as opposed to one displaying the western bias based on the Graeco-Roman histories that have hitherto dominated the literature,

Daryaee's history is overwhelmingly western oriented. It is dominated by the wars with the Romans, with virtually nothing on the wars with the powers to the east. Relations with the Armenians, for example, are written about at length, but there is nothing on the (arguably far more important) relations with the Kushans. Religion in the Sasanian Empire – Zoroastrianism, Manichaeism, Christianity – is rightly discussed at length, but there is no mention of the Buddhists, despite their inclusion in Kartir's inscription.

3 'Roman' used here in the broader – and strictly correct – meaning of incorporating the Byzantine Empire as well.
4 Anthony Pagden (2009), for example, views the entire history of Iran in terms of a perceived 2,500-year Manichaean struggle between east and west, of barbarism and 'a tyrannical and corrupt East' versus 'a free and virtuous West'. Such views reflect commonly held popular assumptions and would ordinarily belong to the realm of popular history, but it must be emphasised that the author is an acknowledged academic and the book is published by a major university press (Oxford). See also my introductory remarks in Ball 2010.
5 Ball 1982 (and new edn forthcoming 2018): map 66. See also maps 67–9.
6 Adams 1965; Wilkinson and Tucker 1995.
7 Sauer et al. 2013. See also chapters 4, 5, 6 and 11 in this volume.
8 Rahbar 2007; Kaim 2002.
9 Rahbar 2007: 472.
10 Summarised by Betts and Yagodin 2007.
11 Ferrier 1857: 229–30.
12 The reports were published in five volumes, the relevant ones being I, II and V (Afghan Boundary Commission 1888).
13 Ball 1982: site 1000. For a summary of the Sasanian reliefs in Iran, see Ball 2000: 118–21.
14 Herzfeld 1941: 183–4 for the Sar-e Pol relief; see Ball 2000: 118–21 for a summary of the Sasanian reliefs.
15 Ball 1982: site 362, with references; Grenet and Lee 1998.
16 Another example of a monument in western Afghanistan once considered non-existent or at least lost concerns unconfirmed ninteenth-century reports of a decorated minaret at Sakhar which, like the Ferrier relief, defied efforts at discovery until its existence was confirmed only recently. See Ball 1982: site 974; Thomas et al. 2014. While hardly relevant to the present discussion, it clearly demonstrates that the mountainous regions of western Afghanistan still have many secrets to yield.
17 Grenet et al. 2007.
18 Ball 1982: sites 630 and 1123.
19 Sims-Williams 2002–7.
20 Ball 1982: 377–81; Alram 2015.
21 Although sherds have been found as far west as Aliabad Kishmar in eastern Iran; personal observation.
22 Ball in McNicoll and Ball 1996: 398.
23 McNicoll in McNicoll and Ball 1996: 235–6; Mac Dowall in McNicoll and Ball 1996: 305–6.
24 Mac Dowall and Ibrahim 1978; 1979.

25 Dupree 1963.
26 For a summary of the evidence see Ball 2000: 139–48. See also Boardman 2015: 167.
27 Ball 1982: site 389. Misattributed to the Kushans, for example, in Knobloch 2002: 82–4.
28 Ball 1982: sites 15 and 260.
29 E.g. compare Ball 1982: regional maps 129–41 of Sistan with the same area for the Sasanian period, maps 66–9: sites dated to the Sasanian period are either solely Sasanian or clearly distinguished ceramically from the subsequent Islamic periods.
30 Whitehouse and Williamson 1973. See also Ball 2000: 130–1 with references.
31 Ball 1982: sites 100, 305 and 508.
32 Lubo-Lesnichenko 1999: esp. 464–7.
33 Bussagli 1978: 16–18 and throughout; Azarpay 1981; Baumer 2014: chs IV and VII.
34 Harper 1981; Juliano and Lerner 2001: 97, 244, 304–9; Ball 2000: 136–7; Daryaee 2009: 136–40; Baumer 2014: ch. VII.
35 Emmerick 1983: 275. See also Gnoli 1980; Sunderman 1986; Klimkeit 1993; Ball 2010: 194–5.
36 Baumer 2006; Ball 2010: 195–7; Wilmshurst 2011.
37 Frye 1984: 298, 371–7; Wieseöfer 1996: 184–5.
38 Grenet et al. 2007: 261.
39 Yarshater 1983a: 402–11, 477. See also Ferdowsi 2006.
40 *Encyclopædia Iranica*, Online Edition, <http://www.iranicaonline.org/articles/garsasp-nama>.
41 For Rustaveli see the translation and commentary by Marjory Wardrop together with the new foreword by Donald Rayfield in Rustaveli 2001. For the *Arabian Nights* see Irwin 2004 and Warner 2011.
42 Bivar 1983; Frye 1984.
43 Howard-Johnston 2006. See also Ball 2010: ch. 6, where I have described it 'as the greatest war in the history of the world' – nothing like a good understatement!
44 This reconstruction is put forward by James Howard-Johnston (1999: 103–4, 183–7).
45 Juliano and Lerner 2001: 221; Daryaee 2009: 37–8.
46 Ball 2010: 195.

BIBLIOGRAPHY

Adams, R. M. (1965), *Land Behind Baghdad: A History of Settlement on the Diyala Plains*, Chicago: University of Chicago Press.

Afghan Boundary Commission (1888), *Records of the Intelligence Party. Vol. I and II: Diary of Major Maitland. Vol. V: Miscellaneous Reports*, Simla: Government Central Press.

Alram, M. (2015), 'From the Sasanians to the Huns: New Numismatic Evidence from the Hindu Kush', *Numismatic Chronicle*, 174 (for 2014), pp. 261–91.

Azarpay, G. (1981), *Sogdian Painting: The Pictorial Epic in Oriental Art*, Berkeley: University of California Press.
Ball, W. (1982), *Archaeological Gazetteer of Afghanistan*, 2 vols, Paris: Editions Recherche sur les civilisations (new edn forthcoming 2018 as *The Archaeology and Monuments of Afghanistan: A Source Book*, Oxford: Oxford University Press).
Ball, W. (2000), *Rome in the East: The Transformation of an Empire*, London: Routledge (new edn 2016).
Ball, W. (2010), *Towards One World: Ancient Persia and the West*, London: East and West.
Baumer, C. (2006), *The Church of the East: An Illustrated History of Assyrian Christianity*, London: I.B. Tauris.
Baumer, C. (2014), *The History of Central Asia. Vol. Two: The Age of the Silk Roads*, London: I.B. Tauris.
Betts, A. V. G. and Yagodin, V. N. (2007), 'The Fire Temple at Tash-k'irman Tepe, Chorasmia', in Cribb and Herrmann 2007, pp. 435–54.
Bivar, A. D. H. (1983), 'The History of Eastern Iran', in Yarshater 1983a, pp. 181–231.
Boardman, J. (2015), *The Greeks in Asia*, London: Thames & Hudson.
Bussagli, M. (1978), *Central Asian Painting. From Afghanistan to Sinkiang*, Geneva: Macmillan.
Cribb, J. and Herrmann, G. (eds) (2007), *After Alexander. Central Asia Before Islam*, Oxford: Oxford University Press.
Daryaee, T. (2009), *Sasanian Persia. The Rise and Fall of an Empire*, London: I.B. Tauris.
Dupree, L. (1963), *Deh Morasi Ghundai: a Chalcolithic Site in South Central Afghanistan*, New York: American Museum of Natural History.
Emmerick, R. E. (1983), 'Iranian Settlement East of the Pamirs', in Yarshater 1983a, pp. 263–75.
Ferdowsi, A. (2006), *Shahnameh: The Persian Book of Kings*, transl. D. Davis, London: Penguin.
Ferrier, J. P. (1857), *Caravan Journeys and Wanderings in Persia, Afghanistan, Turkistan, and Beloochistan*, London: John Murray.
Frye, R. N. (1983), 'The Political History of Iran under the Sasanians', in Yarshater 1983a, pp. 116–80.
Frye, R. N. (1984), *The History of Ancient Iran*, Munich: C. H. Beck.
Gnoli, G. (1980), *Zoroaster's Time and Homeland*, Naples: Istituto Universitario Orientale.
Grenet, F., and Lee, J. L. (1998), 'New Light on the Sasanian Painting at Ghulbiyan, Faryab Province, Afghanistan', *South Asian Studies*, 14, pp. 75–86.
Grenet, F., Lee, J., Martinez, P. and Ory, F. (2007), 'The Sasanian Relief at Rag-i Bibi (Northern Afghanistan)', in Cribb and Herrmann 2007, pp. 243–68.
Harper, P. O. (1981), *Silver Vessels of the Sasanian Period*, New York: Metropolitan Museum of Art.
Herrmann, G. (1976), *The Iranian Revival*, Oxford: Elsevier Phaidon.
Herzfeld, E. E. (1941), *Iran in the Ancient East: Archaeological Studies Presented in the Lowell Lectures at Boston*, New York: Oxford University Press.
Howard-Johnston, J., with Greenwood, T. and Thomson, R. W. (1999), *The*

Armenian History Attributed to Sebeos II: Historical Commentary, Liverpool: Liverpool University Press.

Howard-Johnston, J. (2006), *East Rome, Sasanian Persia and the End of Antiquity*, Aldershot: Ashgate Variorum.

Irwin, R. (2004), *The Arabian Nights: A Companion*, London: Tauris Parke Paperbacks.

Juliano, A. L. and Lerner, J. A. (2001), *Monks and Merchants: Silk Road Treasures from Northwest China. Gansu and Ningxia, 4th–7th Century*, New York: Abrams.

Kaim, B. (2002), *Zaratushtrian Temple of Fire: Five Years of Excavation at Mele Hairam*, Warsaw: Agade.

Klimkeit, H. J. (1993), *Gnosis on the Silk Road*, San Francisco: HarperCollins.

Knobloch, E. (2002), *The Archaeology & Architecture of Afghanistan*, Stroud: Tempus.

Lubo-Lesnichenko, E. (1999), 'Western Motifs in the Chinese Textiles of the Early Middle Age', in M. Alram and D. Klimberg-Salter (eds), *Coins, Art and Chronology: Essays on the Pre-Islamic History of the Indo-Iranian Borderlands*, Vienna: Österreichische Akademie der Wissenschaften, pp. 461–80.

Mac Dowall, D. W. and Ibrahim, M. (1978), 'Pre-Islamic Coins in the Kandahar Museum', *Afghan Studies*, 1, pp. 67–77.

Mac Dowall, D. W. and Ibrahim, M. (1979), 'Pre-Islamic Coins in the Herat Museum', *Afghan Studies*, 2, pp. 45–51.

McNicoll, A. and Ball, W. (1996), *Excavations at Kandahar 1974 and 1975*, BAR International Series 641, Oxford: Tempus Reparatum.

Pagden, A. (2009), *Worlds at War: The 2,500-Year Struggle Between East and West*, Oxford: Oxford University Press.

Rahbar, M. (2007), 'A Tower of Silence of the Sasanian Period at Bandiyan: Some Observations about *Dakhmas* in Zoroastrian Religion', in Cribb and Herrmann 2007, pp. 455–74.

Rustaveli, S. (2001), *The Man in the Panther's Skin*, trans. M. Wardrop, London: Curzon.

Sauer, E. W., Omrani Rekavandi, H., Wilkinson, T. J., Nokandeh, J. et al. (2013), *Persia's Imperial Power in Late Antiquity: The Great Wall of Gorgān and Frontier Landscapes of Sasanian Iran*, British Institute of Persian Studies Archaeological Monographs Series, II, Oxford: Oxbow Books.

Sims-Williams, N. (2002–7), *Bactrian Documents from Northern Afghanistan. I: Legal and Economic Documents. II: Letters and Buddhist Texts. III: Plates*, Cambridge: Cambridge University Press.

Sundermann, W. (1986), 'Mani, India and the Manichaean Religion', *South Asian Studies*, 2, pp. 11–20.

Thomas, D. C., 'Umar, U. S., Ahmad, F. and Smith, D. (2014), 'The Rediscovery of the "Lost" Minaret of Qal'a-i Zārmurgh, Sāghar, Afghanistan', *Iran*, 52, pp. 133–42.

Warner, M. (2011), *Stranger Magic: Charmed States & the Arabian Nights*, London: Vintage.

Whitehouse, D. and Williamson, A. (1973), 'Sasanian Maritime Trade', *Iran*, 11, pp. 29–50.

Wiesehöfer, J. (1996), *Ancient Persia*, London: I.B. Tauris.

Wilkinson, T. J. and Tucker, D. J. (1995), *Settlement Development in the North*

Jazira, Iraq: A Study of the Archaeological Landscape, Warminster: Aris & Phillips.

Wilmshurst, D. (2011), *The Martyred Church: A History of the Church of the East*, London: East and West.

Yarshater, E. (ed.) (1983a), *The Cambridge History of Iran: The Seleucid, Parthian and Sasanian Periods*, 3.1, Cambridge: Cambridge University Press.

Yarshater, E. (1983b), 'Iranian Historical Tradition Iran', in Yarshater 1983a, pp. 343–477.

Zeimal, E. V. (1983), 'The Political History of Transoxiana Iran', in Yarshater 1983a, pp. 232–62.

Part III

Contested Territories and Cultural Contacts Between Persia and Rome

8 Minority Religions in the Sasanian Empire: Suppression, Integration and Relations with Rome

Lee E. Patterson

Gauging the importance of religion to the exercise of political will in the Sasanian world requires enormous care. It is all too easy to take the Great Kings at their word as they championed the doctrines of Zoroastrianism in their political pronouncements, especially as some of them also persecuted Christianity. Whether or not such sentiments were genuine, a closer analysis of the evidence suggests a more pragmatic royal use of religion. The political realities on the ground were more often the deciding factor in how the kings related to the religious sectors of Sasanian society. This state of affairs sometimes set the kings against the Zoroastrian clerics, whose agendas were not always in alignment, and it explains why Christian persecutions were usually motivated more by politics than doctrine. Moreover, this dynamic also explains the prominence of the Christian church in the later Sasanian period as kings employed it as a base of support, much as they had the Zoroastrian hierarchy.

INTRODUCTION

The complexities of religious life in the Sasanian realm, especially at the levels of the political elite, are staggering. No less so are the varied scholarly interpretations of how religion functioned in the state, especially religion's influence on the foreign and domestic policies of the *shahanshahs*, which is the primary concern of the present chapter. One basic fact has long been accepted: although Zoroastrianism was prominent in the Sasanian Empire, it was in fact a vast and diverse empire of many traditions existing in a coherent, if not always harmonious, system. The fortunes of these traditions, including Christianity, Judaism, Manichaeism, Buddhism and so on, fluctuated with the temperaments and policies of each *shahanshah* and, to a lesser extent, other entities such as powerful Zoroastrian *mobads*. Less universally but still commonly argued is another proposition: while religion ostensibly explains the policies of the kings, who usually claim to uphold some sort of Zoroastrian principle, such as orderliness and truth (*asha*), the actual motivations are more often than not informed by the political realities on the ground.

This framework is our starting point, but my purpose is to place greater emphasis on the latter proposition, with two main arguments: first, it is the king, not the priest, who should be our focus. For example, even if we acknowledge a *mobad* as the architect of a Christian persecution, motivated by genuine religious sentiment, the policy serves the political purposes of the king, who might publicly extol the religious virtues of the persecution but in reality regard it as necessary to achieve an immediate political goal. The same applies to policies that followed the opposite path and promoted Christianity (and other non-Zoroastrian traditions). Very often this political goal involved attaining leverage on the Romans, whose presence on the Sasanian western frontier required constant vigilance by the *shahanshahs*. Thus, the position of the king in relation to both internal sectors, such as priests and nobility, and external ones, such as the Romans, depended on political calculations that employed religion to achieve desired outcomes. I am consequently arguing for stronger and more centralised royal control than some others have,[1] partly on the basis of the archaeological record.[2]

The second argument involves how we might more precisely gauge the relationship of kingship and religion in the Sasanian world. That there was an interdependence cannot be denied. But where do we draw the line? Do we deny the close relationship of king and cleric and attribute it to later literary invention, as Gignoux, or embrace it as fundamental to Sasanian royal ideology, as Shaked, who further holds that this ideology required royal control over religious doctrine and practices?[3] I believe the answer lies in between these views. The close relationship of kingship and religion was real but not as later sources depicted it. Whatever religious sentiments any individual Sasanian king may have held – something as impossible to determine as with Constantine – *Realpolitik* should be seen as the fundamental determining factor in the pursuit of Sasanian policy, even when outwardly expressed as the enforcement of a religious doctrine. Thus, for example, the Christianisation of Armenia became a concern for the *shahanshahs* more for its political and strategic consequences than for any doctrinal implications. Religion, however, was the medium through which their policies were given expression, whether or not they felt their official acts also to be pious, and thus control of the religious hierarchies, mainly Zoroastrian and eventually Christian as well, was fundamental to their method.

Aside from the difficulties of our sources, of which space only allows a brief treatment here, we must confront a number of factors that enhance the challenges of the present exercise. They can be listed succinctly as follows: (1) 'policies' determined by individual *shahanshahs*; (2) relations between Romans and Sasanians (diplomatic, military and economic); (3) relations between Sasanian kings and Zoroastrian priests; (4) uncertainties about the cohesion of a Zoroastrian 'church'; (5) relations between Sasanian kings and Persian Christians; and (6) relations between Persian Christians and 'Orthodox' Christians in the Roman Empire. A corollary of numbers (3) and (4) is the fact that Zoroastrianism, and particularly its theology, was not a monolithic phenomenon but probably took on different forms at the hands of the kings, the priests and the general populace. This fact is fundamental to understanding the relationship of the king and the *mobads*. The brands of Zoroastrianism employed may have reflected not only different world views – for example, a purer Avestan ideology versus a mindset that acknowledges the multicultural realities on the ground – but also the sometimes competing interests of the kings and the priests.

THE KING AND ZOROASTRIANISM

A quick look at some of the primary evidence, putting aside late or post-Sasanian material for the moment, reveals how ardently the *shahanshahs* outwardly embraced Zoroastrian doctrine and employed it to cast their policies, achievements and even political position in the appropriate light. The founder Ardashir made clear in his reliefs, most famously at Naqsh-e Rostam,[4] that his rise to power was in accordance with the divine plan of Ohrmazd (Ahura Mazda), from whom he claimed his right to rule over Eranshahr. Ardashir is shown receiving an emblem of power from Ohrmazd while his horse tramples the Arsacid king Artabanus IV, which parallels Ohrmazd's horse trampling Ahriman. In his trilingual inscription from the same location (*ŠKZ*), Ardashir's son Shapur I describes himself as a 'Mazda-worshipping' king who has expanded his rule not only by conquest but by the establishment of sacred fires. The name Eranshahr also had important religious implications, traceable to the Avesta, which added to the legitimacy of the new regime.[5] In his inscription Shapur also cast relations with Rome in Zoroastrian terms when he said that the emperor (probably Philip the Arab) 'lied and did wrong to Armenia',[6] aligning the Romans with the Lie/Chaos (*druy*) and the Sasanians with the Truth/Order (*asha*).[7] 'Mazda-worshipping' also appears on the coins of Ardashir and Shapur, as well as depictions of the fires. In the fifth century, beginning with the coinage of Yazdgerd II, a shift occurred with the removal of *shahanshah Eran* and the addition of *kay*, harking back to the mythical period of the Kayanid kings of the Avesta, which reinforced Yazdgerd's pro-Zoroastrian agenda that would be felt especially acutely in Armenia.[8] A relief from the late period, at Taq-e Bostan, shows Ohrmazd and possibly Anahita investing Khusro II (or possibly Peroz).[9]

Once we get past these public declarations, the situation becomes less simple, partly because of what was happening on the ground and partly due to historiographical issues arising from later Pahlavi, Syriac and Arabic sources. Source interpretation has contributed to an assumption that the royal court and the Zoroastrian hierarchy were, as the *Testament of Ardashir* claims, 'twins', that is to say, working together as a cohesive whole. We find similar attestations in the *Denkard*[10] and the *Letter of Tansar*.[11] All these sources are late or post-Sasanian, but they probably preserve earlier material. The key point here is that most of this material 'came down to us through the channel of the Zoroastrian priesthood'.[12] Shaked's point is essential for understanding the kings' religious policy. The relationship that these sources celebrate was often in reality more antagonistic, primarily because of the kings' policy of blunting any clerical attempt to curb their power. Thus the union claimed by the sources is merely a 'literary theme', a different sort from the association actually employed by the kings, an alliance of king and cleric formed by the former on their terms.[13] In some cases, there may also have been a corresponding aversion to embracing Zoroastrianism, or rather the *mobads*' version of it. If there were in fact at least two strands of Zoroastrianism, one royal and one clerical, we should not be surprised. Even as the religious eclecticism of the Sasanian realm has long been recognised, there is increasing acknowledgement now of the same dynamic within Zoroastrianism itself.[14] We might quickly illustrate this point by considering Shapur I's apparent embrace of Manichaeism.

The status of Mani in Shapur's court has complicated assessments of Shapur's religiosity. Even as he ostensibly espoused Zoroastrianism in his inscriptions, his religious leanings were clearly eclectic. We have an interesting note in the *Denkard* that Shapur was drawn to sources of knowledge beyond Mazdean doctrines.[15] This inquisitiveness probably attracted Shapur to Mani's teachings, which claimed to be a 'reformed Zoroastrianism'.[16] As such Shapur may have seen Manichaeism as an alternative to the more orthodox version. This is mostly supposition, as we cannot know exactly how Shapur perceived Manichaeism or why he found it so attractive, but we must remember, as noted above, that our notions of Zoroastrianism may not match how the Sasanians perceived it.[17] Mani's doctrines may have represented a radical departure from Mazdean tradition, and certainly Kirdir's main interest during and after Shapur's time was to codify and unify Zoroastrianism and tie it more to the state, whereas Manichaeism was more universal in its outlook. But it is possible Shapur understood Manichaeism to be another version of Zoroastrianism.

Still another variant to the orthodoxy of Kirdir and other clerics was the cult of Anahita that the Sasanian royal family maintained at Estakhr. Or at least we can regard this as a variant in the sense that this was more of a family cult than a state religion. Anahita was a water goddess to whom the early Sasanians dedicated the heads of their defeated foes.[18] This shrine was the centre from which Ardashir's father Papak had built his power locally in Fars.[19] This reality stands in contrast to the tradition in the *Denkard* that Ardashir restored the religion of Ahura Mazda after the dark interlude that had begun with Alexander the Great, and that his *mobad* Tansar had gathered the fragments of the Avesta. Tansar's historicity has been questioned, especially as Shapur's *Res Gestae* makes no mention of him. Indeed, Kirdir himself is hardly prominent in Shapur's inscriptions despite his claims in his own later texts that he held supreme authority over Zoroastrians in the empire.[20] Interestingly, this particular divergence in the Zoroastrian tradition took a dramatic turn when the end of Kirdir's supremacy was effectively announced by Ardashir's grandson Narseh through the promotion of Anahita in his Paikuli inscription.[21]

As the cult of Anahita supported Papak and his son's bid for local supremacy in the final years of the Arsacid period, in their claim to be *shahanshah* Ardashir and his successors likewise made astute use of an elaborate religious apparatus. On the practical side this apparatus provided important mechanisms for administering the empire (see next section). No less important were the kings' ideological needs, namely Zoroastrian and later Christian support of the idea of royal supremacy. By way of the renewed Zoroastrian tradition, as Daryaee has noted, the kings managed to cultivate a sense of sacredness and the idea that they were vital to the well-being of the empire. This was achieved in part through their claim of descent from the gods, as in the legends on Ardashir's coins: *shahan shah eran ke čihr az yazdan*, 'King of Kings of *Eran* (Iranians), whose lineage (is) from the gods'. This meant that Ardashir had either elevated his putative ancestor Sasan to divine status or claimed a connection to the gods, the *yazatas*, or both. The claim of a connection to the gods is a specifically Iranian rendering of an old Hellenistic concept going back to Alexander the Great, when royal claims of divine descent were common.[22] The strategy of the later kings, beginning with Yazdgerd II (438–57), changed with the introduction of *kay* into the royal titulature, which connected the kings to the Kayanids of the Avesta. The timing is suggestive: an association with and possible emulation of legendary kings who fought foes in the east as the Sasanians began to confront new dangers on their eastern frontier in the fifth century, with the use of 'Eranshahr' to extend their claim further eastward.[23]

RELIGIOUS ADMINISTRATION OF THE EMPIRE

Just as religion promoted royal legitimacy, centralisation of Sasanian administration strengthened the kings' control of the empire, improving on the Arsacid system of vassal kings. This entailed, for example, the eradication, within the first century of Sasanian rule, of the vassal kings, who were replaced by royal princes and later by *marzpans*; central control of numismatic iconography, an essential propagandistic tool given that coins were an important medium of contact between ruler and subject; and the issuing of royal seals.[24] Other archaeological evidence also reinforces the view of a strong central authority commanding significant resources, with the cooperation of the nobility, which does not always match the characterisation of those who feel the kings were generally weak in the face of recurring noble opposition, as suggested particularly by literary sources.[25] This evidence includes fortresses and fortifications (e.g. the Gorgan Wall), elaborate irrigation systems (e.g. in Mesopotamia and Azerbaijan), and enhanced urbanisation efforts (e.g. Ardashir Khurrah in Fars and Eyvan-e Karkha in Khuzestan).[26]

The multicultural nature of the empire also came to enhance the status of the kings, not only through legitimisation but in administration. At the centre of the elaborate bureaucracy was the king, who exerted control through his relationships with the various groups in power, notably the religious hierarchies who had the training to oversee political, economic and judicial affairs. This power dynamic, widely recognised by scholars, is important for understanding the role of religion in the Sasanian realm, at least as the *shahanshahs* saw it.[27] From such late sources as Ferdowsi's *Shahnama*, supported by Syriac martyrologies along with seals issued by *mobads* and other officials (also attested by Agathias[28]), we learn that Zoroastrian clerics presided over law courts, supervised state finances (including taxation), participated in military campaigns, supervised districts, served as diplomatic emissaries to foreign powers, and so on.[29] From the early fifth century, as we shall see, Christian authorities began to take on some of these responsibilities as well.[30] In the late period, according to the Sasanian law book *Madiyan-e hazar dadistan*, the *mobadan mobad* even issued decrees in his own name, with his own seal, and clearly wielded power comparable to that of the king.[31] In fact an elaborate hierarchy seems to have developed around the *mobadan mobad*, with structures comparable, in Gignoux's mind, to those in the western and eastern Christian churches.[32]

This religious bureaucracy has been interpreted by some as the formation of an organised Zoroastrian church, especially during the dramatic periods of Kirdir (third century) and Mihr Narseh (fifth century). The trend now is to reject this interpretation of the evidence.[33] These controversies have little bearing on the basic argument presented here, that is, the importance of the religious hierarchy, however organised, for royal administration. It bears noting, however, that the apparent free reign granted to Kirdir and Mihr Narseh reminds us that the Zoroastrian clerics had their own agenda, which did not always align with that of the kings. Even the apparent congruence in the outlook of Mihr Narseh and Yazdgerd II does not negate the king's political motivations for the spread of Zoroastrianism (see below).

THE KING AND CHRISTIANITY: ADMINISTRATION

A wide spectrum exists in the scholarship on Persian Christianity in terms of how harmoniously it existed in the Sasanian Empire. A proper starting point for understanding the relationship of the *shahanshahs* and the Christians is the proposition that persecutions were the exception, not the rule, and that their motivations were political. The politics in question involved both domestic affairs, especially the security of the king's position, and foreign, especially relations with the Romans. These persecutions tended to be aimed at elite Christians, whose activities had greater economic and political consequences for the Sasanians. This state of affairs was largely the work of the kings themselves, who began to include Christians in the running of the empire, supplementing the work done by the Mazdean hierarchy.

The Christian presence in Mesopotamia had been steadily growing for centuries, with penetration east of the Tigris perhaps as early as the second century and other movement deeper into Parthian/Persian territory. A major contributing factor to the initial rise of this population was the deportations of Christians by Shapur I after his sack of Antioch and other places in Syria and Cappadocia.[34] By the fifth century, Christianity had made deep inroads into Sasanian society, as attested by frequent Iranian names of clergy and lay officials in official church documents.[35] By the sixth century, if not before, Christians had joined the ranks of the Sasanian aristocracy, along with other newcomers such as the *dehkans*.[36]

More work is still required for a better understanding of how integrated Christians were into Sasanian society, but it seems certain that to some extent Christians experienced an awkward existence in the Sasanian world, partly because of doctrinal differences with Zoroastrianism over treatment of the dead, laws concerning marriage, and so on. Still, as Rist has argued, Christians by and large managed to balance their loyalty to the *shahanshah* and their religious duty. While some of the persecutions resulted from hiccups when Christians fell short of adhering to the former, this state of affairs was not the norm.[37] The material record, moreover, affirms a certain measure of cultural assimilation, as well as an orientation away from Roman Christianity, in theological, liturgical and ideological terms. Such a picture emerges from Stefan Hauser's analysis of the remains of churches (e.g. those at Qasr Serij, Veh Ardashir and Qusair), along with grave styles, as well as seals and other materials, when we see, for instance, Persian Christians eschewing Byzantine architectural styles and depictions of human figures.[38]

Given the enormous presence Christianity came to have, we should not be surprised that the *shahanshahs* saw an opportunity to employ the services of bishops and other officials, especially when it helped to counterbalance the influence of the Zoroastrian hierarchy. Already in the fourth century, bishops were collecting taxes among the Christian communities of Mesopotamia and Khuzestan for the

Sasanian authorities, as we know, for instance, from the East Syriac accounts of the beginning of Shapur II's persecution, which we will deal with more directly below. According to these accounts, the failure of Simeon, bishop of Seleucia-Ctesiphon, to collect a special double tax on the king's Christian subjects led to Simeon's arrest around 340, the matter having some urgency because of the need for revenue in Shapur's Roman wars. Simeon's role in raising revenue was especially important given the primitive status of Sasanian finances in this period, but it anticipates the enhanced role bishops would have in the fiscal and administrative operations of the provinces later.[39]

This enhanced role properly begins with the official organisation of the Church of the East at the Synod of Ctesiphon in 410, presided over by Yazdgerd I, where its structure, procedures and doctrines (including the Nicene Creed) were established.[40] This vitally important development came in a period of, and was partly influenced by, détente between the Romans and the Sasanians. Yazdgerd himself, despite a persecution at the end of his reign (see below), was known for his friendly attitude towards Christianity. Indeed, for this reason, he was described in later sources, including the *Shahnama* and the Arab historians Balkhi, Thaʿalibi and Tabari, as being hostile to the *mobads*, earning him the moniker 'the sinner'.[41] Yazdgerd's good relations with Theodosius II, meanwhile, were fostered by the diplomatic efforts of Marutha, bishop of Sophanene. Indeed, the synod happened because Marutha convinced Yazdgerd to recognise Ishaq, bishop of Seleucia-Ctesiphon, as catholicos, or head of the church.[42] In fact, the primacy of this bishopric served Yazdgerd's purposes. Significantly, the acts of this synod, compiled in the eighth century by the patriarch Timothy I in the *Synodicon Orientale*, draw parallels between Yazdgerd and Constantine. The implication is clear: both leaders sought to enhance their political status by claiming leadership of a powerful religious institution and, no less important, assert universal rule, an interesting appropriation of a Roman claim that may have contributed to the persecutions of Shapur II.[43] Yazdgerd reserved the right to nominate the catholicos and through him exert control of a significant religious apparatus that could reinforce the king's legitimacy among Christians and perform advisory, diplomatic and administrative functions.[44]

In a sense the Church of the East became an even more Persian institution with the schism from the Byzantine church at the Synod of 424 and the embrace of Nestorianism by 484, at the Synod of Beth Lapat. The former meant that the Persian catholicos no longer looked to the Byzantine church for consultation and derived his authority strictly from Christ alone. These developments helped to allay the concerns of most of the *shahanshahs* that Persian Christians might potentially align themselves with the Romans and undermine the Sasanian state.[45]

THE KING AND CHRISTIANITY: PERSECUTION

This state of affairs, however, did not stop persecutions from occurring in the later period. Indeed, the question becomes how we reconcile the increasing reliance on Christian authorities for administration with the periodic persecutions of the fifth to the seventh centuries. Richard Payne challenges the orthodoxy by arguing that the Syriac hagiographers have exaggerated the extent of persecution for the sake of their religious agendas, the reality lying in the realm of pragmatism, as noted in the case of Simeon above.[46] For me pragmatism does indeed help to reconcile the paradox, for the kings only persecuted when it was in their immediate political interests to do. Sometimes this meant bowing to clerical pressure, as with Yazdgerd I, who reversed his stance on Christianity when violence against fire temples forced him to persecute. He was left with no choice, given that the fire temples were important for the functioning of the state as they formed part of the economic and social power of the aristocracy.[47] Likewise, in his dealings with the catholicos Mar Aba, Khusro I had to walk a fine line. On the one hand, Khusro made significant use of the church hierarchy, personally liked Aba, and sought to protect him from the Mazdean clerics. However, Aba was accused of collaborating with the Romans, an accusation that could not be taken lightly given the war that had started in 540. Thus in 542 Aba was removed from office, though he was only exiled rather than killed.[48]

Already near the beginning of the Sasanian engagement with Christians, royal motivation lay in politics. We noted Shapur I's deportations of Christians from sacked Roman cities above, but it bears noting that these moves were not made out of any religious hostility to Christians. For Shapur, these deportees were sources of excellent labour to develop newly founded cities, such as Gondeshapur in Khuzestan and Bishapur in Fars. In fact, according to the *Chronicle of Seert*,[49] Christians in these areas thrived on the lands given to them to develop.[50]

Constantine's conversion to Christianity overshadows most discussions of the first major sequence of persecutions, conducted by Shapur II from c. 340 to the end of his reign in 379. With Christianity now embraced by the Roman Empire, the fear was that Persian Christians might constitute a fifth column in the Sasanian realm.[51] There are many uncertainties about whether Constantine's letter to Shapur II, recorded by Eusebius,[52] is genuine;[53] whether Shapur received it or any other communication articulating Constantine's claim to protect all Christians in the world; and, if so, what the king would have made of it.[54] But whether or not Shapur's concern of a Christian menace in his empire can be traced at all to any correspondence with Constantine, many scholars, as far back as Christensen, recognise that Shapur's concern was not religious or doctrinal but political. To start with, his religious leanings seemed not very anchored, as he re-established the family cult of Anahita in Estakhr and possibly embraced Zurvanism in addition to championing the official Mazdean orthodoxy. Additionally, the 'great persecution' seemed not to apply to the Jewish elements in the Sasanian world.[55]

We noted earlier that Shapur turned against the Christians upon the refusal of Bishop Simeon to collect a special tax for the state. In about 340, Simeon was arrested, and it is likely that the persecutions were limited at this point. Decret has noted a synchronism in 344 between Simeon's execution and Constantius' capture of Singara, an unfortunate (for the Sasanians) development in the continuing drama of the Roman frontier. Decret suggests that the former was partly motivated by the latter and that at this point Shapur stepped up the persecutions.[56] To this we might add another bit of evidence for the political dimension of the 'great persecution'. The anxiety Shapur felt about Christianity can be measured especially by the strategic implications of not only Constantine's conversion but that of Tiridates IV of Armenia in 314. That Armenia should officially become Christian was troubling mainly because such a transformation aligned it with the Romans even more than before.[57] The importance of Armenia to Shapur is amply demonstrated in his response to Constantius' offer of peace in 356: among the most important terms Shapur insisted on was the restoration of Armenia and other territories taken in the Treaty of Nisibis, which was forced upon Narseh in 298 and which Shapur now described, in Ammianus' rendering, as a *composita fraude*.[58] The recovery of Armenia was a high priority for Shapur, and this state of affairs provides the proper context in which to assess the 'great persecution'. Because of Shapur's anti-Christian stance, as Decret has observed, the conflict with Rome 'took on the *appearance* of a war of religions' ('prenait l'*allure* d'une guerre de religions') (my emphasis).[59]

I believe the same dynamic is in play in the massive effort by Yazdgerd II to promote Zoroastrianism in the Sasanian realm as well as Armenia. The latter venture has made Yazdgerd one of the great villains in Armenian historiography, which lionised Vardan Mamikonean and other Armenian Christians who resisted the Sasanians' attempt to suppress Christianity in 451. The architect of this endeavour was Yazdgerd's vizier (*hazarbed*), Mihr Narseh, a member of the powerful Suren clan who had also served Yazdgerd I and Bahram V. In addition to his religious and administrative duties Mihr Narseh served as a general. He was evidently an ardent partisan of the Zurvanite version of Zoroastrianism, which he tried to impose on the Armenians.[60] As for Yazdgerd II, we have a curious paucity of coverage in the Arabic and Persian material, with emphasis on his personal piety and on tensions with the Persian nobility,[61] while the Armenian and Syriac sources make him into a religious zealot; this tradition has made its way into much modern scholarship, beginning with Labourt.[62]

But it is not Yazdgerd's religiosity that best explains his persecution of Christians and Jews in the empire. Control of Armenia continued to be important for securing the Roman frontier, but even more pressing for Yazdgerd was heightened internal instability, including strained relations with the nobility, and the changing situation in the east. We noted above the change in his royal titulature, with the addition of *kay*, invoking the legendary Avestan kings, the Kayanids, who also confronted great challenges in the east. By the fifth century that challenge was a formidable Hunnic confederation which inflicted a series of defeats on Yazdgerd at the beginning of his reign. It is significant that Yazdgerd's moves against the Christians did not begin until his eighth year. According to the Armenian chronicler Łazar P'arpets'i[63] and the Syriac *History of Karka de Beth Selok*, Yazdgerd blamed the Christians for his defeats in the east, apparently because Armenian and Iberian nobles provided much of his cavalry. He began the persecutions by trying to force Christian nobles at Karka to convert to Zoroastrianism. Our main Armenian sources for the revolt of 451 note that Yazdgerd made the same demands of the nobility in Armenia and Iberia.[64] Indeed, of Yazdgerd's persecutions of non-Zoroastrians it is important to point out that they were in fact generally limited, with the noble ranks receiving the brunt, despite Mihr Narseh's poisonous rhetoric about the evils of Christianity. Yazdgerd's main purpose was to counter the internal and external pressures threatening the empire by enhancing royal centralisation in the administration, which required cooperation from the nobility. It was important to establish the terms on which the nobles and priests were to yield to royal authority.[65] This is the reason why Yazdgerd eventually moderated his stance towards

Armenia and through the new *marzpan* Atrormizd Arshakan (i.e. Adhur-Hormizd) allowed religious freedom there for the sake of stability,[66] a position hardly compatible with one taken by a religious zealot. Zoroastrian belief, as McDonough points out, may have been a 'test of personal loyalty' for Yazdgerd,[67] but I do not believe we are dealing with the same motives as in the case of Mihr Narseh.

CONCLUSION

We might conclude with an obversation has that lurked behind much of the foregoing discussion. The persecutions, especially when pursued by the *shahanshahs*, were usually aimed at a focused segment of the Christian populace: the nobility. And to be sure, both Mazdean *mobads* and Christian bishops generally hailed from this sector of society. Whether Zoroastrian or Christian, these officials were essential for the functioning and security of society and, just as important, for promotion of royal legitimacy. The case has been made, I hope, that while religion certainly played an important role in these matters, for the kings it was a means to an end. As a general rule, we may posit contrasting views and uses of Zoroastrianism between the kings and the clerics, the latter usually fostering more genuine religious concerns. Whatever personal piety the kings may have felt, their use of religion was informed by the realities arising from their relations with the nobility and from their relations (friendly and hostile) with the powers on their frontiers, especially the Roman. Both Zoroastrianism and Christianity served the kings well, and when they did not the kings took measures that one should hesitate to regard as indications of their religiosity.

ABBREVIATIONS

ANRm   Relief of Ardashir I at Naqsh-e Rostam
DkM   *Denkard* (ed. Madan)
KKZ   Inscription of Kirdir from the Ka'be-ye Zardosht
PO   *Patrologia Orientalis*
ŠKZ   Inscription of Shapur I the from Ka'be-ye Zardosht

NOTES

1 For example, Pourshariati 2008: 455–6; Rubin 2008: 153–5.
2 See especially Payne 2014.
3 Gignoux 1984; Shaked 1990: 263.

4 *ANRm* I
5 Wiesehöfer 2001: 165–7; Gnoli 1989: 137–9.
6 *ŠKZ* 10.
7 Daryaee 2013: 16.
8 Shayegan 2013: 808–9; Daryaee 2013: 17.
9 Daryaee 2009: 106; Schippmann 1990: 97.
10 E.g. *DkM* 3.58.
11 Gignoux 1984: 72–6; Kreyenbroek 2013: 20–2.
12 Shaked 2008: 105.
13 Gignoux 1984: 80; cf. Shaked 1994: 112–13; Gnoli 1989: 138 no. 13.
14 Pourshariati 2008: 324–6; Gnoli 1989: 167–74. In fact there was even greater complexity (the doctrine of Zurvanism comes to mind, for instance), as well as the likely condition that Zoroastrianism only penetrated upper levels of Sasanian society, with a freer flow of other traditions among the wider classes. 'One must assume that constant Zoroastrian references to the various strata of society that comprise the ordered, harmonious whole are mere wishful thinking' (Russell 1986: 128).
15 *DkM* 412, 17–413, 2.
16 Hutter 1993: 6, cf. Duchesne-Guillemin 1983: 879.
17 See further Kreyenbroek 2008: 7; Shaked 2008: 104.
18 Tabari, *Ta'rikh* 1.819.
19 Schippmann 1990: 92–3.
20 Rubin 2008: 140–1. This matter is uncertain. In his own inscription on the Ka'be-ye Zardosht, Kirdir claims to have had authority over all Zoroastrian officials and affairs throughout the empire in the time of Shapur (*KKZ* 1–2). But he only issued these inscriptions during the reign of Bahram II (276–93), when Kirdir held significant power as a *mobad*. In Shapur's *Res Gestae* Kirdir is only listed as a *herbed*, following a lengthy roll of officials, with no indication of significant responsibility (*ŠKZ* 34 [Pers.], 28 [Parth.]). See further Kreyenbroek 2013: 28–30.
21 Daryaee 2009: 13.
22 Daryaee 2013: 13–15.
23 Shayegan 2013: 807; Daryaee 2013: 17.
24 McDonough 2005: 141–69.
25 To be sure the 'strength' of the *shahanshahs* fluctuated over time, but the question becomes whether this at least partially results from historical circumstances rather than a structural flaw in the system that compromised the position of the kings. This of course is not the place to attempt a resolution, except where religion informs the matter. See further Payne 2014: 4–5, *contra* Pourshariati 2008: 455–6; Rubin 2008: 153–5.
26 Payne 2014: 4–6.
27 Payne 2015: 41; Shaked 1994: 109–10; McDonough 2011: 298.
28 Agathias, *Histories* 2.26.5.
29 Shaked 1990: 268–71; Daryaee 2009: 127–33.
30 Greatrex 2003: 80.
31 Shaked 1990: 269; cf. Gignoux 1984: 78.
32 Gignoux 1983: 258–9.
33 See, for example, Schippmann 1990: 92–3; Rubin 2008: 140–4; Wiesehöfer 2001: 211–13; Hauser 2008: 33.

34 Baum and Winkler 2003: 8–9; Hage 1973: 174–5; cf. Brock 1982: 3.
35 Asmussen 1983: 942.
36 McDonough 2011: 307.
37 Rist 1996: 41–2.
38 Hauser 2007; 2008.
39 Payne 2015: 40–1.
40 In general see Labourt 1904: 92–9; Wood 2012: 58–62; Baum and Winkler 2003: 14–17; Hage 1973: 181–2.
41 Pourshariati 2008: 66; Asmussen 1983: 939–40.
42 Blockley 1992: 48–9; Wood 2012: 58–9. As Blockley has noted, Marutha's Persian diplomacy is well documented. For sources, see Blockley 1992: 196 no. 19.
43 McDonough 2008: 130; Wood 2012: 59; Decret 1979: 150.
44 McDonough 2011: 304–5; Wood 2012: 60.
45 Asmussen 1983: 944–5; Greatrex 2003: 79–80; Hage 1973: 183.
46 Payne 2015: 23–58.
47 McDonough 2008: 131–4; Payne 2015: 47–8.
48 Maksymiuk 2015: 126; Brock 1982: 5.
49 *PO* 4.3, II: 220–3.
50 Decret 1979: 104–5, 110; Rist 1996: 26.
51 Brock 1982: 7–8; Alinia 2008: 53–4; Labourt 1904: 44.
52 Eusebius, *Vita Constantini* 4.9–13.
53 For a useful summary of the main arguments, see Frendo 2001.
54 Cf. Barnes 1985: 136.
55 Christensen 1944: 250; Duchesne-Guillemin 1983: 886; Schippmann 1990: 95.
56 Decret 1979: 145–7.
57 Decret 1979: 138–9; Rist 1996: 30–1.
58 Ammianus Marcellinus 17.5.
59 Decret 1979: 138–9.
60 Pourshariati 2008: 60–2; McDonough 2005: 75; Duchesne-Guillemin 1983: 891.
61 Pourshariati 2008: 70.
62 Labourt 1904: 126–30; Asmussen 1983: 942.
63 Łazar 87 = 2.48.
64 Łazar 43–4 = 2.21–2; Ełishē 17–18 pp.71–2; McDonough 2006: 74; Rist 1996: 34.
65 McDonough 2006: 75–81; Payne 2015: 45–6.
66 Łazar 73 = 2.40; Garsoïan 2004: 347.
67 McDonough 2006: 81.

BIBLIOGRAPHY

Alinia, S. (2008), 'Zoroastrianism and Christianity in the Sasanian Empire (Fourth Century AD)', in S. M. Reza Darbandi and A. Zournatzi (eds), *Ancient Greece and Ancient Iran: Cross-Cultural Encounters*, Athens: National Hellenic Research Foundation, pp. 53–8.

Asmussen, J. P. (1983), 'Christians in Iran', in E. Yarshater (ed.), *The Cambridge*

History of Iran: The Seleucid, Parthian, and Sasanian Periods, 3.2, Cambridge: Cambridge University Press, pp. 924–49.

Barnes, T. D. (1985), 'Constantine and the Christians of Persia', Journal of Roman Studies, 75, pp. 126–36.

Baum, W. and Winkler, D. W. (2003), The Church of the East: A Concise History, London: Routledge.

Blockley, R. C. (1992), East Roman Foreign Policy: Formation and Conduct from Diocletian to Anastasius, ARCA 30, Leeds: Francis Cairns.

Brock, S. P. (1982), 'Christians in the Sasanian Empire: A Case of Divided Loyalties', Studies in Church History, 18, pp. 1–19.

Christensen, A. (1944), L'Iran sous les Sassanides, Copenhagen: E. Munksgaard.

Daryaee, T. (2009), Sasanian Persia: The Rise and Fall of an Empire, London: I.B.Tauris.

Daryaee, T. (2013), 'Sasanian Kingship, Empire and Glory: Aspects of Iranian Imperium', in V. Naddaf, F. Goshtasb and M. Shokri-Foumeshi (eds), Ranj-o-Ganj: Papers in Honour of Professor Z. Zarshenas, Tehran: Institute for Humanities and Cultural Studies, pp. 11–22.

Decret, F. (1979), 'Les conséquences sur le christianisme en Perse de l'affrontement des empires romain et sassanide: de Shâpûr Ier à Yazdgard Ier', Recherches Augustiniennes, 14, pp. 91–152.

Duchesne-Guillemin, J. (1983), 'Zoroastrian Religion', in E. Yarshater (ed.), The Cambridge History of Iran: The Seleucid, Parthian, and Sasanian Periods, 3.2, Cambridge: Cambridge University Press, pp. 866–908.

Frendo, D. (2001), 'Constantine's Letter to Shapur II: Its Authenticity, Occasion, and Attendant Circumstances', Bulletin of the Asia Institute, 15, pp. 57–69.

Garsoïan, N. (2004), 'Frontier-Frontiers? Transcaucasia and Eastern Anatolia in the Pre-Islamic Period', in A. Carile (ed.), La Persia e Bisanzio: convegno internazionale (Roma, 14–18 ottobre 2002), Atti dei convegni Lincei 201, Rome: Accademia nazionale dei Lincei, pp. 327–52.

Gignoux, P. (1983), 'Die religiöse Administration in sasanidischer Zeit: Ein Überblick', in H. Koch and D. N. MacKenzie (eds), Kunst, Kultur und Geschichte der Achamenidenzeit und ihr Fortleben, Berlin: Reimer, pp. 253–66.

Gignoux, P. (1984), 'Church–State Relations in the Sasanian Period', Bulletin of the Middle Eastern Culture Center in Japan, 1, pp. 72–80.

Gnoli, G. (1989), The Idea of Iran: An Essay on Its Origin, Serie Orientale Roma LXII, Rome: Istituto Italiano per il Medio ed Estremo Oriente.

Greatrex, G. (2003), 'Khusro II and the Christians of His Empire', Journal of the Canadian Society for Syriac Studies, 3, pp. 78–88.

Hage, W. (1973), 'Die oströmische Staatskirche und die Christenheit des Perserreiches', Zeitschrift für Kirchengeschichte, 84, pp. 174–87.

Hauser, S. R. (2007), 'Christliche Archäologie im Sasanidenreich: Grundlagen der Interpretation und Bestandsaufnahme der Evidenz', in A. Mustafa, J. Tubach and G. S. Vashalomidze (eds), Inkulturation des Christentums im Sasanidenreich, Wiesbaden: Reichert, pp. 93–136.

Hauser, S. R. (2008), '"Die Christen vermehrten sich in Persien und bauten Kirchen und Klöster": Eine Archäologie des Christentums im Sasanidenreich', in U. Koenen and M. Müller-Wiener (eds), Grenzgänge im östlichen

Mittelmeerraum: Byzanz und die islamische Welt vom 9. bis 13. Jahrhundert, Wiesbaden: Reichert, pp. 29–64.
Hutter, M. (1993), 'Manichaeism in the Early Sasanian Empire', *Numen*, 40.1, pp. 2–15.
Kreyenbroek, P. G. (2008), 'How Pious was Shapur I? Religion, Church, and Propaganda under the Early Sasanians', in V. Sarkhosh Curtis and S. Stewart (eds), *The Sasanian Era*, Idea of Iran 3, London and New York: I.B. Tauris, pp. 7–16.
Kreyenbroek, P. G. (2013), 'Zoroastrianism under the Sasanians', in K. Rezania (ed.), *Teachers and Teachings in the Good Religion: Opera Minora on Zoroastrianism*, Wiesbaden: Harrassowitz, pp. 19–50.
Labourt, J. (1904), *Le christianisme dans l'empire perse sous la dynastie sassanide (224–632)*, Paris: Lecoffre.
McDonough, S. (2005), 'Power By Negotiation: Institutional Reform in the Fifth Century Sasanian Empire', PhD thesis, UCLA.
McDonough, S. (2006), 'A Question of Faith? Persecution and Political Centralization in the Sasanian Empire of Yazdgard II (438–457 CE)', in H. A. Drake (ed.), *Violence in Late Antiquity: Perceptions and Practices*, Aldershot: Ashgate, pp. 69–81.
McDonough, S. (2008), 'A Second Constantine? The Sasanian King Yazdgard in Christian History and Historiography', *Journal of Late Antiquity*, 1.1, pp. 127–41.
McDonough, S. (2011), 'The Legs of the Throne: Kings, Elites, and Subjects in Sasanian Iran', in J. P. Arnason and K. A. Raaflaub (eds), *The Roman Empire in Context: Historical and Comparative Perspectives*, Chichester: Wiley-Blackwell, pp. 290–321.
Maksymiuk, K. (2015), 'Die Politik von Xusrō I. Anōšīrvān (531–579) gegenüber Christen in dem Iran', *Historia i Świat*, 4, pp. 123–34.
Payne, R. E. (2014), 'The Archaeology of Sasanian Politics', *Journal of Ancient History*, 2.2, pp. 1–13.
Payne, R. E. (2015), *A State of Mixture: Christians, Zoroastrians, and Iranian Political Culture in Late Antiquity*, Oakland: University of California Press.
Pourshariati, P. (2008), *Decline and Fall of the Sasanian Empire: The Sasanian-Parthian Confederacy and the Arab Conquest of Iran*, London: I.B. Tauris.
Rist, J. (1996), 'Die Verfolgung der Christen im spätantiken Sasanidenreich: Ursachen, Verlauf und Folgen', *Oriens Christianus*, 80, pp. 17–42.
Rubin, Z. (2008), 'Persia and the Sasanian Monarchy (224–651)', in J. Shepard (ed.), *The Cambridge History of the Byzantine Empire: c.500–1492*, Cambridge: Cambridge University Press, pp. 130–55.
Russell, J. R. (1986), 'Zoroastrianism as the State Religion of Ancient Iran', *Journal of the K. R. Cama Oriental Institute*, 53: 74–142. (Reprinted in Russell, J. R., *Armenian and Iranian Studies*, HATS 9, Cambridge: Harvard University Press, 2004, pp. 65–133.)
Schippmann, K. (1990), *Grundzüge der Geschichte des Sasanidischen Reiches*, Darmstadt: Wissenschaftliche Buchgesellschaft.
Shaked, S. (1990), 'Administrative Functions of Priests in the Sasanian Period', in G. Gnoli and A. Panaino (eds), *Proceedings of the First European Conference of Iranian Studies, Held in Turin, September 7th–11th, 1987 by the Societas*

Iranologica Europea, part 1, Rome: Istituto Italiano per il Medio ed Estremo Oriente, pp. 261–73.

Shaked, S. (1994), *Dualism in Transformation: Varieties of Religion in Sasanian Iran*, London: School of Oriental and African Studies, University of London.

Shaked, S. (2008), 'Religion in the Late Sasanian Period: Eran, Aneran, and Other Religious Designations', in V. Sarkhosh Curtis and S. Stewart (eds), *The Sasanian Era*, Idea of Iran 3, London and New York: I.B. Tauris, pp. 103–17.

Shayegan, M. R. (2013), 'Sasanian Political Ideology', in D. T. Potts, *The Oxford Handbook of Ancient Iran*, Oxford: Oxford University Press, pp. 805–13.

Wiesehöfer, J. (2001), *Ancient Persia from 550 BC to 650 AD*, London: I.B. Tauris.

Wood, P. (2012), 'Collaborators and Dissidents: Christians in Sasanian Iraq in the Early Fifth Century', in T. Bernheimer and A. Silverstein (eds), *Late Antiquity: Eastern Perspectives*, Exeter: Gibb Memorial Trust, pp. 57–70.

9 A Contested Jurisdiction: Armenia in Late Antiquity

Tim Greenwood

Although Roman and Persian engagement with late antique Armenia has been analysed from several perspectives, its juridical dimension has been largely ignored. This chapter provides a reassessment of the legislation pertaining to Roman Armenia from the reign of Justinian, arguing that it offers a reflection of legal practices operating beyond the newly reorganised Roman provinces, in districts of Armenia under Persian hegemony. It may also attest the seeping of Roman legal culture beyond the formal limits of the jurisdiction. Crucially, the local inheritance practices which the legislation prescribes find analogues in Sasanian jurisprudence. Although not every aspect of Persian legal culture will have been replicated in the districts of Armenia or received in the same way, the rich Armenian literary tradition from late antiquity reveals a proximate legal culture, expressed in terms of concepts employed and processes followed. Three illustrations from Łazar P'arpets'i *History* are examined. Furthermore two later compilations preserve valuable evidence of law in practice. The tenth-century compilation titled *History of Ałuank'* contains a collection of documents deriving from the Council of Partav convened in 705 CE. One of these confirms that land across Caucasian Albania was still being bought and sold at this time, that there was current uncertainty over whether the transfer of a village included the village church and its endowment, and that laymen had been represented as holding clerical status to circumvent this. A specific case is then outlined. The late thirteenth-century *History of Siwnik'* on the other hand contains transcripts of fifty-two documents, and summaries of twelve more, recording property transactions in favour of the bishops of Siwnik' and the see of Tat'ev. It is argued that the earliest of these, dating from the middle of the ninth century, preserve clear vestiges of Sasanian legal culture. Armenian sources have much to tell us about law and legal tradition in Sasanian Persia.

Armenia was wholly partitioned between the 'great powers' of Rome and Persia throughout late antiquity. Although the manner and the degree of intrusion on the part of the two imperial powers may have fluctuated over the course of the two centuries following the eclipse of the Arsacid kingdom in 428 CE, every district of Armenia was under the hegemony of one or the other. There was no neutral space, no gap between them into which an independent Armenia might be squeezed. We need to be reminded of this because the rich Armenian literary tradition frequently projects an alternative landscape, an Armenia comprising a single people united around a single confession of faith, inhabiting their own land and relating to those same powers of Rome and Persia in the manner of a sovereign nation. Although this singular construction exercised a powerful influence on Armenian historical memory – and continues to do so today – it obscured a very different reality. Not only was late antique Armenia plural, contradictory and volatile, a world of rival local lordships, of different expressions of Christian doctrine, practice and cult, of multiple historical traditions, even of different forms of spoken Armenian; by virtue of its partition, it was also exposed to Roman and Persian systems of government and administration.[1] The regions of historic Armenia encountered and responded to the evolving institutions and practices of both empires on an individual basis. For much of the fifth and sixth centuries, approximately four-fifths of historic Armenia fell under Persian control, with only those districts to the west of the upper Euphrates fully incorporated into Roman provincial structures. From the last quarter of the sixth century, however, the balance of power across Armenia fluctuated, as a result of both negotiated settlements and military action, and this unstable state of affairs persisted until the first Arab raiders crossed into Armenia from the Jazira in autumn 640. Armenian reception of imperial traditions, therefore, was far from a straightforward or singular process.

Several aspects of Roman and Persian engagement with late antique Armenia have been traced in previous scholarship.[2] The heroic resistance led by Vardan Mamikonean to the imposition of Zoroastrian practices and beliefs by an impious Persian *shahanshah*, Yazdgerd II, which culminated in defeat at the battle of Avarayr in 451 CE, quickly became central to Christian Armenian memory and tradition. This episode, together with the conversion of King Trdat by Grigor the Illuminator at the start of the fourth century, has been studied repeatedly. We should recall, however, that Garsoïan's meticulous examination of the Armenian church in late antiquity also reveals the intrusion of dyophysite challenges from east and west in the course of the fifth, sixth and early seventh centuries; there was much more to Armenian Christianity than Grigor, Trdat and Vardan, significant though they were.[3] Research has also been conducted into how members of the elite were drawn into closer relationship with the great powers, through the award of titles, offices and gifts, and how this enabled Armenian military manpower to be exploited for service on distant frontiers.[4] Finally, there has been some study of the respective provincial structures which overlaid the districts of Armenia, and in particular how the Roman network changed over time; there has been less work on how the Sasanian administration evolved, although there is strong evidence to indicate that it did.[5] To date, however, there has been little in the way of sustained investigation into Armenian jurisprudence and the legal culture, or cultures, which operated across Armenia in late antiquity. Yet since Armenia was wholly partitioned between Rome and Persia in late antiquity, we need to consider the extent to which these twin powers introduced their own legal and judicial traditions, to what purposes and with what results. Late antique Armenia was not only the locus for military, social and cultural competition between the great powers; as we shall see, it was also contested from a juridical perspective.

Let us start by examining the situation of those districts of Armenia under Roman control. Adontz demonstrated in his magisterial study that the provincial reorganisation undertaken at the start of the reign of Justinian was intended to transform the districts of Roman Armenia.[6] For our purposes, it is highly significant that the three pieces of relevant legislation describe both the circumstances prevailing at the time and the new structures, processes and principles being instituted. All three therefore offer an impression of the present state of affairs and a vision of the future.

The first of the three is *Novella XXXI*, dated 18 March 536 CE and addressed to John, most honoured praetorian prefect of the east, second among the *hypatoi* and *patrikioi*. This *Novella* created four new provinces of Armenia. They extended over districts which had hitherto been treated in different ways by the Roman state. The new province of Fourth Armenia, for example, covered land which had not previously been included in the network of provinces but had been settled by various nations, bearing different barbarian names: Tzophanene and Anzitene and Tzophene and Asthianene and Balabitene, under satraps; the name of such a ruler was neither Roman nor known to our ancestors but had been established by the other *politeia*.[7]

This can only be referring to Persia, although the failure to identify it openly as a rival source of political authority is significant. Fourth Armenia overlay districts which had hitherto been outside the Roman provincial framework, and hence beyond the purview of Roman law. By way of contrast, the new Second Armenia was created largely, although not exclusively, from the former First Armenia, and the new Third Armenia seems to have mirrored the former Second Armenia. These regions had been incorporated long before into the Roman provincial network and so had been situated within the limits of Roman jurisprudence.

Two features of *Novella XXXI* merit particular comment. In the first place, the boundaries of three of the four new provinces were defined in terms of cities and their territories. First Armenia had Justinianopolis as its metropolis, together with six other named cities; Second Armenia contained Sebasteia together with four other cities; and Third Armenia included the metropolis of Melitene together with four other cities. By contrast, Fourth Armenia was described in terms of the five satrapies, the city of Martyropolis and the newly constructed fortress of Kitharizon. It was conceptualised therefore in very different terms, as a province without cities. Although Fourth Armenia did contain several historic centres of settlement, such as Angł, which might have qualified as cities, these were left out of the definition. But it could be that its lack of urban centres was intended to be a metaphor for its lack of Romanitas, a cultural as much as a sociological comment. As Maas has noted, the intended audience for the *Novellae* was Roman, both in Constantinople and in the provinces.[8] Secondly, the juridical status of each province was established unequivocally. The governors of First Armenia and Third Armenia were defined as *spectabiles*, the former under the most magnificent *anthypatos*, Acacius, the latter under the Justinianic count, Thomas. The governors of Second Armenia and Fourth Armenia, however, were *ordinarii*. Appeals from Second Armenia in cases worth up to five hundred *solidi* went up to the *anthypatos* in Justinianopolis for final adjudication; appeals from Fourth Armenia in cases with the same limit went up to the Justinianic count in Melitene for final adjudication.[9] Although no evidence of this appellate system survives, these provisions confirm that Roman law was intended to operate across all four provinces, that there was, at least in principle, no space for the continuing operation of existing traditions.[10]

The second of the legal instruments, *Novella XXI*, came into force on the same day as *Novella XXXI*, 18 March 536, and was addressed to the most magnificent Acacius, *anthypatos* of Armenia. It was titled 'Concerning the Armenians, that they should follow the laws of the Romans in everything' and confirmed that there should be no laws among them apart from those which the Romans enacted.[11] Roman law was therefore to be exclusive. Two specific practices were highlighted and repudiated: first, that 'inheritance from parents, brothers and other relatives should no longer be to men alone and never to women, a barbaric custom', but should be equal in all cases, the same for women as for men; and second, that women should not be married without dowries. Although the nature of the assets transferred by inheritance are not described in the prologue, the second chapter of the *Novella*, confirming that the legislation was to come into force from the start of the present fourteenth indiction, stipulated that women should not be treated as sharers in patrimonial estates already divided or inheritances which had taken place in or before the thirteenth indiction.

It has long been recognised that through this legislation, Justinian was trying to subvert customary Armenian inheritance practices and undermine the power of the noble families by precipitating the breakup of the family landholdings. But there are two other features of this enactment which hold particular significance for this chapter. In the first place, the prologue acknowledges that 'this extreme barbarism has been performed among them up to the present day'. This implies a precise knowledge of current inheritance traditions among the Armenian elite, including those newly located within the Roman provincial framework. The prologue goes on to observe that these very harsh customs were not limited to them but 'that other nations acted in a similarly disdainful manner towards nature and had insulted the female sex as if it were not created by God'. The most natural interpretation of this phrase 'other nations' is that it refers to other Armenian princely houses presently situated outside Roman control, in districts of Armenia under Persian control. If they had been located inside the Roman Empire, they would have been subject to Roman laws on inheritance and dowries. That these nations were represented as persisting in their traditions indicates that they were located beyond the present reach of Roman law. Therefore this *Novella* not only reflects the input of someone conversant with present legal traditions, in all likelihood one of the members of the Armenian elite; it also sketches in pejorative terms the encounter between Roman and Persian jurisprudence, for, as noted above, there was no separate Armenian 'space' between the two imperial powers.

The third of the legal regulations comprises an edict or decree preserved in the *Codex Justinianus*, titled 'Concerning the Order of Inheritance of the Armenians' and dated in one manuscript to 1 August 535.[12] In content, there is a considerable overlap with *Novella XXI*, save in one key respect. The edict prescribed that its provisions were to have retrospective force, being effective from the accession of Justinian. The *Novella*, however, provides that its regulations were to be effective from the present fourteenth indiction. As Adontz noted, there can be no doubt that the edict predated, and was partly superseded by, *Novella XXI*.[13] Nevertheless its provisions merit consideration. The prologue reads as follows: 'We want the Armenians to be delivered from their former injustices, to transfer them to our laws in everything and to give to them fitting equality.' The first chapter continues:

> When we learned recently about a certain barbarous and harsh law among them, appropriate neither for Romans nor for the proper justice of our *politeia*, insomuch as men may inherit from their fathers but never women, for this reason we decree through the promulgating of this divine law, to your Magnificence, that succession is to be equal and concerning those matters arranged in the laws of the Romans concerning men and women, all are to prevail in Armenia; for it is on account of this that our laws have been sent down there, for the administering of them.

The final substantive section reads:

> We decree that women shall share in the declared patrimonial estates from the said date. If nevertheless it happens that certain ones are discovered, those who have written all the same that their daughters are to inherit, those who are not included in the intestate succession, then they, and the children born from them, shall have a share in the inheritance of the patrimonial things.

The edict contains several intriguing features. It is not clear exactly to whom it was addressed, although Adontz's suggestion that it was the praetorian prefect of the east, John, rather than Acacius or Thomas, seems more likely. The circumstances in which it was promulgated are not recorded, although the opening words, 'When we learned recently', imply that a concrete case involving a conflict of law had reached the emperor.[14] The issue of what is meant by Armenia and the Armenians is harder to determine. Accepting that it dates from before the full provincial reorganisation described in *Novella XXXI*, it seems improbable that it was directed specifically to the districts of *Armenia Minor*, Lesser Armenia, since these had been divided into the old provinces of First and Second Armenia in the later fourth century under Theodosius I and so had experienced Roman legal tradition for the past century and a half. Having excluded *Armenia Minor*, we are left with *Armenia Magna*, Greater Armenia, sometimes called Interior Armenia, that part of the Arsacid kingdom which fell under Roman hegemony in c. 387 CE and which was governed by the *Comes Armeniae*, or the five satrapies, discussed above. It is unlikely that this issue will be resolved because aspects of the edict seem to point in opposite directions. On the one hand, the tone of the edict implies the recent despatch of Roman law, suggesting it had not been available and accessible previously; this supports the argument that the edict was drafted with the satrapies in mind. On the other hand, the final sentence of the edict, cited above, clearly envisages that some members of the elite had already tried to write testaments leaving a share of their patrimony to their daughters, in contravention of the prevailing custom of intestate succession which was limited to male heirs. This might seem to favour the identification of Interior Armenia, but it is conceivable that some in the satrapies had already begun to adopt practices of Roman law, including the making of a written will disposing of their assets as they wished, before the districts had been incorporated as Fourth Armenia. If so, this would be evidence for the seeping of Roman legal practice beyond the formal limits of Roman jurisdiction. In any event, whether the edict was intended to operate across Interior Armenia, or the satrapies, or both, the situation was short-lived. Within a year, the two *Novellae* had transformed the provincial structure and Roman jurisprudence was established as the only competent authority, at least from a Roman perspective. With regret, lack of evidence prevents us from seeing how these changes were implemented, or how they were received or negotiated.

From the above, it is clear that these local inheritance practices had been followed in the satrapies and perhaps in Interior Armenia for generations, in all likelihood since the end of the fourth century. To what extent they were 'Armenian', however, is less certain. It was suggested above that the 'other nations' who followed these traditions were Armenian noble families settled beyond the frontier in Persian-controlled Armenia. The persistence of these traditions may reflect a light-touch approach to provincial administration on the part of the Persian authorities, similar to the manner in which the satrapies had been treated. But it could reflect a different dynamic, one which found a much closer correspondence between Armenian and Persian legal traditions. Could it be that Armenian legal culture in late antiquity was closely aligned to Persian jurisprudence?

If we examine once again the four principles and practices picked out for specific criticism in the Justinianic legislation – inheritance restricted to men from their fathers and never women; the notion of the patrimonial or family estate; a system of intestate succession as the norm; and the lack of a dowry – we find close parallels in Sasanian jurisprudence. Macuch has proposed that only a freeborn man above the age of fifteen who was a subject of the *shahanshah* and a citizen of Eranshahr, confessing Zoroastrianism and belonging to a noble family, had full legal capacity.[15] A legitimate son stood in direct succession to his father and was heir not only to his property but also to his name and genealogical status, his standing in the community and his rank, *gah*, in society. Conversely a woman never gained full legal capacity, remaining under the legal guardianship of her father, brother, uncle or other male relative who became the family guardian, and then under the guardianship of her husband after marriage. Although there were certain circumstances in which wives and legitimate daughters were entitled to shares of a husband's inheritance, these did not extend to movable and immovable property which had been passed down from the ancestors, *abarmand i pidaran*. Such property was held by the head of a household, *kadag-xwaday*, as *xwastagdar*, possessor of the estate as heir, but it could also be held on the same terms by those to whom a *kadag-xwaday* had bequeathed property. Crucially, all such property was held as *pad abarmand*, as an undivided inheritance, and shares in it remained notional. This meant that ancestral family property was held jointly by the possessors. Its substance, *bun*, was inalienable; its fruit, *bar*, or income, *waxš*, could, however, be disposed. In some respects at least, this corresponds to the modern distinction in English law between a legal and an equitable interest. Although Sasanian law recognised other categories of property which could be acquired, held and disposed of in various ways, the substance of ancestral property was, at least in principle, incapable of alienation, displacement or partition by any means and thereby sealed in perpetuity. This ensured the pre-eminence of an elite comprising a small number of families across very long periods of time. And this seems to be precisely the challenge which confronted Justinian and his legal officers along the eastern frontier, in the satrapies and possibly Armenia Interior, and against which the legislation was drafted.

Yet we should be cautious before accepting that every aspect of

Sasanian jurisprudence was present across the districts of Roman Armenia throughout late antiquity. The satraps and the otherwise anonymous elite of Armenia Interior were neither subjects of the *shahanshah*, nor citizens of Eranshahr, nor, so far as we know, practising Zoroastrians. Conversion to Christianity should have put an end to the complex regulations permitting several different forms of marriage as well as incestuous relationships, all devised to perpetuate a nobleman's lineage.[16] On the other hand, one could certainly envisage a world which was Christianised rather than Christian, loosely integrated into state and ecclesiastical institutions, where traditional practices in relation to inheritance and family property persisted across the generations, even if consanguineous and multiple marriages to ensure succession disappeared. We have seen from the above discussion that notions of ancestral property persisted, and in circumstances where traditional inheritance mechanisms were effective and trusted by the elite, there would have been little impetus for change. So it is possible, even likely, that the legal culture in Roman Armenia was extremely conservative and, outside the original provinces of First and Second Armenia, underwent little change between the late fourth century and the first years of Justinian. If, however, we accept this, it follows that the specific elements referred to in the legislation and analysed above need not be 'Sasanian'. Rather they may reflect even deeper traditions, going back into the Parthian era. It is conceivable therefore that the Justinianic legislation contains a reflection of Parthian jurisprudence.

Let us turn to consider the juridical situation of those districts of Armenia under Persian hegemony, known to Roman contemporaries as Persarmenia. We know that by the sixth and seventh centuries, Sasanian law was, in the words of Macuch, 'by no means less sophisticated than Roman law of the Byzantine era'.[17] There are tantalising references to a large number of works on jurisprudence and commentaries on a range of subjects compiled by legal scholars. We can be confident that there were very many court archives, containing a mass of records of other documents, as well as private archives, holding the legal documents pertaining to individual noble families. There does not appear to have been any systematic treatment of Sasanian law to compare with either the Theodosian Code or Justinian's *Corpus iuris civilis*, but that may be more to do with the vagaries of preservation than anything else. For with the exception of the single seventh-century Sasanian law book, *Hazar Dadestan*, no substantial compilation of Sasanian legal literature survives.[18] Therefore it is not possible to turn to collections of normative statements of Sasanian law and presume that these applied to Persarmenia. Nor, with regret, can we turn to a contemporary Armenian collection, for such a work has not survived, if indeed it ever existed in the first place. Nevertheless this is not quite the end of the trail.

In the first place, there are numerous references in the surviving Armenian literature which attest a proximate legal culture. If we limit ourselves to the *History* of Łazar Pʻarpetsʻi, a work assembled at the very start of the sixth century, we find three significant passages. At the start of book I, King Arshak is described as 'abandoning and deserting the fortunate and original inheritance of his ancestors', *zbari ew zbnik zharangutʻiwn naxneatsʻ iwrotsʻ*.[19] Examining the transliterated forms, it seems more likely that this recorded his abandonment of the *bar* and the *bun*, both the fruit and the substance, of his ancestral inheritance. In other words, he repudiated his full entitlement for ever, extinguishing his own rights and those of his family in perpetuity. This original meaning, however, was lost, either at the time of composition or in the course of transmission – the earliest manuscript to preserve Łazar's *History* is M2639, dated 1672 CE – when the transliterated Middle Persian loanwords were modified.[20] Whilst *bnik* retained something of the sense of *bun*, albeit in adjectival form, the addition of an *ini* to *bar* brought about a significant shift in meaning. The second passage implies that legitimate adult daughters did not have full legal capacity. It records that 'the man of God Sahak gave and sealed the possessions of his villages and estates', *et ew knkʻeatsʻ surb ayrn Astutsoy Sahak zstatsʻuatss geawłitsʻ iwrotsʻ ew agarakatsʻ*, to the three sons of his daughter because he did not have a son; 'he gave to them and to their offspring as an inheritance for ever', *et notsʻa i zharangutʻiwn ew zawaki notsʻa minchʻew tsʻyawitean*.[21] It appears that his daughter was not legally competent to inherit. Rather than follow Sasanian legal practice and Zoroastrian tradition in creating a legal male heir, Sahak transferred his property to his three grandsons. And finally, when setting out his demands to the messengers of Nixor Vshnaspdat, Vahan Mamikonean requests that 'you allow us our patrimonial and original religion', *zhayreni ew zbnik orēns mer i mez tʻołukʻ*.[22] This is a striking phrase, applying *bun*, the formal term for the substance or full legal title of a material property, possession or asset, to an immaterial, spiritual asset, in the form of Christian belief. Thus when Łazar represented Vahan making this request, he was employing meaningful legal terminology, asserting that Christianity was an inalienable possession of the

Armenian people. Evidently the technical sense of *bun* still held meaning at the start of the sixth century. As Thomson notes, it had also held meaning to the author of the *Buzandaran*, writing in the 480s, but looking back to the events of the fourth century. Thomson further observes that by the time Ełishē was composing his *History*, perhaps in the 570s, the term *bnik* was no longer in use; the same sense could be conveyed through the use of the term *hayreni*.[23] This suggests that legal terminology was not static and that within his *History*, Ełishē was reflecting these changed circumstances.

Łazar's so-called Defence, a separate letter sent by him from exile in the city of Amida, and appended to his *History* in M2639, also offers insight into contemporary legal practice. In response to the accusations that he had abused his position when serving as abbot, Łazar observes that 'three brothers loved the monastic community of the Holy Cathedral with fruits and all necessities' and that 'the gift of each of them was known and set down in writing in the place', *orots' iwrak'anch'iw' uruk' turn yaytni ēr ew grov mnats' i tełwojn*.[24] Elsewhere he notes that 'the things I brought from Ałuank' and Virk' and Siwnik' and Arsharunik', and the things from the nephews of your Lordship, each gift was set down separately in the place'.[25] These incidental remarks indicate that every gift to the community was set down in writing, that the monastery had its own archive recording both the donors and their gifts. No such archive survives; the closest we can get is to interpret a small corpus of Armenian building inscriptions on these terms, as records of the donation and the identity of the donor(s) on the endowment itself.[26]

It follows therefore that traces of Armenian legal culture are reflected in Łazar's *History*, and careful analysis of other late antique texts – notably the *Buzandaran* and Ełishē's *History*, referred to previously, and the *Girk' T'łt'ots'*, *Book of Letters*, a collection of ecclesiastical correspondence assembled at the start of the seventh century – reveals other instances which cannot be discussed here for reasons of space.[27] These traces appear to correspond to features of Sasanian law. We have to look elsewhere, however, for more substantial evidence of this legal culture. Fortunately two later compilations preserve such material.

The first body of evidence is preserved in a collection of documents recording the circumstances and the decisions of a council of the church of Ałuank'held at Partav in 705 CE and preserved in a composite work assembled in the tenth century, titled *History of Ałuank'*.[28] Beyond observing that there is no reason to question the authenticity of this bundle of documents, the details of the whole council do not concern us here. The final document in the collection, however, merits close attention. It is described as an ordinance, established by Simeon, the newly-installed catholicos of Ałuankʻ. Simeon expresses a general determination to reform the institutions of the church, but identifies one abuse in particular. According to Simeon, unworthy men and soldiers had been gaining possession of church property: 'No one shall have authority to entrust a church of God to unworthy men or soldiers, nor to sell it, as if a possession, nor to give it to princes or to their tutors as a gift.'[29] Furthermore Simeon asserts that 'the churches of God are free [*azat*] and under the authority of no one other than bishops and those to whom they have given the churches, that is to say, chaste and true holy priests and not unworthy soldiers'.[30] He continues, 'Today, all the laymen have this rule, that when they sell their own villages [*zgiwłs iwreantsʻ sephakans*], they write the deed [*zktakn*] in this way, "apart from the church and the soil of the church"'.[31] Since we lack contemporary documents recording property transfers, either in the districts of Ałuankʻ or in Armenia, it is impossible to know whether Simeon was trying to introduce this condition into all future transactions or was reflecting current practice. Nor can we judge how effective it was. In any event, he notes, 'I hear grumbling from many people, that in many places, soldiers are taking possession of the churches of God through the status of being an abbot.'[32] Not only were churches and church assets being transferred to soldiers; by asserting that they held the status of abbot, they were also employing a legal fiction to secure those assets.

This ordinance therefore attests several features of legal practice. It confirms that at the start of the eighth century, villages were still being bought and sold by laymen in Ałuankʻ and that title was transferred by written instrument. Evidently there was some uncertainty as to whether the transfer of such properties included or excluded the church in the village and its endowment. Simeon was at pains to stress that it did not, that title to churches and church assets were vested in the bishop and could only be transferred to priests. Whether this had always been the case is hard to tell but the widespread use of the fiction, whereby laymen were represented as having clerical status to enable them to take possession of churches and their endowments, suggests that church property had been regarded as separate from other categories of property for some time before 705 CE.

The ordinance contains one further surprise. In its conclusion, Simeon sets out a brief summary of a recent property dispute:

Concerning which as well K'shik abbot of Nersmihr, brought up in holiness and *tanutēr* of the monastery, has written that Varaz Trdat, prince of Aluank', gave this very small village of Holy Cross for service for the sake of his soul. Now a cavalryman, P'usan Veh by name, a layman, who has lived in debauchery, presents documents that 'the prince of Aluank' gave that church to me through the office of abbot because of my tutorship'. With regard to that, O beloved ones, this law shall exist from now on for the future: it shall not be for P'usan Veh to hold that church in accordance with the command of the Holy Spirit; but unsullied and pure priests shall have control over the church, because that man does not have authority from God or from us.[33]

K'shik was not an obscure individual. He appears as a signatory to the undertaking signed by both clerics and laymen of Aluank' at the council of Partav by which they repudiated Nersēs Bakur and were reconciled to the Armenian church under its catholicos Elia. He was the first named of several abbots after Simeon and four other bishops, implying that he was a leading cleric at the time.[34] Furthermore, K'shik was one of two abbots with whom Elia deposited a signed and sealed document confirming that he had received the undertaking.[35] The location of the monastery of Nersmihr is unknown but it was evidently a prominent community. As well as being entrusted with the safe-keeping of such important documents, the above confirms that the community had been endowed by the prince of Aluank', Varaz Trdat. The figure of P'usan Veh is also unknown. Evidently he too had enjoyed close ties to a prince of Aluank', conceivably the same Varaz Trdat. The reference to Varaz Trdat supplies a secure historical context. He was the nephew of Prince Juanshēr and succeeded the latter as prince of Aluank' after Juanshēr's murder in September 669 CE. Varaz Trdat seems to have held power until c. 699, when he was imprisoned by the emperor Justinian II in Constantinople. It was during his five-year absence that Nersēs Bakur induced, or worked in concert with, Spram, the wife of Varaz Trdat, to introduce dyophysite teachings into Aluank', prompting the intervention of Elia and the council of Partav.[36]

Two striking features merit comment. The first is that we find Simeon exercising judicial authority, preferring the suit of K'shik to that of P'usan Veh, despite the latter presenting documents before him. This corresponds to the legal identity and self-determination granted to other religious communities within the Sasanian Empire, arrangements which persisted after its demise. The second is that K'shik is titled *tanutēr* of the monastery.[37] This term has long presented a challenge to historians. Although its meaning has always been clear enough, 'lord of the house', its apparent overlap with other social terms, including *tēr*, *naxarar* and others, has always remained something of a mystery. Yet if we treat it as an Armenian calque on the Middle Persian *kadag-xwaday*, master of the household or *pater familias*, its true meaning becomes clear. It is used to describe someone's legal status, someone in whom the inalienable property of the family, whether genealogical or spiritual, was vested.

It is clear from the above that the country ofAłuankʻ possessed a sophisticated legal culture at the start of the eighth century. From where did it come? The most straightforward solution is to propose that it reflected pre-conquest Sasanian legal principles, practices and language, that legal process in Ałuankʻ in the century after the conquest, at least with respect to property transactions, was closely related to legal process before the conquest. The traditional mechanisms for transferring property continued to be used because all parties to a transaction trusted in their efficacy. Even the endowment by Varaz Trdat of a small village to the monastery of Nersmihr for the sake of his soul had a clear parallel in Sasanian law, albeit in a Zoroastrian rather than a Christian context; 'property of the soul', *xwastag i ruwan*, was intended to provide income for rites and ceremonies to be performed after a person's death. Admittedly there are some aspects which are unclear. Had the catholicos always been involved in adjudicating disputes or was this a development of the post-conquest era, or perhaps even a temporary state of affairs following the detention of Varaz Trdat in the Byzantine Empire? Should we treat the repeated references to soldiers and cavalrymen obtaining church property as evidence of recent political turmoil – perhaps linked to Khazar raids and Umayyad counter-offensives from 685 CE – or, in the alternative, increasing confidence on the part of the catholicos Simeon to protect the interests of the church against familiar abuses? These questions may never be resolved. That the legal culture pervading Caucasian Albania at the start of the eighth century was strongly informed by Sasanian tradition is, however, evident.

We must advance to consider the second compilation. The *History of the Province of Siwnikʻ* was assembled by the metropolitan bishop of Siwnikʻ, Stepʻanos Orbelean, in 1299 CE. It treats the whole of Siwnian history from its mythical origins to the year of completion, drawing upon a wealth of written sources going back centuries, including ecclesiastical correspondence, theological treatises and a large number of documents recording property transactions in favour of the bishops of Siwnikʻ and the monastery and churches of Tatʻev where they were based. Indeed, it preserves the full text of no fewer than fifty-two such deeds, together with summaries of, or substantial extracts from, a further twelve documents. The earliest is dated to the year 288 of the Armenian era (30 April 839–29 April 840 CE).[38] They are distributed unevenly across time, with twenty-four dating to the period between 839 and 945 but none at all between 1089 and 1223. Stepʻanos does not reveal exactly where he found them, but he admits that one of the original deeds was so old and worn around the edges that it was only possible to read some of the words and 'on account of its length we reckoned it would be tedious to our audience and so we have not included it'.[39] Evidently he had access to the actual documents, some of which were in poor condition. Furthermore it is significant that the charters incorporated by Stepʻanos tend to appear in clusters within his composition, in small groups of three or four. They repeatedly disrupt the narrative and the chronological progression of the text. One of the clusters, of three late ninth-century conveyances, moves backwards in time.[40] Arguably this reflects the sequence that he found them in, indicating that they were stored in a bundle with the oldest at the bottom. In this one instance, picking them off the pile in front of him, he forgot to reverse the sequence. There seems little doubt therefore that Stepʻanos exploited the episcopal archives when assembling his *History*, and that these contained bundles of documents recording endowments, just as Łazar Pʻarpetsʻi had described.

The earliest cluster comprises four charters which record villages being bought, exchanged and given to the see. The following is a translation of one of them:

> In two hundred and ninety-three of the Armenian calendar [29 April 844–28 April 845], a wish came upon me, Pʻilippē, son of Vasak, lord of Siwnikʻ. I gave Tatʻev for the sake of my soul to you, lord Davitʻ, bishop of Siwnikʻ, which had arrived in my inheritance from my father *anxuēš kʻarē* with all its boundaries, mountain and plain, vines and walnut trees, water-meadows and mill, and whatever are its entire boundaries. And may no one dare after my passing, my sons or my brothers or descendants, to remove that village from that church and that Holy Cross; otherwise may he be condemned by God and by that holy church and by that Holy Cross and may he endure curses from that spiritual lord. And I have given with open heart and mind to you, lord Davitʻ, bishop of Siwnikʻ, to enjoy throughout a peaceful lifetime, and those others who succeed after you to that see, may they enjoy until the coming of Christ. If they remain, may they exist in that way; but if they go, may they not dare to remove that village with its definition from that church, or to sell, or to exchange, or to establish as security [*gravakan dnel*]; but those who are servants of the church shall be master [*išxan*] of all the boundaries. And the witnesses shall be the God-protected lord [*tēr*] Grigor, lord of Siwnikʻ, lord Atrenerseh son of Vasak, lord of Siwnikʻ, lord Grigor, son of Sahak, lord Hrahat and lord Aruman, sons of Sahak, lord Hrahat and lord

Gagik, sons of Grigor lord of Siwnikʻ ... [and a further twenty-eight named lay figures and clerics] And for the sake of further confirmation, I have set my customary seal and those of my sons and the other nobles.⁴¹

This deed gives important insights into the prevailing legal culture in mid-ninth-century Siwnikʻ. It retains two phrases which are transliterations of Middle Persian: *anxuēš kʻarē*, a seemingly garbled form which must be related to *xwēših*, ownership with the right to dispose of the property, and which speaks to the nature of the rights conveyed to lord Pʻilippē from his father; and *gravakan*, in Middle Persian *grawgan*, a form of mortgage giving the creditor access to the increase, *bar*, of the property, until the loan was repaid.⁴² It is highly likely that these phrases were vestigial by the time this deed was executed, carried over from earlier documentation but retained nevertheless. Legal instruments tend to possess an inherent conservatism in form and language – even to the point of retaining elements which no longer function or reflect the present circumstances – for as long as all parties believe that they are effective in fulfilling their intentions. The deed contains other formulaic phrasing in the generic description of the property being transferred and in the range of transactions prohibited once the transfer has been performed. These lists imply an underlying legal culture of sophistication, one that was capable of envisaging and prescribing various dealings in the future. The statement that the transaction occurred through the wish of the donor is also significant because this was a necessary element of a binding contract under Sasanian law. Moreover, in expressing anxiety that his sons, brothers or descendants might try to disrupt or overturn his endowment, Lord Pʻilippē appears to deny agency to any female relative, a feature we have observed previously.

In its terminology, formulae and legal principles, therefore, this deed reflects late antique Sasanian legal culture. It is not the only example. All four of the documents in the earliest cluster do so. The oldest document describes the purchase of the village of Artsiv in similar, though not identical, terms to those seen previously, 'with its boundaries, mountain and plain, the arid [*zostin*] and the watered [*zjrarbin*] and the pasture [*zarawt erkir*], field and meadow [*zart ew zmarg*]'.⁴³ Unlike the above, it defines the limits of the property being conveyed in terms of specific local topographical features – named watercourses, valleys, rocks, hills, paths and even 'the field of Vardan' – along its eastern, western and southern boundaries respectively.⁴⁴ Another of the four refers to the *grawgan* form of mortgage.⁴⁵ A deed of exchange dated 320 of the Armenian era (23 April 871–21 April 872) states that the transaction was in accordance with the will of both parties to the transaction: 'And we have undertaken the transfer with both parties willing and in agreement, I and lord Sołomon.'[46] This document also refers to the two villages 'in accordance with its definition and the royal *nepak*', a word which seems to be a transliteration of the Middle Persian term *nipek*, meaning document or perhaps list.[47] This could be referring to a formal record of the property – and perhaps a process of registration – in the provincial archives or *diwan*. If so, it too would be vestigial, another distant echo of a process followed in late antiquity but long since abandoned. This might seem anomalous: should not all the deeds include such a provision? But we should not expect absolute consistency of expression across all the deeds. They do not derive from a single template. In the absence of a supervening judicial authority, to monitor and regularise, arguably each form of transaction – purchase, sale, exchange, partition, endowment – developed its own patterns and nuances, reflecting Sasanian legal culture in its own way.

In support of this remarkable persistence of Sasanian legal tradition, it is worth recalling that Siwnik' was an eastern region of historic Armenia, bordering Ałuank', and never under direct Roman control, even at its greatest extent. It was also a remote highland region, hard to access and difficult to administer, lacking an urban centre through which to transmit alternative legal cultures. Unlike many of the districts of Ałuank' to the east or Armenia to the north and west, it did not experience Arab or Persian settlement in the second half of the eighth century, and was apparently not subjected to a more intensive regime of provincial government. Rather it was left to its own devices, with minimal intrusion or interference. We should not, therefore, be altogether surprised that the oldest documents uncovered and preserved by Step'anos Orbelean retain features of Sasanian legal practice two hundred years after the demise of the last *shahanshah*. Yet it is also striking that several of these features vanish in the second half of the ninth century. This is accompanied by a greater awareness of Islamic practice and jurisprudence. The expressions *halal* and *haram* appear in the deeds, with the former being applied in one instance to the source of a donor's wealth.[48] Moreover there is a much greater prominence afforded to protective curses, situated at the end of the document and now directed specifically at Christians or Muslims who dare to meddle with the transaction.[49] These developments may have been responses to the harsh campaigns of Bugha the Elder across the whole of Armenia, including Siwnik', in the mid-850s.[50] Alternatively it may be that when Mariam, the daughter of Ashot I Bagratuni, settled in Siwnikʻ as the wife of Vasak, lord of Siwnikʻ, she preferred to use Bagratuni legal traditions for her many foundations and endowments; she was living in Siwnikʻ by 874/5 and was still active in 903/4. Unfortunately, we have no contemporary legal documents from the Bagratuni-held lands in central Armenia with which to make comparison. Whatever the stimulus, the documents attest an awareness of, and engagement with, the contemporary Islamic legal culture as well as a need for greater spiritual protection – hence the evocation of divine sanction on any Christian or Muslim who contravened the terms. As a result, towards the end of the ninth century, the reflection of Sasanian legal culture in the deeds of the see of Siwnikʻ began to fade.

Armenia in late antiquity was therefore a site of juridical contestation. The western districts under Roman hegemony after the fourth century experienced different administrative arrangements. Those incorporated into the provincial network fell within the jurisdiction of Roman law; those associated with the Roman Empire by treaty or agreement persisted in their own traditions, which owed much to Persian – and perhaps even Parthian – legal culture. The Justinianic reforms transformed this plural legal landscape, replacing – or more probably overlaying – local traditions with Roman law. Although the intention of the legislation is clear, its reception is harder to discern; no legal documents survive from the four new provinces of Armenia, and we have no sense of local reactions or responses. Conversely several Armenian sources composed in those districts of central and eastern Armenia under Sasanian hegemony attest an ongoing familiarity with contemporary Sasanian legal principles, concepts and terminology. Some terms were absorbed and preserved in transliteration; others were rendered in Armenian translation. Although again no legal records survive, evidently Persarmenia was suffused with Sasanian law. It is only through two later historical compositions that we obtain sustained insight into the reception – and retention – of that law in specific regions. Legal culture in Caucasian Albania at the start of the eighth century continued to be informed by Sasanian practices and traditions. The evidence from the composition of Stepʻanos Orbelean suggests that the same was true of Siwnikʻ in the middle of the ninth century, although this was about to change. Extending Garsoïan's thesis of the 'Iranian' index of medieval Armenia, Armenians living under Sasanian rule acknowledged and used Sasanian law, although we cannot be certain how it was received and used in every district in every period.[51] Nevertheless the Armenian evidence has the potential to reveal as much about

Sasanian law and the nature of the Sasanian Empire as it does about Armenian experiences within that empire.

NOTES

I should like to express my sincere thanks to Professor Caroline Humfress for her generous and stimulating comments on an earlier draft. All Greek, Latin and Armenian translations are my own. For the Armenian transcription, I have adopted the system followed in Thomson and Howard-Johnston 1999, with one minor revision.

1. Step'anos Siwnets'i 1970: 187. In his commentary on Dionysius Thrax, this eighth-century scholar identified dialects of Armenian from the districts of Korch'ayk', Tayk', Xoyt', Fourth Armenia, Sper, Siwnik' and Arts'ax.
2. Garsoïan 1985; Mahé and Thomson 1997.
3. Garsoïan 1999a.
4. Charanis 1959: 28–36; Thomson and Howard-Johnson 1999: 2, 173–91; Garsoïan 1999b: 53–62.
5. Adontz 1970: 7–164; Garsoïan 2009. One significant development involved the transfer of the *diwan* of Siwnik' from Dvin to P'aytakaran 'so that the name of Armenians would no longer be applied to them'; see Sebēos 1979: 67–8 (ch. 8). For the experience of other Christian communities within the Sasanian Empire, see now Payne 2015.
6. Adontz 1970: 103–64.
7. *Nov. Just.* 31.1.
8. Maas 1986: 18–19, 25–7; 1992: 20, 26.
9. *Nov. Just.* 31.1.1–3.
10. Humfress 2005: 162, 176–8.
11. Maas 2010: 238–9, 292–3.
12. Edict III, *De Armeniorum Successione*, in *CJC* III.760–1.
13. Adontz 1970: 145.
14. I am indebted to Professor Humfress for this suggestion.
15. Macuch 2011.
16. Macuch 2003: 232–3, noting modifications made by Christian communities to family and inheritance law.
17. Macuch 2004: 182.
18. Perikhanian 1997. See Bakhos and Shayegan 2010 and Macuch 2014 for recent research on the Babylonian Talmud and legal pluralism in the Sasanian Empire.
19. Łazar 1904: 9, lines 13–14 (ch. 7).
20. Thomson 1991: 3.
21. Łazar 1904: 37, lines 21–7 (ch. 18).
22. Łazar 1904: 161, 12 (ch. 89).
23. Thomson 1991: 28–9.
24. Łazar 1904: 195, 17–19.
25. Łazar 1904: 196, 21–4.
26. Greenwood 2004.
27. *Girk' T'łt'ots'* 1901. For a partial French translation, see Garsoïan 1999a: 411–583.

28 Movsēs Kałankatuats'i 1983: 293.1–311.5 (book III, chs. 3–11).
29 Movsēs Kałankatuats'i 1983: 308, 17–19 (book III, ch. 11).
30 Movsēs Kałankatuats'i 1983: 309, 5–7.
31 Movsēs Kałankatuats'i 1983: 309, 3–5.
32 Movsēs Kałankatuats'i 1983: 309, 10–12.
33 Movsēs Kałankatuats'i 1983: 309, 14–23.
34 Movsēs Kałankatuats'i 1983: 300, 5–9 (book III, ch. 8).
35 Movsēs Kałankatuats'i 1983: 303.20–304.4 (book III, ch.9).
36 Greenwood 2008: 344–6; Movsēs Kałankatuats'i 1983: 311.6–312.7 (book III, ch.12).
37 Garsoïan 1989: 563.
38 Step'anos Orbelean 1861: 149.22–150.21 (ch. 38).
39 Step'anos Orbelean 1861: 167.18–22 (ch. 41).
40 Step'anos Orbelean 1861: 156.18–161.4 (ch. 39). The three deeds are dated 330 Armenian era (20 April 881–19 April 882), 320 Armenian era (23 April 871–21 April 872) and 316 Armenian era (24 April 867–22 April 868) respectively.
41 Step'anos Orbelean 1861: 151.1–152.9 (ch. 38).
42 Macuch 2011: 190, 191.
43 Step'anos Orbelean 1861: 149.25–6 (ch. 38).
44 Step'anos Orbelean 1861: 149.26–150.3 (ch. 38).
45 Step'anos Orbelean 1861: 153.13 (ch. 38).
46 Step'anos Orbelean 1861: 158.23–4 (ch. 39).
47 Step'anos Orbelean 1861: 159.16–18 (ch. 39): 'We have received Bex in accordance with its definition and royal *nepak* and we have given Aruk's in accordance with its definition and the royal *nepak*, which was twelve drams.'
48 Step'anos Orbelean 1861: 170.17 (ch. 42): 'may the *halal* become *haram*', *halaln haram ełits'i*. See also 157.15 (ch. 39): 'from my own *halal* labours', *i halal vastakots' imots'*. This appears in a deed dated 330 Armenian era (20 April 881–19 April 882).
49 These later developments lie outside the remit of this chapter and merit separate treatment. The earliest sanction clause to protect from violations by Christians and Muslims appears in a deed dated 320 Armenian era (23 April 871–21 April 872): 'And from now on, may no one dare to oppose this inviolable deed [*anxaxt vchŕis*], whether one of ours or a stranger. But if anyone attempts this, may he not be successful in his action and may he be condemned by the three Holy Councils, may he receive the lot of Judas and be liable for our sins. And if some Muslim lord [*tachik awag*] should come and attempt to seize, may he be *apiłar* [rejected, separated from?] by his Muhammad and may a thousand thousand *nalat'* [Ar., read *lanat*, curses] from his law be upon him, and may he be forsaken by, and black-faced before, his God.'
50 These events receive extended treatment in Armenian historical tradition: see T'ovma Artsruni 1885: 122.1–200.32 (book III, chs. 1–13).
51 Garsoïan 1996.

BIBLIOGRAPHY

Adontz, N. (1970), *Armenia in the Period of Justinian*, ed. and trans. N. G. Garsoïan, Lisbon: Calouste Gulbenkian Foundation.
Bakhos, C. and Shayegan, M. R. (eds) (2010), *The Talmud in its Iranian context*, Tübingen: Mohr Siebeck.
Charanis, P. (1959), 'Ethnic Changes in Seventh-Century Byzantium', *Dumbarton Oaks Papers*, 13, pp. 23–44.
Garsoïan, N. G. (1985), *Armenia between Byzantium and the Sasanians*, London: Variorum.
Garsoïan, N. G. (1989), *The Epic Histories (Buzandaran Patmut'iwnk')*, Cambridge: Harvard University Press.
Garsoïan, N. G. (1996), 'The Two Voices of Armenian Mediaeval Historiography: The Iranian Index', *Studia Iranica*, 25, pp. 7–43.
Garsoïan, N. G. (1999a), *L'Église arménienne et le grand schisme d'Orient*, CSCO vol. 574, t. 100, Louvain: Peeters.
Garsoïan, N. G. (1999b), 'The Problem of Armenian Integration into the Byzantine Empire', in H. Ahrweiler and A. E. Laiou (eds), *Studies on the Internal Diaspora of the Byzantine Empire*, Cambridge: Harvard University Press, pp. 53–124.
Garsoïan, N. G. (2009), 'Armenian Sources on Sasanian Administration', *Res Orientales*, 18, pp. 90–114.
Girk' T'łt'ots' (1901), ed. Y. Izmireants', Tiflis: T. Ṙawtineants' and M. Sharadzē. (Partial trans. in Garsoïan 1999a, pp. 411–583.)
Greenwood, T. W. (2004), 'A Corpus of Early Medieval Armenian Inscriptions', *Dumbarton Oaks Papers*, 58, pp. 27–91.
Greenwood, T. W. (2008), 'Armenian Neighbours (600–1045)', in J. Shepard (ed.), *The Cambridge History of the Byzantine Empire c. 500–1492*, Cambridge: Cambridge University Press, pp. 333–64.
Humfress, C. (2005), 'Law and Legal Practice in the Age of Justinian', in M. Maas (ed.), *The Cambridge Companion to the Age of Justinian*, Cambridge: Cambridge University Press, pp. 161–84.
Łazar P'arpets'i (1904), *Patmut'iwn Hayots' ew T'ułt' aṙ Vahan Mamikonean*, eds. G. Tēr-Mkrtch'ean and S. Malxasean, Tiflis: Mnatsakan Martiroseants'. (Reprinted 1985, Delmar: Caravan Books.)
Maas, M. (1986), 'Roman History and Christian Ideology in Justinianic Reform Legislation', *Dumbarton Oaks Papers*, 40, pp. 17–31.
Maas, M. (1992), *John Lydus and the Roman Past: Antiquarianism and Politics in the Age of Justinian*, London and New York: Routledge.
Maas, M. (2010), *Readings in Late Antiquity: A Sourcebook*, London and New York: Routledge.
Macuch, M. (2003), 'Zoroastrian Principles and the Structure of Kinship in Sasanian Iran', in C. G. Cereti, M. Maggi and E. Provasi (eds), *Religious Themes and Texts of Pre-Islamic Iran and Central Asia: Studies in Honour of Professor Gherardo Gnoli on the Occasion of his 65th Birthday on 6 December 2002*, Beiträge zur Iranistik 24, Wiesbaden: Reichert, pp. 231–46.
Macuch, M. (2004), 'Pious Foundations in Byzantine and Sasanian Law', in G. Gnoli (ed.), *La Persia e Bisanzio: Convegno internazionale, Roma, 14–18*

ottobre 2002, Atti dei convegni Lincei 201, Rome: Accademia nazionale dei Lincei, pp. 181–96.

Macuch, M. (2011), 'Judicial and Legal Systems. iii: Sasanian Legal System', in *Encyclopædia Iranica*, 15, New York: Encyclopædia Iranica Foundation, pp. 181–96.

Macuch, M. (2014), 'Jewish Jurisdiction Within the Framework of the Sasanian Legal System', in U. Gabbay and S. Secunda (eds), *Encounters by the Rivers of Babylon: Scholarly Conversations Between Jews, Iranians and Babylonians in Antiquity*, Tübingen: Mohr Siebeck, pp. 147–60.

Mahé, J.-P. and Thomson, R. W. (1997), *From Byzantium to Iran: Armenian Studies in Honour of Nina G. Garsoïan*, Atlanta: Scholars Press.

Movsēs Kałankatuats'i (1983), *Patmut'iwn Ałuanits' Ashxarhi*, ed. V. Aṙakelyan, Erevan: Haykakan SSH GA Hratarakch'ut'yun.

Payne, R. E. (2015), *A State of Mixture: Christians, Zoroastrians, and Iranian Political Culture in Late Antiquity*, Los Angeles: University of California Press.

Perikhanian, A. (1997), *The Book of a Thousand Judgements (A Sasanian Law-Book)*, trans. N. G. Garsoïan, Costa Mesa: Mazda.

Sebēos (1979), *Patmutiwn Sebēosi*, ed. G. V. Abgaryan, Erevan: Haykakan SSH Gitut'yunneri Akademiayi Hratarakch'ut'yun.

Step'anos Orbelean (1861), *Patmut'iwn tann Sisakan*, ed. N. O. Ēmin, Moscow: Tparani Lazarean chemarani arewelean lezuats'.

Step'anos Siwnets'i (1970), *Meknut'iwn k'erakanin*, in N. Adontz (ed.), *Denys de Thrace et les commentateurs arméniens*, Louvain: Bibliothèque arménienne de la Fondation Calouste Gulbenkian: Imprimerie Orientaliste.

Thomson, R. W. (trans.) (1991), *The History of Łazar P'arpec'i*, Atlanta: Scholars Press.

Thomson, R. W. and Howard-Johnston, J. (trans. and ed.) (1999), *The Armenian History Attributed to Sebeos*, TTH 31, 2 vols, Liverpool: Liverpool University Press.

T'ovma Artsruni (1887), *Patmut'iwn tann Arcruneats'*, ed. K'. Patkanean, St Petersburg: Tparan N. Skoroxodov. (Reprinted 1991, Delmar: Caravan Books.)

10 Cultural Contacts Between Rome and Persia at the Time of Ardashir I (c. AD 224–40)

Pierfrancesco Callieri

There has been much scholarly interest in the relationship between Rome and Persia in the Sasanian era. Historians have devoted detailed studies to the intensified political and military contacts following Ardashir I's accession to the throne of Iran. Most art historians and archaeologists, by contrast, have argued that cultural contacts between Rome and Sasanian Persia were only established under Shapur I. There is, however, architectural and artistic evidence to suggest that such contacts commenced, in fact, during the reign of Ardashir I. As far as architecture is concerned, Dietrich Huff has made a persuasive case, as we shall see later,[1] that architects and masons from the eastern provinces of the Roman Empire were involved in the construction of the fire temple in the city of Ardashir Khurrah (Firuzabad).

This chapter argues that rock reliefs also imply similar cultural influence, even though the case is more difficult to prove. I examine the chronology of the five rock reliefs accomplished under Ardashir, as well as the workshops involved in producing them. The earliest relief, at Firuzabad I, shows traits characteristic of Elymaean craftsmen. Subsequently, new techniques and styles appear, and the relief at Naqsh-e Rostam I seems to imitate Persepolitan sculpture. Since numismatic evidence suggests that the reliefs were all carved within about ten years, only the involvement of experienced sculptors, perhaps from the Syro-Mesopotamian regions invaded by Ardashir, can explain such a major and rapid change of style.

One of the central topics of this volume is the relationship between Rome and Persia in the Sasanian period. This is a subject which has attracted the attention of many scholars, particularly historians but also art historians and archaeologists. Historians have investigated in detail the long series of political and military contacts which started immediately after the accession to the throne of Iran of Ardashir I, the local ruler of Fars who had succeeded in taking power from the last of the Arsacid kings.

There is no space here for a review of these contacts. It is worth noting, however, that even before Shapur I's celebrated victorious campaigns against Rome, from AD 242 to AD 261, Ardashir was seriously engaged in confrontation on the western boundary of his kingdom, starting with raids into the Roman provinces of Syria and Mesopotamia from AD 230 onwards and culminating in the conquest of northern Mesopotamia and the capture of Nisibis and Carrhae in AD 235/236[2] or AD 237/238.[3] Confrontation with Rome continued under his heir, Shapur I.[4]

When we turn to art history and archaeology, most scholars assign the beginning of cultural contacts between Rome and Sasanian Iran to the reign of Shapur I. It is during his reign that there is circumstantial evidence for Roman influence at Bishapur, notably the mosaic floor decoration and iron clamps with western parallels used in stone masonry. Western influence is also evident in aspects of the iconography and style of the rock reliefs accomplished by the artists at Bishapur,[5] as well as in the hydraulic works of Susiana, rightly considered the result of employing specialised Roman craftsmen, allegedly deportees.

On careful scrutiny, however, cultural contacts between Sasanian Iran and the Roman Empire appear to have started earlier, during the reign of Ardashir I (c. AD 224–40). I wish to present here two different strands of evidence; these may allow us to adopt a new perspective.

A crucial piece of evidence for this interaction is already well known, albeit frequently forgotten. It is represented by one of the buildings at Ardashir Khurrah, the circular city founded by Ardashir I in the plain near present Firuzabad, in southern central Fars. In the central area of the city there still stands the lower part of an imposing *chahar taq* structure, built in dressed stone masonry with four *ivans* projecting from the central square block originally supporting the dome in bricks: a low mound with the collapsed ruins covered by soil debris (Fig. 10.1) was all that could be seen of the monument until 2005, when an Iranian–German excavation exposed, within one of the four front *ivans*, the well-preserved masonry of one of the four external sides of the *chahar taq* down to the original floor level (Fig. 10.2). The

Fig. 10.1 Ardashir Khurrah (southern central Fars, Iran): Takht-e Neshin, general view before the excavations (photo P. Callieri).

Fig. 10.2 Ardashir Khurrah (southern central Fars, Iran): Takht-e Neshin, the south-east face of the *chahar taq* (photo D. M. Meucci).

building is known as the Takht-e Neshin, and its peculiar masonry had prompted an attribution to the Achaemenid period in the past.[6] Careful investigation has now shown, however, that there is sufficient evidence for dating it to the early Sasanian period: the use of dressed stone masonry, with its undeniable Achaemenid flavour, is in fact one of the instruments which Ardashir used in order to link his new power to the builders of Persepolis. They are likely to correspond to the 'ancestors' (*ahenagan*) mentioned in the inscription of Shapur I at Naqsh-e Rostam,[7] and the building programme evidently carried a clear ideological message.[8] This structure has been convincingly interpreted by Dietrich Huff as the first Sasanian fire temple, built by Ardashir I and mentioned in the sources.[9]

The building technique has traits of Persian tradition, such as the dovetail shape of the clamp sockets. Huff's observation, however, that a measurement unit of 29.27cm, corresponding to a Roman foot (*pes*) of 29.60cm, was used, instead of the oriental ell of 46.50cm, proves that Roman architectural traditions were observed in the construction. This important technical detail suggests that Ardashir I, wishing to have a monumental building in dressed stone masonry, long abandoned on the Iranian Plateau, resorted to architects and masons from the eastern provinces of the Roman Empire. These worked alongside Persian masons, even prior to the deportation of Roman craftsmen by Shapur I:

> Es darf daher weiterhin angenommen werden, dass bei der Errichtung des Takht-i Nishin Bauleute der östlichen Mittelmeerländer mitgewirkt haben, die nicht erst in Verbindung mit den Kriegszügen Shapurs, sondern bereits von Ardashir unter noch unbekannten Umständen nach Iran gebracht worden sind.[10]

When Huff published his architectural study of the monument, there had been no evidence for Ardashir's military advances into the Roman east, which is why the German scholar lamented the lack of sources for the historical context of the construction project: 'Vergleichbare Nachrichten, die den historischen Hintergrund für die Errichtung des Takht-i Nishin aufhellen würden, fehlen.'[11] A similar approach was adopted by Lionel Bier when discussing the appearance of dressed stone masonry in Sasanian Iran.[12] Now, after the works by Kettenhofen, Edwell, Dignas and Winter, and others, it is clear in what historical context this contact occurred.

Rock reliefs similarly point to cultural contacts between the two empires at an early stage. I am fully aware of the fact that in this case we have no firm factual proof to date, but technical and stylistic interpretation provides circumstantial evidence. Dietrich Huff's studies have offered profound insights into the ideology underpinning the cultural policy of Ardashir I, from town planning (such as the circular plan of Ardashir Khurrah) to coinage.[13] This cultural policy, despite the anti-Arsacid propaganda, shows strong continuity with the late Arsacid period.[14]

Fig. 10.3 Tang-e Ab (southern central Fars, Iran): Firuzabad I rock relief (photo P. Callieri).

In this context, rock reliefs, intended to propagate royal ideology, appear to resume the ancient Iranian tradition of rock reliefs. They also have an iconographic antecedent in the pre-Sasanian graffiti of Persepolis, even if much smaller and less visible.[15] When we examine the five rock reliefs produced in the reign of Ardashir I, we see tremendous changes in technique and style which, in the light of their production within a short period of time, can in my opinion only be explained by external influence.

My discussion is based on the chronology of these reliefs: the equestrian combat scene at Firuzabad I (Fig. 10.3) and the investiture at Firuzabad II (Fig. 10.4), both in the Tang-e Ab Gorge near Firuzabad; the investiture at Naqsh-e Rajab III (Fig. 10.5); the mounted investiture and victory scene at Naqsh-e Rostam I (Fig. 10.6), near the historic town of Estakhr; and finally the mounted scene at Salmas (Fig. 10.7), near Lake Urmia in eastern Azerbaijan. The last of these, which iconography places at the end of the sequence in the light of the presence of the heir Shapur I, but which is stylistically primitive, is clearly the product of a very inexperienced local workshop, geographically isolated from the main workshops in Fars. It has often

Fig. 10.4 Tang-e Ab (southern central Fars, Iran): Firuzabad II rock relief (photo P. Callieri).

Fig. 10.5 Naqsh-e Rajab (central Fars, Iran): Naqsh-e Rajab III rock relief (after Hinz 1969: pl. 57).

Fig. 10.6 Naqsh-e Rostam (central Fars, Iran): Naqsh-e Rostam I rock relief (photo P. Callieri).

Fig. 10.7 Salmas (eastern Azerbaijan, Iran): Salmas rock relief (after Hinz 1969: pl. 69).

been disregarded by art historians, and we will follow Walther Hinz, in assigning it to the end of the sequence,[16] and Matthew Canepa, who points out that it has been accomplished by a less experienced artist.[17]

As to the other four reliefs, with Naqsh-e Rajab III not being always taken into consideration, the views of scholars as to the sequence of production differ, particularly on the chronological position of Firuzabad I.

Vladimir Lukonin postulated, from comparisons with the crowns featuring on coinage, that Firuzabad II and Naqsh-e Rajab III should be dated to the end of the AD 230s, earlier than Naqsh-e Rostam I, which he dates between the end of the 230s and the beginning of the 240s: Firuzabad I, on the contrary, shows no crown but a battle headdress[18] and cannot therefore be dated through comparison with coinage. We may add that the subject of Firuzabad I, the battle of Hormizdegan, places the relief evidently after AD 224/225.

Walther Hinz, the only scholar to include the Salmas relief, suggests a sequence as follows: Firuzabad I – Firuzabad II – Naqsh-e Rajab III – Naqsh-e Rostam I – Salmas.[19] Louis Vanden Berghe agrees with the sequence proposed by Hinz.[20]

Georgina Herrmann, on the contrary, places the investiture scene at Firuzabad II at the beginning of the sequence: 'this relief is simple in design and technique, with little improvement on Elymaian reliefs'; the second relief would be the combat scene at Firuzabad I, and Herrmann remarks that 'although the depth of relief is relatively shallow, the modelling is excellent and the finished surface finely worked and polished'; the relief at Naqsh-e Rostam would represent the final step, illustrating 'Ardashir's success in developing a distinctive visual language suitable for reproduction on a large scale'.[21] Herrmann is correct in observing that at Firuzabad I 'the modelling is excellent and the finished surface finely worked and polished', but we are offered no explanation as to how 'Ardashir's sculptors were improving both in their vivid design and in their technique of carving'[22] as compared to the investiture scene of Firuzabad II. It is interesting that, on the basis of the study of the traces of stone-working, Herrmann confirms that Firuzabad I and Naqsh-e Rajab III, carved in medium relief and only partially polished, should be earlier than Naqsh-e Rostam I, carved in high relief and polished.[23]

Bruno Overlaet discusses the dating of Ardashir I's reliefs in his 2013 paper offering a new interpretation of the Sasanian investiture reliefs, which aims to show that the king does not face the god

Ohrmazd, but a priest. The Belgian scholar follows Touraj Daryaee in dating the relief at Firuzabad II as early as AD 205/206, thought to be the year of the foundation of the town of Ardashir Khurrah,[24] and he links the relief at Naqsh-e Rajab III to the instalment of Ardashir as king of Persis;[25] these would therefore be the two earliest reliefs. Overlaet himself, however, also observes that the numismatic evidence would suggest that the three investiture reliefs date to the period between AD 228/229 or 229/230 and AD 238/239, because the *korymbos* on the royal crown is present only on Ardashir's coins minted after the victory over Ardavan IV, as also pointed out, after Lukonin, by Michael Alram.[26] Nevertheless Overlaet dismisses these late dating proposals, suggesting instead that the 'korymbos had been in use in Fars long before this headdress was used on coins'.[27] The relief at Naqsh-e Rostam I, featuring, of course, the Arsacid king under the horse of Ardashir, would evidently need to be later than the battle of Hormizdegan of AD 224/225, depicted on the relief of Firuzabad I.[28]

Matthew Canepa, who mainly investigates the stylistic evolution of these reliefs, argues on the contrary for the precedence of Firuzabad I, which he attributes to a 'burgeoning workshop that descended from the elaborate early preimperial graffiti etched into the window frames at Persepolis'.[29] According to Canepa, the reliefs of Firuzabad II and Naqsh-e Rajab III were accomplished next. He believes that these were products of the same workshop. The 'turning point' would be Naqsh-e Rostam I, 'where the sculptural forms themselves become more measured and refined and the composition more carefully thought out' and where 'the figures themselves were finished to a polish'.[30] As already observed by Leo Trümpelmann,[31] Canepa also recognises in this relief the presence of 'formal cues from Achaemenid sculpture visible at Persepolis and in the tombs'.[32]

This is just a brief review of some of the mainstream opinions. In my view, it is first of all important to draw a clear distinction between iconography on the one hand and its technical and stylistic rendering on the other. In terms of iconography, Ardashir's reliefs belong to the Iranian tradition of the Arsacid age. For the equestrian combat scene of Firuzabad I, Canepa has rightly pointed out that 'composition and subject matter responded to Arsacid precedents, such as the equestrian victory of Gotarzes Geopothros at Bisotun'.[33] Investiture scenes are also known from the Arsacid period, such as the very late scene of the Susa satrap Khwasak being invested by Ardavan IV. They also feature on the pre-Sasanian graffiti at Persepolis.[34]

I will now shift my focus to the second aspect, that of stylistic rendering and in particular the technical and organisational aspects. Ardashir required, of course, a workshop capable of producing reliefs with the chosen subjects. As far as we know, no sculpture had been produced in Fars for centuries. The only known stone sculptures between the end of Achaemenid rule and the Sasanian era are the reliefs from the so-called Frataraka Temple at Persepolis and the relief at Qir-Karzin in southern Fars;[35] these are no later than the first century BC and other sculptures, such as the heads from Qal'a-ye Now[36] and Tomb-e Bot,[37] can now quite possibly be dated to the early Sasanian period too.[38]

In attempting to identify the workshop which accomplished Firuzabad I, I do not agree on linking it with the craftsmen who produced the Persepolis graffiti, as proposed by Canepa:[39] these works of art should in my opinion, despite iconographic parallels, not be attributed to the same workshop, in the light of the significant difference between tiny etchings of small dimensions and rock carvings of large dimensions, the former resembling drawings, the latter being major works of sculpture.

On the other hand, the equestrian combat scene at Firuzabad I is reminiscent of the rock reliefs of Elymais, particularly as regards the technical and stylistic aspects. They are also not far apart in terms of chronology and geographic location, as these reliefs are commonly dated to the second–third centuries AD, and Elymais is on the western border of Fars.

Herrmann has suggested that 'the carvings of Elymais inspired Ardashir to employ rock reliefs as an official art form'.[40] Prudence O. Harper has been more explicit when proposing that the rock reliefs in Elymais could be 'the most probable source for the early Sasanian artisans'.[41] Recently, Fabrizio Sinisi has reiterated this explanation,[42] with which I also fully agree. It seems reasonable to suggest not only an Elymaean inspiration, but also the possibility that the new *shahanshah* had resorted to craftsmen from Elymais, a region where rock reliefs had a strong tradition: Elymaean craftsmen were able to provide the necessary know-how lacking in Fars.

The working technique and instruments used may enable us to test this hypothesis. Here we may rely only on the studies by Malcolm A. R. Colledge for Hellenistic and early Arsacid Iran[43] and by Herrmann for the Sasanian period,[44] to which we can add the recent Iranian–Italian investigations[45] in Elymais. A detailed comparative study of traces of working technique and instruments used in these two groups of sculptures is, however, beyond the scope of this chapter, and I will limit myself to general observations to underline the similarities.

On the whole, in both the productions of Elymais and those of what I consider the first Ardashir relief, Firuzabad I, the figures are produced by recessing the background so as to make the figures project. On the figures themselves details are indicated either with minor projections or with incisions: plasticity is limited to the upper parts of the figures only. It is also important to note that the lower part of the Firuzabad I relief is abraded, if ever finished.[46]

The composition and iconography of the Firuzabad I relief too, despite the effort to convey a feeling of movement, are quite simple, and the rendering of the figures of the three combat scenes is very far from naturalism: the horses in particular have large bodies and short legs, which recall the Elymaean relief of Tang-e Sarvak, Rock III[47] (Fig. 10.8). Even though the head of the horseman at Tang-e Sarvak is frontal, while the heads of the horsemen at Firuzabad are shown in profile, the frontal position of the busts is strikingly similar.

Most probably, the investiture reliefs are the subsequent step, starting with the scenes with standing figures at Firuzabad II and Naqsh-e Rajab III.

Fig. 10.8 Tang-e Sarvak (Khuzestan, Iran): Rock III, relief (after Vanden Berghe and Schippmann 1985: pl. 47).

As regards the style of these reliefs, we notice that figures gradually acquire a greater plasticity, which progressively distances them from two-dimensional drawings. However, the bad preservation and the odd location of the Firuzabad II relief, which prevent close inspection, do not allow us to offer detailed stylistic evaluation: at any rate the judgement of Herrmann, who considers the relief 'simple in design and technique, with little improvement on Elymaian reliefs',[48] predating Firuzabad I, does not seem persuasive. The relief at Naqsh-e Rajab, on the contrary, can be examined fully despite the fact that its lower parts have not been finished. All the figures are completely detached from the background and have acquired sculptural qualities which are absent from the Firuzabad I relief. Also, the composition is more balanced, capturing the solemnity of the moment in which the king stands in front of Ohrmazd, slightly larger than the king.[49]

The third investiture scene is that on horseback, carved out of the fortification wall enclosing the Achaemenid rock-cut tombs near an Elamite water sanctuary at the southern end of the Naqsh-e Rostam cliff. Herrmann considers this sculpture 'the finest relief of the Sasanian period'.[50] Her authoritative description is worth quoting:

> the scene was carved in high relief, practically in the round. The dramatic effect of the sculpted figure was enhanced by a high polish, set against a background which was deliberately left rough. Although this relief is static when comparing with the jousting scene, nevertheless there is movement in the ribbons of the diadem and the god's fluttering cloak – a breeze is blowing from the king.[51]

The technical and stylistic distance between the Firuzabad I and the Naqsh-e Rostam I reliefs is in fact huge, as rightly observed by Canepa. But how was this evolution possible? How could the simple craftsmen who produced Firuzabad I be able to 'closely study Achaemenid sculpture, with the reliefs sculpture of Persepolis and Naqsh-e Rostam providing ready examples to king and artisans alike'?[52] Let us remember that, as we have seen above, the numismatic and historical evidence would in fact suggest dating all four reliefs, of Firuzabad I, Firuzabad II, Naqsh-e Rajab III and Naqsh-e Rostam I, to the period between AD 224/225 and AD 238/239; that is, within less than fifteen years!

Throughout antiquity we see that craft traditions are transmitted within workshops, evolving slowly, wherever there is sufficient evidence. The technical perfection of the Persepolis reliefs, for example, is the result of an activity that started at Pasargadae with the reported involvement of Lydian and Ionian craftsmen on the instigation of Cyrus the Great,[53] together with the possible participation of Assyrian craftsmen, as the reliefs of Palaces R and S seem to suggest.

When observing the limited technical capacities of the craftsmen who carved Firuzabad I and the two following investiture scenes, I do not think that a close study of Achaemenid sculpture alone could have enabled them to make the huge technical leap forward between that relief and the one at Naqsh-e Rostam. Is such a change possible in less than fifteen years without the guidance of an experienced master?

Craft activity cannot be understood out of the socio-cultural context of its actual production. The various classes of artefacts reflect different levels of complexity. Stone sculpture is one of the most complex, involving the use of various tools for carving, the realisation of large-scale compositions and the establishment of a complex workshop.[54] For this reason, more than one scholar has suggested that for the first large rock relief at Firuzabad I craftsmen from Elymais, where rock reliefs had a strong tradition, had been involved. The only event which in my opinion has made the development from Firuzabad I to Naqsh-e Rostam I possible in a short period of time was the intervention of an experienced master from outside, having technical skills enabling him to achieve that skilful imitation of isolated iconographic details from the Persepolitan reliefs, combined with a harmonious rendering of the figures and a technical perfection in stone-working and polish.

Just this last aspect, which Herrmann had interpreted as an intentional stylistic choice with deep ideological linkage to the Achaemenids, provides no explanation of the practical implications: who had been able to bring this technical perfection, going back to a tradition developed with great financial effort by Cyrus and Darius, back to life?

The British scholar rightly underlines that 'Ardashir's choice of a polished finish for sculptures may reflect his admiration for, and desire to copy, the Achaemenids',[55] but does not pose what, in my view, is the crucial question as to who was able to accomplish this, given the high technical level of stone workmanship.

Copying the Persepolis reliefs, with their rich iconography and sophisticated stone polish, was not an easy task. We should remember that Cyrus and Darius had resorted to craftsmen with previous experience in stone workmanship from other provinces of the empire: this non-Persian presence is commonly accepted by scholars, and not only because it is mentioned in the Achemenid inscriptions and in the administrative Elamite tablets from Persepolis.

For the Bishapur reliefs of King Shapur I also, Ernst Herzfeld explicitly stressed 'how strongly not only foreign influence but foreign hands must have been at work during that period of Sasanian art'.[56] A long line of scholars has adopted the same position since, including recently Canepa who also acknowledges for the reliefs of Bishapur (II) and (III) 'some influence of Roman sculptural and compositional elements on the early Sasanian style'.[57] On the contrary, oddly enough for the birth of the workshop which has produced the masterpiece of Sasanian sculpture at Naqsh-e Rostam I, until now the problem of its origin has never been posed.

As already mentioned, it has been acknowledged that, in order to build the monumental complex of the Takht-e Neshin at Ardashir Khurrah, the Sasanian king resorted to craftsmen from the eastern provinces of the Roman Empire (see above). When we study the possibility of employing more experienced sculptors than the craftsmen first available to him, Ardashir could have resorted to developed traditions both in the east – in north-western India and Afghanistan – and in the west – in the eastern provinces of the Roman Empire. In both areas the Sasanian king had conducted military campaigns. However, on the basis of the greater cultural continuity and particularly on the evidence from Ardashir Khurrah in architecture, which belongs to the same period as the reliefs, I think it is more reasonable to look for a possible origin of the craftsmen employed by Ardashir I in the Syro-Mesopotamian region.

Ardashir I invaded in the course of his campaigns the area between Nisibis in the east and Carrhae and Edessa in the west. These territories saw limited penetration of Hellenistic-Roman traditions, with no known major site of monumental architecture. The vicinity of major art workshops in nearby Syria, however, probably resulted in the circulation of works of art as well as of craftsmen, as attested by the series of stone reliefs and sculptures conserved in the Museum at Sanlıurfa, the site of ancient Edessa, of a technical level much superior to that of the Elymais reliefs. Even among the interesting mosaics of Edessa, alongside panels rendered in a local stylistic approach, we have other works in the Hellenistic-Roman style.

With the contribution of a sculptor from this area, Ardashir's craftsmen may have been able to receive and transform suggestions from Persepolis to arrive at the high sculptural quality of the Naqsh-e Rostam I relief. A detailed investigation of the working techniques of Ardashir's reliefs will perhaps provide proof for this hypothesis.

NOTES

1. See also notes 9–11 below.
2. Kettenhofen 1995: 177; Dignas and Winter 2007: 19.
3. Edwell 2008: 167, 178; 2013: 843.
4. There is no space to discuss Ardashir's alleged ambition to reconquer the territories of the former Persian Empire of the Achaemenids, recurring in Roman literary sources (see Edwell 2013: 842).
5. Callieri 2014: 146–7.
6. Schippmann 1971: 116–18.
7. See Callieri 2011: 189 ff.
8. Callieri 2011: 192.
9. Huff 1972.
10. Huff 1972: 540.
11. Huff 1972: 539.
12. Bier 2009: 19.
13. Huff 2008.
14. Sinisi 2014: 50.
15. Callieri 2006.
16. Hinz 1969: 115–43.
17. Canepa 2013: 873.
18. Lukonin 1969: 47–8; 1977: 180; 1979: 18–19.
19. Hinz 1969: 115–43.
20. Vanden Berghe 1983: 62.
21. Herrmann 2000: 38–9.
22. Herrmann 2000: 38.
23. Herrmann 1981: 156.
24. Overlaet 2013: 326.
25. Overlaet 2013: 324; cf. Daryaee 2010: 251.
26. Alram and Gyselen 2003: 148.
27. Overlaet 2013: 326.
28. Overlaet 2013: 327.
29. Canepa 2013: 873.
30. Canepa 2013: 873.
31. Trümpelmann 1991: 62.
32. Canepa 2013: 873.
33. Canepa 2013: 862. Within the Sasanian period, the relief at Firuzabad I, which B. Goldman and A. M. G. Little define as 'a rather hesitant work', has remarkable similarities in composition and flat rendering with the mural paintings of similar date at Dura-Europos (Goldman and Little 1980: 287–8), as well as in a graffito recectly discovered in the Kashan area, representing a galloping horseman (Sowlat 2012).
34. Callieri 2006; see Canepa 2013: 873.
35. Callieri 2007: 144–5.
36. Kawami 1987: 138–9, 222.
37. Asgari Chaverdi 2002.
38. Callieri 2007: 138–9.
39. Canepa 2013: 873.
40. Herrmann 2000: 36.

41 Harper 1981: 96.
42 Sinisi 2014: 46–7.
43 Colledge 1979.
44 Herrmann 1981.
45 Messina et al. 2014.
46 Callieri 2014: 138, no. 403.
47 Von Gall 1990: fig. 1; Kawami 2013: fig. 38.10.
48 Herrmann 2000: 38.
49 The total height of the figure of the king is greater than that of the investing figure; however, this only applies if we include the *korymbos*, while the investing figure is on the whole taller, with his eyes looking at the king from a superior position.
50 Herrmann 2000: 39.
51 Herrmann 2000: 39.
52 Canepa 2010: 576.
53 See Nylander 1970.
54 Kawami 2013: 751.
55 Herrmann 1981: 159.
56 Herzfeld 1941: 314.
57 Canepa 2013: 873.

BIBLIOGRAPHY

Alram, M. and Gyselen, R. (2003), *Sylloge Nummorum Sasanidarum Paris – Berlin – Wien, Band I, Ardashir I.–Shapur I.*, Veröffentlichungen der numismatischen Kommission, 41, Vienna: Österreichische Akademie der Wissenschaften.

Asgari Chaverdi, A. (2002), 'Recent Post-Achaemenid Finds from Southern Fars, Iran', *Iran*, 40, pp. 277–8.

Bier, L. (2009), 'Palais B at Bishapur and its Sasanian Reliefs', in R. Gyselen (ed.), *Sources pour l'histoire et la géographie du monde iranien (224–710)*, Res Orientales, XVIII, Bures-sur-Yvette: Association pour l'Avancement des Études Iraniennes, pp. 11–40.

Callieri, P. (2006), 'At the Roots of Sasanian Royal Imagery: The Persepolis Graffiti', in M. Compareti, P. Raffetta and G. Scarcia (eds), *Ērān ud Anērān: Studies Presented to Boris Il'ič Maršak on the Occasion of his 70th Birthday*, Venezia: Cafoscarina, pp. 129–48.

Callieri, P. (2007), *L'archéologie du Fārs à l'époque hellénistique: Quatre leçons au Collège de France 8, 15, 22 et 29 mars 2007*, Persika, 11, Paris: De Boccard.

Callieri, P. (2011), 'Les Sassanides étaient-ils les héritiers des Achéménides? L'évidence archéologique', in C. Lippolis and S. de Martino (eds), *Un impaziente desiderio di scorrere il mondo: Studi in onore di Antonio Invernizzi per il suo settantesimo compleanno*, Monografie di *Mesopotamia*, XIV, Florence: Le Lettere, pp. 187–200.

Callieri, P. (2014), *Architecture et représentations dans l'Iran sassanide*, Studia Iranica, Cahier 50, Paris: Association pour l'Avancement des Études Iraniennes.

Canepa, M. P. (2010), 'Technologies of Memory in Early Sasanian Iran:

Achaemenid Sites and Sasanian Identity', *American Journal of Archaeology*, 114.4, pp. 563–96.
Canepa, M. P. (2013), 'Sasanian Rock Reliefs', in D. T. Potts (ed.), *The Oxford Handbook of Ancient Iran*, New York: Oxford University Press, pp. 856–77.
Colledge, M. A. R. (1979), 'Sculptors' Stone Carving Techniques in Seleucid and Parthian Iran and Their Place in the "Parthian" Cultural Milieu: Some Preliminary Observations', *East and West*, 29.1–2, pp. 221–40.
Compareti, M. (2011), 'The State of Research on Sasanian Painting', *E Sasanika Archaeology* 8, <http://www.sasanika.org/esasanika/the-state-of-research-on-sasanian-painting-2/>.
Daryaee, T. (2008), 'Kingship in Early Sasanian Iran', in V. Sarkhosh Curtis and S. Stewart (eds), *The Sasanian Era*, The Idea of Iran, 3, London: I.B. Tauris, pp. 60–70.
Daryaee, T. (2010), 'Ardaxšīr and the Sasanians' Rise to Power', *Anabasis: Studia Classica et Orientalia*, 1, pp. 236–55.
Dignas, B. and Winter, E. (2007), *Rome and Persia in Late Antiquity: Neighbours and Rivals*, Cambridge: Cambridge University Press.
Edwell, P. (2008), *Between Rome and Persia: The Middle Euphrates, Mesopotamia and Palmyra under Roman Control*, London and New York: Routledge.
Edwell, P. (2013), 'Sasanian Interactions with Rome and Byzantium', in D. T. Potts (ed.), *The Oxford Handbook of Ancient Iran*, New York: Oxford University Press, pp. 840–55.
Goldman, B. and Little, A. M. G. (1980), 'The Beginning of Sasanian Painting and Dura-Europos', *Iranica Antiqua*, 15, pp. 283–98.
Harper, P. O. (1981), *Silver Vessels of the Sasanian Period. Vol. One: Royal Imagery*, New York: Metropolitan Museum of Art.
Herrmann, G. (1981), 'Early Sasanian Stoneworking: A Preliminary Report', *Iranica Antiqua*, 16, pp. 151–60.
Herrmann, G. (2000), 'The Rock Reliefs of Sasanian Iran', in J. Curtis (ed.), *Mesopotamia and Iran in the Parthian and Sasanian Periods: Rejection and Revival c. 238 BC–AD 642. Proceedings of a Seminar in Memory of Vladimir G. Lukonin*, London: British Museum, pp. 35–45.
Herzfeld, E. (1941), *Iran in the Ancient East*, New York and London: Oxford University Press.
Hinz, W. (1969), *Altiranische Funde und Forschungen*, Berlin: de Gruyter.
Huff, D. (1972), 'Der Takht-i Nishin in Firuzabad: Mass-Systeme Sasanidischer Bauwerke I', *Archäologischer Anzeiger*, pp. 517–40.
Huff, D. (2008), 'Formation and Ideology of the Sasanian State in the Context of Archaeological Evidence', in V. Sarkhosh Curtis and S. Stewart (eds), *The Sasanian Era*, The Idea of Iran, 3, London: I.B. Tauris, pp. 31–59.
Kawami, T. S. (1987), *Monumental Art of the Parthian Period in Iran*, Acta Iranica 26, Leiden: Brill.
Kawami, T. S. (2013), 'Parthian and Elymaean Rock Reliefs', in D. T. Potts (ed.), *The Oxford Handbook of Ancient Iran*, New York: Oxford University Press, pp. 751–65.
Kettenhofen, E. (1995), 'Die Eroberung von Nisibis und Karrhai durch die Sasaniden in der Zeit Kaiser Maximins (235/236 n. Chr.)', *Iranica Antiqua*, 30, pp. 159–77.

Lukonin, V. G. (1969), *Kul'tura sasanidskogo Irana: Iran v III–V vv. Očerki po istorii kul'tury*, Moscow: Nauka.
Lukonin, V. G. (1977), *Iskusstvo drevnego Irana*, Moscow: Iskusstvo.
Lukonin, V. G. (1979), *Iran v III veke: Novye materialy i opyt istoričeskoj rekonstrukcii*, Moscow: Nauka.
Messina, V., Rinaudo, F. and Mehr Kian, J. (2014), '3D Laser Scanning of Parthian Sculptural Reliefs: The Experience of the Iranian–Italian Joint Expedition in Khuzestan (Iran)', *Journal of Field Archaeology*, 39.2, pp. 151–61.
Nylander, C. (1970), *Ionians in Pasargadae: Studies in Old Persian Architecture*, Acta Universitatis Upsaliensis – Boreas. Uppsala Studies in Ancient Mediterranean and Near Eastern Civilizations, 1, Uppsala: Academia Upsaliensis.
Overlaet, B. (2013), 'And Man Created God? Kings, Priests and Gods on Sasanian Investiture Reliefs', *Iranica Antiqua*, 48, pp. 313–54.
Schippmann, K. (1971), *Die iranischen Feuerheiligtümer*, Berlin and New York: De Gruyter.
Sinisi, F. (2014), 'Sources for the History of Art of the Parthian Period: Arsacid Coinage as Evidence for Continuity of Imperial Art in Iran', *Parthica*, 16, pp. 9–60.
Sowlat, F. (2012), 'Nowyâfteha̍'i az dowre-ye sâsâni dar Kâshân [New Sassanid Finds from Kashan Area]', *Bāstānpazhūhi*, 4–5/8–9, pp. 97–102.
Trümpelmann, L. (1991), *Zwischen Persepolis und Firuzabad: Gräber, Paläste und Felsreliefs im alten Persien*, Mainz: von Zabern.
Vanden Berghe, L. (ed.) (1983), *Reliefs rupestres de l' Irān ancien*, Brussels: Musées Royaux d'Art et d'Histoire.
Vanden Berghe, L. and Schippmann, K. (1985), *Les reliefs rupestres d'Elymaïde (Iran) de l'époque parthe*, Suppléments à *Iranica Antiqua*, 3, Leuven: Peeters.
von Gall, H. (1990), *Das Reiterkampfbild in der iranischen und iranisch beeinflussten Kunst parthischer und sasanidischer Zeit*, Teheraner Forschungen VI, Berlin: Gebr. Mann.

Part IV
Imperial Power Balance and International Relations

11 *Innovation and Stagnation: Military Infrastructure and the Shifting Balance of Power Between Rome and Persia*

Eberhard W. Sauer, Jebrael Nokandeh, Konstantin Pitskhelauri and Hamid Omrani Rekavandi

The Roman Empire, and its eastern and western successor states, controlled the majority of Europe's population for approximately half a millennium (first century BC to fifth century AD), holding dominant power status from the second century BC to the seventh century AD, longer than any other state in the western world in history, and it was also the only empire ever to rule over the entire Mediterranean. Its ability to integrate ethnic groups and its well-organised military apparatus were instrumental to this success. From the third century onwards, however, the balance increasingly shifted; the physical dimensions of fortresses and unit sizes tended to decrease markedly in the Roman world, and the tradition of constructing marching camps and training facilities seems to have been abandoned. By contrast, the Sasanian Empire increasingly became the motor of innovation. Already in the third century it matched Rome's abilities to launch offensive operations, conduct siege warfare and produce military hardware and armour. Jointly with the Iberians and Albanians, the empire also made skilful use of natural barriers to protect its frontiers, notably by blocking the few viable routes across the Caucasus. By the fifth/sixth century, it pioneered heavily fortified, large, rectangular campaign bases, of much greater size than any military compounds in the late Roman world. These military tent cities, filled with rectangular enclosures in neat rows, are suggestive of a strong and well-disciplined army. Like these campaign bases, the contemporary c. 200km-long Gorgan Wall, protected by a string of barracks forts and of distinctly independent design, is not copied from prototypes elsewhere. The evidence emerging from recent joint projects between the Iranian Cultural Heritage, Handcraft and Tourism Organisation and the Universities of Edinburgh, Tbilisi and Durham suggests that in late antiquity the Sasanian army had gone into the lead in terms of organisational abilities, innovation and effective use of its resources.

EIGHT CENTURIES OF GREAT POWER STATUS – SEVEN CENTURIES OF RIVALRY

Some 1,400 years ago, in AD 614/615 and again in AD 626, Sasanian armies had reached the Bosporus. They stood opposite what was at the time by far the richest and most populous city in Europe: Constantinople, the capital of the Roman Empire.[1] The Roman Empire had dominated Europe and the Mediterranean, militarily and economically, for almost 800 years, vastly longer than any other state in world history. In the early seventh century, the Sasanian army pushed the western world's most enduring mega-empire to the brink of annihilation.

The Sasanian Empire in the late AD 610s, and for much of the 620s, stretched from Egypt and Syria to the west of the Indian subcontinent and from the Caucasus and the southern margins of the Steppes of Eurasia to Yemen (Fig. 11.1). Not just in terms of territorial extent, but also in terms of duration of dominance, the Sasanian Empire was arguably an equal rival to Rome, lasting for over four centuries; that is longer than most other political entities of comparable size, and this timespan can be doubled if we bear in mind that it was not a new empire established from scratch in the third century. Instead, the Sasanian Empire should be considered a successor of the Parthian Empire on which a new dynasty had been imposed via internal revolt (rather than conquest by an external foe). So it is logical to think of just one, Partho-Sasanian, Empire – which was the major military and economic power in the Near East for roughly the same period of time as the Roman Empire had been in the west, from the second century BC to the seventh century AD. The Sasanian Empire, with its centre of dynastic power in south-western Persia, differed no more from the Parthian Empire, with its northern Persian core, than the early Roman Empire, where Italians held the reins of political and military power up to the first century AD, differed from the high to late Roman Empire, when most of the army and the emperors themselves were recruited from within the frontier provinces. It is needless to stress that during the eight centuries or so when the Roman and Partho-Sasanian Empires enjoyed great power status, both underwent numerous fundamental changes; indeed, that they were adaptable to the challenges of the time explains their longevity. Gradual bestowal of citizenship on conquered peoples and the shift of power from conqueror to conquered within the Roman Empire greatly reduced the risk of rebellion, and contributed as much to the empire's stability and longevity as the efficacy of its armed forces. The late Roman Empire may have had little in common with the second-century BC Republic – and the late Sasanian state little in common with the Parthian Empire centuries earlier – except that they had never been completely defeated and subdued by an external force, and remained the most dominant political entities in the west and Near East respectively for some three quarters of a millennium. For seven centuries they confronted each other, from Pompey's conquest of Syria in 64 BC, soon followed by the annihilation of Crassus' army at Carrhae in 53 BC, to the Arab conquest of Roman and Sasanian possessions in the Near East in the AD 630s. Only two other pre-medieval empires in south-west Asia and the Mediterranean had reached similar geographic size, and neither was as long-lasting as the Roman and Partho-Sasanian Empires had been: the Achaemenid Empire, retaining its vast dominion for over two centuries, and Alexander's short-lived realm thereafter.[2]

It seems logical to see the Parthian and Sasanian eras as two phases in the history of one empire, but there is no attempt here to downplay the changes the Sasanian dynasty brought about. Notably in terms of military capabilities, the Sasanian era saw a series of major innovations, spread over centuries. It is also the Sasanian era, for which we have significant new evidence, and the focus of this chapter is thus on this period.

FASHIONABLE RELATIVISM AND PERSISTENT EUROCENTRISM

The Sasanian Empire's territorial extent and further expansion in the later sixth and early seventh centuries, well beyond what had been controlled by the Parthian kings, is a remarkable phenomenon. It is astonishing that some believe nonetheless that the Sasanian army had been disorganised, largely or exclusively non-professional, and that successful defence of an empire of such extraordinary size depended on haphazard arrangements, indeed that there had been no standing army at all for the first three centuries of the Sasanian Empire's existence.[3] Major monuments in the east, such as the Gorgan Wall,

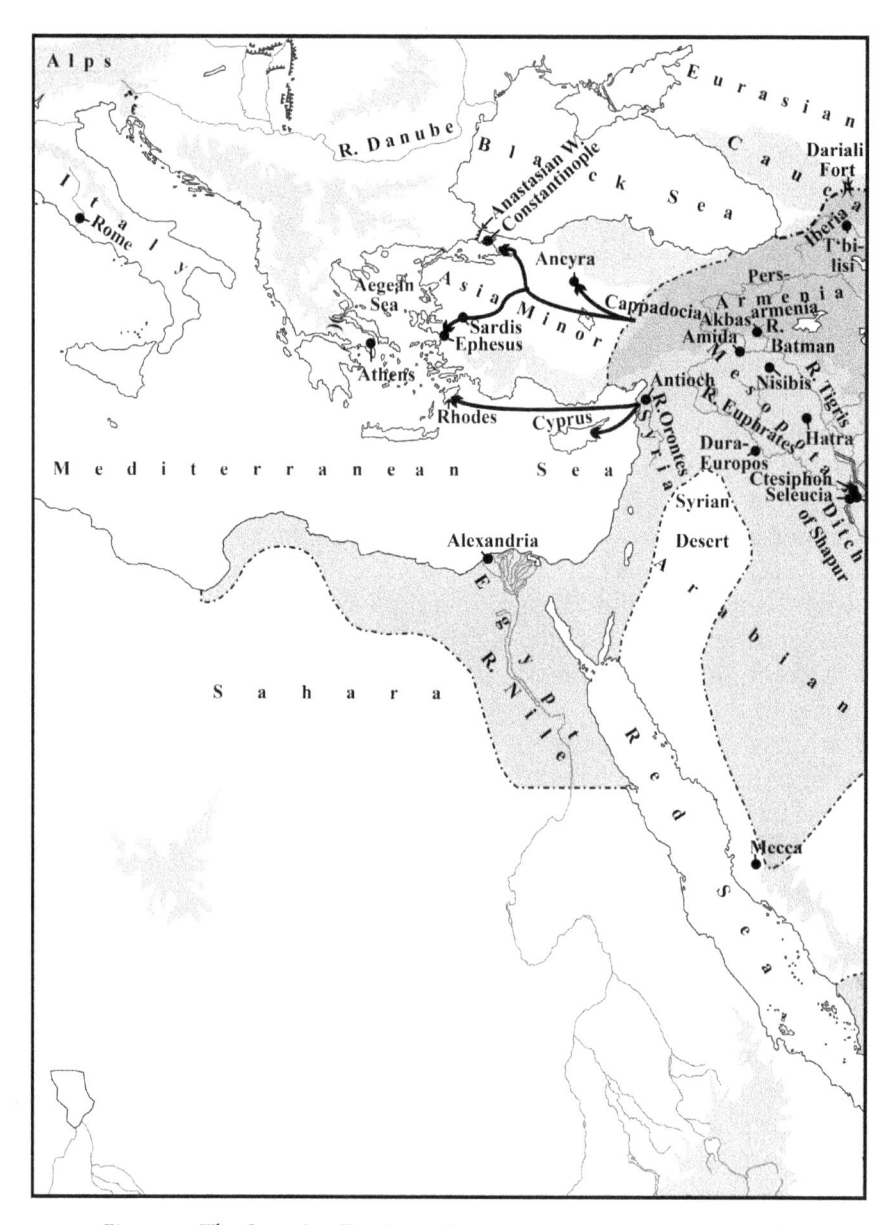

Fig. 11.1 The Sasanian Empire at its greatest extent in c. AD 619–28.

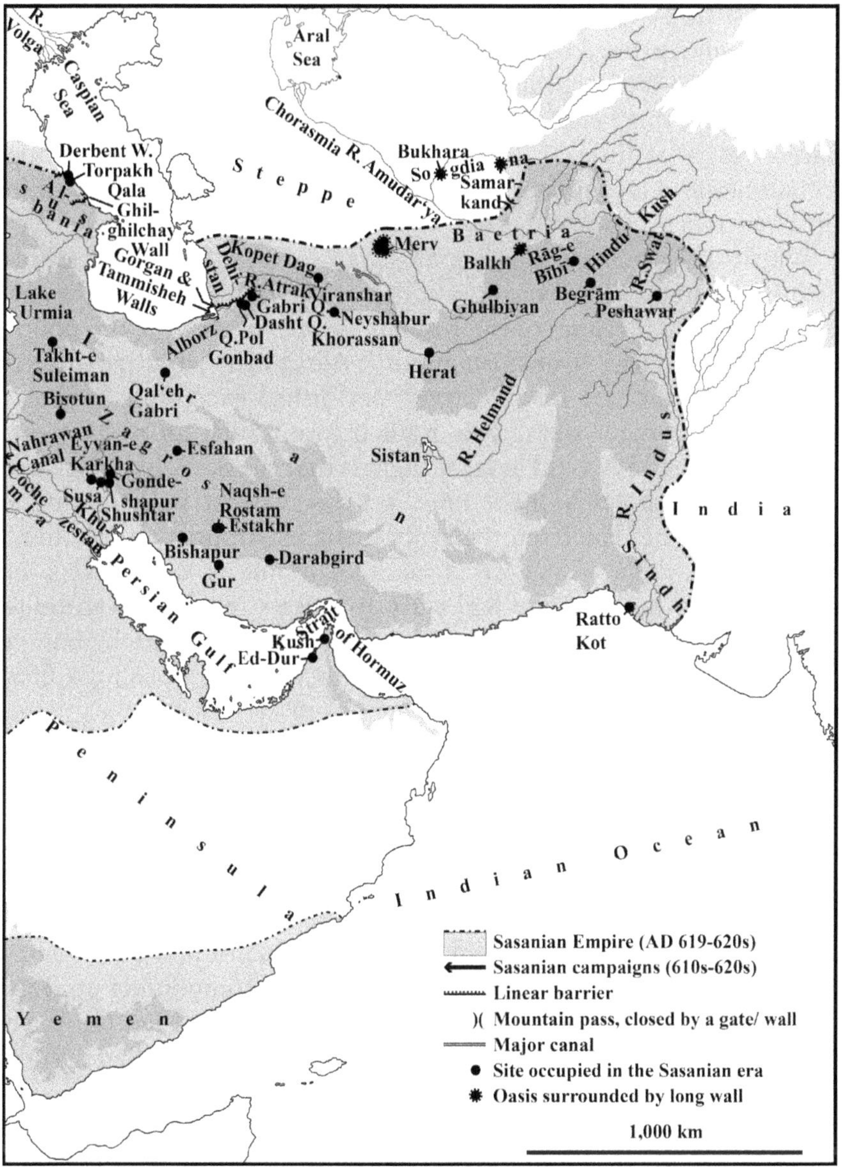
R. Volga
Caspian Sea
Aral Sea
Chorasmia
R. Amudar'ya
Steppe
Bukhara
Sogdiana
Samarkand
Derbent W.
Torpakh Qala
Ghilghilchay Wall
Albania
Gorgan & Tammisheh Walls
Dehistan
Kopet Dag
R. Atrak
Viranshar
Gabri Q.
Dasht Q.
Neyshabur
Khorassan
Merv
Bactria
Balkh
Rāg-e Bībī
Hindu Kush
R. Swat
Begrām
Peshawar
Ghulbiyan
Lake Urmia
Takht-e Suleiman
Alborz
Q.Pol Gonbad
Qal'eh Gabri
Bisotun
Herat
R. Helmand
Sistan
Nahrawan Canal
Eyvan-e Karkha
Esfahan
Zagros
Iran
Coche
Susa
Gondeshapur
Shushtar
Naqsh-e Rostam
Estakhr
Khuzestan
Bishapur
Darabgird
Gur
Persian Gulf
Kush
Ed-Dur
Strait of Hormuz
R. Indus
Sindh
India
Ratto Kot
Peninsula
Indian Ocean
Yemen
Sasanian Empire (AD 619-620s)
Sasanian campaigns (610s-620s)
Linear barrier
)(Mountain pass, closed by a gate/ wall
Major canal
Site occupied in the Sasanian era
Oasis surrounded by long wall
1,000 km

are often assumed by default to be imitations of prototypes from the west[4] – sometimes probably a result of subconscious Eurocentrism, not a conscious ideology but a bias towards what we know best. Similarly, if our (mainly western or much later) written sources provide little evidence for permanent Sasanian frontier troops, it is all too easily assumed that there were none. Lack of firm archaeological proof for a well-organised standing army until recently seemingly corroborated this belief. As was perhaps to be expected, this was in part a result of little, if any, fieldwork and state-of-the-art dating techniques at relevant sites, and the picture has radically changed in the twenty-first century.

Whilst often underestimating Sasanian capabilities, recent scholarship has frequently overrated those of the late Roman state and questioned the 'decline' of the Roman Empire, preferring the politically correct term 'transformation'.[5] Alexander Sarantis argued recently that the late Roman army 'performed exceptionally well', just facing stronger opponents than before.[6] Such an assessment, even if persuasive, would at least suggest that the army had not kept up with developments of the time. Yet the evidence paints a rather different picture. Far from the army being as strong as it had been before, the evidence suggests a marked decline in capabilities. In the early and high empire legionary fortresses reached an average size of 20–5 ha, housing some 5,000–6,000 soldiers each, but in late antiquity they tend to be 4–5 ha large, perhaps housing a fifth of the garrison. Not only had the legions massively shrunk in size, but there were no longer compounds even approaching the size that was widespread up to the third century. There is far less evidence for late antique military barracks than for those of the first three centuries of the Christian era. Were there fewer soldiers? If written sources can be trusted,[7] the Roman army had increased in numbers in late antiquity. This, if true, will apply to urban garrisons, which are hard to trace archaeologically, not to mention the *foederati*. The number of troops in permanent military compounds appears to have shrunk massively and those that remained relied on much more heavily defended compounds than Rome's soldiers had needed before.

Training similarly appears to have declined. We are not aware of a single training ground, practice camp or new marching camp that is certain to be late antique. Whilst admittedly, none of these installations are easy to date, and whilst there are very few training grounds in total, the complete absence of firm proof for any late antique installations of this kind is significant.[8] Even if there is still the odd reference to late antique camps in the sources, such as during Julian's invasion of Sasanian Mesopotamia in AD 363, defences (if any) were basic, consisting of wooden stakes or shields, whereas ditches and ramparts or walls appear to have been exceptional.[9] Vegetius, lamenting that soldiers in his time no longer were involved in regular training or built marching camps, to keep them safe from surprise attacks,[10] will not have been far off the truth.

The post-war generations of the twentieth and twenty-first centuries, mostly fortunate enough never to have personally experienced war and never confronted with the reality and logic of warfare, have often dismissed the loss of capabilities of the late Roman army or doubted the effectiveness of major military fortifications.[11] The pendulum of fashion in the Anglo-American world has swung from an obsession with military history in the earlier twentieth century to widespread scepticism towards any notion that military strength or weakness can be key factors in the success or failure of political entities. Relativism is in part to blame too. Any notion of superlatives or decline seems suspect and old-fashioned, and contemporary scholars often argue for the middle ground, refusing to entertain the idea that military success or failure can be the result of the strength or weakness of a state's military apparatus and relevant factors, such as numbers, quality of training, leadership, strategy, organisation, quality of equipment and defensive architecture. There is, of course, no question that it was more than loss of military capabilities that led to the takeover of the Western Roman Empire by its enemies as well as the military setbacks of the more prosperous and naturally well protected Eastern Empire. Multiple other factors were involved, but the decline in military capabilities and over-reliance on foreign fighters were surely amongst the most decisive weak points.

Fashion has led to scholars frequently downplaying the role of military strength and weakness in the Roman Empire's successes and setbacks. It was, by contrast, to a significant extent lack of evidence that has led many to underestimate the Sasanian army's size, level of organisation and capabilities. The widespread lack of interest in military matters of course has been a contributing factor nonetheless. Even without new evidence, the hypothesis that the Sasanian Empire could have maintained its vast dominion for centuries without a strong army and whilst relying on ad hoc conscription of mercenaries or peasant soldiers[12] would hardly have been credible.

BALANCE OF POWER UP TO THE FOURTH CENTURY

In the second century, the Roman army had captured Ctesiphon three times: in AD 116–17, AD 165 and AD 197/198. It had also once, in AD 116, ventured as far as the Persian Gulf and repeatedly operated in Transcaucasia. Then and for the next 500 years, until the AD 620s, it never reached any part of the highlands of Persia (such as the third-century palaces in Fars) and it may have been convenient to portray Ctesiphon as the eastern neighbour's centre of power. Nonetheless, it is worth noting that in the second century Roman armies penetrated deeper into the Parthian Empire's sphere of control than vice versa. Furthermore, Rome annexed territory, pushing its frontiers further east, temporarily in AD 114–17 and permanently in AD 165, and notably in c. AD 198, when establishing the province of Mesopotamia (Fig. 11.2). In the third century, by contrast, especially after the rise of the Sasanian dynasty and during the half century when Rome was much weakened through a string of civil wars (AD 235–80s), the armies of Rome's eastern neighbour repeatedly ventured deep into Rome's provinces in the Near East and Asia Minor. The military initiative was now very much with the Sasanian Empire, whilst Rome repeatedly suffered defeat and humiliation, including the temporary capture of Antioch, the largest city in the Roman Near East, and a string of defeats – of Gordian III, Philip I and Valerian, the last of whom was the first and only Roman emperor ever to be taken a prisoner of war (Fig. 11.3).[13] The remains of siege works and (probably Sasanian) camps at Dura-Europos[14] and Hatra[15] provide material evidence for the number of men the Sasanian Empire was capable of mustering and for its capabilities, which now matched those of its western rival. It was only towards the end of the century that Rome temporarily regained the initiative. Emperor Carus captured Ctesiphon in AD 283. Aside from Odaenathus of Palmyra's successful military campaigns in the AD 260s, this was the first time in over eighty years a Roman army had been able to penetrate victoriously so deep into Mesopotamia. In AD 298 Galerius won a victory that resulted in Rome gaining territory on the Upper Tigris.

Yet, whilst the first Tetrarchy (AD 293–305) resulted in Rome regaining some of its offensive capabilities, the century had seen major changes to the Roman army. At the beginning of the third century, Roman legions, and the fortresses they occupied, had been as large as they had been for the previous two centuries. Under the

Fig. 11.2 The Arch of Septimius Severus at Rome, commemorating the Parthian Wars of the AD 190s.

Fig. 11.3 Rock relief at Bishapur (II): Shapur I triumphant over the dead Gordian III (AD 238–44), a kneeling emperor, probably Philip I (AD 244–9), and a standing emperor, probably Valerian, taken prisoner of war in AD 260. (See above, 'Cover Images', on the proposed identification of the figures.)

soldier emperors (AD 235–84/285), notably in the AD 250s-70s, a string of civil wars led to the depletion of frontier garrisons, triggering invasions of unprotected provinces by external enemies, insecurity, depopulation and a severe economic downturn. When by the late third century Rome emerged from the troubles, legions and the fortresses they occupied had shrunk massively in size and relied on much heavier defences. Of course, as noted above, written sources claim that the late antique Roman army was numerically stronger than its early and high imperial predecessors, but, if this is true, most military personnel no longer appear to have occupied purpose-built military compounds. The number of troops may not have decreased, but the number of well-organised forces may well have plummeted.

The Sasanian army, unlike its Roman counterpart, is not easy to trace archaeologically in this century, other than when involved in siege operations. Yet this would similarly be true of Caesar's army which had conquered Gaul in the 50s of the first century BC. The Roman Empire expanded most rapidly under the late Republic without its powerful military forces normally erecting forts, fortresses and camps that allow the modern archaeologist to evaluate its capabilities, with few exceptions.[16] It preferred to reoccupy existing towns and hillforts, leaving few traces of its presence. Only the invasion of Germany, which was largely devoid of fortifications or defended urban settlements suitable for reoccupation, forced the Roman army under Augustus to pioneer the systematic erection of large geometric compounds from scratch.[17] The Sasanian army of the third century is similarly elusive and for similar reasons to those that applied to Caesar's forces in Gaul: evidently, it was also content to reuse existing infrastructure, thus evading the archaeologist – other than when, like Caesar's army three centuries before, forced to engage in siege operations when there was no alternative to erecting military architecture from scratch. The scale of Caesar's siege works at Alésia[18] and of their Sasanian counterparts some 300 years later at Hatra, with a circumvallation and a 184ha siege camp (excluding an additional 101ha outer perimeter)[19] provides us with rare glimpses of the size, level of organisation and engineering skills of the military apparatus late Republican Roman generals and third-century Sasanian kings could mobilise. Very important is the recent discovery by Simon James and his colleagues of three camps at Dura, measuring 117ha, 121ha and 124ha. Perhaps it is no coincidence that the surface area of each is similar to the 125ha campaign bases at Torpakh Qala and Qal'eh Pol Gonbad, whereas

Fig. 11.4 Dura-Europos on the River Euphrates, taken by Shapur I with overwhelming force in AD 256.

Roman marching camps tend to be significantly smaller. Were they Roman in origin and reoccupied by the Sasanian siege army, as Simon James argues,[20] or Sasanian? The evidence, which there is no space here to discuss in detail, is circumstantial and does not permit us to rule out either attribution, but the existence of Sasanian compounds of almost identical size, whilst we know of no Roman match,[21] is a strong argument for assigning them to Rome's eastern neighbour. The spot, where a large Sasanian army could have been easily supplied via the Euphrates, may have been used on the occasion of the siege of Dura-Europos (Fig. 11.4) as well as on successive Sasanian campaigns to the west as a gathering point for large field armies. Whether the Dura camps were Sasanian or Roman, written testimony for the sustained success of both armies leaves no doubt that siege operations were unusual only in leaving such clear traces – whilst the deployment of troops of similar numbers and skills, at the major theatres of war, was perfectly normal. There is no space to discuss weapons and armour in detail, but as widely acknowledged, advances in arms technology also often occurred in the east, sometimes later copied in the west. The *catafracti*, heavy cavalry foreshadowing medieval knights, are just one example of the phenomenon.[22]

For much of the fourth century, the Sasanian army has left even fewer archaeological traces detected to date than in the third, whereas the Roman army continued to erect a significant number of heavily fortified compounds, albeit none of them coming close to the size of fortresses of the first to third centuries. Written sources suggest that the armed forces of Rome's eastern neighbour were at least as powerful as they had been in the third century. Emperor Julian when invading central Mesopotamia in AD 363 paid with his life, and the empire with the loss of territory, for underestimating Sasanian military might and ability to devise a successful defensive strategy. The effective use of skilled archers, fortified cities and knowledge of the terrain, when cutting off supplies to the Roman army and devising attacks, gave the Persians the upper edge.

THE LATE FOURTH TO SIXTH CENTURIES

It was in the late fourth, fifth and sixth centuries that circumstances arose which led the Sasanian army to emerge from its archaeological shadow – and step by step build up the most massive military infrastructure of late antiquity, if not of the ancient world as a whole. Evidence for the phenomenon has emerged at multiple frontiers. Recent fieldwork by Jaafar Jotheri has established that water flowed in the massive, multifunctional Khandaq Shapur ('Shapur's Ditch') in central Mesopotamia after AD 420 and before 570, an obstacle for any hostile forces approaching from the south.[23] The sample dates to a time when the canal, evidently dug before this date and used beyond, was already operational. This allows for the possibility that the traditional attribution to Shapur II (AD 309–79) is correct, and it certainly proves the existence of the Khandaq Shapur in the later Sasanian era. Our latest results indicate that the most likely date for the construction of Dariali Fort (Fig. 11.5), controlling traffic across the central Caucasus, was AD 390/430, probably related to the Hunnic raid of AD 395. In the fifth century another dangerous new neighbour appeared on the northern frontiers: the Hephthalites, requiring Sasanian kings repeatedly to focus their attention on the fertile Gorgan Plain. To protect this more effectively, the decision was taken to build the Gorgan Wall on the right bank of the River Gorgan, where fewer tributaries had to be negotiated. In the steppes north of the river, there were no settlements of sufficient size and with appropriate defences to accommodate the estimated 20,000–30,000-strong garrison, let alone to spread it evenly along over 200km of wall (Fig. 11.6).[24] It ran, like earlier Roman frontier barriers (the *Limes*,

Fig. 11.5 Recent excavations by the University of Edinburgh and Tbilisi State University have shown that the well-built mortared outer walls (right) and casemates of Dariali Fort, blocking the key route across the Caucasus, most probably date to the AD 390s or early fifth century when the site was under Sasanian control.

Hadrian's Wall and the Antonine Wall) through thinly populated lands – and the Sasanian army, undoubtedly independently, followed the same logic as the high imperial army of Rome had done: it erected geometric forts alongside the linear barrier. Much larger compounds in the hinterland, such as Qal'eh Kharabeh, dated like the Gorgan Wall to the fifth and/or early sixth century, provided a safe retreat for mobile forces, probably parts of the field army whilst deployed here at times of crisis. At least one of these, the 36ha fortification of Gabri Qal'eh, was erected prior to the Gorgan Wall, yielding a *terminus ante quem* of AD 422 (based on a sample dating to between AD 337 and AD 422 at 95.4 per cent probability) and may have developed into a Sasanian town, to judge by the quantity of redeposited Sasanian material from an access causeway.

Similarly, when confronting Rome in Upper Mesopotamia, geometric compounds were erected on arid land where no suitable compounds were available for reuse. These barracks forts may be of similar date to their counterparts on the Gorgan Wall, but we also have to allow for the possibility that they could be earlier (or later) – as Persia had already taken over the territories, where it

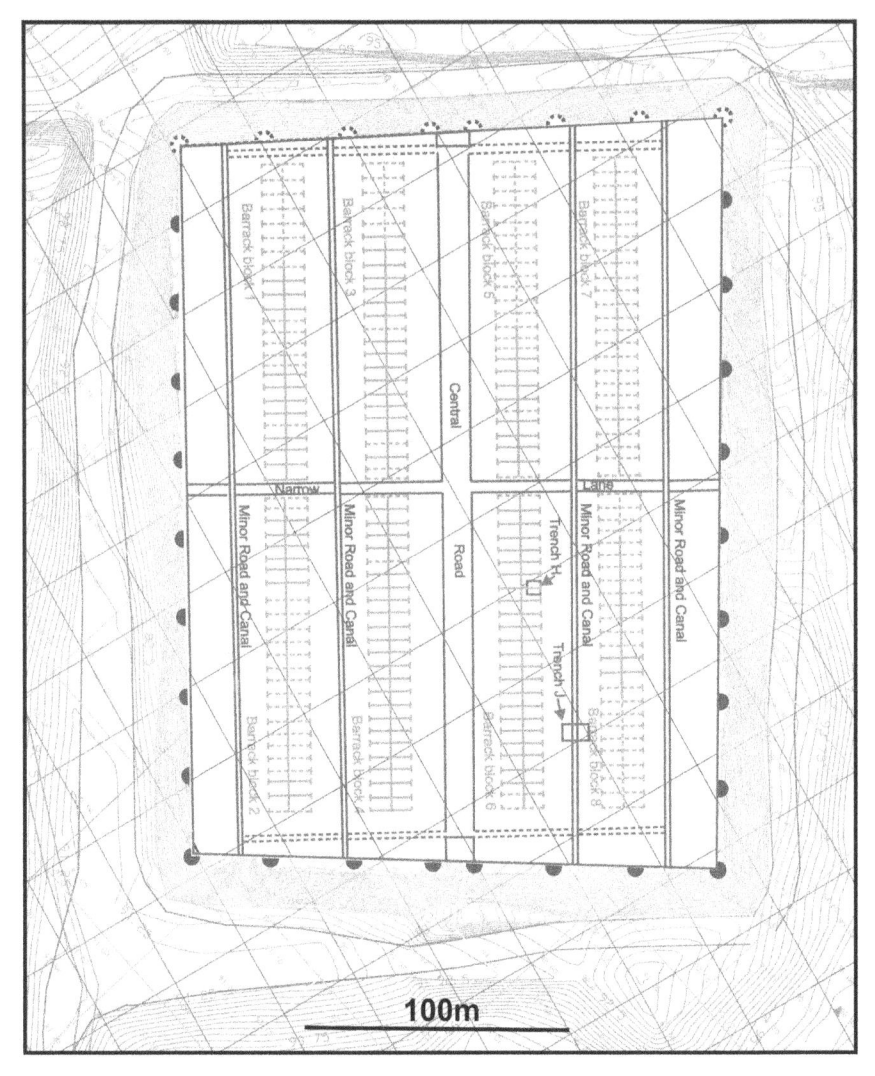

Fig. 11.6 Plan of Fort 4, based on fieldwork by the ICHHTO, the University of Edinburgh and Abingdon Archaeological Geophysics. The neat organisation of space, with barracks providing accommodation for a permanent garrison, demonstrates that the Sasanian Empire possessed a well-organised frontier army.

subsequently appears to have built barracks forts, partially in the third century and partially after AD 363.[25]

The Roman Republican army and the Sasanian army of the third century both achieved significant successes against their opponents, and written sources attest that both were more often victorious than suffering defeat. Yet both have left few purpose-built military monuments, other than those associated with a siege (Table 11.1). Armies can evidently be strong without leaving much material evidence. If this is accepted, can we conclude that the reduction in maximum and average size of late Roman military compounds, as well as a reduction of their combined size and the combined size of barracks therein, in comparison with first- to third-century bases, marks a loss in strength? The Sasanian army of the fifth–sixth centuries AD was capable of erecting and manning vast compounds (Fig. 11.7), not to mention major linear barriers, greater than any military monuments in the late Roman world. Does this prove that it was much stronger than the contemporary Roman army – or indeed much stronger than the early Sasanian army had been (which has left no geometric compounds of similar scale identified as such to date)? Not necessarily; indeed, an army can be strong and largely invisible, as were the Roman Republican and third-century Sasanian armies – or it can be strong and visible, as were the high imperial Roman and late antique Sasanian armies. Yet, whilst any simplistic conclusions, based on quantitative differences of what we can see, ought to be avoided, the visible remains of military infrastructure can be highly revealing, if interpreted in context. Early imperial Roman marching camps significantly reduced the risk of a successful surprise attack when operating in enemy territory, as did late Sasanian campaign bases mostly erected in frontier zones where there was a real possibility of coming under attack (Fig. 11.8). That the late Roman army appears to have abandoned building temporary bases, whilst the Sasanian army at the same time engaged in constructing such compounds on an impressive scale, provides evidence that the latter avoided unnecessary risks and had the capabilities to do so. This gave it the competitive edge.

NATURAL BARRIERS

Pragmatic armies avoid unnecessary work. This is why under the Roman Republic, when the empire kept expanding and mainly controlled territories with settlements suitable for reoccupation, few forts and linear barriers were built. The construction of geometric forts and artificial barriers on a significant scale only commenced when expansion stalled, the empire having reached on most frontiers the edge of territories of lesser economic interest and with terrain difficult to control: forested, mountainous or desert. It made sense, where no further expansion was anticipated and where no

Table 11.1 The archaeology of Roman and Partho-Sasanian military infrastructure (disregarding long walls and military equipment).

Period	Archaeological visibility		Permanent bases		Temporary bases	
	Roman	Partho-Sasanian	Roman	Partho-Sasanian	Roman	Partho-Sasanian
2nd–late 1st c. BC	Low–medium	Low	Largely invisible	Largely invisible	Siege camps	Largely invisible
Late 1st c. BC–mid-3rd c. AD	High	Low	Numerous forts and fortresses often up to c. 25ha and, exceptionally, over 50ha, if for more than one legion	Largely invisible	Numerous lightly fortified marching camps, up to c. 70ha, as well as siege camps	Largely invisible
Mid-3rd–4th c. AD	Medium–high	Low–medium	Numerous forts, not normally larger than 5ha	Mostly invisible	Largely invisible	Siege camps
5th–6th c. AD	Medium	Medium–high	Some forts, not normally larger than 5ha	Some forts, not normally larger than 5ha	Largely invisible	Several heavily fortified campaign bases up to c. 170ha

Archaeological visibility: an estimate as to the overall proportion of military establishments that has left traces and provides a testimony to the army's size and level of organisation.

- Low: material evidence does not provide us with a reliable idea of the size of the army; largely reoccupying existing settlements or housed in compounds defended, if at all, so lightly so as to be invisible.
- High: size and number of compounds provide significant insights into the size and organisation of the army.
- Largely invisible: compounds either did not exist or were lightly defended, so as to leave little or no trace. Note that in addition to archaeologically easily traceable (even if often as yet undated), heavily fortified campaign bases, Vegetius (3.10) implies that the Sasanians also built marching camps, defended only with sacks of sand. The evidence for these will in many instances literally have been blown away, whilst others may well survive, even if not easy to trace.

Permanent versus temporary bases: too little research has been done to date on Sasanian campaign bases for secure classification. Whilst there is no evidence for permanent barracks in any of them so far, other than rows of small mudbrick structures at Qal'eh Kharabeh and casemates at Qal'eh Gabri at Varamin, it is possible that some saw longer-term occupation. The c. 170ha heavily fortified compound of Qal'eh Gabri was in an ideal location to dispatch troop to trouble-spots in the north-east or north-west of the empire, such as the Gorgan Plain, Torpakh Qala south of the Derbent Wall, or the Lake Urmia area as a staging post to Transcaucasia. Whether the absence of barracks signals temporary occupation or that the field army preferred tented occupation, being in a permanent state of readiness, is hard to tell.

(On Qal'eh Gabri, see Kleiss 1989; Sauer et al. 2013: 321–2, 360, 372. Important recent fieldwork has been carried out at the site by Dr Mohammad-Reza Nemati, to whom we are very grateful for having provided us with a guided tour of this most impressive fortress in 2015. Estimated dimensions are based on Google Earth. See Kleiss 1989: 301, 306 fig. 20 on the campaign base at Leilan; Ełišē 105 (trans. Thomson 1982: 157) and Sauer et al. 2013: 321 on a campaign base in Her and Zarevand province; Gadzhiev and Magomedov 2008 on Torpakh Qala; and Sauer et al. 2013: 303–81, Alizadeh 2011 and Lawrence and Wilkinson (this volume) on other campaign bases and towns that may have originated as military fortifications.)

Fig. 11.7 At c. 170ha, perhaps the largest fortress in the late antique world: Qal'eh Gabri near Varamin, a probable Sasanian campaign base.

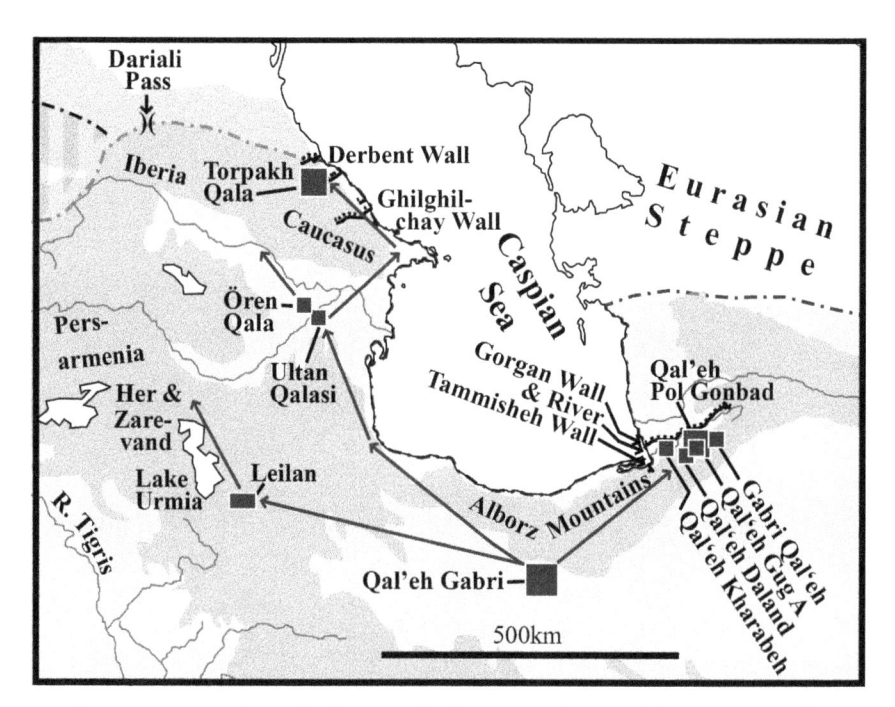

Fig. 11.8 Hypothetical schematic deployment scheme of the Sasanian field army and its possible use of large (c. 125–70ha: large squares) and medium-size (c. 30–70ha: small squares and rectangles) campaign bases.

infrastructure suitable for reuse or reoccupation existed, to erect military architecture on an unprecedented scale (including Hadrian's Wall and a long string of forts along the frontier in Continental Europe and in North Africa). Here too the same principle of avoiding unnecessary work – and unnecessary risk – still applied. Where there were natural features facilitating border or frontier zone surveillance and defence, forts were skilfully placed behind them, in preference to erecting labour-intensive linear barriers or using more permeable and insecure roads or tracks. Such natural features include evidently major rivers, notably the Rhine, the Danube and the Euphrates, as well as arid lands, notably the Syrian Desert and the Sahara. The rivers considerably enhanced and facilitated frontier control whilst well guarded, but were worthless for control if not. It is for this reason that the European river frontiers by and large kept the empire secure up to the early third century, but not when the frontier garrison had been depleted during the civil wars later in the century or in the early fifth century. Despite the loss of Dacia and the *Limes* territory, the Western Roman Empire's natural defences were as strong in AD 400 as they had been in AD 100 and 200; it was the army guarding them that had massively diminished in strength. The Eastern Roman Empire, facing similar problems along the lower Danube, survived, as its stronger natural defences – the Black Sea, the Bosporus and the Aegean – kept its richest provinces secure.[26]

The Partho-Sasanian Empire benefitted from effective natural river barriers in the west. The Euphrates and Tigris could be used for defensive advantage. In late antiquity, the River Batman divided Roman and Persian territory in eastern Anatolia, and some fortifications, such as the heavily contested stronghold of Akbas, employed natural defences for added protection and were placed on hilltops.[27] In the east, arid and mountainous lands provided a buffer zone.

The Indus could have been used as a control and communication line too during those periods when the empire stretched so far. It was, however, in the north that the empire was provided with the most formidable natural defences: the Hindu Kush, the Alborz Mountains and the Caucasus (Fig. 11.9). This massive mountain chain provided a far superior barrier to that of the Roman Empire in Europe. The Rhine and Danube could have been crossed at many points by boat or even swimmers, but the sheer cliffs of the Caucasus formed insurmountable obstacles to human movement, let alone mounted soldiers. Even the few paths across were difficult

Fig. 11.9 The Sasanian Empire was the first mega-empire to control temporarily the main passes across Europe's highest mountain range, the Caucasus. View from Dariali Fort over the narrow gorge north.

to negotiate and dangerous, notably in inclement weather. As in the case of military architecture, the Sasanian era saw significant advances in the effective use of natural obstacles. Whilst the main path across Europe's highest mountain chain, the Dariali Gorge in the Caucasus, and the coastal route at Derbent were outside Parthian dominion, the Sasanian Empire recognised their strategic significance. Shapur I had already brought the Dariali Pass under Sasanian control, and between AD 390 and AD 430 construction works appear to have started on Dariali Fort at one its narrowest points. This heavily fortified bastion blocked the main route across the central Caucasus more effectively than ever before. It was subsequently, in the fifth to sixth century, that a series of linear fortifications was built to block the coastal route, notably the Ghilghilchay (Figs 11.10 and 11.11) and Derbent Walls. The former is not well dated, but is almost certainly also late Sasanian, perhaps slightly earlier than the other major Sasanian barriers, to judge by the less durable building material and the less standardised fort design.[28] The Great Wall of Gorgan, protecting the fertile Gorgan Plain and the approaches to the Alborz, rose up probably between the AD 420s and 480s, and certainly no later than the AD 530s, on the eastern flank of the world's largest inland sea: the Caspian – itself a

Fig. 11.10 The coastal section of the Ghilghilchay Wall in modern Azerbaijan, with its tower mounds, survives in places to a height of up to 7m and must have been much higher prior to the decay of its mudbricks: a possible indicator how high the robbed-out Gorgan and Tammisheh Walls, made of sought-after fired bricks, may have been.

Fig. 11.11 A tower on Chirakh Qala, a fortification on the Ghilghilchay Wall, may perhaps have originated as a Sasanian fire temple, with the spaces between the pillars blocked up later.

formidable natural barrier. A canal and reservoir to the north of this long-wall provide further evidence that Sasanian strategists not only made use of natural defences, effectively blocking all major gaps, but also used canalised water to enhance defensive barriers further where there were no natural rivers of suitable size.

CONCLUSION

Notions of military decline and superiority have both been similarly unfashionable. It seems undeniable, however, that in the Roman world military capabilities had markedly diminished in late antiquity in comparison to the late Republic and the early and high empire. In the Partho-Sasanian Empire we see the opposite trend. The most significant advances, in the effective use of both architecture and natural assets to boost the mega-empire's impregnability, occur at around the same time as the Western Roman Empire ceased to exist, collapsing under enemy pressure whereas the Sasanian Empire's defences held firm by and large.

Unprecedented prosperity in the Sasanian era was made possible through effective defence and at the same time provided the resources the large military apparatus needed. There are, of course, exceptions that prove the rule, notably the major defeat inflicted on the overconfident Sasanian Empire by the Hephthalites in AD 484 or Justinian's re-conquest of about a third of the Roman Empire's lost western half. Both empires remained formidable players on the world stage, but the trend is clear. New archaeological discoveries provide evidence for unprecedented military innovation in the east and stagnation if not a downwards trajectory in the west. The Sasanian military apparatus was significantly stronger and more sophisticated than had been realised until recently. The most monumental and elaborate defensive barrier of late antiquity was Persian. The largest Persian fortresses, Torpakh Qala, Qal'eh Gabri and Qal'eh Pol Gonbad, are not just the largest military fortresses in the Persianate world, but in the ancient world as a whole, exceeding not just the late Roman, but also their early imperial and Republican, counterparts in scale. As in AD 484, overconfidence, based on Persia's formidable military strength, led to incautious strategies – culminating in almost thirty years of war in the early seventh century, weakening both empires and thus paving the way for the victory of the Caliphate.

NOTES

1 A much more appropriate term for the one surviving legal successor to Rome than the 'Byzantine Empire'.
2 None of the successor states of Alexander's empire ever reached the same size. The largest initially, the Seleucid Empire, rapidly lost ground in Asia and never reached the size of the Sasanian Empire at the zenith of its power.
3 E.g. Rubin 1995: 279–91.
4 See for example Yarshater (1983: lxiv) and James (2011a: 216, 258) on alleged western prototypes for this linear barrier.
5 E.g. Webster and Brown 1997.
6 Sarantis 2013: 3, cf. 67.
7 Agathias 5.13.7 (ed. Keydell 1967: 180); Ioannis Lydus, *Liber de mensibus* 1.27 (ed. Wuensch 1898: 13), cf. Jones 1964: 59–60, 679–86, 1449–50 tab. XV; Nicasie 1998: 74–6; and further references in Sauer et al. 2013: 627 no. 191.
8 Training was not abandoned altogether in the late Roman army (Janniard 2012), but written and material evidence suggest that it featured much more prominently under the early and high empire (Sauer et al. 2013: 622–3 with references).
9 Ammianus Marcellinus (24.5.3, 24.5.12, 24.8.7–25.1.2, 25.6.5, cf.

25.3.1) implies that Julian's army built lightly fortified marching camps where there was particular danger, i.e. near the conurbation of Coche, Seleucia and Ctesiphon.
10. Vegetius 1.8, 1.20–1, 2.18, 3.10.
11. See Sauer et al. 2013: 621–4, 629 and Spring 2015: *passim*, e.g. 325–6 for examples.
12. E.g. Rubin 1995: 282–3, 291.
13. Primary sources and modern scholarly works for the well-known military campaigns of the second and third centuries are far too numerous to list. For some detailed recent treatises, see Johne 2008; Millar 1993; Mosig-Walburg 2009; Winter 1988. See Barnes 2009 and Glas 2014: 96–7, 108, 324–6 on the Persian sack of Antioch and the controversy in modern scholarship on chronology and whether Antioch was taken once or twice, which there is no space to discuss here.
14. James 2011b; 2013: 94–100; 2015a; 2015b; Leriche 2013: 143.
15. Hauser and Tucker 2009; Hauser 2013; Foietta 2015.
16. Other than the well-known siege camps, it is worth noting recent discoveries in Gaul and Italy, the former probably also associated with a siege: Hornung 2012; Urbanus 2015.
17. Sauer 2005: 137–47.
18. Reddé and Schnurbein 2001.
19. Hauser 2013: 124, fig. 3.
20. James 2015a; 2015b.
21. See Jones 2012: 117–18 on the size of Roman marching camps.
22. James 2006.
23. Jotheri et al. 2016: 182 fig. 5D, 184 fig. 6C, 185 tab. IV, 186; Lawrence and Wilkinson, this volume.
24. See Sauer et al. 2013: esp. 230–4, 614–15.
25. Sauer et al. 2013: 234–9.
26. As correctly pointed out by Ward-Perkins 2005: 58–62.
27. Whitby 1983. The location of Akbas, held by the Persians in the AD 580s and twice captured by Rome in AD 583 and 589 (Theophylact Simocatta 1.12.1–3, 4.2.1 [ed. De Boor and Wirth 1972: 62–3, 150, trans. Whitby and Whitby 1986: 37, 104], John of Ephesus, *Ecclesiastical History* 6.36–7 [trans. Payne Smith 1860: 447–8 and Schönfelder 1862: 265–6]; cf. Whitby 1988: 130, 199, 246, 255 map 12, 272, 277–8, 290, 292), is a matter of debate. Sinclair 1989: 428–9, cf. 277, 381–2 locates it on a prominent hill, but to the west of the River Batman.
28. Aliev et al. 2006; Lawrence and Wilkinson, this volume; personal observations on a visit, 25 August 2012.

BIBLIOGRAPHY

Aliev, A. A., Gadjiev, M. S., Gaither, M. G., Kohl, P. L., Magomedov, R. M. and Aliev, I. N. (2006), 'The Ghilghilchay Defensive Long Wall: New Investigations', *Ancient West & East*, 5, pp. 143–77.

Alizadeh, K. (2011), 'Ultan Qalasi: A Fortified Site in the Sasanian Borderlands (Mughan Steppe, Iranian Azerbaijan)', *Iran*, 49, pp. 55–77.

Barnes, T. (2009), 'The Persian Sack of Antioch in 253', *Zeitschrift für Papyrologie und Epigraphik*, 169, pp. 294–6.
De Boor, C. and Wirth, P. (eds) (1972), *Theophylacti Simocattae historiae*, Stuttgart: Teubner.
Foietta, E. (2015), 'The Defences of Hatra', in G. Affanni et al. (eds), *Broadening Horizons*, 4, BAR International Series 2698, Oxford: Archaeopress, pp. 295–302.
Gadzhiev, M. S. and Magomedov, R. G. (2008), 'Торпах-Кала', in N. I. A. Merpert and S. N. Korenevskiĭ (eds), *Археология Кавказа и Ближнего Востока*, Moscow: Российская Академия Наук, Институт археологии, pp. 276–97.
Glas, T. (2014), *Valerian*, Paderborn: Ferdinand Schöningh.
Hauser, S. R. (2013), 'Where is the Man of Hadr, Who Once Built It and Taxed the Land by the Tigris and Chaboras?', in L. Dirven (ed.), *Hatra*, Oriens et Occidens, 21, Stuttgart: Franz Steiner, pp. 119–39.
Hauser, S. R. and Tucker, D. J. (2009), 'The Final Onslaught: The Sasanian Siege of Hatra', *Zeitschrift für Orient-Archäologie*, 2, pp. 106–39.
Hornung, S. (2012), 'Eine Episode des Gallischen Krieges auf deutschem Boden? Aktuelle Forschungen im spätrepublikanischen Militärlager von Hermeskeil, Kreis Trier-Saarburg', *Funde und Ausgrabungen im Bezirk Trier*, 44, pp. 28–38.
James, S. (2006), 'The Impact of Steppe Peoples and the Partho-Sasanian World on the Development of Roman Military Equipment and Dress, 1st to 3rd Centuries AD', in M. Mode and J. Tubach (eds), *Arms and Armour as Indicators of Cultural Transfer: The Steppes and the Ancient World from Hellenistic Times to the Early Middle Ages*, Wiesbaden: Reichert, pp. 357–92.
James, S. (2011a), *Rome & the Sword*, London: Thames & Hudson.
James, S. (2011b), 'Stratagems, Combat, and "Chemical Warfare" in the Siege Mines of Dura-Europos', *American Journal of Archaeology*, 115.1, pp. 69–101.
James, S. (2013), 'The Archaeology of War', in B. Campbell and L. A. Tritle (eds), *The Oxford Handbook of Warfare in the Classical World*, Oxford: Oxford University Press, pp. 91–127.
James, S. (2015a), 'Ancient Campaign Camps at Dura-Europos, Syria: A Preliminary Note', in L. Vagalinski and N. Sharankov (eds), *Limes XXII: Proceedings of the 22nd International Congress of Roman Frontier Studies, Ruse, Bulgaria, September 2012*, Sofia: National Archaeological Institute, pp. 307–12.
James, S. (2015b), 'Of Colossal Camps and a New Roman Battlefield: Remote Sensing, Archival Archaeology and the "Conflict Landscape" of Dura-Europos, Syria', in D. J. Breeze et al. (eds), *Understanding Roman Frontiers: A Celebration for Professor Bill Hanson*, Edinburgh: John Donald, pp. 328–45.
Janniard, S. (2012), '*Campicursio*, pyrrhique et *campidoctores*: Entraînement aux mouvements collectifs et instructeurs dans l'armée romaine tardive', in C. Wolff (ed.), *Le métier de soldat dans le monde romain*, Paris: De Boccard, pp. 275–83.
Johne, K.-P., with Hartmann, U. and Gerhardt, T. (eds) (2008), *Die Zeit der Soldatenkaiser*, 1–2, Berlin: Akademie.

Jones, A. H. M. (1964), *The Later Roman Empire 284–602*, 1–2, Oxford: Blackwell.
Jones, R. H. (2012), *Roman Camps in Britain*, Stroud: Amberley.
Jotheri, J., Allen, M. B. and Wilkinson, T. J. (2016), 'Holocene Avulsions of the Euphrates River in the Najaf Area of Western Mesopotamia: Impacts on Human Settlement Patterns', *Geoarchaeology*, 31, pp. 175–83.
Keydell, R. (ed.) (1967), *Agathiae Myrinaei historiarum libri quinque*, Berlin: De Gruyter.
Kleiss, W. (1989), 'Qal'eh Gabri bei Veramin', *Archäologische Mitteilungen aus Iran*, 20, for 1987, pp. 289–307.
Leriche, P. (2013), 'Europos-Doura sur l'Euphrate', *Revue Archéologique*, 2013.1, pp. 135–43.
Millar, F. (1993), *The Roman Near East*, Cambridge: Harvard University Press.
Mosig-Walburg, K. (2009), *Römer und Perser*, Gutenberg: Computus.
Nicasie, M. J. (1998), *Twilight of Empire: The Roman Army from Diocletian to the Battle of Adrianople*, Amsterdam: J.C. Gieben.
Payne Smith, R. (trans.) (1860), *The Third Part of the Ecclesiastical History of John, Bishop of Ephesus*, Oxford: Oxford University Press.
Reddé, M. and Schnurbein, S. von (eds) (2001), *Alésia*, 1–2, Paris: De Boccard.
Rubin, Z. (1995), 'The Reforms of Khusro Anūshirwān', in A. Cameron (ed.), *The Byzantine and Early Islamic Near East III: States, Resources and Armies*, Princeton: Darwin Press, pp. 227–97.
Sarantis, A. (2013), 'Waging War in Late Antiquity', in A. Sarantis and N. Christie (eds), *War and Warfare in Late Antiquity: Late Antique Archaeology*, 8.1, for 2010, Leiden and Boston: Brill, pp. 1–98.
Sauer, E. W. (2005), *Coins, Cult and Cultural Identity: Augustan Coins, Hot Springs and the Early Roman Baths at Bourbonne-les-Bains*, Leicester Archaeology Monographs, 10, Leicester: University of Leicester.
Sauer, E. W., Omrani Rekavandi, H., Wilkinson, T. J., Nokandeh, J. et al. (2013), *Persia's Imperial Power in Late Antiquity: The Great Wall of Gorgān and Frontier Landscapes of Sasanian Iran*, British Institute of Persian Studies Archaeological Monographs Series, II, Oxford: Oxbow Books.
Schönfelder, J. M. (trans.) (1862), *Die Kirchen-Geschichte des Johannes von Ephesus aus dem Syrischen übersetzt*, Munich: J.J. Lentner.
Sinclair, T. A. (1989), *Eastern Turkey: An Architectural and Archaeological Survey*, 3, London: Pindar Press.
Spring, P. (2015), *Great Walls and Linear Barriers*, Barnsley: Pen & Sword.
Thomson, R. W. (trans.) (1982), *Ełishē: History of Vardan and the Armenian War*, Cambridge: Harvard University Press.
Urbanus, J. (2015), 'Rome's Earliest Fort', *Archaeology*, 68.4, p. 18.
Ward-Perkins, B. (2005), *The Fall of Rome and the End of Civilization*, Oxford: Oxford University Press.
Webster, L. and Brown, M. (eds) (1997), *The Transformation of the Roman World*, London: British Museum Press.
Whitby, M. (1983), 'Arzanene in the Late Sixth Century', in S. Mitchell (ed.), *Armies and Frontiers in Roman and Byzantine Anatolia*, BAR International Series 156, Oxford: British Archaeological Reports, pp. 205–18.
Whitby, M. (1988), *The Emperor Maurice and His Historian: Theophylact Simocatta on Persian and Balkan Warfare*, Oxford: Clarendon Press.

Whitby, M. and Whitby, M. (trans.) (1986), *The History of Theophylact Simocatta*, Oxford: Clarendon Press.
Winter, E. (1988), *Die sāsānidisch-römischen Friedensverträge des 3. Jahrhunderts n. Chr.*, Frankfurt: Peter Lang.
Wuensch, R. (ed.) (1898), *Ioannis Laurentii Lydi Liber de mensibus*, Leipzig: Teubner.
Yarshater, E. (1983), 'Introduction', in E. Yarshater (ed.), *The Cambridge History of Iran*, 3.1, Cambridge: Cambridge University Press, pp. xvii–lxxv.

12 The Arabian Frontier: A Keystone of the Sasanian Empire

Craig Morley

From a Roman perspective the Arabian Peninsula was frequently relegated to a peripheral position on the edge of the empire. In contrast, in different stages of Sasanian history the Arabian frontier acted as a keystone of their empire. Sasanian control, both direct and indirect, of the Arabian Peninsula strengthened its economic prosperity and military security. It was for these reasons that the empire's activities on their southern frontier in Arabia peaked during three distinct periods: during the early Sasanian period, principally in the reigns of Ardashir I and Shapur I; during the reign of Shapur II; and, perhaps most importantly, during the sixth century in renewed hostilities with the Roman Empire.

As Warwick Ball, Dan Lawrence, Tony Wilkinson and Kristen Hopper have analysed the nature and importance of the Sasanian Empire's northern, western and eastern frontiers elsewhere in this volume, it is now time to turn our attention to the empire's southern frontier in Arabia. From a western, Roman-centric perspective the Arabian Peninsula has often been regarded as an insignificant periphery of the ancient world; however, for the Persians it was arguably of much more central importance. The geopolitical position the Sasanians found themselves in after overthrowing the Parthians in 224 necessitated close relations with Arab tribes and a degree of authority over the Arabian Peninsula.[1] Indeed, from the foundation of the Sasanian Empire Arabia played a significant role in its security and economic prosperity. As such, it will be argued here that the southern frontier in Arabia was a keystone of the Sasanian Empire at various points throughout its history. In understanding the important role the southern frontier fulfilled this chapter will have two main areas of focus. First, it will be necessary to show at what points in Sasanian history it acted as a keystone of empire. Secondly, an attempt will be made to show why Arabia was important and what strategies the shahs employed to ensure their control of the region.

It is important to stress that Sasanian activity and involvement in Arabia fluctuated over time in response to developments on the southern frontier itself and also to events elsewhere in the empire. Fortunately, there is both literary and archaeological evidence which allows us to trace the development of Sasanian activity on the southern frontier.

Although frustration at the lack of written sources which originate from the Sasanian Empire itself is commonly acknowledged, those that we do have, namely Shapur I's *Res Gestae* at Naqsh-e Rostam, the Paikuli inscription of Narseh and those of Kirdir, as well as the later *Shahrestaniha-ye Eranshahr*, cast some light on the history of the Arabian frontier. By comparing these sources we can identify when, and to what degree, Arabia was considered an integral part of the empire, as part of the *Eranshahr*, throughout Sasanian history. For example, that Shapur I claimed Oman (Mazun) was a fully integrated territory of his empire indicates that the region was considered an integral part of the empire in the first half of the third century.[2] Yet shortly afterwards, during the reign of Shapur's successor, Hormizd, the empire's chief Magian, Kirdir, in his own inscription does not include Arabia as part of the *Eranshahr*. This absence suggests that once the Sasanian Empire was fully established and secure the Arabian frontier lost some of its importance, as other regions became the focus of imperial attention and concern.[3] Indeed, it has been argued that after Shapur I Arabia's importance underwent a hiatus during the reigns of his immediate successors, who had more pressing internal concerns to deal with.[4] According to our sources, this time from the later Arab writer Tabari, Arabia did not become a priority again until the beginning of the fourth century, when Shapur II led a major military campaign in the region.[5] After this, it is not until the sixth century that Arabia is next mentioned in Sasanian sources, and when it is, in the *Shahrestaniha-ye Eranshahr*, it is once more considered an intrinsic part of the *Eranshahr*. In this document the Sasanian Empire is divided into four distinct regions (*kusts*), of which Arabia is included in the south-west district (*kust-ye xwarbaran*) and heralded as a site where many Sasanian cities where founded.[6] Given that the division of the Sasanian Empire into

Table 12.1   Sasanian coins found in eastern Arabia.

Ruler	Reign	Number of coins	Century
Ardashir I	c. 224–40	3	Third century
Shapur I	c. 240–72	1	
Shapur II	309–79	22	Fourth century
Yazdgerd I	399–420	1	Fifth century
Balash	484–8	1	
Kavad I	488–96/7 and 499–531	10	
Khusro I	531–79	7	Sixth and seventh centuries
Bahram VI	590–1	1	
Khusro II	590–628	1	

four districts was not begun until the reigns of Kavad I (488–96/7 and 499–531) and his successor Khusro I (531–79) and was only completed in the reign of Khusro II (590–628), it is likely that the *Shahrestaniha-ye Eranshahr* itself was first compiled at this time, or at least reflected the geographical situation of the empire at this time.[7] Therefore, it can be suggested that Arabia, as part of one of these districts, was once again important in the sixth and seventh centuries.

Although these literary sources only provide snapshots of Arabia's position and importance to the Sasanian Empire, the general historical trend described above is supported by archaeological evidence: primarily Sasanian coins uncovered in Arabia (Table 12.1). Coins are useful in identifying chronological and geographical patterns, and, as such, Sasanian coins uncovered in Arabia are used here to help identify in what periods Sasanian activity in the southern frontier peaked and, therefore, in which periods it can be claimed Arabia had more significance.[8] In this regard, it is revealing that the number of Sasanian coins found in different periods coincides with and thus supports the evidence from the literary sources, as seen in Table 12.1.[9] For example, from the reign of Shapur II, twenty-two Sasanian coins have been located at different locations throughout eastern Arabia, namely Jabal Berri, Al Khobar, Jabal Kenzan and Hofuf. Nineteen coins which date from the sixth century (or late fifth to early seventh centuries), from the reigns of Kavad I, Khusro I, Bahram VI and Khusro II, have also been uncovered in eastern Arabia. Compare this with the reigns of Yazdgerd I and Balash from the end of the fourth to the late fifth centuries, from each of which which only one coin has been discovered, and it suggests, just as the literary sources do, that while Arabia was important in the early fourth and sixth centuries it was less so in the fifth century. Although there is danger in putting too much weight on the distribution of coins in making assessments of imperial activity in different regions, that there is agreement with the literary sources is worth noting.

From this analysis of the available sources it can justifiably be claimed that the Arabian frontier had three distinct periods of importance. The first was during the early Sasanian period, namely the reigns of Ardashir I and Shapur I, when the founder of the empire and his successor campaigned extensively to stamp Sasanian authority on the frontiers of their newly won empire.[10] For example, Ardashir's early campaign in 240 aimed to bring Ahvaz and Meshan under Sasanian control, and it has also been claimed he campaigned as far as Bahrain,[11] while, as already seen, Oman was considered a part of the Sasanian Empire during the reign of Shapur I. Secondly, the reign of Shapur II, who launched a ferocious campaign deep into Arabia in 325/6 that saw the construction of Shapur's Ditch (Khandaq Shapur), an extensive fortification in southern Iraq, and the deportation of the most troublesome Arab tribes to less strategically sensitive regions, in retaliation for an earlier Arab raid into the province of Fars.[12] The savagery of this campaign and Shapur's treatment of captive Arabs earned him the nickname Do'l-aktaf ('piercer of shoulders'). Thirdly, and perhaps most importantly, in the sixth century renewed conflict with Rome, after the brief respite of the peaceful fifth century, reignited the Arabian frontier as a region of imperial competition.[13] Arabian trade routes provided a valuable alternative to the more traditional routes in Mesopotamia and Armenia which became difficult to traverse, or were closed down completely, during conflicts with Rome.[14] These fluctuations in Sasanian involvement in Arabia and its importance to the security of the empire reinforce the fact that the Sasanian Empire was not a static and unchanging entity, but was, like all long-lasting empires, one that underwent changes and shifts in priorities as and when different crises and threats arose.

Arabia, particularly the north-east of the peninsula, was important to the security and prosperity of the Sasanian Empire for two reasons. First, its close proximity to the important cities of Ctesiphon and Veh Ardashir, as well as the agricultural and political heartlands of the empire in Fars, Khuzestan and lower Mesopotamia, and the fact that it was a frontier partially shared with the Roman Empire, made it a strategically sensitive gateway into the soft underbelly of the Sasanian Empire. Secondly, north-east Arabia was important in accessing and controlling the lucrative trade routes of the Persian

Gulf. The economic prosperity of the Sasanian Empire, like that of most ancient states, depended predominantly on agriculture and trade, and as such, the Arabian frontier, given the vital role it played in both of these, was intrinsically important to the success of the empire.[15]

Successive shahs spent vast resources on improving the infrastructure of their empire. This was achieved primarily through increased urbanisation and expansion of agricultural land in Khuzestan and southern Mesopotamia, regions in close proximity to the Arabian frontier, through the development of sophisticated irrigation systems.[16] The resources the Sasanians expended on making these regions the most economically lucrative of their empire ensured they had a vested interest in safeguarding their investment by cementing their dominant position on the nearby Arabian frontier. Certainly, the fact that Arab tribes were able to launch damaging raids into Fars at the start of the fourth century reveals the extent to which the empire's economic heartlands were vulnerable to attack.

Arguably even more important to the economy of the Sasanian Empire was control of the Persian Gulf.[17] It has been suggested that control of the lucrative Gulf trade was the key component of Sasanian economic strength, and thus of the empire's ability to survive and prosper for as long as it did.[18] This view is given extra credence by the fact that the fourth-century Roman historian Ammianus Marcellinus knew that the Persian Gulf was an important region for trade; the riches of the Gulf were evidently well known in the ancient world.[19] The economic benefits of controlling the Persian Gulf were certainly apparent to the Sasanians from an early stage. For example, Ardashir's determination to cement Sasanian control of its trade routes is apparent in his construction of forts on both the east and west coasts of the Persian Gulf. Likewise, it has also been claimed that the Sasanians began to divert Gulf trade to their coastal outposts and cities on both the eastern and western shores as early the fifth century.[20] The geographical position of the Sasanian Empire allowed it to act as the profitable middleman in east–west trade in late antiquity, and control of the Persian Gulf, alongside their control of major branches of the so-called Silk Road, was an instrumental part of this.[21] This position ensured they could profit from trade with, as well as the flow of goods between, the Roman Empire, China and India.[22] Certainly, that Sasanian silver coins have been found as far as the south-east coast of China underlines the vast commercial reach that control of the Persian Gulf granted Persian merchants, or at least Persian goods.[23] That the majority of these coins have been dated to the sixth and seventh centuries also reinforces the claim that Sasanian activity and control of their southern frontier, and as such the Persian Gulf, reached a peak in this period. Furthermore, it has been argued that the increase in the minting of coinage in Fars during the reigns of Khusro I and II was linked to the increase of maritime trade in this period.[24]

If the Sasanians wished to profit from the economic benefits Arabia had to offer, as well as protect their capital and most important agricultural lands, they had to ensure their control of the southern frontier. They did this through the establishment of what will be labelled here as a two-tier defensive system, based on a fortified zone and a system of alliances with local Arab tribes.

The first part of this system was the construction of a defensive line that stretched from Hit in the north to Basra in the south.[25] Central to this was a series of large forts and fortified cities which were designed to hold back or impede any unexpected raids launched from within the Arabian Peninsula.[26] Smaller fortlets, such as those discovered at Ruda, Ukhaydir and Qusayr, were used to protect the important communication routes between their larger counterparts.[27] Further protection was added by the aforementioned Shapur's Ditch, an extensive military installation, which lay in front of these forts.[28] The construction of large-scale defensive fortifications in the ancient world was a projection of a state's power and resources to those who might seek to challenge it. As such, they were constructed not only as straightforward defensive structures, but also to intimidate enemies. In this regard, the construction of Shapur's Ditch indicates that the Sasanians felt threatened enough on their southern frontier to feel it necessary to construct such a military installation to ward off and intimidate any would-be Arab raiders. Likewise, the construction of such large-scale military installations required the investment of vast resources, both financial and manpower; therefore, that the Sasanians were willing to expend these resources on defending their southern frontier reveals how seriously they took that defence.[29] Indeed, that the construction of Shapur's Ditch was ordered by Shapur II in response to the Arab raids that had caused devastation as far as Fars indicates it was purposely designed to offer protection to the important political and agricultural heartlands behind it.[30]

Beyond this fortified zone, the Sasanians added further protection to their southern frontier through a policy of indirect rule which cemented their authority and influence throughout eastern and into central Arabia. This was based on the creation of a system of alliances, principally with the Nasrids of al-Hira, to act as an outer shield for imperial defence. The claim that centralisation was a key component of Sasanian imperial control has been challenged in recent years, and it is now accepted that there was much more flexibility and negotiation on the peripheries of the Sasanian Empire.[31] Importantly, Arabia has long been recognised as a region that was controlled through degrees of indirect rule.[32]

The Nasrids performed a variety of functions in their role as the outer shield of Sasanian defence and authority in northern Arabia. They defended against raids from hostile tribes, protected trade routes and fought in Sasanian campaigns against the Romans and their Arab allies.[33] In order to perform this role better the Nasrids were granted hegemony over other Arab tribes allied to the Sasanian Empire.[34] The success of the Nasrids in defending Sasanian interests on their southern frontier is underlined by the fact that it prompted imitation by the Romans, who promoted one of their own allied Arab tribes, the Jafnids, to an equally high rank and to perform the same roles, in the hope of improving their own frontier defence in the region.[35] In return for these services the Nasrids benefitted from Sasanian patronage, which granted them the financial and political clout to ensure their internal dominance over their own followers and in al-Hira.[36] In this regard, the Sasanian–Nasrid relationship was similar to the *Carayut'iwn* relationship that existed between the shahs and the Armenian *nakharars*, in that it was based on rewards for services rendered by the allies to their imperial patron.[37]

It is because of the nature of this indirect rule, and because the shahs preferred to create relationships with individual leaders rather than with wider or larger groups, that we should refer to the Sasanians' principal allies at al-Hira as Nasrids rather than by the more traditional term, Lakhmids.[38] Sasanian–Arab relations were highly personal, fundamentally at the level of the shah, as the imperial patron, and of the Arab tribal chief, as the client. Two rulers and political leaders are more likely to share, in general terms at least, similar values, attitudes and ambitions as well as recognition of common interest, and from the perspective of the Sasanian patron this made them easier to control.[39] Certainly, in the Paikuli inscription 'Amr, the 'king of Lakhm', not a wider Lakhmid polity, is designated as the vassal and ally of the Sasanian Empire.[40] As such, it is better to view the Sasanians' allies at the level of individual leaders or dynasties rather than kingdoms; therefore, labelling their principal Arab allies as Nasrids, which designates an individual dynasty, is more appropriate than using 'Lakhmids', which suggests that the empire was dealing with a coherent and centralised polity.[41]

Although it is not known exactly when al-Hira and the Nasrids came to prominence, it is believed they did so at the same time as the Sasanians themselves came to power, in the early third century, presumably due to the patronage of the Sasanian shahs.[42] That their alliance with the Nasrids was established by the early shahs, to cement their presence in Arabia, reinforces the importance the region had during the formative years of the empire.[43] Certainly, given the Sasanian mercantile interests in Arabia it seems more than a coincidence that their chosen allies' political centre, al-Hira, was located on the lucrative caravan routes between the Persian Gulf and the Red Sea.[44] Likewise, the importance Arabia had in the sixth century, due to renewed conflict with Rome in the region, is supported by the fact that the Sasanians dispatched a force of their feared *catafracti* (*dosar shahba*) to al-Hira to bolster the defence and power of Nasrids in this period.[45] Indeed, it was also in the sixth century that the Sasanians extended Nasrid authority over their Arab allies in Bahrain and Yamama.[46] It was in the same period that the Sasanians pursued closer relations with the Al Jolanda in Oman, in a bid to extend their influence over this economically important region of Arabia.[47] Both of these moves allowed the Sasanians to increase their political and economic control over the east coast of Arabia, further underlining the importance Arabia and Persian Gulf trade had in the sixth century.

Although the authority and power of the Nasrids over other Arab tribes in region rested substantially on the patronage of the Sasanians, their relationship was not completely one-sided. The Nasrids' importance to the Sasanians was evident in Yazdgerd I's decision to send his son, Bahram V, to be raised and educated in al-Hira.[48] Likewise, Yazdgerd also attempted to use his Nasrid allies as a political counterweight to the Sasanian nobility in the internal power struggles of the early fifth century.[49] Thus there was deep interdependence between the Sasanians and Nasrids; their security and prosperity were intrinsically intertwined. This was never more evident than in the fate of the Sasanians' southern frontier after Khusro II deposed and killed Nu'man b. al-Mundhir, the last Nasrid leader, after his conversion to Christianity at the end of the sixth century. Shortly after this fateful decision the Sasanians were defeated by Arab armies on the 'day of Dhu Qar' at some point between 604 and 611, and lost their ascendancy over north-eastern Arabia.[50]

This two-tier defensive system, with its multi-layered fortifications in the north supported by the Nasrid, and other, Arab allies further south and east, offered the Sasanians a form of defence in depth on their southern frontier. The success of this frontier system is suggested by the fact that we do not hear of any other major Arab raids into the Sasanian heartlands after the construction of Shapur's Ditch until the Arab conquests in the seventh century. Likewise, despite repeated Roman attempts to challenge Sasanian dominance in the region, by building up alliances with Himyar and Aksum, the Romans were never able to dislodge the Sasanians from their entrenched and ascendant position in north-eastern Arabia.[51] However, once one part of the two-tier system was removed, with Nu'man b. al-Mundhir's deposition and death on the order of Khusro II, the southern frontier was left exposed and was soon overrun by the Arabs in the seventh century.

In their bid to control Persian Gulf trade, the Sasanians' domination of the north-eastern Arabian coastal regions was of paramount importance. Significantly, the evidence of Sasanian activity and presence in Arabia does suggest that they focused their attention on the north-east.[52] For example, in relation to our review of Sasanian coins it is noticeable that the majority of these finds came from north and north-eastern Arabia, and that coin finds become rarer the further south one travels.[53] Similarly, later Arabic sources claim that the Sasanians controlled and lived on the coasts while the Arabs themselves were forced to move into the desert, and although the veracity of this statement has been debated it does reinforce the importance the Sasanians placed on control of, or at least access to, the coasts of the Persian Gulf.[54] Northern Oman and the Strait of Hormuz, which reaches out into the Gulf like a greedy hand, were also strategically important sites in the control of late antique Gulf trade, and it is no surprise that Sasanian activity also concentrated on these areas.[55] For instance, the Sasanian fort uncovered at Jazirat Umm al-Ghanam was probably used to facilitate and supervise trade passing through the Strait of Hormuz.[56] That these forts were used to facilitate trade, not as docking yards for the Sasanian navy, reinforces the primacy that economic interests had for the Sasanians in the Persian Gulf.[57] The commercial chokehold the Sasanians established over the Persian Gulf ensures it is not an exaggeration to suggest that it represented their very own *mare nostrum*.[58] Indeed, despite numerous Roman attempts to bypass Sasanian ascendancy in the region, the Romans were never able to succeed, and thus were not able to profit from Gulf trade as their rivals did.[59]

Although Arabia did not see consistent Sasanian attention as did its northern and western frontiers, there were periods, namely in the reign of Shapur II and during the sixth century, when it was arguably one of the most important regions in the empire. Control over the southern frontier was integral to the overall defence and economic prosperity of the Sasanian Empire. Indeed, once this keystone was removed and the southern frontier was overrun by the Arab tribes in the seventh century, the empire did not survive long.

ABBREVIATIONS

ŠKZ   Inscription of Shapur I from the Ka'be-ye Zardosht.

NOTES

1. Isaac's (1992: 268) claim that Arabia was largely unimportant to the Roman and Sasanian Empires alike is indicative of the Roman-centricity which has affected our understanding of Arabia's position and importance to the Sasanians. For a more in-depth discussion on historical Arab–Persian links see Bosworth (1983; 1986) and Toral-Niehoff (2013b: 116).
2. ŠKZ 3.17.
3. As agreed with by Potts (1990: 329–30). For more information on these other frontiers see the relevant chapters by Ball, Lawrence and Wilkinson, and Hopper, this volume.
4. Ulrich 2011: 379. The internal difficulties affecting the empire at this time are evident in the short and troubled reigns of Shapur I's successors; Hormizd (270/2–3), Bahram I (273–6), Bahram III (293) and Narseh (293–302). The internal stability and dominance of Ardashir and Shapur I had been achieved primarily through their military achievements; however, their three immediate successors, especially Bahram I and III, were too young to be able to create their own legitimacy through military victory (Potter 2004: 291).
5. Tabari 1.836–9.
6. *Shahrestaniha-ye Eranshah* 21; Daryaee 2002: 29.
7. Daryaee 2002: 2–4; 2005: 132.
8. Kennet 2008a: 58.
9. Following Kennet's (2008a: 60) warning that Sasanian coins from three Islamic hoards discovered in eastern Arabia probably came into the region during the early Islamic period, rather than the Sasanian period, these hoard coins have not been included in Table 12.1. For more detailed information and studies on Sasanian coins uncovered in Arabia see Potts and Cribb (1995: 126–30) and Kennet (2008a), which were insightful for this brief survey.
10. Tabari 1.820; Potts 2012.
11. Wiesehöfer 1996: 196; Potts 2012. There is much debate among scholars about Ardashir's 240 campaign in Arabia. This debate is focused on whether the campaign was limited to the conquest of the north-east of the peninsula, namely Bahrain, or whether he instead campaigned throughout

Arabia, from Oman to Hajar (Piacentini 1985: 66; Daryaee 2002: 54). Further adding to the debate, Widengren (1971: 775) and Altheim and Stiehl (1965) believe that this campaign has actually been confused with Ardashir's conquest of Hatra in c. 240.
12 Thaalibi 517–20; Tabari 1.836–9. The Taghlib tribe were sent to al-Khatt, the Abd al-Qays and Tamim tribes to Hajar, while the Bakr b.Wa'il tribe was sent to Kerman and Hanazila in Ramila (Daryaee 2009a: 16–17). On the Arab raid on Sasanian territory see *Bundahishn* (33.16).
13 Frye 1992.
14 Daryaee 2003: 5; 2010: 408; Dignas and Winter 2007: 200.
15 Brosius 2006: 182; Wiesehöfer 1996: 195; Daryaee 2010: 401. Ulrich (2011) argues that the traditional idea of the Sasanian period being a time of prosperity and investment in eastern Arabia should be tempered with some caution (for this traditional view see Morony 2001–2). Ulrich believes that, compared to the earlier Parthian and later Islamic periods, Sasanian Arabia was a period of economic decline. Kennet (2008b) takes a similar view. Although this is an important argument in gaining a wider understanding of Sasanian Arabia, it is not of immediate concern here, as our focus is on Arabia as the Sasanian Empire's southern frontier. In other words, Arabia will be investigated in this chapter as a frontier of the empire, not as a province. As such, rather than debate whether eastern Arabia as a whole prospered under the shahs we are more interested in showing how control of the Arabian frontier benefitted and secured the empire, not how the empire benefitted Arabia itself. As long as the shahs benefitted from the trade routes that led through Arabia, via the Gulf, they were unlikely to be overly concerned with the prosperity of Arabia as a whole. This is evident in the fact that they only tried to maintain their control over the north-eastern coastal regions of the peninsula rather than fully conquer and assimilate Arabia as a whole, as will be shown below.
16 On the increased urbanisation of these regions under the Sasanians see Rubin (2000: 652), Adams (1981), Pourshariati (2008: 38–9) and Simpson, this volume. On these irrigation systems and the expansion of agricultural land see Ammianus Marcellinus 24.3.10, Wenke (1975–6; 1987: 253–5) and Adams (1962).
17 ŠKZ (1–3) and *Shahrestaniha-ye Eranshah* (25, 52) both express the importance of the Persian Gulf to the Sasanian Empire. On the importance of the Persian Gulf to the Sasanian economy see Wiesehöfer (2006: 191–7), Daryaee (2003; 2010), Brosius (2006: 182–3) and Whitehouse and Williamson (1973: 11).
18 Piacentini 1985: 59; Haussig 1971: 138.
19 Ammianus Marcellinus 23.6.11.
20 Howard-Johnston 1995: 204–5.
21 Confirming this profitable position, Cosmas Indicopleustes (*Christian Topography II*) speaks of the competition that existed between Roman merchants and the Sasanian middlemen. That the Romans made numerous attempts to bypass the Sasanian's dominant position in east–west trade also underlines its profitability (Dignas and Winter 2007: 202; Procopius, *Bella* 1.20.9, 8.17.1–8).
22 Chinese sources indicate Sasanian goods arrived by sea, and Sasanian

bullae, used in the transfer of goods from one region to another, have been found as far away as modern Sri Lanka (Wink 1990: 48–50).
23 Nia 1974: 107.
24 Daryaee 2003: 12.
25 For more detailed discussion on Sasanian fortifications in this region see Finster and Schmidt (1976).
26 One example of these was the fort at Qasr Yeng, which measured 150 × 150m (Howard-Johnston 2012: 97–8).
27 Howard-Johnston 2012: 97–8.
28 Frye 1977; Mahamedi 2004; Lawrence and Wilkinson, this volume, with Fig. 5.2.
29 Howard-Johnston 2012: 93. Bachrach's (2010) study of the Roman fortification of Gaul after the third-century crisis provides a useful comparison for understanding the levels of financial and manpower resources these vast fortification construction projects would have required.
30 McDonough (2013: 611–12) also agrees that the primary function of Shapur's Ditch was to defend the revenue-generating provinces further north.
31 Pourshariati 2008.
32 Lecker (2002: 109–15), Donner (1981: 44–8) and Kister (1968: 155–6) show that Sasanian policy in Arabia was built on indirect rule, through building alliances with local leaders and dynasties.
33 Bosworth 1986.
34 Kister 1968: 150–3.
35 Procopius, *Bella* 1.17.40–1.
36 In this regard, Potts (1993: 197) has identified a Sasanian lead horse uncovered in north-east Arabia as a gift that was probably given to Sasanian clients in the region. There is no reason this could not have been given to the Nasrids, or, as Kennet (2008a: 58) suggests, by the Nasrids to their own clients.
37 Preiser-Kapeller 2010.
38 Fisher 2011: 1–5. Indeed, the same is true in Armenia, where the Sasanians were eager to abolish the Arsacid monarchy in order to focus on building relationships with individual Armenian *nakharars*.
39 Dignas and Winter 2007: 169; Hoyland 2009: 118.
40 Humbach and Skjærvø 1983: 71.
41 Fisher 2011: 91–2. Likewise, the Romans, who pursued a similar strategy of indirect rule in Arabia and who actually imitated Sasanian policy towards the Nasrids with their own Jafnid allies (see Procopius, *Bella* 1.17.40–1), only mention individual leaders such as Arethas and Alamoundaras in their historiography, and not wider tribal groups (Procopius, *Bella* 2.28.12–14). Similarly, Syriac sources only speak of 'Beth Harith' or 'Beth Mundhir', 'The House of Harith' or 'The House of Mudhir', never the names of the clans themselves; as pointed out by Hoyland (2009: 119, citing John of Ephesus' *Church History*).
42 Toral-Niehoff 2013b: 119.
43 For more on the cultural and political links between the Sasanians and Nasrids, see Toral-Niehoff (2013a).
44 Fisher 2011: 92.

45 Toral-Niehoff 2013b: 119; Kister 1968: 167.
46 Tabari 1.958.
47 Wilkinson 1975.
48 Tabari 1.854–5. On the dating of this battle between 604 and 611 see Bosworth (1983: 603).
49 Rubin 1986: 679.
50 Tabari 1.1016, 1.1032.
51 Procopius, *Bella* 1.20.9–10.
52 Wiesehöfer 1996: 196; Kennet 2008a: 57.
53 Although Potts and Cribb (1995: 130–5) note that this may be due to a comparative lack of archaeological work undertaken in the south.
54 Awtabi 2.862; Hoyland 2001: 28; Wilkinson 1973. Ulrich (2011: 378) believes this claim is dubious. However, scholars such as Potts and Cribb (1995: 136) use this to further their argument that the Sasanians used isolated military garrisons to control Arabia with little or no interaction with the local population. Daryaee (2010: 406) also seems to take this idea at face value.
55 Ulrich 2011: 381–2; Kennet 2008a: 57.
56 Kennet 2007: 90; de Cardi 1972: 308.
57 Daryaee 2003: 6; 2010: 405
58 Daryaee (2009b: 57) also agrees with this assessment.
59 Procopius, *Bella* 1.10.12.

BIBLIOGRAPHY

Adams, R. M. (1962), 'Agriculture and Urban Life in Early Southwestern Iran', *Science*, 136, pp. 109–22.
Adams, R. M. (1981), *Heartland of Cities: Surveys of Ancient Settlement and Land Use on the Central Floodplain of the Euphrates*, Chicago: Chicago University Press.
Altheim, F. and Stiehl, R. (1965), *Die Araber in der Alten Welt* II, Berlin: De Gruyter.
Bachrach, B. S. (2010), 'The Fortification of Gaul and the Economy of the Third and Fourth Centuries', *Journal of Late Antiquity*, 3, pp. 38–64.
Bosworth, C. E (1983), 'Iran and the Arabs Before Islam', in E. Yarshater (ed.), *The Cambridge History of Iran: The Seleucid, Parthian and Sasanid Periods*, 3.1, Cambridge: Cambridge University Press, pp. 593–612.
Bosworth, C. E. (1986), 'Arab i: Arabs and Iran in the Pre-Islamic Period', in *Encyclopædia Iranica*, 2.2, London: Routledge, pp. 201–3.
Brosius, M. (2006), *The Persians: An Introduction*, London: Routledge.
Daryaee, T. (2002), *Šahrestānīhā ī Ērānšahr: A Middle Persian Text on Late Antique Geography, Epic and History*,Costa Mesa: Mazda.
Daryaee, T. (2003), 'The Persian Gulf Trade in Late Antiquity', *Journal of World History*, 14.1, pp. 1–16.
Daryaee, T. (2005), 'Ethnic and Territorial Boundaries in Late Antique and Early Medieval Persian (Third to Tenth Century)', in F. Curta (ed.), *Borders, Barriers and Ethnogenesis: Frontiers in Late Antiquity and Middle Ages*, Turnhout: Brepols, pp. 123–38.

Daryaee, T. (2009a), *Sasanian Persia: The Rise and Fall of an Empire*, London: I.B. Tauris.
Daryaee, T. (2009b), 'The Persian Gulf in Late Antiquity: The Sasanian Era (200–700 C.E)', in L.G. Potter (ed.), *The Persian Gulf in History*, New York: Palgrave Macmillan, pp. 57–70.
Daryaee, T. (2010), 'Bazaars, Merchants, and Trade in Late Antique Iran', *Comparative Studies of South Asia, Africa and the Middle East*, 30.3, pp. 401–9.
De Cardi, B. (1972), 'A Sasanian Outpost in Northern Oman', *Antiquity*, 46, pp. 305–10.
Dignas, B. and Winter, E. (2007), *Rome and Persia in Late Antiquity: Neighbours and Rivals*, Cambridge: Cambridge University Press.
Donner, F. M. (1981), *The Early Islamic Conquests*, Princeton: Princeton University Press.
Finster, B. and Schmidt, J. (1976), 'Sasanidische und frühislamische Ruinen im Iraq', *Baghdader Mitteilungen*, 10, pp. 179–92.
Fisher, G. (2011), *Between Empires: Arabs, Romans and Sasanians in Late Antiquity*, Oxford: Oxford University Press.
Frye, R. N. (1977), 'The Sasanian System of Walls for Defence', in M. Rosen-Ayalon (ed.), *Studies in Memory of Gaston Wiet*, Jerusalem: Institute of Asian and African Studies, pp. 7–15.
Frye, R. N. (1992), "Commerce III: In the Parthian and Sasanian Periods", in *Encyclopædia Iranica*, 6, Costa Mesa: Mazda, pp. 61–4.
Haussig, H. W. (1971), *A History of Byzantine Civilisation*, London: Praeger.
Howard-Johnston, J. (1995), 'The Two Great Powers in Late Antiquity: A Comparison', in A. Cameron (ed.), *The Byzantine and Early Islamic Near East. III: States, Resources and Armies*, Princeton: Darwin Press, pp. 157–226.
Howard-Johnston, J. (2012), 'The Late Sasanian Army', in T. Bernheimer and A. Silverstein (eds), *Late Antiquity: Eastern Perspectives*, Exeter: Short Run Press, pp. 87–127.
Hoyland, R. G. (2001), *Arabia and the Arabs: From the Bronze Age to the Coming of Islam*, London: Routledge.
Hoyland, R. G. (2009), 'Late Roman Provincia Arabia, Monophysite Monks and Arab Tribes: A Problem of Centre and Periphery', *Semitica et Classica*, 2, pp. 117–39.
Humbach, H. and Skjærvø, P. O. (1983), *The Sasanian Inscription of Paikuli 3.1*, Wiesbaden and Munich: Reichert.
Isaac, B. (1992), *The Limits of Empire: The Roman Army in the East*, 2nd edn, Oxford: Oxford University Press.
Kennet, D. (2007), 'The Decline of Eastern Arabia in the Sasanian Period', *Arabian Archaeology and Epigraphy*, 18, pp. 86–122.
Kennet, D. (2008a), 'Sasanian Coins from 'Uman and Bahrayn', in D. Kennet and P. Luft (eds), *Current Research in Sasanian Archaeology, Art and History*, BAR International Series 1810, Oxford: Archaeopress, pp. 55–64.
Kennet, D. (2008b), 'Transformations in Late Sasanian and Early Islamic Eastern Arabia: The Evidence from Kush', in C. Robin and J. Schiettecatte (eds), *L'Arabie à la veille de l'Islam*, Paris: De Boccard, pp. 135–61.
Kister, M. (1968), 'Al-Ḥīra: Some Notes on its Relations with Arabia', *Arabica*, 15, pp. 143–69.

Lecker, M. (2002), 'The Levying of Taxes for the Sassanians in Pre-Islamic Medina', *Jerusalem Studies in Arabic and Islam*, 27, pp. 109–26.
Mahamedi, H. (2004), 'Walls as a System of Frontier Defence During the Sasanid Period', in T. Daryaee and M. Omidsalar (eds), *The Spirit of Wisdom [Mēnōg ī Xrad]: Essays in the Memory of Ahmad Tafazzoli*, Costa Mesa: Mazda, pp. 145–59.
McDonough, S. (2013), 'Military and Society in Sasanian Iran', in B. Campbell and L. A. Tritle (eds), *The Oxford Handbook of Warfare in the Classical World*, Oxford: Oxford University Press, pp. 601–20.
Morony, M. G (2001–2), 'The Late Sasanian Economic Impact on the Arabian Peninsula', *Nāme-ye Irān-e Bāstān*, 1, pp. 25–37.
Nia, H. (1974), 'A Survey of Sasanian Silver Coins Found in China', *K'ao Ku 'Hsüeh Pao*, 1, pp. 91–110.
Piacentini, V. F. (1985), 'Ardashīr I Pāpakān and the Wars Against the Arabs: Working Hypothesis on the Sasanian Hold of the Gulf', *Proceedings of the Eighteenth Seminar for Arabian Studies*, 15, pp. 57–77.
Potter, D. S. (2004), *The Roman Empire at Bay*, London: Routledge.
Potts, D. T. (1990), *The Arabian Gulf in Antiquity*, 2, Oxford: Clarendon Press.
Potts, D. T. (1993), 'A Sasanian Lead Horse from Northeastern Arabia', *Iranica Antiqua*, 28, pp. 193–9.
Potts, D. T. (2012), 'Arabia ii: The Sasanians and Arabia', in *Encyclopædia Iranica*, Online Edition, <http://www.iranicaonline.org/articles/arabia-ii-sasanians-and-arabia>.
Potts, D. T. and Cribb, J. (1995), 'Sasanian and Arab-Sasanian Coins from Eastern Arabia', *Iranica Antiqua*, 30, pp. 123–37.
Pourshariati, P. (2008), *Decline and Fall of the Sasanian Empire: The Sasanian–Parthian Confederacy and the Arab Conquest of Iran*, London: I.B. Tauris.
Preiser-Kapeller, J. (2010), '*Erdumn, Uxt Carayut'iwn*: Armenian Aristocrats as Diplomatic Partners of the Eastern Roman Emperors 387–884/5 A.D.', *Armenian Review*, 52, pp. 139–217.
Rubin, Z. (1986), 'Diplomacy and War in the Relations between Byzantium and the Sassanids in the Fifth Century', in P. Freeman and D. Kennedy (eds), *The Defence of the Roman and Byzantine East*, BAR International Series 297, Oxford: British Archaeological Reports, pp. 677–95.
Rubin, Z. (2000), 'The Sasanid Monarchy', in A. Cameron, B. Ward-Perkins and M. Whitby (eds), *The Cambridge Ancient History XIV. Late Antiquity: Empire and Successors AD 425–600*, Cambridge: Cambridge University Press, pp. 638–61.
Toral-Niehoff, I. (2013a), *Al-Hira: Eine Arabische Kulturmetrople im Spätantiken Kontext*, Leiden: Brill.
Toral-Niehoff, I. (2013b), 'Late Antique Iran and the Arabs: The Case of al-Hira', *Journal of Persianate Studies*, 6, pp. 115–26.
Ulrich, B. (2011), 'Oman and Bahrain in Late Antiquity: The Sasanians' Arabian Periphery', *Proceedings of the Seminar for Arabian Studies*, 41, pp. 377–86.
Wenke, R. J. (1975–6), 'Imperial Investments and Agricultural Developments in Parthian and Sasanian Khuzestan: 150 BC to AD 640', *Mesopotamia*, 10–11, pp. 31–221.
Wenke, R. J. (1987), 'Western Iran in the Partho-Sasanian Period: The Imperial Transformation', in F. Hole (ed.), *The Archaeology of Western Iran: Settlement*

and Society from Pre-History to the Islamic Conquest, Washington: Smithsonian Institution Press, pp. 251–81.

Whitehouse, D. and Williamson, A. (1973), 'Sasanian Maritime Trade', *Iran*, 11, pp. 29–49.

Widengren, G. (1971), 'The Establishment of the Sasanian Dynasty in the Light of New Evidence', in *Atti del Convegno internazionale sul tema: La Persia nel Medioevo*, Rome: Accademia Nazionale dei Lincei, pp. 711–84.

Wiesehöfer, J. (1996), *Ancient Persia: From 550 B.C to 650 A.D.*, London: I.B Tauris.

Wilkinson, J. C. (1973), 'Arab–Persian Land Relationship in Late Sasanid Oman', *Proceedings of the Sixth Seminar for Arabian Studies*, 3, pp. 40–51.

Wilkinson, J. C. (1975), 'The Julanda of Oman', *Journal of Oman Studies*, 1, pp. 97–108.

Wink, A. (1990), *Al-Hind: The Making of the Indo-Islamic World I: Early Medieval India and the Expansion of India*, Leiden: Brill.

13 The India Trade in Late Antiquity

James Howard-Johnston

The effects of long-distance maritime trade on the economic and political development of the hinterlands of port-cities are as evident on either side of the Red Sea as in South-East Asia. Both great powers of the west profited from the India trade in the fifth century, but with the deterioration in their relations after the 502–5 war, the Persians imposed an embargo on Roman trade with India, which Justinian tried and failed to break. Hence it was mainly through Persia that the products of the south and the east, including garnets from south India and Sri Lanka, reached Europe. The gold received in tribute from the Romans was probably destined for India. Close attention should be paid to references to trade in contemporary writings by members of elites which were largely indifferent to economic matters. They reveal *inter alia* the existence of a powerful business lobby in the Sasanian Empire.

While the early Roman centuries marked the high point of Mediterranean economic activity before the early modern period, it was in late antiquity that the growth of commerce gathered way in the wider world. There was increased traffic across Eurasia, from the late fourth century, when the city-states of Sogdia took control of the overland routes between China and the west, as well as those running south across the mountains to the subcontinent.[1] This development in the north was dwarfed by the growth of long-distance trade by sea and of a series of interconnected maritime markets, itself facilitated by the extension of the Indian cultural zone over South-East Asia, as nascent states on the mainland and islands adopted Indian modes of rule and Buddhist beliefs.[2] To the west of the subcontinent, in the Indian Ocean, there was increasing activity. Manufactured goods and natural products were exchanged between the Roman Empire, south Arabia, East Africa, the Persian Gulf, India and Sri Lanka. Growth continued in late antiquity, boosted, in the fifth century, by the opening of a direct sea route, through the Straits of Malacca, between the southern and eastern oceans. This facilitated trade between the Indian Ocean world and south China, and opened up the Java Sea as an active zone of exchange.[3]

Competition between the port-cities of South-East Asia, on both the mainland and the great western islands, gave an added push to commercial exchange, into which, with time, the easternmost islands of the Indonesian archipelago were drawn. New precious commodities thus entered the transoceanic market: camphor from north-west Sumatra and Borneo, pepper from west Java, cloves, nutmeg and mace from the Moluccas, sandalwood from Timor ... The new demand which was generated in distant developed markets of the east and west contributed to further commercial growth. So too did the gradual extension and integration of political entities in South-East Asia, as port-cities intensified their grip on their hinterlands and nascent centralised states appeared on the rice-growing plains of the mainland and islands. Increasing market activity behind maritime façades both increased the supply of prized commodities from South-East Asia to the transoceanic market and magnified local demand for imported goods, thereby imparting another twist to the series of virtuous economic circles at work.[4] It thus became easier and cheaper to convey Indian products – cotton textiles, glass beads, pearls, precious and semi-precious stones, pepper, teak and soforth – and spices from South-East Asia to the Roman, Persian and Chinese markets and for goods of various sorts to flow back – glass, silver plate, fine tableware, metalwork, coral, woollen and linen cloth and so forth – from the west, together with south Arabian aromatics, and from China principally silks.[5]

The growth of production and exchange within South-East Asia thus acted as a stimulus to transoceanic trade. There was the same interplay between the level of activity within the other great markets (south China, the Indian subcontinent and, in the far west, the Roman and Sasanian Empires) and long-distance exchange. South China, relatively immune from the troubles of the north and with an elite boosted by aristocratic migrants from the north, generated an increasing demand for goods from overseas. Merchants achieved increasing prominence, entering the apparatus of government in the fifth century.[6] While there is less evidence, archaeological and literary, than previously about cities, manufacturing and trade in India, it does not follow that economic decline set in or that long-distance trade with the far west and China collapsed. Cities and markets continue to feature in the fifth–sixth-century Tamil epics. Merchants, goldsmiths, bronze workers, leather workers and so forth, along with trade associations (of oil manufacturers, silk weavers ...), are attested on inscriptions, in particular on copper plate records of charitable endowments. Several words connected with cotton textiles – weaver, loom, thread, coarse and fine fabric – appear in the *Amarakosha* (Sanskrit lexicon). The most striking single piece of evidence about commerce, though, comes from outside, from a sixth-century Egyptian merchant's account of the flourishing emporium on the north-west coast of Sri Lanka (of which more below). It was, above all, the opening up of South-East Asia which boosted Indian trade, certain commodities acquiring enhanced value with the spread of Indian mores and religions.[7]

There can be little doubt about the high level of commercial activity and enterprise encouraged by the ease of maritime transport around and across the Mediterranean while it was united under Roman rule. The troubles of the third century, when the stress of defending a beleaguered empire was exacerbated by hyper-inflation, had a significant dampening effect on trade, but a revival gathered pace once order was restored by the Tetrarchate. Cities recovered their old vigour, the notables eager to display their wealth and win the gratitude of their fellow-citizens by endowing public buildings and spectacles, and, increasingly, by channelling funds to the poor through the church. Ceramic evidence makes it plain that trade revived throughout the Mediterranean in the fourth century and that there was plenty of east–west traffic in the fifth century, despite the destruction of the empire in the west and the establishment of independent Germanic regimes in Gaul, Spain, North Africa and Italy. Growth was sustained in the east in the sixth century, only halted by the wildfire spread of bubonic plague in 541–2 and the demographic shock which it induced.[8]

There was therefore continuing demand for exotic commodities from abroad and continuing interest in exporting Mediterranean specialities (e.g. wine) and manufactured goods. Roman merchants, both those investing in trading ventures and those conducting business in person, kept up the high level of involvement in Indian Ocean commerce documented for the first and second centuries AD by an anonymous captain's report on commercial conditions in the Red Sea, East Africa and south Arabia, and by a papyrus which gives some idea of the profits to be made from just one of the hundred or more voyages which Strabo reports were made in a year from Myos Hormos to India.⁹ Myos Hormos was in decline in the fourth century, as its lagoon was silting up. It was supplanted – the archaeological evidence is unequivocal – by Berenike, its nearest neighbour on the Egyptian coast of the Red Sea, which likewise was linked by road to Koptos on the Nile. Black peppercorns, rice, coconut husks, teak beams recycled in buildings, gems, glass beads, fragments of cotton cloth, cooking pots, camel girths and so forth testify to ongoing trade with India. The city became one of three important Roman emporia on the Red Sea, migrating east and developing a new quarter on an artificial platform made of thousands of tons of broken early and late Roman pottery. The other two were Clysma and Aila, which, despite their positions at the end of the two northern horns of the Red Sea, remained important centres in late antiquity, Clysma doubling probably as the main Roman naval base, and Aila benefitting from its position at the southern end of the caravan route running north to the Syrian *badiya* and from copper mines in the Wadi Faynan. Carrot-shaped amphorae made at Aila are to be found throughout the Red Sea, indicators perhaps of the distribution of copper vessels also manufactured there.¹⁰

The sort of consolidation and extension of political authority discernible in South-East Asia is paralleled in non-Roman lands fronting the Red Sea. On the African mainland, the rise of Aksum as a regional power seems to have begun in the first century AD, when the growing population of the capital spilled out from the original settlement on the hill of Beta Giyorgis and Roman manufactured goods were being imported, probably in considerable quantity, through Adulis, 150km away on the Red Sea. For a while, in the third century, the *neguš*' authority was projected over large parts of south Arabia – later kings continued to claim suzerainty over Himyar, Raydan, Saba and Salhan in their official titulature – but in the first half of the fourth century they turned their attention to extending and consolidating their rule in Africa, pushing west to Nubia and north over the territory of the Bega (Blemmyes) between the Nile and the Red Sea coast. Both these military and political ventures may be viewed as responses to growing commercial activity in the Red Sea, as Adulis, Aksum's main outlet to the regional and transoceanic markets, generated increasing revenues and needed an enlarged hinterland. Finds of Aila amphorae and African red slip ware testify to its involvement in long-distance trade, as do finds of Aksumite exports in Egypt and India, and the minting of gold coins with Greek legends.¹¹

A similar process of military expansion and political consolidation can be observed on the Arabian side of the Red Sea, as the kingdom of Himyar enveloped four pre-existing states and, we may conjecture, led the resistance to Aksum. The rise of Himyar as a unitary power in south Arabia by the end of the third century, a power capable of projecting its influence deep into the interior of the peninsula, may have been prompted by the Aksumite threat, but it was assuredly facilitated by growing activity in the principal emporium of south Arabia. Qana, on the coast of Hadramawt, was integrated, like Adulis, into the Roman-dominated commerce of the Red Sea, to judge by the high proportion of amphorae found which originated from Aila.[12] As in South-East Asia, increased domestic production and exchange were a likely consequence of territorial expansion and intensification of authority, and acted, in turn, as a stimulant to regional economic activity and transoceanic exchange. In this context, it should cause little surprise that monotheist beliefs took hold in both nascent states in the fourth century. The colouring in Himyar was Jewish, an indication perhaps of the sojourning of Mesopotamian traders in Himyarite ports, while Aksum was more exposed to Christian proselytising (from Egypt).[13]

Before turning to the fifth great market, that of the Sasanian Empire, we should glance south, down the East African coast. This was not untouched by long-distance commerce. In late antiquity it lay within the commercial horizons of Roman traders operating out of the Red Sea, as it had done in the first century AD. Finds of Roman ceramics, transport jars and tableware, in the farming and fishing villages of the coast leave no doubt about this. But there is no evidence of the development of emporia or growth in exchange networks linking coast to interior analogous to that documented for South-East Asia, and none of any consolidation of political power akin to that discernible in Ethiopia and south Arabia. The market remained rudimentary, appreciated above all as a source of high-quality ivory. The chief export, apart from ivory, was the plague bacillus, which percolated down to the coast and then followed the sea-lanes to Alexandria in late 541.[14]

The very diversity of lands ruled by Sasanian kings promoted interregional commercial exchange. Outside their heartlands on the Iranian Plateau and the adjoining irrigated lowlands of Mesopotamia, their control reached from the fertile uplands of Transcaucasia in the west to the Oxus and Indus in the east and south-east, and down both shores of the Persian Gulf in the south. Theirs was a great unitary state, with a developed urban economy and a stable currency.

It had good internal communications by land, river and canal, and easy access to the Indian Ocean via the Persian Gulf. The cumulative demand generated by aristocratic houses in Iran, by court and capital (the twin cities of Ctesiphon–Veh Ardashir) in Mesopotamia, and by the army was one of the principal drivers of the economy. We should envisage a two-way traffic in goods, agricultural and manufactured, between the capital and the grainlands of the Diyala basin and Jazira, between country houses and nearby villages, between town and country, between regional centres all over the empire – as well as the hoovering up of supplies from designated provisioning areas by troop concentrations in frontier zones, and longer-distance commerce with distant markets overseas and overland.

There is less material evidence than from the Roman Empire, but enough – in the form of ceramic finds, workshops and merchant establishments – to confirm the hypothesis.[15] The merchant was a familiar figure. It was recognised that economic prosperity lay at the base of state power.[16] Hence the promotion of craft production in the early phase of empire-building in the third century when captured Roman artisans were resettled in Khuzestan. Hence the sensitivity of the political classes to the charge of impeding commerce which was brought against Khusro II towards the end of his reign.[17] Hence the promotion of ports on the Persian side of the Gulf at the expense of those on the opposite Arabian shore. The rise of Siraf, which has been excavated, may have antedated the coming of Islam. Growing prosperity in the hinterland of Bushire (Sasanian Rev-Ardashir) is suggested by surface survey. As for the Arabian shore, there is archaeological evidence from several sites of a marked decline in population and prosperity.[18] The only new constructions found so far which date from the Sasanian period are a fort for the projection of Sasanian authority over the interior of Bahrain from the north and an isolated tower at Kush, on the coast 80km inside the Straits of Hormuz.[19]

It is hard for us to know what interest the governments of the two great powers of the west took in the distant markets of the Indian Ocean and the South China Sea. It is seldom possible to discover whether or not these powers pursued commercial policies, let alone to define what those policies might have been. Their governing classes did not advertise involvement in trade. Roman aristocrats maintained an attitude of studied indifference to the business of earning money, whether from the land or from trade. This can be shown up for what it was, an artificial pose, with respect to agriculture, thanks to the voluminous estate records preserved on papyrus from the Nile valley, whereas records of commercial transactions (with a single exception, the Muziris papyrus) do not survive from the Delta.[20] The same stance was almost certainly prevalent in the Sasanian aristocracy, to judge by the exclusive focus on political and religious achievements, above all victory in war, in Sasanian monumental inscriptions and reliefs and by the evidence of aristocratic literary tastes provide by preserved reading matter. As for high-style writers, including historians, it is rare indeed to find any reference to trade or manufacture in works which were, after all, written for the delectation and education of the governing elites.[21] Such references are to be treasured and handled with the utmost care. For the implication of their being made is surely that the matter in question was of the utmost importance, and that it managed not only to attract the attention of government but also to make its way in the teeth of cultural disdain into a work of literature.

This is a point of great methodological importance. It must be impressed upon western historians who, in the decades of the Cold War, were all too ready to reject the prominence accorded by their Soviet counterparts to economic factors, at the expense of ideas, *imaginaires*, and all the immaterial concerns which had an impact on social formations. So, I repeat: *we should pay close attention to any substantive notices in late antique texts which deal with commerce and government commercial policy.*

War and diplomacy dominated the first century and a half of Persian–Roman relations after the seizure of power by the Sasanian dynasty in the 220s. There were two long bouts of warfare, the first (early 230s–298) initiated by the Persians in the latter stages of the phase of dynamic expansion of Sasanian power, the second (337–late 380s) planned by Constantine I not long before he died. The intensity of the conflict diminished after the failure of the climactic Roman campaign, Julian's disastrous invasion of Mesopotamia in 363.[22] Considerations of cost and war-weariness doubtless began to prey upon minds. But it was an external threat which prompted both sides to seek a lasting accommodation. This threat took the form of a formidable adversary in the north, the rump of Xiongnu/Chionitai/Huns who had been expelled from China around 350 and such other tribes as they had drawn into dependency as they migrated west. They impinged first, in the 350s, on the inner Asian frontiers of Iran and then, in the 370s, on the eastern approaches to the lower Danube and the Roman Balkans.[23] Both southern powers realised that a major geopolitical change had occurred and that they now had a strong common interest in confronting the new danger together. In addition they could not but acknowledge that the strategic defences which each side had built up greatly reduced the chances of making worthwhile gains from warfare against each other.

A comprehensive peace treaty was negotiated in the late 380s, which was subsequently extended and refined in the first half of the fifth century. The existing frontier in north Mesopotamia was recognised. It was agreed to formalise the de facto division between Roman and Persian spheres of influence north of the Armenian Taurus in a partition which left the Persians in control of four-fifths of Transcaucasia. A division of northern Arabia into spheres of influence was probably agreed; hence the Persians' later insistence (probably in 440) that none of their Beduin should be granted asylum by the Romans. An important clause, dating probably from 408–9, regulated commerce across their mutual frontier. It was to be channelled through three officially designated emporia: Artaxata in Transcaucasia, Nisibis in northern Mesopotamia and Callinicum on the Euphrates. Apart from the advantage to both sides of their being able to monitor and tax transactions, both were left free to police the uplands of western Armenia and the desert south of the Euphrates, well away from the main trade routes, and to crack down as they chose on illicit trade and those involved. Another clause (probably introduced in 422 to formalise an existing arrangement) prohibited the construction of new fortresses or improvement of existing ones in frontier zones. This prevented a new arms race, which would have seen rival fortification programmes extend beyond north Mesopotamia. A shared concern with the northern danger was, we may assume, openly acknowledged from the first, each giving a vague commitment to support the other. The Romans accepted that the Persians were likely to bear the heavier burden and undertook informally (perhaps as late as 440) to contribute to the cost of Caucasus defence. For much of the fifth century they were ready to provide substantial sums of gold in offset payments.[24]

Apart from fleeting crises in 421–2 and 440, relations remained good throughout the fifth century.[25] It follows that there was no interruption to the ordinary course of commercial activity and rivalry between the various participants – Roman, Arab, Aksumite, Persian, Indian and Sri Lankan – in the India trade. Flourishing commerce, as has been seen, helps to explain the development of Aksum and Himyar in late antiquity. Likewise, while the revived prosperity of Berenike from the middle of the fourth century, manifest above all in the eastward extension of the city, must be partly explained by the general stabilisation of the Roman economy and governmental system achieved by the Tetrarchate at the end of the third century, new opportunities and increased commercial profits, in an era of good relations between the great powers and unimpeded trade in southern waters, undoubtedly made an important contribution. Imports from India/Sri Lanka excavated in late antique strata at Berenike leave no doubt about the revival of long-distance trade. What survives is, of course, but a minuscule portion of what passed through the port, namely those durable and archaeologically discernible items which were sold or spilled or discarded in transit through the emporium, such as black peppercorns (but not other, more valuable spices), some cotton cloth (preserved in exceptionally dry contexts), Indo-Pacific glass beads (obtained probably *via* Sri Lanka) and other items noted above.[26]

Given the favourable geographical position of the Persian Gulf, so much closer than the Red Sea to all parts of the western seaboard of the subcontinent, we should probably envisage the merchants of southern Mesopotamia, Khuzestan and the Gulf coast of Persia proper as taking a leading role in the India trade. There is scattered evidence for this contention: first the presence of a Sasanian fortress at Ratto Kot, which controlled access to the emporium of Daybal (modern Banhore) at the mouth of the Indus – a distant southern analogue of Qal'at al-Bahrayn, which commanded a narrow bay to the north of the abandoned site of Tylos on Bahrain;[27] second, the presence of Sasanian ceramic containers, so-called torpedo jars, in larger numbers than those of late Roman amphorae at sites on the Gujarat and Konkan coasts, as well as in Sri Lanka (it should be remembered, though, that they form but a small proportion of total ceramic finds);[28] and third, a tantalising piece of evidence about the acquisition of precious and semi-precious stones, in this case garnet (a translucent, red, semi-precious stone), from south India and Sri Lanka – a garnet-inlaid pendant with a Pahlavi inscription, signifying manufacture in a Sasanian workshop, which was found at Wolfsheim in the Rhineland, in a Migration Era burial loosely datable to the late fourth or fifth century by the find of a *solidus* of Valens.[29]

An idea of the scale of the Persians' India trade may be obtainable if evidence can adduced about the size of any imbalance between imports and exports. It is likely, of course, that imports, which, in addition to precious and semi-precious stones (such as garnets), included silk (brought to the subcontinent both overland, across the Pamirs and down the Indus valley, primarily by Sogdian merchants, and shipped in via South-East Asia),[30] were worth considerably more than Persian exports (which are harder to define, but presumably included cloth, glassware and natural produce unique to Mesopotamia or Iran, such as nuts and dried fruit). The need to fund a continuing balance-of-payments deficit explains the otherwise baffling Persian appetite for Roman gold – baffling because the Sasanian regime did not put gold to use apart from rare, ceremonial issues of gold dinars and (presumably) sales of bullion to goldsmiths for the fabrication of jewellery.[31] It is hard to see how the annual contributions to Caucasus defence paid in gold in the fifth century or the larger payments of tribute in the sixth century (including lump sums of 11,000 pounds in 532 and a little under 3,000 in 562), conveyed probably in the compact form of ingots, benefitted the Sasanian Empire, unless the gold was put to commercial use – enabling Persian merchants to buy up more high-value commodities in India and Sri Lanka than they could pay for with their exports, commodities which could then be sold in their home market and to foreign buyers at a considerable profit.[32]

The era of peaceful symbiosis came to end at the beginning of the sixth century. The equilibrium had been disturbed by the determination of Peroz (457–84) to assert Sasanian authority over the Hephthalites, who had succeeded Xiongnu and Kidarites as the hegemonic power in central Asia. The annihilation of the Persian expeditionary army and the death of Peroz in 484 inaugurated a period of political, social and religious upheaval. The *shahanshah* was reduced to the status of Hephthalite client-king and was obliged to pay tribute. Tension in relations with the Romans grew when they halted the customary offset payments, on the not unreasonable grounds that sums intended to keep a northern power at bay were now being passed on as tribute to that same northern power. It was probably to raise his prestige at home after his second installation by the Hephthalites that Kavad I (488–98 and 501/502–31) launched a surprise attack (surely cleared beforehand with the Hephthalites) on the Roman Empire in autumn 502, which netted two key frontier cities: Theodosiopolis and Amida. The war which followed was hard fought, the Romans eventually deploying nearly a hundred thousand men in their successful drive to recover Amida.[33]

Kavad's war was the first of five fought in the course of the sixth and early seventh centuries. Unprovoked aggression of that sort could not but sour relations. The Romans were ready to negotiate an end to the fighting in 505–6 but refused to agree a full peace on the old terms.[34] This left the regimes of Anastasius (491–518) and

Justin I (518–27) free to embark on a twenty-year programme of military building along the frontier from Palmyra to Tzanica and the Black Sea coast in the north, at the same time making diplomatic forays into Lazica, Iberia and the steppes north of the Caucasus and helping on the percolation of Christianity into south Arabia. There was no question of their renewing the fifth-century offset payments or of their cooperating in the management of commerce across their common frontiers. It was an armistice, an interlude between two rounds of warfare, the second of which would occur at a time of the Romans' choosing. In effect they were beginning a slow-moving offensive in stone, with ancillary subversion, which was designed to strengthen their strategic position and to prepare the ground for a renewal of military action.[35]

Kavad doubtless instituted a fortification programme of his own. It is to him that should be attributed the inception of schemes to seal off Ctesiphon–Veh Ardashir from attack on the left bank of the Tigris (the 'Cut of Khusro') and to upgrade defences on both sides of the Caspian.[36] His most effective riposte, however, could be made in the commercial sphere. Making use of the natural dominance of the Persian Gulf, the Sasanians could intervene to exclude Roman merchants from the India trade, whether by negotiating agreements with trading partners in the subcontinent, from the Gupta in the north to the rulers of Sri Lanka in the south, or by direct naval or military action against Roman vessels. Indian vessels could also be intercepted by Persian merchants as they made their way north along the coast, long before any Roman traders who flouted the embargo could make contact. There is clear evidence that this policy was adopted by Kavad. It comes from the pen of Cosmas Indicopleustes, an Egyptian merchant who travelled widely and had eccentric views about the architecture of the cosmos. In what is now an appendix to his *Christian Topography* (probably written in the middle or late 540s), he describes the fauna and flora of India, Taprobane (Sri Lanka) and its trade. He refers to a friend of his, Sopatros, a merchant operating out of Adulis in Aksum, who had died thirty-five years before the time of writing and who had been in the main port of Taprobane when a Persian mission (probably one of many dispatched over the years to different emporia) arrived to negotiate a preferential trade treaty. A *terminus ante quem* of 515 is obtained. Sopatros argued the Romans' case, asserting their superiority over the Persians on the basis of their coinage (the gold *solidus* as against the silver drachm). But despite the consternation this argument is said to have induced in the Persian envoy, there is no reason to suppose that he failed to secure the trade treaty which he sought.[37]

Confirmation that Persian merchants achieved something close to a monopoly over the India trade (i.e. over deals with Indian and Sri Lankan parties, both merchants and resident traders) is provided by a passage in Procopius' history of Justinian's wars, which deals with an episode datable to 531. By then the war long planned by the Romans, which had broken out in 527, was calming down after successive grand offensives by the Romans (in 528) and the Persians (in 530), neither of which had made much headway. The only substantive Roman gain was made by surrogates in the south in 528: an Aksumite naval and military expeditionary force, including a large Roman naval contingent, defeated and killed the proselytising Jewish ruler of Himyar who had seized power in 522–3, and reimposed the authority of the Christian *neguš* of Aksum.[38] In 531 Justinian was trying to follow up this success with two more offensive moves against the Persians: a military push from Himyar towards the Gulf, and an Aksumite commercial push into the Indian Ocean to gain a share of the silk trade. Both failed. The plan for a joint Himyar–Ma'add expedition east was thwarted by reluctance on the part of the Aksumite client-ruler of Himyar to take the first step of installing a pro-Roman leader over the Ma'add. The commercial initiative came to nothing too. Persian importers of raw silk went out to meet Indian shippers at their first port of call on Sasanian territory, and bought up all their merchandise, while Persian shippers probably continued to patronise the markets of India and Sri Lanka.[39]

Nothing seems to have been said about the India trade in the peace treaty which brought the second sixth-century war to an end in 532. It is conceivable that the Sasanians lifted the embargo for a while (although that is hard to square with what Procopius writes), but it would undoubtedly have been reimposed during the third war, initiated by a surprise invasion of Syria by Khusro I in 540 and only brought to an end twenty-two years later. The treaty of 562, we know, included no clause about free navigation in the Indian Ocean, which suggests that the Roman side did not press it as an issue during the negotiations.[40] The restrictions on Roman merchants are likely to have remained in force for the rest of the century, before and after a fourth round of warfare (573–91), and help explain the sharp decline of Berenike, the Romans' main commercial port on the Red Sea, from the second quarter of the sixth century.[41] Dependence on the Persians for supplies of raw silk and silk cloth – as necessary to a developed monarchy as precious metal – was galling to Justinian, and even more so to his successor, Justin II (565–78), who was determined to assert his imperial status. Justinian's response was, around 545, to give his approval to a scheme proposed by two monks to smuggle silkworm eggs out of China. This was a scheme which worked, the eggs arriving around 552, but many decades would pass before an indigenous silk industry of any scale could be developed.[42] Justin II, for his part, proved receptive to the proposal for an alliance from the new central Asian power, the Turkish khaganate, brought by a Turco-Sogdian embassy in 568–9. He was tempted primarily by the prospect of victory over the Sasanians but also, we may suspect, by knowledge that the khaganate had access to virtually unlimited supplies of Chinese silk.[43]

Before considering the background to the Turkish diplomatic démarche to the Romans and its fateful consequences, let us pick up two telling pieces of evidence for the northern reach of the India trade, in the era of Sasanian dominance. The first is a single object: a bronze figurine of the Buddha seated on a double lotus flower. It is of very high quality, well modelled and well made, with caste mark, eyelids and lips picked out with silver, tin and niello inlay. To judge by the style and technique, it was made – probably as a reliquary (it has a hollow interior) – in the Swat Valley in what is now Pakistan in the sixth century. It was excavated at an important emporium and cult centre in Sweden, the island of Helgö in Lake Mälaren, the late antique and early medieval predecessor of Birka. The figurine was probably acquired as an example of fine craftsmanship by a metalworker, at the latest in the eighth century.[44] The second piece of evidence is the impressive number of garnets found in the north. Their provenance from south India and Sri Lanka is well established. There was an alternative source of supply in Bohemia, but it was only exploited (the garnets were inferior) when the supply of southern garnets began to dry up in the seventh century (a consequence, I suspect, of political instability in the Middle East, as the fifth and final great war was fought between Romans and Persians [603–30], followed all too soon by the Arab campaigns of conquest [634–52]).[45]

Brooches, pendants, sword pommels and other items decorated with inlaid garnets, in geometrical or medallion patterns, are characteristic finds from the Germanic world of the fifth and sixth centuries (extending into the seventh in the case of Britain). They have been found, mainly in burials, in large quantities.[46] Stocks of unworked garnet have also been unearthed in high-status settlements (e.g. the royal complex at Gamla Uppsala) and emporia (e.g. Pavliken I on

Gotland, or Ribe or Ipswich). Such caches indicate the presence of workshops producing garnet-inlaid metalwork.[47] While garnets still reached the Mediterranean in the fifth century, only one workshop is known to have produce cut garnet stones in any quantity, mainly for seals – and the main inspiration seems to have been Sasanian.[48] Garnet-inlaid metalwork of the sort found in the north was *not* manufactured in the Eastern Roman Empire. The Sasanians, by contrast, have already been shown to be implicated in the garnet trade with the north by the Wolfsheim pendant. The penchant for garnet decoration and for cloisonné inlay can be traced back to the Kushan Empire in the first three centuries AD; that is, to eastern Iranian lands and a surrounding zone extending from the steppes through Afghanistan to Pakistan.[49] It is from there, it may be conjectured, that demand for garnet-inlaid metalwork spread into the steppes, creating a fashion within the Hunnic Empire of the fourth–fifth centuries, which was picked up by their Germanic subjects. The key intermediaries in the garnet trade would then be Persian merchants operating from the Gulf and their Indian and Sri Lankan counterparts.

I shall end with the Gulf merchants, a powerful constituency within the Sasanian Empire. Their lobbying could exercise a decisive influence on foreign policy, as can be demonstrated from the course of negotiations between Persians and Turks. Khusro I (531–79), a great reforming king, was well aware of the strength of the Turks and their Sogdian partners. He handled them carefully. When they first entered the field of Sasanian diplomatic vision, he negotiated an agreement, under which he received Hephthalite territory up to the Oxus in return for giving political backing to the Turks' attack on the Hephthalites.[50] He then closed down his western war, making a substantial concession (Lazica) to the Romans. But at a new round of talks in the middle 560s, when a Sogdian delegation was seeking permission to sell silk inside the Sasanian Empire, he refused them entry and, after a high-level debate, on the advice of a refugee Hephthalite leader, bought the whole consignment of silk on offer and had it publicly burned. When a second, purely Turkish embassy failed to alter the Persian position and several of its members died, Turks and Sogdians sent off the embassy to Constantinople, which led ultimately to a plan for co-ordinated attacks by Romans and Persians on the Sasanians, scheduled for 573.[51]

Such an outcome was foreseeable, albeit as a fairly remote possibility. So the question arises as to how Khusro I was manoeuvred into antagonising the great central Asian power of the time. It cannot have been the influence of a single Hephthalite refugee, however important. We should look instead to interests which would be harmed by any trade deal struck with the Sogdians – namely the Gulf merchants, who had gained a virtual monopoly over the India trade and much of whose wealth came from the importation and resale of silk. The various scattered pieces of evidence which have been assembled above suggest that great fortunes could be made and that the merchants formed a powerful lobby, which not even the king of kings could resist.

So it was that Khusro I found himself forced to break off diplomatic relations with the Turks. Soon afterward, in 571, he seems to have been cajoled into taking direct control of Himyar and thus cutting off Roman access to East Africa as well as the Indian Ocean.[52] After the prelude of a Roman-sponsored rising in Persarmenia in 572, the war he had probably feared for some years began with Roman and Turkish offensives in 573.[53] The future of the Sasanian Empire was imperilled as never before and only once subsequently – when the Arabs launched their attack on Mesopotamia in 636.

NOTES

1 De la Vaissière 2002: 99–191.
2 Heirman and Bumbacher 2006; Hall 2011: 15–17, 46–54, 65–6, 114–19.
3 Findlay and O'Rourke 2007: 33–7.
4 Hall 2011: 12–32, 53–9, 67–76, 106–16.
5 Liu 1994: 7–9, 53–75; Young 2001: 14–18; Hall 2011: 157–62.
6 Lewis 2009: 6–7, 31–7, 51–85.
7 Chakravarti 2001: 72–6; Singh 2009: 408–18, 500–4; Hall 2011: 58–9; Cosmas Indicopleustes, 11.13–16.
8 Brown 1992: 71–117; Liebeschuetz 2001: 29–136, 284–317; Ward-Perkins 2001.
9 Casson 1989; Rathbone 2001; Strabo, 2.5.12, 17.1.13.
10 Tomber 2008: 57–87; Power 2012: 28–30, 31–2, 38–41.
11 Tomber 2008: 88–93; Power 2012: 47–8; Phillipson 2012: 63–5, 69–90, 195–201, 203; Marrassini 2014: 28–32.
12 Hoyland 2001: 36–51; Tomber 2008: 103–8; Power 2012: 50–1.
13 Phillipson 2012: 91–106; Gajda 2009: 39–41, 223–54.
14 Horton and Middleton 2000: 26–46; Sarris 2002: 169–72.
15 See, for example, Whitcomb 1985: 102–3 and Simpson 2014: 132–4.
16 Grignaschi 1966: 103–8, 129–35 (*Book of Crown*).
17 *Chronicle of Seert*, 220–1; Movses Daskhurants'i, 145.8–10 (trans. 89).
18 Whitehouse and Williamson 1973: 29–42; Priestman and Kennet 2002: 265–7; Carter et al. 2006: 63–9, 96–9; Kennet 2007.
19 Kervran 1994: 325–7, 330–5; Kennet 2009: 144–51, 157–9.
20 Sarris 2006: 43–9, 193–8.
21 Christensen 1944: 50–74; Herrmann 1977: 85–98, 104–6.
22 Matthews 1989: 130–79; Dignas and Winter 2007: 18–34, 71–94, 119–30.

23 Matthews 1989: 61–3; Barfield 1989: 101–3; Heather 1995; Lewis 2009: 74–6, 145–8; Golden 2011: 33–4.
24 Rubin 1986: 32–9; Blockley 1992: 42–5, 50–1, 57–8, 60–1.
25 Greatrex and Lieu 2002: 36–45.
26 Sidebotham 2011: 260–4, 268–79; Power 2012: 38–41.
27 Kervran 1994: 325–7, 335–8.
28 Tomber 2008: 126–8, 145–7, 167–8.
29 Ebert 1914: 58–65; Bernhard 1982: 82–5.
30 De la Vaissière 2002: 77–97, 174–80.
31 Alram et al. 2003–12.
32 Joshua the Stylite, ch. 8, with Rubin 1986: 39, no. 150; Procopius, *Bella*, 1.22.3–5; Menander Protector, fr. 6.1.134–54.
33 Greatrex 1998: 73–115; Bonner 2015: 80–6.
34 Greatrex 1998: 115–18; Greatrex and Lieu 2002: 82–228.
35 Whitby 1988: 207–13; Howard-Johnston 2013: 872–82.
36 Howard-Johnston 2012: 96–108.
37 Cosmas Indicopleustes, 11.17–19; cf. Kominko 2013: 4–9, 12–13.
38 Procopius, *Bella*, 1.20.1; Ioannes Malalas, 18.15; *Martyrium S. Arethae*, chs 28–39; Tabari, 1.925–30 (trans., 204–12); cf. Beaucamp et al. 1999–2000: 55–83; Robin 2010: 69–79; Beaucamp 2010: 206–15.
39 Procopius, *Bella*, 1.20.9–12; Ioannes Malalas, 18.56; cf. Beaucamp 2010: 197–206.
40 Procopius, *Bella*, 1.22.1–19; Menander Protector, fr. 6.1.304–423.
41 Sidebotham 2011: 279–82.
42 Procopius, *Bella*, 8.17.1–8; cf. Zuckerman 2013: 333–6, who envisages a much more rapid development of an indigenous silk industry.
43 Menander Protector, fr. 10.1.1–2, 47–95; cf. de la Vaissière 2002: 230–7.
44 Gyllensvärd 2004; Arrhenius 2011.
45 Drauschke 2011: 38–43, 209–13. Von Freeden 2000: 97–122 puts the dwindling of the supply of southern garnets in the second half of the sixth century and blames it on the closure of the Red Sea. See also Adams et al. 2011.
46 Arrhenius 1971; 1985; Drauschke 2011: 37, 43–8; Hamerow, forthcoming 2017.
47 Hamerow, forthcoming 2017; Ljungkvist and Frölund 2015.
48 Spier 2007: 87–93.
49 Adams 2000; 2011.
50 Bonner 2015: 107–12.
51 Menander Protector, fr. 10.1.1–47; cf. de la Vaissière 2002: 222–30.
52 Photius, *Bibliotheca*, cod. 64 (Theophanes of Byzantium); Tabari, 1.946–58 (trans., 235–52); cf. Potts 2008: 206–11; Gajda 2009: 149–67.
53 Whitby 1988: 250–8; Howard-Johnston 2010: 46–57.

BIBLIOGRAPHY

Adams, N. (2000), 'The Development of Early Garnet Inlaid Ornaments', in C. Bálint (ed.), *Kontakte zwischen Iran, Byzanz und der Steppe im 6.-7. Jahrhundert*, Varia Archaeologica Hungarica 10, Budapest: Archaeological Institute, Academy of Sciences, pp. 13–70.

Adams, N. (2011), 'The Garnet Millennium: The Role of Seal Stones in Garnet Studies', in Entwistle and Adams 2011, pp. 10–24
Adams, N. et al. (2011), 'Lithois Indikois: Preliminary Characterisation of Garnet Seal Stones from Central and South Asia', in Entwistle and Adams 2011, pp. 25–38.
Alram, M., Gyselen, R., Schindel, N. et al. (2003–12), *Sylloge Nummorum Sasanidarum: Paris – Berlin – Wien*, 3 vols, Philosophisch-historische Klasse, Denkschriften 317, 325, 422, Vienna: Österreichische Akademie der Wissenschaften.
Arrhenius, B. (1971), *Granatschmuck und Gemmen aus nordischen Funden des frühen Mittelalters*, Stockholm: University of Stockholm.
Arrhenius, B. (1985), *Merovingian Garnet Jewellery: Emergence and Social Implications*, Stockholm: Kungliga Vitterhets Historie och Antikvitets Akademien.
Arrhenius, B. (2011), 'Helgö: Pagan Sanctuary Complex', in B. Arrhenius and U. O'Meadhra (eds), *Excavations at Helgö. XVIII: Conclusions and New Aspects*, Stockholm: Kungliga Vitterhets Historie och Antikvitets Akademien, pp. 11–43.
Barfield, T. J. (1989), *The Perilous Frontier: Nomadic Empires and China*, Oxford: Blackwell.
Beaucamp, J. (2010), 'Le rôle de Byzance en mer rouge sous le règne de Justin: Mythe ou réalité?', in Beaucamp et al. 2010, pp. 197–218.
Beaucamp, J., Briquel-Chatonnet, F. and Robin, C. J. (1999–2000), 'La persécution des chrétiens de Nagran et la chronologie himyarite', *ARAM*, 11–12, pp. 15–83.
Beaucamp, J., Briquel-Chatonnet, F. and Robin, C. J. (eds) (2010), *Juifs et chrétiens en Arabie aux Ve et VIe siècles: Regards croisés sur les sources*, Paris: Association des Amis du Centre d'Histoire et de Civilisation de Byzance.
Bernhard, H. (1982), 'Germanische Funde des Spätantike zwischen Strassburg und Mainz', *Saalburg Jahrbuch*, 38, pp. 72–109.
Blockley, R. C. (1992), *East Roman Foreign Policy: Formation and Conduct from Diocletian to Anastasius*, Leeds: Francis Cairns.
Bonner, M. R. J. (2015), *Al-Dinawari's Kitab al-Ahbar al-Tiwal: An Historiographical Study of Sasanian Iran*, Res Orientales 23, Bures-sur-Yvette: Groupe pour l'étude de la civilisation du Moyen-Orient.
Brown, P. (1992), *Power and Persuasion in Late Antiquity: Towards a Christian Empire*, Madison: University of Wisconsin Press.
Carter, R. A., Challis, K., Priestman, S. M. N. and Tofighian, H. (2006), 'The Bushehr Hinterland: Results of the First Season of the Iranian-British Archaeological Survey of Bushehr Province, November-December 2004', *Iran*, 44, pp. 63–103.
Casson, L. (ed. and trans.) (1989), *The Periplus Maris Erythraei*, Princeton: Princeton University Press.
Chakravarti, R. (2001), *Trade in Early India*, Delhi: Oxford University Press.
Christensen, A. (1944), *L'Iran sous les Sassanides*, Copenhagen: Ejnar Munksgaard.
Chronicle of Seert, ed. and trans. A. Scher (1908), *PO* IV, pp. 220–1.
Cosmas Indicopleustes, *Topographia Christiana*, ed. and trans. W. Wolska-Conus (1968–73), 3 vols, Paris: Éditions du Cerf.

De la Vaissière, É. (2002), *Histoire des marchands sogdiens*, Paris: Collège de France.
Dignas, B. and Winter, E. (2007), *Rome and Persia in Late Antiquity: Neighbours and Rivals*, Cambridge: Cambridge University Press.
Drauschke, J. (2011), *Zwischen Handel und Geschenk: Studien zur Distribution von Objekten aus dem Orient, aus Byzanz und aus Mitteleuropa im östlichen Merowingerreich*, Rahden: Marie Leidorf.
Ebert, M. (1914), 'Der Wolfsheimer Platte und die Goldschale des Khosrau', in *Baltische Studien zur Archäologie und Geschichte*, Berlin: Gesellschaft für Geschichte und Altertumskunde der Ostseeprovinzen Russlands, pp. 57–95.
Entwistle, C. and Adams, N. (eds) (2011), *'Gems of Heaven': Recent Research on Engraved Gemstones in Late Antiquity c.AD 200–600*, London: British Museum.
Findlay, R. and O'Rourke, K. H. (2007), *Power and Plenty: Trade, War, and the World Economy in the Second Millennium*. Princeton: Princeton University Press.
Gajda, I. (2009), *Le royaume de Himyar à l'époque monothéiste*, Paris: Académie des Inscriptions et Belles-Lettres.
Golden, P. B. (2011), *Central Asia in World History*, Oxford: Oxford University Press.
Greatrex, G. (1998), *Rome and Persia at War, 502–532*, Leeds: Francis Cairns.
Greatrex, G. and Lieu, S. N. C. (2002), *The Roman Eastern Frontier and the Persian Wars, Part II: AD 363–630: A Narrative Sourcebook*, London: Routledge.
Grignaschi, M. (1966), 'Quelques spécimens de la littérature sassanide conservés dans les bibliothèques d'Istanbul', *Journal Asiatique*, 254, pp. 1–142.
Gyllensvärd, B. (2004), 'The Buddha Found at Helgö', in H. Clarke and K. Lamm (eds), *Excavations at Helgö. XVI: Exotic and Sacral Finds from Helgö*, Stockholm: Kungliga Vitterhets Historie och Antikvitets Akademien, pp. 11–27.
Hall, K. R. (2011), *A History of Early Southeast Asia: Maritime Trade and Societal Development*, Lanham: Rowman and Littlefield.
Hamerow, H. (forthcoming 2017), 'The Circulation of Garnets in the North Sea Zone, ca.400-700', in A. Hilgner, S. Greiff and D. Quast (eds), *Gemstones in the First Millennium AD*, Mainz: Römisch-Germanisches Zentralmuseum, pp. 71-84.
Heather, P. J. (1995), 'The Huns and the End of the Roman Empire in Western Europe', *English Historical Review*, 110, pp. 4–41.
Heirman, A. and Bumbacher, S. P. (2006), *The Spread of Buddhism*, Leiden: Brill.
Herrmann, G. (1977), *The Iranian Revival*, Oxford: Elsevier-Phaidon.
Horton, M. and Middleton, J. (2000), *The Swahili: The Social Life of a Mercantile Society*, Oxford: Blackwell.
Howard-Johnston, J. (2010), 'The Sasanians' Strategic Dilemma', in H. Börm and J. Wiesehöfer (eds), *Commutatio et contentio: Studies in the Late Roman, Sasanian and Early Islamic Near East – In Memory of Zeev Rubin*, Düsseldorf: Wellem, pp. 37–70.
Howard-Johnston, J. (2012), 'The Late Sasanian Army', in T. Bernheimer

and A. Silverstein (eds), *Late Antiquity: Eastern Perspectives*, Exeter: Gibb Memorial Trust, pp. 87–127.

Howard-Johnston, J. (2013), 'Military Infrastructure in the Roman Provinces North and South of the Armenian Taurus in Late Antiquity', in A. Sarantis and N. Christie (eds), *War and Warfare in Late Antiquity: Current Perspectives*, Late Antique Archaeology, 8.2, Leiden: Brill, pp. 853–91.

Hoyland, R. G. (2001), *Arabia and the Arabs: From the Bronze Age to the Coming of Islam*, London: Routledge.

Ioannes Malalas, *Chronographia*, xviii.15, ed. J. Thurn (2000), CFHB 35, Berlin: De Gruyter; trans. E. Jeffreys, M. Jeffreys and R. Scott (1986), *The Chronicle of John Malalas*, Byzantina Australiensia 4, Melbourne: Australian Association for Byzantine Studies.

Joshua the Stylite, ed. and trans. P. Martin (1876), *Chronique de Josué le Stylite, écrite vers l'an 515*, Abhandlungen für die Kunde des Morgenlandes 6.1, Leipzig: Harassowitz.

Kennet, D. (2007), 'The Decline of Eastern Arabia in the Sasanian Period', *Arabian Archaeology and Epigraphy*, 18, pp. 86–122.

Kennet, D. (2009), 'Transformations in Late Sasanian and Early Islamic Eastern Arabia: The Evidence from Kush', in J. Schiettecatte and C. J. Robin (eds), *L'Arabie à la veille de l'Islam: Bilan clinique*, Orient et Méditerranée 3, Paris: De Boccard, pp. 135–61.

Kervran, M. (1994), 'Forteresses, entrepôts et commerce: Une histoire à suivre depuis les rois sassanides jusqu'aux princes d' Ormuz', in *Itinéraires d'Orient: Hommages à Claude Cahen*, Res Orientales 6, Bures-sur-Yvette: Groupe pour l'étude de la civilisation du Moyen-Orient, pp. 325–51.

Kominko, M. (2013), *The World of Kosmas: Illustrated Byzantine Codices of the Christian Topography*, Cambridge: Cambridge University Press.

Lewis, M. E. (2009), *China between Empires: The Northern and Southern Dynasties*, Cambridge: Belknap Press.

Liebeschuetz, J. H. W. G. (2001), *The Decline and Fall of the Roman City*, Oxford: Oxford University Press.

Liu, X. (1994), *Ancient India and Ancient China: Trade and Religious Exchanges AD 1–600*, Delhi: Oxford University Press.

Ljungkvist, J. and Frölund, P. (2015), 'Gamla Uppsala: The Emergence of a Centre and a Magnate Complex', *Journal of Archaeology and Ancient History*, 16 <www.arkeologi.uu.se/Journal/no-16-ljungkvist-.>.

Marrassini, P. (ed.) (2014), *Storia e leggenda dell' Etiopia tardoantica: Le iscrizioni reali aksumite*, Brescia: Paideia.

Martyrium S. Arethae, ed. M. Detoraki, trans. J. Beaucamp (2007), *Le Martyre de Saint Aréthas et de ses compagnons*, BHG 166, Paris: Association des Amis du Centre d'Histoire et de Civilisation de Byzance.

Matthews, J. (1989), *The Roman Empire of Ammianus*, London: Duckworth.

Menander Protector, ed. and trans. R. C. Blockley (1985), *The History of Menander the Guardsman*, Liverpool: Francis Cairn.

Movses Daskhurantsʻi, ed. V. Arakʻeljan (1983), *Movses Kałankatuatsʻi: Patmutʻiwn Ałuanitsʻ*, Erevan: Hayastan; trans. C. J. F. Dowsett (1961), *Moses Dasxurancʻi's History of the Caucasian Albanians*, London: Oxford University Press.

Phillipson, D. W. (2012), *Foundations of an African Civilisation: Aksum and the Northern Horn, 1000 BC–AD 1300*, Woodbridge: James Currey.
Photius, *Bibliotheca*, ed. and trans. R. Henry (1959–77), 8 vols, Paris: Les Belles Lettres.
Potts, D. T. (2008), 'The Sasanian Relationship with South Arabia: Literary, Epigraphic and Oral Historical Perspectives', *Studia Iranica*, 37, pp. 197–213.
Power, T. (2012), *The Red Sea from Byzantium to the Caliphate AD 500–1000*, Cairo and New York: American University in Cairo Press.
Priestman, S. M. N. and Kennet, D. (2002), 'The Williamson Collection Project: Sasanian and Islamic Pottery from Southern Iran', *Iran*, 40, pp. 265–7.
Procopius, *Bella*, ed. J. Haury, J., rev. G. Wirth (1962–3), 2 vols, Leipzig: Teubner; trans. H. B. Dewing (1914–28), 5 vols, Cambridge: Loeb.
Rathbone, D. (2001), 'The "Muziris" Papyrus (SB XVIII 13167): Financing Roman Trade with India', in *Alexandrian Studies II in Honour of Mostafa el Abbadi*, Alexandria: Société d'archéologie d'Alexandrie, pp. 39–50.
Robin, C. J. (2010), 'Nagran vers l'époque du massacre', in Beaucamp et al. 2010, pp. 39–106.
Rubin, Z. (1986), 'The Mediterranean and the Dilemma of the Roman Empire in Late Antiquity', *Mediterranean Historical Review*, 1, pp. 13–62.
Sarris, P. (2002), 'The Justinianic Plague: Origins and Effects', *Continuity and Change*, 17, pp. 169–82.
Sarris, P. (2006), *Economy and Society in the Age of Justinian*, Cambridge: Cambridge University Press.
Sidebotham, S. E. (2011), *Berenike and the Ancient Maritime Spice Route*, Berkeley: University of California Press.
Simpson, St J. (2014), 'Merv: An Archaeological Case Study from the Northeastern Frontier of the Sasanian Empire', *Journal of Ancient History*, 2, pp. 116–43.
Singh, U. (2009), *A History of Ancient and Early Medieval India: From the Stone Age to the 12th Century*, Delhi: Pearson.
Spier, J. (2007), *Late Antique and Early Christian Gems*, Wiesbaden: Reichert.
Strabo, *Geographica*, ed. and trans. H. L. Jones (1917–32), 8 vols, London and New York: Loeb.
Tabari, ed. M. J. de Goeje et al. (1881), *Annales quos scripsit Abu Djafar Mohammed ibn Djarir at-Tabari*, III.2, Leiden: Brill; trans. C. E. Bosworth (1999), *The History of al-Ṭabarī. V: The Sasanids, the Byzantines, the Lakmids, and Yemen*, New York: State University of New York Press.
Tomber, R. (2008), *Indo-Roman Trade: From Pots to Pepper*, London: Bristol Classical Press.
Von Freeden, U. (2000), 'Das Ende engzelligen Cloisonnés und die Eroberung Südarabiens durch die Sasaniden', *Germania*, 78, pp. 97–122.
Ward-Perkins, B. (2001), 'Specialisation, Trade, and Prosperity: An Overview of the Economy of the Late Antique Eastern Mediterranean', in S. Kingsley and M. Decker (eds), *Economy and Exchange in the East Mediterranean During Late Antiquity*, Oxford: Oxbow Books, pp. 167–78.
Whitby, M. (1988), *The Emperor Maurice and His Historian: Theophylact Simocatta on Persian and Balkan Warfare*, Oxford: Clarendon Press.
Whitcomb, D. S. (1985), *Before the Roses and Nightingales: Excavations at Qasr-i Abu Nasr, Old Shiraz*, New York: Metropolitan Museum of Art.

Whitehouse, D. and Williamson, A. (1973), 'Sasanian Maritime Trade', *Iran*, 11, pp. 29–49.
Young, G. K. (2001), *Rome's Eastern Trade: International Commerce and Imperial Policy 31 BC–AD 305*, London: Routledge.
Zuckerman, C. (2013), 'Silk "Made in Byzantium": A Study of Economic Policies of Emperor Justinian', in C. Zuckerman (ed.), *Constructing the Seventh Century*, Travaux et Mémoires 17, Paris: Association des Amis du Centre d'Histoire et de Civilisation de Byzance, pp. 323–50.

Index

Page numbers in *italics* refer to illustrations, those followed by 'n' are notes, 't' are tables, and 'm' are places named on maps. Some maps use a different transliteration systems for geographic names to that used in the text. The index refers to place names as they appear in the text (but lists variants that differ substantially in parentheses to enable the reader to find relevant map entries). Geographic terms that are not discussed in the text are listed verbatim as they appear on the maps, even if a different transliteration system is used.

Aba, Mar, 190
Abbasi, G., 138
Abd al-Qays tribe, 278n
Abdullaev, 15n
Abhar, 152m
Abingdon Archaeological Geophysics, 254
Abivard, 52m
Abu Skhair, 36m
Acacius, 202–4
Achaemenid Empire, 2, 4, 9–10, 41, 51, 60–4, 68–70, 92, 169, 223–4, 230, 235n, 243
Achaemenid sculpture, 229, 232–3
Adams, R. M., 34–5
Adontz, N., 201, 204
Adulis, 287–8, 294
Ādurbādagān, 152m
Aegean Sea, 244m
aerial photographs, 24, 27, 28, *30*, *32*, *33*, 136
Afghan Boundary Commission, 155
Afghanistan, vii, 7, 23m, 151–71, *154*, *157*, 174n, 234, 297
Afrasiab, 164
agriculture, 4–5, 13, 22, 30, 43–4, 55, 67–9, 104, 106, 117–20, 131, 272, 289–90
Ahangaran, 163
Ahura Mazda, 183, 185; see also Ohrmazd
Ahwāz, 152m
Aila, 287–8
Akbas, 52m, 244m, 259, 264n
Akbora [Buzung Sabur], 22
Ak-Depe, 52m
Aksum, 276, 287–8, 291, 294–5; see also Ethiopia
Al Jolanda, 275
Alamoundaras, 279n
Albania, 52m, 199, 212, 216, 241, 245m; see also Azerbaijan
Alborz Mountains, 4–5, 7, 52m, 54–6, 61–4, 68–70, 75, 117, 119, 129m, 131–2, 138, 245m, 258m, 259–60
Alborz Pass, 139m
Alésia, 250
Alexander the Great, 151, 185–6, 243, 263n
Alexandria, 244m
al-Hira, 274–5
Aliabad Kishmar, 174n

Aliyev, Tevekkul, 114–15
Alizadeh, K., 115
al-Khatt, 278n
Al-Khir, 105m
alliances, 11, 104, 273–6, 279n
al-Ma'aridh, 33, 40
Almalou Lake, 52m, 53t, 56–7, *57*, 62–5, 67–9
Alps, 244m
al-Qutqitana, 31–2
Alram, Michael, 229
Altheim, F., 278n
Ałuank', 209–12, 215
Amida, 244m
Ammianus Marcellinus, 26, 191, 263–4n, 272
Amudar'ya River, 52m, 245m
An Lushan, 172
Āna, 52m
Anahita cult, 184–5, 191
Anastasian Wall, 244m
Anastasius, 293–4
Anatolia, 62, 100, 259
Ancyra, 244m
'Aneran', 170
animal exploitation, 4–5, 26, 40–1, 57, 60, 65, 74–93, 130–2, 141–3
Ansari, Ali, 2
anthypatos, 202–3
Antioch, 22, 23m, 244m
Antioch, sack of, 33–4, 188, 248, 264n
Aphoumon, 22
Arab conquest, 11, 21, 26, 31–2, 44, 115, 160–2, 172–3, 200, 243, 276
Arabia, vii, 23m, 270t, 277n, 277–8n, 278n, 279n, 280n
Arabian frontier, 268–77, 278n
Arabian Nights, 170–1, 175n
Arabian Peninsula, 244m
Arabic sources, 184, 276
Aral Sea, 245m
Araz (or Aras) River, 6, 52m, 103, 114–15, 116m, 119, 122n
arboreal pollen (AP), 67
arboriculture, 4–5, 62, 67–70
Archaeological Gazetteer of Afghanistan, 161
archaeozoology, 74–93
Ard Kaskar (Mesene), 35

Ardashir I, 9–10, 43, 183–6, 221–34, 235n, 268, 271–2, 277–8n, 277n
  coins, 270t
Ardashir Khurrah (or Ardaxšīr-Xvarrah or Gur, near Firuzabad), 9, 23m, 24, 24, 37, 52m, 152m, 186, 221–4, 223, 229, 234, 245m
Ardashir Papakan, 24–6
Arethas, 279n
Armenia (or Armēn), 8–9, 52m, 152m, 172, 174n, 199–217, 217n, 218n, 244m, 271, 274, 279n, 291
  Christianity, 8–9, 182–4, 191–3, 200–1
  First, 202, 205, 207
  Fourth, 201–2, 205, 217n
  Interior, 205, 207
  Magna, 205
  Minor, 205
  Persarmenia, 207–8, 216, 244m, 258m, 298
  Second, 202, 205, 207
  sources, 192
  Third, 202
ar-Rumiyya, 34
Arsacid kingdom, 183, 185–6, 200, 205, 222, 224, 229–30, 279n; see also Parthian Empire
Arshak, 208
Arshakan, Atrormizd (Adhur-Hormizd), 193
Arts'ax, 217n
Asia Minor, 244m
Asōrestān, 52m, 152m
Aspanabr (or Asfanabr), 25, 33, 40
Astarabadh Ardashir, 35
Athens, 244m
Atrak River, 129m, 131, 140, 245m
at-Taqtaqanah, 31–2
Aves, 81t, 83t, 86, 87
Avesta, 183–6, 192
Awedi River, 107m
Azerbaijan, 5–6, 99, 103, 109, 112, 114–15, 151, 187, 225, 261; see also Albania

Bab al Mandab, 12
Bābil, 152m
Babylon, 23m, 36m
Babylonian Talmud, 40, 217n
Bachrach, B. S., 279n
Bactria, 52m, 245m
Bactrian documents, 7, 151, 160–1
Baghdad, 152m
Bagratuni, Smbat, 172
Bagratuni legal traditions, 216
Bahrain, 271, 275, 277–8n, 289, 292
Bahram I, 277n
Bahram II, vii, 171, 194n
Bahram III, 277n
Bahram V, 170, 192, 275
Bahram VI, 270
  coins, 270t
Bahusir see Veh Ardashir
Bakhtiyari, 88–92, 89, 90
Bakr b.Wa'il tribe, 278n
Balash, 270–1
  coins, 270t
Balkh, 52m, 162, 171, 245m
Balkhi, 189
Ball, Warwick, 7, 175n
Bamiyan, 164
Bandiyan, 23m, 52m, 151, 153
Bansaran Fort, 64, 75–93
Barda, 6, 115, 116n
Basra, 35, 104, 132m, 273
Batinah Plain, 77
Batman River, 244m, 259, 264n

Bay-Shapur see Bishapur
bear, 85
Begram, 52m, 245m
Berenike, 287, 291–2, 295
Berghe, Louis Vanden, 228
Beshbarmark Fort, 109, 110m, 116m, 119
Beshbarmark Wall, 110m, 116m
Beta Giyorgis, 287
Beth Harith, 279n
Beth Mundhir, 279n
Beylaqan, 114
'Beyşehir occupation phase', 62, 67
Bier, Lionel, 224
bin Yusuf, Hajjaj, 27
bioarchaeological studies, 74–93
Bishapur (or Bīšābuhr), 22, 23m, 28, 28, 37, 44, 52m, 77, 152m, 156, 190, 222, 245m
Bishapur rock reliefs, vii–viii, 155–6, 159, 234, 249
Bisotun, 52m, 245m
Bivar, David, 156
Black Sea, 23m, 52m, 76m, 109, 244m, 259, 294
Blockley, R. C., 195n
boar, 75, 78
Borsippa, 36m
Bos taurus, 80t, 82t, 86, 87
Bosworth, C. E., 133
Bouara Lake, 52m, 53t, 58, 59, 62–4
Brak region, 120
Breeze, David, 100, 118–19
British Institute of Afghan Studies, 7
British Institute of Persian Studies, 2
Browicz, K., 60
Bruno, Andrea, 156
Buddha figurine, 296
Buddhism, 8, 170–1, 174n, 182, 284
  art, 162–3
  cave paintings, 164, 165
  stupa-monastery, 163
  texts, 161
Bugha the Elder, 215
built environment, 34–44
Bukhara, 52m, 245m
Bustan Kisra, 34
Buzandaran, 209
Byzantine Empire, 174n, 263n

Callieri, Pierfrancesco, 9–10
camel, 78, 287
canals, 4, 6, 13, 15, 22, 24, 25, 30, 33, 35, 44, 64, 103–4, 114–15, 117, 119–20, 122n, 130–1, 133, 252, 262, 289
Canepa, Matthew, 228–30, 232, 234
Canidae, 80t, 82t
Capillaria, 56t
Cappadocia, 244m
Capra hircus, 80t, 82t
Caprini, 80t, 82t
carnivores, 80t, 82t
Carrhae, 222, 234, 243
Carus, Emperor, 248
'Caspian Gates', 12, 114; see also Dariali Fort; Dariali Gorge/ Pass
Caspian Sea, 10, 23m, 52m, 54–6, 68, 76m, 77–8, 92, 103, 109, 110m, 111, 113m, 114, 116m, 117–20, 128m, 129m, 131, 152m, 153, 245m, 258m, 260–2, 294
Caspian Sea coast, 101m
Castanea sativa Mill (sweet chestnut), 55t, 56t, 57t, 58t, 59t, 60–1, 60t, 61t, 69
Castellum, 108, 130, 132
catafracti, 251, 275

cats, 85
cattle, 67, 74, 79, 85, 91, 92-3
Caucasian Walls, 52m
Caucasus, 6, 11-12, 23m, 52m, 60-2, 74, 77-8, 84, 99-100, 101m, 110m, 116m, 120, 244m, 258m
  defence, 259-60, 291, 293-4
  routeways, 127-30, 144n, 241-2, 252, 253, 260
  southern, 109-16, 116, 118-19
  see also Albania; Iberia
Central Asia, 2, 11, 23m, 38, 62-3, 77, 118, 138, 153-5, 164, 167, 170-2, 293, 296-7
Centro Scavi di Torino, 38-41
ceramic evidence, 4, 103, 114-15, 130, 138, 140-1, 161-3, 175n, 286, 288-9, 292
ceramics, 32, 36-7, 122n, 164
Cerealia-t., 55t, 56t, 57t, 58t, 59t, 60t, 61t
cereals, 65
chahar taq, 24, 222-4, 223; see also fire temples
Chai Qushan-e Kuchek canal, 133
Charax Spasinu, 35
Chilburi, 52m
China, 11-12, 62, 164, 166-7, 170, 172, 272, 278n, 284-6, 289-90, 296
Chionites, 171, 290
Chirakh Qala, 6, 15n, 109, 110m, 112-14, 113m, 116m, 262
Christian Topography, 278n, 279n, 294
Christianity, 174n, 181-93, 217n, 246, 276, 288
  Arabia, 294-5
  Armenian, 8-9, 192, 200-1, 207-9
  China, 167
  churches, 187
  freedom of worship, 34
  Greek Orthodox, 170
  Justinian, 12
  legal culture, 208-9, 212, 215-16, 218n
  Nestorian, 8, 167, 189
  Persian, 183, 187-91
  subsistence economy, 75
  tolerance of, 8-9, 14
Christians, 217n
  deportation of, 188, 190
  persecution of, 181-2, 189-93
Chronicle of Se'ert, 22, 190
Church of the East, 167, 189
Clysma, 287
Coche *see* Veh Ardashir
Codex Justinianus, 204-5
coins, 1, 12, 155-6, 161-2, 171, 184, 186, 228-9, 270-3, 276, 277n, 287
  Sasanian, 162, 270t, 277n
  silver, 272-3
Colledge, Malcolm A. R., 230-1
Comes Armeniae, 205
Constantine, 182, 189-91, 290
Constantinople, 3, 23m, 167, 202, 211, 242, 244m, 297
Constantius, 191
coprophilous fungi, 53, 53t, 56, 56t, 57t, 60t, 65-7
CORONA imagery, 27, 99, 102, 110-12, 114, 117, 122n, 130, 132-6, 140
Council of Partav (705 CE), 199, 209, 211
Cribb, J., 280n
Ctesiphon (or Tēsfōn), 23m, 25-6, 25, 32-3, 36m, 52m, 104, 151, 152m, 189, 244m, 248, 264n, 271, 289, 294
Ctesiphon synod (AD 410), 8, 189
cultural contacts between Rome and Persia, 221-39
Curtis, Vesta Sarkhosh, 2

Curzon, Lord, 100
Cyrus the Great, 233

Daghestan, 99, 109, 112
Damghan, 37
Damghan Plain, 35-6
Danube, 244m
Dara, 23m, 107m
Darabgird, vii-viii, 26-7, 27, 35, 52m, 152m, 245m
Dariali Fort, 6, 12, 74-93, 76m, 114, 130, 244m, 252, 260, 260
  animal exploitation at, 79-85
  cattle population at, 91
  coins, 12
  goat populations at, 90
  recent excavations of, 253
  sheep population of, 89
  Trench F, 78-85, 80t, 81t, 82t, 83t, 86, 87
Dariali Gorge/ Pass, 52m, 74-93, 101m, 114-15, 127-30, 128m, 258m, 260
Darius, 233
Darrehgaz, 52m
Daryaee, Touraj, 1, 173-4n, 186, 229, 280n
Dasht Qal'eh, 3-5, 7, 30, 37, 52m, 56, 75-93, 76m, 89, 90, 117, 120, 129m, 138, 139m, 245m
Dasht-e Archi, 163
Daybal (Banhore) emporium, 292
Decret, F., 191
Defence, 209
Deh Luran, 22
Deh Morasi Ghundai, 162
Dehistan, 52m, 133, 139-40, 245m
Denkard, 40, 184-5
Derbent, 109-11, 260
Derbent Wall, 52m, 99, 110m, 116m, 119, 245m, 257, 258m, 260
Dez River, 30, 52m
Dezeridan, 32, 34
Dezfūl, 52m
Digital Elevation Models (DEMs), 102
Dinawari, 33-4
Dionysius Thrax, 217n
Diospyros lotus L. (ebony tree), 55t, 56t, 57t, 58t, 59t, 60t, 61t
Diospyrus lotus L. (ebony tree), 61-2, 68-9
diwan, 217n
Diyala Basin, 32-3, 35, 153, 289
dogs, 85
domestic caprines, 86, 87
domestic fowl, 78
Donner, F. M., 279n
dress, 164-6, 167, 228-9
Dukhtar-e Nushirvan, 164
dung-associated beetles, 55t, 56t, 65-7, 66
Dura-Europos (or Dura), 164-6, 235n, 244m, 248, 250-1, 251
Dvin, 217n

East, Edward, 6
East Africa, 165, 285-8, 298
Ed-Dur, 52m, 245m
Egypt, 13, 64, 242, 244m, 286-8, 295
Elia, 211
Elishē, 209, 257
Elymais reliefs, 221, 228-34
Emesa, viii
Emmerick, R. E., 167
Ephesus, 244m
Equidae, 80t, 82t, 86, 87
Equus caballus, 80t, 82t

'Eran', 170
Eranshahr, 183–4, 186, 206–7
Ērān-Vinnārd-Kavād, 152m
Eridu-Ur region, 30–31
Esfahan, 52m, 245m
Eski Kifri, 32
Estakhr (or Istakhr or Staxr), 23m, 37–8, 44, 52m, 152m, 185, 191, 225
Ethiopia, 12, 288; *see also* Aksum
Euphrates, 6, 23m, 31, 35, 36m, 52m, 105m, 106, 132, 152m, 200, 244m, 251, 251, 259, 291
Eurasia, 52m
Eurasian Steppe, 244m, 258m
Eurocentrism, 243–7
European Pollen Database, 53–70
European Research Council, 2, 75
European travellers, 126, 132
Eusebius, 191
Eynibulak Forts 1, 2 and 3, 113m
Eyvan-e Karkha (or Aivān-e Karkheh or Ērān-Xvarrah-Šābuhr or Ivān-i Karkha), 30, 31, 52m, 152m, 186, 245m

Fallujah, 104, 105m
Falōxt-ī frōdar, 152m
Farg'ona, 52m
Fars, 10–11, 27–8, 77, 151, 152m, 185, 187, 191, 222, 225, 248, 271–3
  arboriculture, 4, 68–70
  rock reliefs, 9, 229–30
Fasā, 152m
faunal spectra, 75–9, 84–8, 86, 87, 92, 143, 294
Febvre, L., 102
Felis catus, 80t, 82t
Ferdowsi, 170, 187
Ferrier, General J. P., 155–7, 174n
fire temples, 8, 153–5, 159–60, 184, 190, 221, 224, 262; *see also chahar taq*
First Armenia, 202, 205, 207
Firuzabad *see* Ardashir Khurrah
Firuzabad I rock relief, 221, 225, 225, 228–33, 235n
Firuzabad II rock relief, 225, 226, 228–9, 232
fish, 78, 81t, 83t, 85
food production, 2, 5, 14, 51, 65, 69–70, 75
Fourth Armenia, 201–2, 205, 217n
fox, 85
Frataraka Temple rock relief, 230
Fraxinus ornus L. (manna ash), 55t, 56t, 57t, 58, 58t, 59t, 60t, 61t, 62, 67–8
freshwater fish, 78, 85
frontiers, 5, 7, 10–14, 31–2, 58, 74–5, 98–174, 182, 186, 191–3, 201, 205–6, 241–2, 246, 248, 250, 252–3, 263n, 277n, 289–94
  Arabian, 268–77, 278n
  natural, 109, 255–62
Frye, R. N., 173n
Fulayj Fort, 77

Gabri Qal'eh, 3, 245m, 253, 258m
Gallus gallus, 81t, 83t
Galūl, 152m
Gandharan art, 162–3
Ganzak Šahrestān, 152m
Gargarāyān, 152m
Garmēgan, 152m
garnets, 12, 284, 292, 296–7, 299n
Garondagan, 25–6
Garshaspnama, 170
Garsoïan, N. G., 201, 216
Gates of Sul, 133
Gaul, 250, 264n, 279n, 286

Gay, 152m
gazelle, 78
Gēlān, 152m
Georgia, 6, 74–93, 76m, 99, 114, 127–30, 170; *see also* Iberia; Lazica
Georgios of Izla, Bishop, 41
Germany, 250
Ghilghilchay River, 112–14, 113m
Ghilghilchay Wall, 6, 52m, 99, 109, 110m, 111–14, 113, 116m, 119, 245m, 258m, 260, 261, 262
Ghirshman, R., 28–30
Ghulbiyan, 52m, 245m
Ghulbiyan painting, 151, 157, 158, 159, 164
Gignoux, P., 182, 187
Girk' T'łt'ots', Book of Letters, 209
glassware, 40, 166, 285, 287, 292–3
goats, 5, 41, 74, 78–9, 85, 88, 90, 92–3
Goebekil, 52m
gold, 12, 169, 284, 286–7, 291, 293–4
Goldman, B., 235n
Gomishan Lagoon, 52m, 53t, 54, 55, 61–5, 68–9
Gonbad-e Kavus, 3, 136
Gondeshapur, 22, 27–32, 29, 31, 190, 245m
Gordian III, vii, viii, 155–6, 248, 249
Gorgan Plain (or Gurgān), 10–11, 15n, 30, 37, 63–5, 69, 100, 101m, 111, 128m, 129, 152m, 169–70, 257
  animal exploitation, 74–93
  ceramics, 103
  frontiers, 252, 260
  hollow ways, 134–8
  irrigation, 117–20
  routeways, 6–7, 126–44
  see also Jurjan
Gorgan River, 44, 52m, 54–6, 75, 117, 129m, 131–3, 141, 252–3, 258m
Gorgan Wall, 23m, 52m, 129m, 129, 139m, 146n, 151, 153, 243–6, 245m, 258m, 261
  animal exploitation, 74–93
  Fort 4, 64, 74–93, 76m, 91, 129m, 133–4, 254
  Forts 12 and 13, 7, 134–6, 135, 137, 138, 139m
  frontiers, 127, 130, 252–3, 260
  hollow ways, 142
  linear barrier, 99, 117, 119
  military infrastructure, 12, 146n, 173, 186, 241–2
  routeways, 5–7, 131–4, 135, 138, 140–3
Gōymān, 152m
Greenwood, Tim, 8–9
Grenet, Frantz, 159, 170
Grigor the Illuminator, 201
Guldara, 163, 163
Gunespan, 76m, 88, 89, 90, 91
Gur *see* Ardashir Khurrah

Habbaniyah Lake, 105m
Hackin, Carl, 155–6
Haftavan (or Haftavan Tappeh/ Tepe), 52m, 76m, 88, 89, 90, 91
Hajar, 278n
Hamadān, 152m
Hamrin, 36m
Hanazila, 278n
Hansman, J., 35–6
hare, 85
Hari River, 52m
Harper, Prudence O., 230
Hasanlu, 76m, 88, 89, 90, 91
Hatra, 52m, 244m, 248, 250, 278n
Hauser, Stefan, 188
Hazar Dadestan, 207
Hecatompylos, 35–6

Index

Hegmantaneh, 76m, 88, 91
Helgö, 296
Helmand River, 52m, 245m
Hephthalites
  campaigns against, 138–9, 145n
  coins, 162
  crossing points, 143
  defence against, 10, 118, 160, 252
  interregnum, 161
  invasion by, 169, 171, 263
  Kavad I, 293
  Khusro I, 297
  wars, 173
Her & Zarevand, 257, 258m
Heraclius, 22, 32, 44, 171
Herat, 52m, 245m
Herat Museum, 162
Herrmann, Georgina, vii, 173n, 228, 230–3
Hērt, 152m
Herzfeld, Ernst, 234
Hillah, 105m
Himyar, 276, 287–8, 291, 295, 298; *see also* Yemen
Hind, 152m
Hindu Kush, 52m, 245m, 259
Hinz, Walther, 228
Hira, 23m, 36m
History of Aluank', 199, 209–12
History of Karka de Beth Selok, 192
History of Siwnik,' 199–200
History of the Province of Siwnik', 212–17
hollow ways, 6–7, 130, 134–8, 137, 140–1, 142
Hopper, Kristen, 6–7, 119
Hormizd, 269, 277n
Hormizd III, 171
Hormizdegan, battle of, 228–9
Hormuz, Straits of, 52m, 245m, 276, 289
horse, vii, 84, 111, 183, 229, 231–2, 235n, 279n
Howard-Johnston, James, 11–13, 122n, 132, 171, 175n, 217n, 279n
Hoyland, R. G., 279n
Huff, Dietrich, 221, 224
Hunnic confederation, 192
Hunnic Empire, 171, 297
Hunnic raid, 252
Huns, 10, 171, 290
hunting, 7, 78, 84–5, 93, 159
Hūzestān-vacar, 152m
Hyrcanian Forest, 54–6, 60–1, 68–9

Iberia, 8, 52m, 192, 241, 244m, 258m, 294
ICHHTO *see* Iranian Cultural Heritage, Handcraft and Tourism Organisation
iconography, 186, 222, 225, 229–30, 231, 233
'immortals', 9
India, 11–12, 23m, 155, 167, 170, 234, 242, 245m, 272, 284–98
Indian Ocean, 2, 11–13, 23m, 52m, 164, 245m, 284–7, 289, 295, 298
Indicopleustes, Cosmas, 278n, 294
Indus River, 7, 11, 13, 22, 23m, 52m, 159, 164, 245m, 259, 288, 292
insect records, 53–6, 53t
Interior Armenia, 205, 207
investiture scenes, 225, 228–9, 231–3, 236n
Ionian craftsmen, 232–3
Iran, 6, 7, 10, 21, 27, 31, 38, 41, 51, 52m, 54, 74–93, 76m, 99, 103–4, 126–44, 151, 153, 156, 157, 163–4, 166, 170–1, 173–4n, 174n, 186, 188, 216, 221–34, 245m, 293, 297
  European travellers, 155
  frontiers, 169, 172–3
  redistribution of populations, 106

religion, 167
trade, 289–90
unexcavated urban centres, 35–6
Iranian Cultural Heritage, Handcraft and Tourism Organisation (or ICHHTO), 24, 242, 254
Iranian plateau, 224, 288
  agriculture, 56–70
  routeways, 32, 132–3, 139
Iran-Iraq war, 30, 35
Iraq, 21, 22, 30–1, 36, 99, 104–6, 118–19, 156, 271; *see also* Mesopotamia
Iron Gates, 52m
irrigation, 4, 13–14, 51, 69, 99, 100, 104–6, 114–20, 132–3, 186, 272, 278n, 288
Isaac, B., 277n
Isfahani, Hamza, 26–7
Ishan al-Jahariz, 36m
Ishaq, Bishop, 189
Islam, 11, 75, 77, 155, 215–16, 218n, 289
Islamic conquest, 22, 44
Islamic period, 3, 13, 38–9, 61–70, 88, 92, 103, 105, 108, 115, 122n, 126, 131–2, 136, 138, 163, 171, 175, 277n, 278n
Islamic pottery, 36–7
Islamic structures, 29
Italy, 244m, 264n

Jafnids, 274, 279n
Jaghjagh River, 106, 107m, 108–9, 128n, 130
James, Simon, 2, 250–1, 263n
Jari Saʿdeh *see* Khandaq Shapur
Jarrah River, 107m
Java Sea, 285
Jazira, 107m, 108, 153, 200, 289
Jazirat Umm al-Ghanam, 276
Jebel Sinjar, 107m
Jerusalem, 23m
Jordan, 104–6, 118
Jotheri, Jaafar, 6, 121n, 252
Juanshēr, Prince, 211
Judaism, 8, 75, 182, 191–2, 288, 295
Juglans regia L. (common or Persian walnut), 55t, 56t, 57t, 58t, 59t, 60t, 61t, 62–3, 67–9
Julian, 26, 44, 247, 252, 264n, 290
Jurjan, 7, 129n, 132, 136, 138, 139m
Justin I, 294
Justin II, 296
Justinian, 12, 171, 199, 201, 203–4, 206–7, 216, 263, 284, 295–6
Justinian II, 211
Justinianopolis, 202

Kaʿbe-ye Zardosht, 194n
Kakrak, 164
Kal-e Garkaz canal, 133
Kandahar, 162, 167
Karabakh Hills, 115
Karağ, 152m
Karbala, 105m
Karkhal, 152m
Kartir, 170, 174n
Kashan (or Kāšān), 52m, 152m, 235n
Kaskar, 35, 36m
Kavad I, 162, 270, 293–4
  coins, 270t
kay, 184, 186, 192
Kayanids, 184, 186, 192
Kāzerūn, 152m
Kennet, D., 277n, 278n, 279n
Kermān, 152m, 278n
Khabur Basin, 101m, 106, 107, 108, 109, 130, 132

Khabur River, 107m
Khandaq Shapur, 11, 52m, 101m, 105, 105m, *105*, 244m, 271
  canal, 6, 44, 104, 252
  defence, 118–19, 273, 276, 279n
  frontiers, 32
  irrigation, 106
Khanly Depe, 140
Khanzir River, 107m
Khazar Khaganate, 118, 212
Khizael Castle, 105m
Khorassan, 245m
Khusro I, 33–4, 170–1, 190, 270, 273, 294–5, 297–8
  coins, 270t
Khusro II (Parviz), 32, 171–2, 184, 270, 273, 275–6, 289
  coins, 270t
Khuzestan (or Xūzistān), 52m, 104, 130, 152m, 186, 188–9, 190, 245m, 271–2, 289, 292
Khwarezm (or Chorasmia or Xvāresm), 52m, 139–40, 152m, 245m
Khwasak, 229
Kiani, M. Y., 134, 136
Kirdir, 8, 185, 187, 194n, 269
Kirkūk, 152m
Kish, 36m
Kister, M., 279n
Knight in the Panther's Skin, 170
Kohna Masjid, 160, *161*
Kone Kishman, 52m
Kongor Lake, 52m, 53t, 54–6, 56, 61–5, 67–9
Kopet Dag, 52m, 245m
Korchʻaykʻ, 217n
Kʻshik, 211–12
Kucha reliquary, 164, *166*
Kūfa, 152m
Kura River, 114, 116m, 122n
Kura-Araz Basin, 101m
Kušān, 152m
Kush, 52m, 245m
Kushan Empire, 7, 159–63, 169, 171, 174n, 175n, 289, 297
Kushanshahr, 170
'Kushanshahs', 171
Kutha, 36m

Lakhmids, 274–6
Landsat 8, 102
Lawrence, Dan, 5, 144n
Łazar Pʻarpetsʻi, 192, 199, 208–9, 213
Lazica, 294, 297
Le Strange, G., 132
Lecker, M., 279n
Lecomte, O., 145n, 146n
Lee, Jonathan, 156–9
legal culture, 9, 99, 161, 199–217, 217n
Leilan, 257, 258m
Lepus europaeus, 81t, 83t
Letter of Tansar, 184
Limes Arabicus, 143, 252–3, 259
limes-style, 146n
literary and historical tradition, 169–73
Little, A. M. G., 235n
Liverani, M., 119
long-distance maritime trade, 284–98
long-distance resettlement, 3
long-distance trade, 43, 278–9n
Lukonin, Vladimir, 228, 229
Lullubi, 156
Lut Desert, 152m
Lydian craftsmen, 232–3

Maʻadd, 295
Maas, M., 202
McDonough, S., 193, 279n
Macuch, M., 206–7
Madiyan-e hazar dadistan, 187
Maharlou Lake, 52m, 53t, 59–60, *61*, 62–4, 67–9
Makrān, 152m
Malacca, Straits of, 285
Mälaren Lake, 296
mammals, 65, 67, 78, 81t, 83t, 84–5, 92
Mani, 171, 184–5
Manichaeism, 167, 174n, 182, 184–5
manufactured goods, 40, 284–9, 297
maps, 134–6
  Afghanistan, *154*
  case study areas (northern and western borderlands), *101*
  Caspian Sea-Upper Caucasus coastal strip, *110*
  Ctesiphon conurbation, *25*
  Ghilghilchay Wall sections and fortifications, *113*
  Gorgan Plain showing Gorgan Wall and archaeological sites, *131*
  Gorgan Wall Forts 12 and 13 hollow ways, *137*
  Gorgan Wall hollow ways, *142*
  Gorgan Wall possible crossing points, *135*
  Khabur Basin, *107*
  Khandaq Shapur region, *105*
  locations and key sites (animal exploitation), *76*
  locations mentioned in the text (route systems), *128*
  possible route system (Gorgan Plain), *139*
  Sasanian Empire, *23*, *152*
  Sasanian Empire at its greatest extent, *244–5*
  Sasanian Empire with location of palaeoecological sites, *52*
  Sasanian sites and canals in central and southern Iraq, *36*
  Sasanian sites in the Ctesiphon conurbation, *25*
  southern Caucasus region, *116*
Maricq, Andre, 156
maritime supremacy, 164
maritime trade, 273, 278–9n, 284–98
markets, 40–1, 160, 284–9, 293, 295
Marutha, Bishop, 189, 195n
Marv Dasht Plain, 37–8
Marw Habor, 22
Mashkour, Marjan, 5
Masjid-i Suleiman, 23m
Mavrakta, 41
Mazdean, 183–5, 188, 190–1, 193
Meadow, Richard, 88
Mecca, 244m
Median Wall, 52m
Medina (Tell ad-Dhibaʾi), 35
Mediterranean Sea, xv, 11–13, 23m, 60, 62–4, 68, 241–3, 244m, 284, 286, 297
Mele Hairam, 153
Meles meles, 80t, 82t
Melitene, 202
merchants, 12, 166, 272, 278n, 285–6, 289, 292–8
Merv (or Marv), 23m, 26, 38, 41, 43, 44, 52m, 119, 152m, 245m
Mēšān, 152m
Mesopotamia, 5, 6, 10–11, 38, 44, 52m, 99, 101m, 106, 151, 186, 221, 234, 244–5m, 247, 253, 293, 298
  ceramics, 103–4
  Christianity, 188–9
  frontiers, 248, 271–2
  hollow ways, 130
  irrigation, 35, 100, 119

Index

Julian, 252
routeways, 32, 138
Shapur I, 222
trade, 288–92
water buffalo, 78
Mēšūn, 152m
Mihr Narseh, 187, 192–3
Mil Plain/ Steppe, 5, 103, 114–15, 117, 119–20, 122n
Mil Plain/ Steppe Survey, 114–15
military infrastructure, 3, 5, 9–11, 13–15, 21–2, 26–8, 44, 51, 74–8, 99, 118–20, 241–63, 256t, 258, 268, 273, 280n, 294
  boundaries, 126–7, 130–1, 143–4
  siege works, 248, 250–1
  soldiers, 51, 201, 246–7
  training, 246–7
Mingechevir Reservoir, 116m
mints, 22, 26, 38, 171, 229, 273, 287
Misrian Plain, 128m, 140, 145n
mobads, 182–93, 194n
molluscs, 81t, 83t
Morley, Craig, 11, 15n
Mossul, 152m
Mughan Steppe, 52m, 115, 117, 119, 122n
Mundhir, Nuʿman b. al, 275–6, 279n
Murghab River, 52m
Murray, John, 155
Mustawfi, 132
Myos Hormos, 287

Nagorno Karabakh range, 114–15, 116m, 119
Nahāvand, 52m
Nahrawan, 36m, 52m, 245m
Nahr-Malki, 152m
Naisan, 35
Najaf, 105m
Naqsh-e Rajab (or Naqš-i Raǧab) rock reliefs, 152m, 156, 159–60, 170, 183
Naqsh-e Rajab III rock relief, 225, 226, 228–9, 231–2
Naqsh-e Rostam (or Naqš-i Rustam), 23m, 52m, 152m, 227, 245m; *see also* Kaʿbe-ye Zardosht
Naqsh-e Rostam I rock relief, vii–viii, 156, 159–60, 169–70, 170, 183, 221, 224–5, 227, 228–9, 232–4, 269
Nargiz Tepe, 114–15, 116m
Narseh, 170, 185, 191, 269, 277n
Narynqala, 109–10, 110m, 116m
Nasrids, 274–6, 279n
Neely, James A., 13
Nēhāvand, 152m
Neor Lake, 52m, 53t, 54, 55, 62–7, 66
Nersmihr monastery, 211–12
Nestorian Christians, 8, 22, 167, 189
Nēv-Dārāb, 152m
Neyshabur, 52m, 245m
Niebuhr, Carsten, 104
Nile River, 244m, 287, 289–90
Nineveh, 23m
Ningxia, 166, 168
Nippur, 36m
Nippur Survey, 35
Niriz, 152m
Nisa, 9
Nisibis, 23m, 52m, 106, 107m, 120, 122n, 191, 222, 234, 244m, 291
Nōd-Ardaxšīragān, 152m
North Jazira Project, 107m, 108
Novella XXI, 203–5
Novella XXXI, 201–3, 205

Ohrmazd (Ahura Mazda), 183–4, 229, 232; *see also* Ahura Mazda
Ohrmazd-Ardaxšīr, 152m
Olea europaea L. (olive), 55t, 56t, 57t, 58t, 59t, 60t, 61t, 63, 69
Oman (Mazun), 77, 269, 271, 275–6, 278n
Optically Stimulated Luminescence (OSL), 103
Ören Qala, 3, 6, 114–15, 116m, 120, 258m
Orontes River, 244m
Ortadepeslik, 140
Overlaet, Bruno, vii–viii, 228–9
Ovis aries, 80t, 82t
Ovis orientalis, 80t
Oxford University, 115

Pagden, Anthony, 174n
Pahlav, 152m
Pahlavi inscription, 292
Pahlavi sources, 184
Paikend, 52m
Paikuli inscription, 151, 152m, 170, 185, 269, 274
Pakistan, 7, 21, 166, 296–7
palaeoecological records, 51–70
Palestine, 105–6
Palmyra, 164–6, 248, 294
Panjikent, 164, *165*
Pārdan, 152m
Parishan Lake, 52m, 53t, 58–9, 60, 62–5, 68
Partav, 199, 209–12
Parthian Empire, 1, 4, 10, 13, 22, 25, 31, 33, 35–7, 61–70, 103, 108, 117, 120, 130, 141, 146n, 151, 160, 162, 169, 188, 207, 216, 242–3, 248, 260, 268, 278n; *see also* Arsacid kingdom
Parthian Wars (AD 190s), 249
Partho-Sasanian Empire, 2, 164, 242–3, 256t, 259, 262
Pasargadae, 232–3
Patterson, Lee, 8
pax Sasanica, 8
Payne, Richard, 8, 190
Pʿaytakaran, 217n
Perm, *168*
Pērōz, 170–1, 173, 184, 293
Pērōz-Šābuhr, 152m
Pērōz-Šābuhr-Pātin, 152m
Persarmenia, 207–8, 216, 244m, 258m, 298
Persepolis, 52m, 60, 224
  graffiti, 225, 229–30
  reliefs, 221, 232–4
'Persia & Rum' conference, xv, 2
'Persia and its Neighbours' project, xv, 2, 75
Persian Christianity, 183, 187–91
Persian Gulf, 11, 13, 23m, 52m, 76m, 77, 152m, 164, 245m, 248, 271–6, 278n, 285, 288–9, 292, 294, 297–8
Peshawar, 52m, 166, 170, 245m
Philip I, Emperor, vii, viii, 156, 184, 248, 249
pig, 75, 93
Pʿilippē, 213–14
Pistacia vera L. (pistachio), 55t, 56t, 57t, 58t, 59t, 60t, 61t, 63–4, 69
plans
  Gondeshapur inverted siphon and bridge, *31*
  Gondeshapur remains, *29*
  Gorgan Wall Fort 4, *253*
  Qasr-e Abu Nasr excavated architecture, *42*
  Ruqbat al-Madaʾin, *37*
  Veh Ardashir excavated area, *39*
Platago lanceolata-t., 55t, 56t, 57t, 58t, 59t, 60t, 61t
Platanus orientalis L. (plane tree), 55t, 56t, 57t, 58t, 59t, 60t, 61t, 64, 67–8

pollen records, 4, 52–70, 53t
pottery *see* ceramics
Potts, D. T., 277n, 279n, 280n
Procopius, 295
Pʿusan Veh, 211

Qala Tepe, 6, 114–15, 116m
Qalaichi (near Bukan), 76m, 88, *89*, *90*, *91*
Qalʿat al-Bahrayn, 292
Qalʿa-ye Now, 230
Qalʿeh Daland, 117, 258m
Qalʿeh Dokhtar, 52m
Qalʿeh Gabri (at Varamin), 52m, 111, 245m, 257, 258m, *258*, 263
Qalʿeh Gug A, 117, 129m, 138–9, 139m, 258m
Qalʿeh Kharabeh, 64, 75–93, 76m, *89*, *90*, 117, 253, 257, 258m
Qalʿeh Pol Gonbad, 111, *112*, 117, 129m, 138–9, 139m, 245m, 250–1, 258m, 263
Qalʿeh-ye Zal, 52m
Qana, 288
Qarniareq Qalʿeh, 134
Qasr Muqatil, 31–2, *33*
Qasr Serij, 188
Qasr Yeng, 279n
Qasr-e Abu Nasr, 23m, 38, 40–2, 42
Qasr-e Shirin, 151
Qianling, *172*, 172
Qir-Karzin relief, 230
Qizil, 164, *165*
Qizlar Qalʿeh, 129m, 134, *135*
Qohandez, 76m, *89*, *90*
Qusair, 188

radiocarbon dating, 51, 53t, 54–60, 67, 78, 84, 103–4, 122n, 138
Rag-e Bibi, 52m, 245m
Rag-e Bibi relief, 7, 151, 159–60, *160*, 164, 170
Ramila, 278n
Rām-Ohrmazd, 152m
Ratto Kot fort, 13, 245m, 292
Ratzel, Friedrich, 100–2
Rayy (or Ray), 23m, 38, 152m, 172
Razazza Lake, 105m
red deer, 78
Red Sea, 12, 23m, 244m, 275, 284, 286–8, 292, 295, 299n
religion, 8, 16n, 75, 153–5, 167, 174n, 181–93, 194n, 208, 286; *see also under individual religions*
Rend, 152m
Rēv-Ardaxšir, 152m
Rezakhani, Khodadad, 1–2
Rhodes, 244m
Rich, Claudius, 32
Ricinus communis L. (castor oil plant), 55t, 56t, 57t, 58t, 59t, 60t, 61t, 64, 68–9
Rishahr, 23m
Rist, J., 188
Ritter, Nils, 12
Roman Empire, 5, 221, 224, 234, 241–3, 246–7, 250, 259, 262–3, 277n, 279n, 285
  ceramics, 287
  Christianity, 8, 14, 182–3, 190–1
  conflict with, 271–2, 275
  frontiers, 99–120
  garnets, 297
  gold, 293
  legal culture, 199–217
  literary and historical tradition, 169–73
  literary sources, 235n
  military campaigns in, 22
  miltary infrastructure, 256t, 263n
  relations with, 151, 184, 188, 190, 222, 268, 293–4
  trade, 12, 276, 278n, 289, 291–2, 294–5
  urban development, 3
Roman Republic, 243, 250, 254–9, 262–3
Rome, xv, 244m, 249
routeways, 6–7, 103, 114, 127–34, *139*, 141–3
Rōyān, 152m
Rum, xv, 2, 170
Rumagan, 34
Rumzan River, 107m
Rupicapra/*Capreolus*, 80t, 82t
Ruqbat al- Madaʾin, 35, 37
Russia, 1, 15n, 75, 127, 166, *168*
Rustaveli, Shota, 170, 175n

Sadd-e Eskander, 52m
Sadd-e Garkaz aqueduct, 129m, 133
Sagestan, vii
Sagzabad, 76m, 88, *89*, *90*, *91*
Sahak, 208, 213–14
Sahara, 244m
Saibakh, 52m, 108, 130, 132
Sakastān, 152m
Sakhar, 174n
Salmas, 227
Salmas rock relief, 225–8, *227*
Samarkand, 52m, 245m
Samawah, 31, 32
Sanlıurfa Museum, 234
Sarakhs, 151, 153
Sarantis, Alexander, 246
Sardis, 244m
Sar-e Pol, 155–6, *157*
Sarli Makhtum canal, 129m, 133, *135*
Sasanian art, 7, 10, 78, 157, 164, 234
Sauer, E. W., 9–10, 111, 117
seals, 22, 186–8, 297
Searight, Anne, *158*
Second Armenia, 202, 205, 207
Sēgān, 152m
Seleucia, 25, *25*, 33, 38, 52m, 189, 244m, 263n, 264n
Septimius Severus Arch at Rome, 33, 249
Sērāz, 152m
Sevan Lake, 116m
Shah Nishin, 52m
shahanshahs, 181–93, 194n, 200, 206–7, 215, 230, 293
Shahnama, 170–1, 187, 189
Shahr-e Qumis, 35–6
Shahrestan-e Yazdegird, 145n
Shahrestaniha-ye Eranshahr, 269–70, 278n
Shaked, S., 182, 184
Shapur [Bishapur] *see* Bishapur
Shapur I
  Christianity, 188, 190
  coins, 270t
  Dariali Fort, 260
  frontiers, 268, 271
  inscriptions, 269
  literary and historical tradition, 169–70
  Mazda, 183–5
  military achievements, 251, 277n
  relations with Rome, 221–2, 224–5
  Res Gestae, 185, 194n, 269
  rock reliefs, vii, viii, 7, 156, 159, 234, 249
  settlement, 22, 28
Shapur II
  Arabs, 11
  Christianity, 189, 191

coins, 270–1, 270t
expeditions, 170–1
frontiers, 268, 277
rock reliefs, vii
settlement, 32, 106
see also Khandaq Shapur
Shapur's Ditch *see* Khandaq Shapur
sheep, 5, 74, 78–9, 84–5, 88–93, *89*
Shemkir, 115, 116m
Shiraz, 38, 41, 68
Shumilovskikh, Lyudmila, 4–5
Shushtar (or Šuštar), 152m, 245m
Siah Mansour, 29–30
Siberia, 166
silk, 12, 285–6, 292, 295–8, 299n
Silk Road, 272
silver, 166, 168, 169, 296
  coins, 22, 162, 272–3, 294
Simeon, Bishop, 189–91, 209–12
Simpson, St John, 3–4, 106
Sinbad cycle, 171
Sindh, 52m, 245m
Singara, 52m, 191
Sinisi, Fabrizio, 230
Sippar, 36m
Siraf, 52m, 289
Sistan, 52m, 164, 169–70, 173, 175n, 245m
Siwnikʻ, 199–200, 209, 212–17, 217n
'Size Index Method', 88
Smith, Monica, 119
Social Darwinism, 100
Sod Shapur [Sadh-Shapur], 22
Sogdian wall paintings, 164, *165*
Sogdiana, 52m, 245m
Sogdians, 166, 172, 292–3, 296–8
South China Sea, 164, 289
South-East Asia, 12, 284–98
South-West Asia, 63, 75, 243
Spahān, 152m
Sper, 217n
Sri Lanka, 12, 279n, 284–6, 291–7
Stepʻanos Orbelean, 212–13, 215–16, 217n, 218n
Strabo, 287
subsistence economy, 22, 74–93, 131
Surkh Kotal, 159–60, *161*
Sus scrofa, 80t, 82t, *86*, *87*
Susa (or Šuš), 23m, 52m, 152m, 245m
Suse Khersan, 76m, 88, *90*
Susiana, 22, 28, 222
Swat River / Valley, 52m, 245m, 296
Sweden, 296
Syārazūr, 152m
Synod (424), 189
Synod of Beth Lapat (484), 189
Synod of Ctesiphon (410), 8, 189
Synodicon Orientale, 189
Syria, 21, 26, 58, 99, 242–3, 244m, 259
  art, 234
  ceramics, 103
  Christianity, 188
  desert castles, 105–9
  Khusro I, 295
  linear barrier, 118
  routeways, 130
  settlement, 120
  Shapur I, 222
  trade, 287
Syriac hagiographers, 190
Syriac martyrologies, 187
Syriac sources, 184, 189, 192, 279n
Syrian Desert, 244m

Tabari, 11, 26, 33–4, 133, 189, 269
Tabriz, 23m
Taghlib tribe, 278n
Takht-e Neshin, 24, 223–4, *223*, 234
Takht-e Suleiman, 23m, 40, 52m, 151, 245m
Tamim tribe, 278n
Tammisheh Wall, 63–4, 75, 117, 119, 129m, 245m, 258m, 261
Tang Dynasty, 172, *172*
Tang-e Ab, 225, *225*, 226
Tang-e Sarvak rock relief, 231–2, *231*
Tansar, 184–5
Taq-e Bostan relief, 23m, 151, 184
Taq-e Kisra, 40
Tarm, 152m
Tatʻev, 199–200, 212–13
Taykʻ, 217n
Tʻbilisi, 52m, 244m
Tedzhen, 52m
Tell ad-Dhibaʼi, 35
Tell Baruda, 25–6, 38–41
Tell Bâti, 52m
Tell Beydar, 106–9
Tell Beydar Survey (TBS), 107m, 108–9, *108*
Tell Brak, 106–9
Tell Brak Sustaining Area Survey (TBSAS), 107m, 108–9, *108*
Tell Hamoukar, 106–9
Tell Hamoukar Survey, 107m, 108–9, *108*
Testament of Ardashir, 184
Testudo sp., 81t, 83t
textile arts, 164–6, 285–6
textual sources, 1, 9–10, 100, 106–8, 115, 126, 139–40, 145n
Thaʻalibi, 189
Theodosius I, 205
Theodosius II, 189
Third Armenia, 202
Thomson, R. W., 209, 217n
Tigris River, 22, 23m, 25, *25*, 33–5, 36m, 52m, 104, 105m, 106, 107m, 132, 152m, 188, 244m, 248, 258m, 259, 294
Timothy I, 189
Tiridates IV, 191
Tole Qalʻeh Seyfabad (TQS), 77–93
Tomb-e Bot, 230
Torpakh Qala, 109, 110m, 111, *111*, 116m, 245m, 250–1, 257, 258m, 263
trade, 4, 6, 11–13, 43–4, 75, 106, 143, 166, 167, 271–6, 278n, 284–98
Transcaucasia, 8–12, 75, 248, 257, 288, 291
travel accounts, 104, 126, 132–3, 140, 155–6, 294
Trdat, King *see* Varaz Trdat
Treaty of Nisibis (298), 191
Trinkaus, Maurer, 36
Trümpelmann, Leo, vii, 229
Tulul al-Ukhaidir, 105m, 106
Tulul Bawi, 33
Tur Abdin Foothills, 107m
Turan, 54–7, 170–1
Turgistān, 152m
Turkey, 23m
Turkmenistan, 21, 75, 117, 133, 153
Turks, 10, 12, 169, 171–2, 297–8
Tūs, 52m
Tusi, Asadi, 170
Tuska Tchal peat bog, 52m, 53t, 56, *57*, 61–5, 67–9
Tylos, 292

Uerpmann, Hans-Peter, 88
Uerpmann, M., 88

Ulrich, B., 278n, 280n
Ultan Qalasi, 3, 6, 52m, 103, 114, 116m, 258m
Ulu Kizylli, 145n
Umayyad period, 26–7, 106, 212
Umm Kheshm, 36m
University of Chicago, 38
University of Durham, 121n, 242
University of Edinburgh, 242, 253, 254
University of Tbilisi, 242, 253
Ur, J., 122n
Uranius Antoninus, vii–viii
urban development, 2–15, 21–45, 51, 56, 75, 104, 106, 109, 115, 117–20, 138, 186, 202, 215, 246, 250, 272, 278n, 289
urbanism, 2–4, 11, 21–2
Urmia Lake, 52m, 56–7, 64, 68, 152m, 225, 245m, 257, 258m
Ursus arctos, 80t, 82t
Uyun at-Taff, 31–2

Vahan Mamikonean, 208–9
Vahman-Ardaxšir, 152m
Valasapat, 25
Valaxšbād, 152m
Valens, 292
Valerian, vii, viii, 156, 248, 249
Van Lake, 52m, 53t, 57, 58, 61–5, 68–9
Varamin *see* Qalʿeh Gabri
Varaz Trdat, 200–1, 211–12
Vardan Mamikonean, 192, 200–1
Vegetius, 247, 257
Veh Ardashir (or Coche or Veh-Ardaxšir-Šahrestan), 23m, 25–6, 25, 36m, 38–41, 39, 52m, 152m, 188, 245m, 264n, 271, 289, 294
Veh-Andiyōk-Šābuhr, 152m
Veh-az-Antiok-Khusro, 25, 34
Veh-az-Amid-Kavād, 152m
Veh-Kavād, 152m
Viranshar, 52m, 245m
Virozān, 152m
Vitis vinifera L. (grapevine), 55t, 56t, 57t, 58t, 59t, 60t, 61t, 64–5, 67–8
Volga River, 245m
von den Driesch, Angela, 85–7

Von Freeden, U., 299n
Vshnaspdat, Nixor, 208
Vulpes sp., 80t, 82t

Warka, 36m
Wasit, 36m, 152m
water birds, 77–8
water buffalo, 78
water supply, 3, 6, 13, 29–30, 34–5, 38, 41, 43–4, 117, 131, 133, 252
Weber, U., vii
'West Test', 38
Western Desert, 101m, 104, 105m, 118, 120
Whitcomb, D. S., 27, 37–8
Widengren, G., 278n
Wiesehöfer, J., 173n
wild *Capra*, 80t, 82t, 86, 87
Wilkinson, Tony, xvi, 5–6, 117, 144n
Wolfsheim, 292, 297
Wright, Henry, 30–1

Xinjiang, 164, 165, 166
Xiongnu, 290, 293
Xoytʿ, 217n
Xusrō-Šād-Kavād, 152m
Xusrō-Šād-Ohrmazd, 152m

Yamama, 275
Yarshater, E., 170
Yazdgerd I, 8, 189–90, 192, 270–1, 275
  coins, 270t
Yazdgerd II, 145n, 184, 186–7, 191–3, 200
Yemen, 11–12, 242, 245m; *see also* Himyar
Yenikend Fortress, 113m

Zagros Mountains, 52m, 56–60, 62–9, 66, 88, 245m
Zar-Tepe, 52m
Zendan-e Suleiman, 76m, 88, 91
Zeribar Lake, 53, 53t, 58, 59, 62–4
Zibliyat, 36m
Ziyaran, 88–92, 89, 90
Zororastrianism, 8, 75, 159–60, 166–7, 171, 174n, 181–93, 194n, 200, 206–8, 212
Zuckerman, C., 299n
Zurvanism, 191–2, 194n

Printed in the USA
CPSIA information can be obtained
at www.ICGtesting.com
LVHW010729281123
765138LV00036B/879